Frommer's®

New York City with Kids

12th Edition

by Alexis Lipsitz Flippin

WILEY

Wiley Publishing, Inc

ABOUT THE AUTHOR

Alexis Lipsitz Flippin is a freelance writer and editor who lives in Manhattan's Greenwich Village with her husband, daughter, and springer spaniel. She is a former senior editor at Frommer's and the author of *Frommer's New York City Day by Day, Frommer's Portable Turks & Caicos,* and *Frommer's St. Maarten/ St Martin, Anguilla & St. Barts,* and coauthor of *Frommer's 500 Extraordinary Islands.*

Published by:
WILEY PUBLISHING, INC.

111 River St.
Hoboken, NJ 07030-5774

ISBN 978-0-470-63100-3 (paper); ISBN 978-1-118-01947-4 (ebk); ISBN 978-1-118-01948-1 (ebk); ISBN 978-1-118-01949-8 (ebk)

Editor: Cate Latting
Production Editor: Erin Amick
Cartographer: Roberta Stockwell
Photo Editor: Richard Fox
Production by Wiley Indianapolis Composition Services
Front cover photo: Central Park with midtown skyline in background ©Russell Kord / Alamy Images.
Back cover photo: Young girls, New York City ©Walter Zerla / AGE Fotostock, Inc.

For information on our other products and services or to obtain technical support, please contact our Customer Care Department within the U.S. at 877/762-2974, outside the U.S. at 317/572-3993 or fax 317/572-4002.

Wiley also publishes its books in a variety of electronic formats. Some content that appears in print may not be available in electronic formats.

Manufactured in the United States of America

5 4 3 2 1

CONTENTS

5 FAMILY-FRIENDLY ACCOMMODATIONS 56

6 FAMILY-FRIENDLY DINING 89

7 EXPLORING NEW YORK CITY WITH YOUR KIDS 139

LIST OF MAPS

ACKNOWLEDGMENTS

This book is dedicated with much love and appreciation to my own mom and dad, Lee and Lil Lipsitz, who first introduced me to all that was wonderful about New York.

—*Alexis Lipsitz Flippin*

HOW TO CONTACT US

In researching this book, we discovered many wonderful places—hotels, restaurants, shops, and more. We're sure you'll find others. Please tell us about them, so we can share the information with your fellow travelers in upcoming editions. If you were disappointed with a recommendation, we'd love to know that, too. Please write to:

Frommer's New York City with Kids, 12th Edition
Wiley Publishing, Inc. • 111 River St. • Hoboken, NJ 07030-5774
frommersfeedback@wiley.com

AN ADDITIONAL NOTE

Please be advised that travel information is subject to change at any time—and this is especially true of prices. We therefore suggest that you write or call ahead for confirmation when making your travel plans. The authors, editors, and publisher cannot be held responsible for the experiences of readers while traveling. Your safety is important to us, however, so we encourage you to stay alert and be aware of your surroundings. Keep a close eye on cameras, purses, and wallets, all favorite targets of thieves and pickpockets.

FROMMER'S STAR RATINGS, ICONS & ABBREVIATIONS

Every hotel, restaurant, and attraction listing in this guide has been ranked for quality, value, service, amenities, and special features using a **star-rating system.** In country, state, and regional guides, we also rate towns and regions to help you narrow down your choices and budget your time accordingly. Hotels and restaurants are rated on a scale of zero (recommended) to three stars (exceptional). Attractions, shopping, nightlife, towns, and regions are rated according to the following scale: zero stars (recommended), one star (highly recommended), two stars (very highly recommended), and three stars (must-see).

In addition to the star-rating system, we also use **seven feature icons** that point you to the great deals, in-the-know advice, and unique experiences that separate travelers from tourists. Throughout the book, look for:

special finds—those places only insiders know about

fun facts—details that make travelers more informed and their trips more fun

kids—best bets for kids and advice for the whole family

special moments—those experiences that memories are made of

overrated—places or experiences not worth your time or money

insider tips—great ways to save time and money

great values—where to get the best deals

The following **abbreviations** are used for credit cards:

AE	American Express	DISC	Discover	V	Visa
DC	Diners Club	MC	MasterCard		

TRAVEL RESOURCES AT FROMMERS.COM

Frommer's travel resources don't end with this guide. Frommer's website, **www.frommers. com**, has travel information on more than 4,000 destinations. We update features regularly, giving you access to the most current trip-planning information and the best airfare, lodging, and car-rental bargains. You can also listen to podcasts, connect with other Frommers. com members through our active-reader forums, share your travel photos, read blogs from guidebook editors and fellow travelers, and much more.

HOW TO FEEL LIKE A NEW YORK CITY FAMILY

t goes without saying that New York is a city of unparalleled cultural richness, boasting world-class museums, performing-arts troupes, and restaurants. But what isn't so widely known is how much of New York is accessible to families. Before we had our daughter, my husband and I dined out in restaurants whenever we felt like it, went to movie theaters in the afternoon, and spent hours leisurely strolling through art galleries and museums. As grown-ups, we found that there was no shortage of fun. After Maisie came along, I felt it was my duty to ensure that the city was as hospitable to children as it was to us. So I did some digging. And promptly discovered that it's already a kids' wonderland. Who knew that metropolitan New York has some 1,000 playgrounds—and that Central Park alone is outfitted with 21 magical playgrounds, where kids can scamper on fanciful stone bridges, porpoise sprinklers, and 45-foot-long curved slides? Or that regular story-time hours are held all over the city, including on and around the Alice in Wonderland statue in Central Park? Or that the original Winnie-the-Pooh bear resides in the New York Public Library—and you can see it for free? While I was gallivanting around Manhattan untethered by children, a number of forward-thinking pioneers were busily making the city a better place for kids.

And as Maisie has grown, we've discovered even more: We've found that the public parks are a godsend for families whose habitat is the concrete urban jungle. We've learned that the city's museums have unparalleled collections and thrillingly innovative programs for children. We've found that the zoos are some of the finest and most forward-thinking in the country. And we've found ourselves, as parents, falling in love with the city all over again. It's like mining a vein of gold in your own backyard.

Still, even with the parks, the museums, the boat rides, and the seasonal spectacles, sometimes the most memorable New York moments are the serendipitous ones you encounter as you stroll about the city. You can see the most amazing things just by turning a corner. We've stumbled upon ballet aerialists swinging from the New York Stock Exchange. We've seen dragon dances on Chinatown streets. We've listened to Brazilian drummers doing impromptu concerts on the street. Some company is always handing out free energy drinks or ice cream cones. Movie sets pop up all over the city, and you never know when you'll stumble upon a major production with megawatt stars hanging out in hair rollers and eating a bag of chips (stars: they're just like us!). Why, just last Sunday, while pushing our daughter in a stroller, we encountered a gentleman with two parrots on his shoulders, one of whom was named Gazpacho. To my daughter's delight, Gazpacho clambered onto my hand and gave me a tweak with his beak. What can beat that?

On Your Mark, Get Set, Go!

This is a big place to tackle in just a few short days. The pulse and tempo of New York City can be discombobulating at first if you're not used to it—my North Carolina nephew actually got dizzy from his first encounter with the noise and commotion—but once you attune yourself, you'll find it a tremendously exciting place, especially for youngsters. It's easy to spot a native New York City kid: They tend to stride down the sidewalk with an unerring radar for other people, bikes, and cars. But I've also seen many kids who've been here only a few days shed their skittishness and start to walk with that same savvy, confident stride, smoothly maneuvering their way around the city. Kids are sponges, remember? They learn fast, and the city's got a lot to teach them.

This guidebook is filled with all the wonderful things you and your family can do in the city. So let's dispense with some of the negatives right from the get-go. First of all: **Yes, there's crime in New York.** But the good news is that crime rates have fallen dramatically in the past 10 years. So dramatically, in fact, that when a mugging occurs in my neighborhood, it's a shock. Still, the city is *not* the place to drop your guard. Stay alert, and follow the tips in "Crime & Safety," in chapter 3.

Second: **It's noisy.** Really noisy. Prepare for a bone-rattling symphony of horns and sirens and garbage trucks and folks having full-throated "discussions" on the street. Children have especially sensitive hearing, and it may take them a little while to acclimate. I recommend avoiding the main thoroughfares if possible (side streets are quieter and less crowded), and even though much of it is pedestrianized, I would never take a toddler to Times Square during the day and especially during show times—the streets can be thick with crowds and latter-day barkers.

Third: **Yes, it's deliriously easy to spend money here.** Whenever I visit the suburbs or go down to my native state of North Carolina, I'm always convinced I'm being vastly undercharged at grocery and convenience stores. Why on earth do businesses charge such high prices in New York City? *Because they can.* You are a captive shopper on this island, and there's so much to do and see, who has time to schlep to a discount store in another borough just to save a few bucks?

But there *are* ways to cut costs with your family in tow. (Back in the day, we used to crash art openings in SoHo for the free hors d'oeuvres and wine, but, oh, never mind . . .) Grocery stores are costly enough in the Big Apple, but Korean delis, the convenience stores of the city, *really* inflate prices. Four soft drinks will cost you six bucks—seven if you throw in a small bag of chips. If your hotel has a **kitchenette,** stock up on drinks and snacks at a local chain supermarket. Also take advantage of **complimentary breakfasts** or—even better—hotels that have a **"Kids Eat Free" policy.** Hit the city's **greenmarkets** for fast, healthy, inexpensive snacks like delicious apples, breads, fruit, cheeses—you'll be supporting local farmers in the process. Check out **www.cenyc.org/greenmarket** to find out what's in season and whether there's a greenmarket near you. **Eat ethnic**—good, cheap Chinese restaurants can be found everywhere in the city, and Ninth Avenue between 57th and 34th streets is just one great ethnic eatery after another, from Brazilian to Thai to Peruvian. It's a tourist trap, but Little Italy will fill your kids up with their three-course prix-fixe lunches, and decent pizza places are on every corner of the city. And don't forget **transportation costs.** Buy unlimited-ride MetroCard passes if you plan to crisscross the city by bus or subway. Or walk: It's the cheapest and best way to get the flavor of the city by far.

Finally: **Street people remain a reality of life in 21st-century New York.** In your travels, you and your kids will likely spot homeless people sleeping in doorways or combing corner trash bins. Some may even have something to say to you; politely move on. If you're asked for money, it's certainly your prerogative to offer some change. But it's also fine to smile and simply say "Sorry," and move along. While these encounters may be uncomfortable at times, that's just the flip side of one of this city's great pluses: Everybody, from the Wall Street banker to the greengrocer to the starving actor waiting tables, shares the streets. It's all part of the fabric of this crazy quilt we call New York City.

FROMMER'S FAVORITE NEW YORK CITY FAMILY EXPERIENCES

o **Spending the Christmas Holidays in New York:** Crusty old New York turns unabashedly giddy with celebration during the holidays. At Christmas you really feel the heart of the Big City. In December, Rockefeller Plaza is an especially thrilling holiday sight, with the city's biggest Christmas tree (a real doozy) twinkling with lights. The tiny Rockefeller Center ice rink is lively with the clash of blades and the tinny blare of piped-in music. Two spectacular holiday shows run the length of the season: The New York Botanical Garden's **Holiday Train Show** and **Radio City Music Hall's Christmas Spectacular.** *The Nutcracker* ballet is produced in two different venues. See chapter 11.

o **Taking a Boat Ride Around Manhattan:** When you're out on the sparkling waters of New York Harbor, with the salt air in your hair and the sea gulls gliding overhead, you'll thrill to the Manhattan skyline in all its glory. It's a fantastic way to see the town. See "Getting Around," in chapter 4.

o **Visiting Chinatown:** The kids I know from out of town always head down here for good food, cheap toys, and excellent street theater. The neighborhood always feels exotic to me too. Come during the Chinese New Year for thrilling dragon dances in the street. See chapters 6 and 8.

o **Spending a Sunday Afternoon at the American Museum of Natural History:** Weekends are definitely family time at this magnificent big museum on the Upper West Side, but the more, the merrier—these dim, cool, high-ceilinged halls never seem too crowded. Head for the musty old back corners where there are old-fashioned dioramas or stop by the Natural Science Center in the early afternoons for hands-on puttering with plants and live animals (for ages 4 and older). See p. 142.

o **Talking to the Animals in the New York Zoos:** The Central Park Zoo is perfect for toddlers: It's small and compact but still spacious enough to feel like a real nature outing. Check out the feeding schedule as you walk in the front entrance—the Sea Lion Pool is the centerpiece of this tidily landscaped little gem of a zoo. Don't expect fancy tricks, but there'll be enough barking and diving and splashing to satisfy everybody. Just yards away is the charming Tisch Zoo, where little ones can feed baby llamas, sheep, and goats as the traffic above on Fifth Avenue whizzes by. In the world-class Bronx Zoo, forward-thinking zoo officials have created enclosures as close to animals' natural habitats as possible, where visitors can see lions, tigers, and gorillas. See p. 153, 153, and 148.

o **Riding a Bike Through the Canyons of Wall Street on Sunday:** The suits have the weekend off, and the streets are quiet and pretty empty. Rent a bike and cruise the narrow corridors with the muscular skyscrapers of the 1920s looming above. It's a thrill. See chapter 8.

o **Playing in Central Park:** It's kiddie land in every way, with a breathtaking array of playgrounds, pools, and attractions to keep children busy and happy for hours, days, weeks. Point toddlers to the Carousel, the Central Park Zoo, Conservatory Water, and the Swedish Marionette Theater; and send the older kids to the state-of-the-art playgrounds, ball fields, and pools. Grab a snack or dine lakeside at the Loeb Boathouse for smashing views all around. See chapter 9.

o **Root, Root, Rooting for the Home Team:** On a sunny summer afternoon, there are few pleasures more fully satisfying than heading to the Bronx to see the Bronx Bombers play in Yankee Stadium, or to Flushing, Queens, to catch the Mets at Citi Field. In either case, nobody minds if your kids make noise, you can leave early if they get tired, and there's plenty of food available—especially the overpriced hot dogs that are so much a part of the experience. In the winter, head to Madison Square Garden to watch the Knicks (basketball) or the Rangers (hockey) play—and, if you can snag tickets, take a bus over to Jersey to the New Meadowlands Stadium, spanking-new home of the New York Giants and the New York Jets. See "Spectator Sports," in chapter 11.

THE best HOTEL BETS

o **Most Family-Friendly:** The **Doubletree Guest Suites,** 1568 Broadway (© **800/ 222-8733** or 212/719-1600; p. 72), provides not only standard two-room accommodations sleeping four or six, but also kitchenettes, baby equipment, childproof rooms, and a super toddler playroom. The Upper East Side's **The Loews Regency,** 540 Park Ave. (© **212/759-4100;** p. 68), offers kids all sorts of amenities, including their own concierge; and **Le Parker Meridien,** 118 W. 57th St. (© **800/543-4300** or 212/245-5000; p. 73), has special welcoming packets for young guests; concierges at both of these hotels are full of great tips for kids visiting NYC.

o **Best Suite Deals:** The **Doubletree Guest Suites,** 1568 Broadway (© **800/222-8733** or 212/719-1600; p. 72), is a sensible family option, sleeping the whole crew in one unit for a relatively easy price. The **Embassy Suites New York,** 102 North End Ave. (© **800/EMBASSY** [362-2779] or 212/945-0100; p. 85), offers some very favorable rates on weekends for its roomy, sleek suites.

o **Most Peace & Quiet:** It's all relative in New York, of course, but the **Excelsior,** 45 W. 81st St. (© **800/368-4575** or 212/362-9200; p. 58), is buffered by Central Park and the park surrounding the Museum of Natural History, and the **Gracie Inn,** 502 E. 81st St. (© **212/628-1700;** p. 68), is tucked away on an Upper East Side street near the East River. Even in Midtown you can find residential quiet at the **Millennium U.N. Plaza,** 1 United Nations Plaza (© **866/866-8086** or 212/758-1234; p. 80), and the **Holiday Inn Midtown 57th Street,** 440 W. 57th St. (© **888/HOLIDAY** [465-4329] or 212/581-8100; p. 75).

- **Best Views:** Two downtown hotels feature dynamite New York Harbor views starring Lady Liberty and Ellis Island: The **Ritz-Carlton New York,** 2 West St. (© **800/241-3333** or 212/344-0800; p. 84), wins hands down for its glorious open westward views from a majority of guest rooms, but there are several rooms with great harbor views also at the **Marriott New York Downtown,** 85 West St. (© **800/228-9290** or 212/385-4900; p. 86).

- **When Price Is No Object:** Our vote goes to **The Carlyle,** 35 E. 76th St. (© **800/227-5737** or 212/744 1600; p. 66), for its dignified East Side calm; its well-nigh-perfect service; and the spaciousness of its designer-decorated rooms, which really deserve to be called apartments. Spring for a suite with a Central Park view and a grand piano. The **Four Seasons,** 57 E. 57th St. (© **800/819-5053** or 212/758-5700; p. 77), has a stylish Midtown address, sleek if somewhat small rooms (but then, you can afford a suite, right?), fabulous service, and a surprisingly kid-friendly gourmet restaurant.

- **When Price Is Your Main Object.** You can't go wrong with the **Travel Inn,** 515 W. 42nd St. (© **800/869-4630** or 212/695-7171; p. 76), which delivers roomy, clean, fairly quiet motel rooms, plus a huge pool and free parking, for around $150 to $200 a night.

- **Best Lobby:** You've gotta love the classic Art Deco lobby of the **Waldorf Astoria,** 301 Park Ave. (© **800/WALDORF** [925-3673], 800/HILTONS [445-8667], or 212/355-3000; p. 79), with its marble-faced pillars, deep carpeting, ornamental plasterwork, the magnificent Park Avenue entry chandelier, and that amazing clock near the front desk.

- **Best Pool:** The pool at the **Millennium U.N. Plaza Hotel,** 44th Street and First Avenue (© **866/866-8086** or 212/758-1234; p. 80), has it all: views, cleanliness, handsome tile work, and not much of a crowd.

- **Tops for Toddlers:** When all is said and done, the **Hotel Wales,** 1295 Madison Ave. (© **212/876-6000;** p. 67), wins for its Carnegie Hill location, friendly staff, breakfast buffet, residential calm, and Puss-in-Boots theme. The **Doubletree Guest Suites,** 1568 Broadway (© **800/222-8733** or 212/719-1600; p. 72), scores big here, too, for its suite convenience and toddler playroom.

- **Tops for Teens:** Budding bohemians may want to be in Greenwich Village at the **Washington Square Hotel,** 103 Waverly Place (© **800/222-0418** or 212/777-9515; p. 82), while trendsetters will gravitate to the way-cool decor and hipster cachet of **The Paramount,** 235 W. 46th St. (© **866/760-3174** or 212/764-5500; p. 75), or the Meatpacking District cool of the **Hotel Gansevoort,** 18 Ninth Ave. (© **877/426-7386;** p. 82).

THE best DINING BETS

- **Best Place to Eat Outside:** It's a seasonal occupation, of course, but when the city starts to thaw after a long, chilly winter, everyone heads outside—and you should, too. It's clichéd and often overrun with tourists (and the pond has a sickly green cast), but the **Loeb Boathouse** (© **212/517-2233;** www.thecentralparkboathouse.com) in the middle of Central Park is simply lovely—you can grab a quick bite, dine casually at the grill (a nice-sized bucket of french fries for $2.50), or get the full-service treatment at the more formal restaurant—all are pillowed in a leafy hollow facing the rowboat pond. The **Boat Basin Café,** W. 79th St., at the Hudson River (© **212/496-5542;** p. 105) has spectacular Hudson River views and a vaulted limestone setting; just follow the scent of burgers sizzling on an outdoor grill.

- **Best Genuine Time Warp:** The city's vintage venues are a dying breed these days, but you can always count on the **Lexington Candy Shop,** 1226 Lexington Ave. (© **212/288-0057;** p. 108), for good old-fashioned vibes. It's a living relic from 1925, with wooden booths, chrome-rimmed stools, and a classic New York egg cream.

- **Best Store Dining: American Girl Café,** 609 Fifth Ave. (© **877/247-5223;** p. 110), will thrill your American Girl aficionado as much as it impresses her parents. The food is actually good, and there are special doll seats where girls can prop their American Girl dolls while they eat.

- **Best Dinner Entertainment:** Even seen-it-all city kids get a kick out of the table show at **Benihana,** 47 W. 56th St. (© **212/581-0930;** p. 111), the trailblazing Japanese steakhouse where flying knives and dexterous teppanyaki chefs became a showbiz standard. But it's the little ones whose eyes will light up at the spectacle.

- **Best Tea Party:** Afternoon tea couldn't be cozier than at the whimsical **Alice's Tea Cup,** at 102 W. 73rd St. (© **212/799-3006**) or 156 E. 64th St. (© **212/ 486-9200**).

- **Best Healthy Comfort Food:** You may not think that a place that specializes in healthy, organic, sustainable foods would draw kids by the barreful—but when a place like **The City Bakery,** 3 W. 18th St. (© **212/366-1414;** p. 121), includes unbeatable versions of fried chicken, mac 'n' cheese, French toast, and quesadilla, why wouldn't they come? A spinning chocolate wheel, fresh hot chocolate (with homemade marshmallows), and the city's best chocolate chip cookies don't hurt either.

- **Best Breakfast:** TriBeCa's **Bubby's,** 120 Hudson St. (© **212/219-0666;** p. 137), welcomes kids for breakfast until 4pm daily; the weekend brunches are especially popular.

- **Best Pancakes:** Okay, so our daughter has rarely met a pancake she doesn't like, but the big, thick numbers at **The Smith,** 55 Third Ave. (© **212/420-9800;** p. 127), leave her speechless; they also come with a cinnamon-dusted banana-and-walnut topping.

- **Best Family-Friendly Restaurant for Grown-ups:** For further proof that this truly is the golden age of children in NYC, witness as more and more city restaurants develop kid-friendly menus and attitudes. Our favorite is **Odeon** 145 W. Broadway (© **212/233-0507;** p. 136), which has transcended its trendy 1970s past to become a great neighborhood *boîte,* with solid food for the whole family (and no cutesy kids' menu).

- **Best Food Court:** The **Grand Central Dining Concourse** is much better than it needs to be—we'd even go out of our way to eat there at lunch. It's got Two Boots Pizza, Brothers Barbecue, Manhattan Chili, Junior's, Zocalo, and Hale and Hearty Soups, among others (oh, and you can stop at the little takeout window outside Grand Central Oyster Bar for some great clam chowder). But our favorite food court—and the perfect place for a sit-down family lunch—is **Chelsea Market** (75 Ninth Ave.; p. 123). It's a cool place, set in an old biscuit factory whose hard-working industrial parts have been transformed: a waterfall here, castle torches there. The food is great, from the Cleaver Company's delicious sustainable fare to Buon Italia's pastas, frittatas, and pizzas to Fat Witch's rich brownies.

- **Best Theme Restaurant:** If you must dine in a theme restaurant (and I know that sometimes you have no choice in the matter), head to **Ellen's Stardust Diner,** 1650 Broadway (© **212/956-5151;** p. 115), where the waitstaff belt out their favorites to a karaoke machine in this Times Square cafe's weekend dinner shows.

- **Good Neighbor Award:** This award goes to James Beard Award–winning restaurateur **Keith McNally,** whose painstakingly re-created French bistros and Italian trattoria have become warm, comfortable neighborhood favorites among both the cognoscenti and families alike. Neat trick, that. You and your children will be treated well at **Pastis, Morandi,** and **Schiller's Liquor Bar.**
- **Best Venue for a Children's Party:** You can have a party in any number of restaurants these days, but the big downstairs space makes for top-notch kids' celebrations at **Hill Country,** 30 W. 26th St. (© **212/255-4544;** p. 122). And few places will leave the barbecue-loving grown-ups happier.
- **Best Dim Sum:** When it comes to the Chinatown lunchtime tradition of dining on small servings of dumplings, skewers, rolls, and other delectables right at your table, you can't go wrong with **Ping's,** 22 Mott St. (© **212/602-9988;** p. 135) or **Golden Unicorn,** 18 E. Broadway (© **212/941-0951;** p. 134). For true spectacle, head to **Jing Fong,** at 18 Elizabeth St. (© **212/964-5256;** p. 135), whose giant Hong Kong–style banquet hall is pure Vegas.
- **Best Pizza:** The location near City Hall may be a little out of the way, but the nod goes to **Farinella,** 90 Worth St. (© **212/608-3222**), where delicious, lighter-than-air Roman-style pizzas are sold in 4-foot-long *palams* or by the square slice.
- **Best Family-Style Italian:** If you can't get to the Bronx's authentic Little Italy, then head to **Carmine's,** 200 W. 44th St. (© **212/221-3800**); or 2450 Broadway (© **212/362-2200;** p. 115 and 102), for great big platters of Southern Italian–style pasta, salads, and more. The food is remarkably good and the ambience properly clamorous (and amazingly satisfying) for a place of this size. It's quite an efficient assembly line.
- **Best Desserts:** Yes, it's often packed and probably overexposed, but the hot-fudge sundaes and whimsical decor at **Serendipity 3,** 225 E. 60th St. (© **212/838-3531**), make children very, very happy.

NEW YORK
CITY IN DEPTH

2

When one thinks of New York City, I'm not sure children are necessarily the first thing that pops into mind. The New York of lore and noir is a sexy, smoky Jazz Age city of grown-up folks doing grown-up things—men in crisp fedoras moving smoothly into the blue-black night, women singing torch songs of love and loss. But this city of grown-ups has also raised millions of children over the years. For a century, kids have been riding the hand-carved horses on the Central Park Carousel. For 200 years they've played along the banks of the Hudson and East rivers. And the first immigrant to pass through Ellis Island was red-haired Annie Moore, who arrived in New York harbor on her 15th birthday. New York has been home for children in good times—as evidenced in Helen Levitt's wonderful 1930s photographs of children playing in the streets, opening fire hydrants, and being kids—and in hard. Children were once a big part of the labor force in New York, and many grew up within the impermeable walls of city slums. When I moved here, in the 1980s, crack dealers and users—many of whom could only be described as children—hung out in doorways and storefronts, projecting a defensively menacing air.

So it may be reasonable to say that I don't think children have ever had it as good as they do in the New York of the early 21st century. In fact, this may be the **golden age of the family in New York City.** These days, being a child in New York can be a wonderful existence. Not only is crime at record lows (the FBI has rated New York as the safest big city in the United States), but streets are cleaner than they ever were and parks safer and spiffier. According to the Citizens' Committee for Children of New York (CCC), which measures and tracks the well-being of New York City's children, greater numbers of children are enrolled in child-care, preschool, and out-of-school time; more children have health insurance—92.4% of all NYC kids were insured in 2008!—and academic achievement is improving across all race and ethnic groups and age ranges. In my own neighborhood, I see the progress in small but telling details. I see city parks bursting with flower beds that remain untouched over the summer. Newspapers dropped on door stoops are there until the owners retrieve them. Small children chase fireflies on July nights in once-forbidding city parks.

Still, these are both the best of times and the worst of times: The ongoing global recession is having a measurable effect on the families of New

York. The CCC, in tracking the early impacts of the 2008 economic downturn, has reported a dramatic rise in **family homelessness** and **food stamp applications** and a spike in **citywide unemployment.** Government budget cuts have forced the MTA to **cut vital bus and subway lines** and **reduce the frequency of mass-transit arrivals.** Even more alarming: The CCC reported that some 28% of all NYC children lived **below the Federal Poverty Line** in 2008, a rate that has not subsided. A hefty percentage of New Yorkers spend **one-half or more of their income on rent.** The social safety net is being stretched to its limits.

Yes, this is still a city of slums and children in wretched situations. But big progress has been made, and New Yorkers are a community-based bunch. The city has never been more welcoming to families than it is today, with more and more restaurants, hotels, museums, and retail shops going out of their way to cater to children and parents alike. Welcome to the Big Apple.

NEW YORK CITY TODAY

In the past 10 years New York has undergone a renaissance. This rebirth helped bring in nearly 46 million tourists in 2009; even more are projected in the next few years. And many are deciding to stay longer. In fact, it's predicted that New York City will add one million more residents by 2030.

At the same time, these are uneasy times. The economy is sputtering, corporations have made big cutbacks, beloved mom-and-pop stores have shuttered their doors all over the city, and residents are struggling mightily under the loss of jobs and homes. On the other hand, people are raising children in the city in record numbers, reflecting a long-view commitment to the urban life, circa 21st-century New York. The city's schools, both public and private, are bursting at the seams; new schools are in the works in every sector of the city.

For visitors, the city has never been more welcoming—and since statistics show that families compose the largest group of travelers to New York City, that means that children are getting the royal treatment as well. It's a pretty cool time to be a child in New York, whether living here on a permanent basis or an unofficial New Yorker for a few glorious days.

LOOKING BACK AT NEW YORK CITY
Colonial Days (1524–1776)

The area that became New York City was the home to many Native Americans before Giovanni da Verrazano arrived in 1524. And it wasn't until 1609, when Henry Hudson, while searching for the Northwest Passage, claimed it for the Dutch East India Company, that New York was recognized as a potential, profitable settlement in the New World.

Hudson (the river that separates Manhattan from the mainland is named after him) said of New York, "It is as beautiful a land as one can hope to tread upon." The treading didn't really start until years later, but by 1625, Dutch settlers established a fur trade with the locals and called their colony New Amsterdam. A year later, Peter Minuit of the Dutch West India Company made that famous deal for the island. He bought New Amsterdam from the Lenape Tribe for what has widely been reported as $24.

New Amsterdam became a British colony in the 1670s, and during the Revolutionary War it was occupied by British troops. England controlled New York until 1783, when it withdrew from the city 2 years *after* the end of the American Revolution.

Two years after that, New York was named the first capital of the United States. The first Congress was held at Federal Hall on Wall Street in 1789, and George Washington was inaugurated president. But New York's tenure as the capital didn't last long. A year later, the government headed south to Philadelphia for a decade, and eventually, to the newly created District of Columbia.

A Melting Pot City

By 1825, New York City's population swelled to 250,000, and it rose again to a half-million by midcentury. The city was a hotbed of Union recruitment during the Civil War; in the 1863 draft riots, Irish immigrants violently protested the draft and lynched 11 African Americans.

With industry booming, the late 19th century was termed the "Gilded Age." New York City was an example of this label in action; millionaires built mansions on Fifth Avenue, while rows of tenements teeming with families (made up of the cheap, mostly immigrant laborers who were employed by the industrial barons) filled the city's districts. In 1880, the city's population boomed to 1.1 million.

More European immigrants poured into the city between 1900 and 1930, arriving at Ellis Island and then fanning out into such neighborhoods as the Lower East Side, Greenwich Village, Little Italy, and Harlem. With the city population in 1930 at seven million and a Depression raging, New York turned to a feisty mayor named Fiorello La Guardia for help. With the assistance of civic planner Robert Moses, who masterminded a huge public works program, the city was remade. Moses did some things well, but his highway, bridge, tunnel, and housing projects ran through (and sometimes destroyed) many vibrant neighborhoods.

NEW YORK CITY TIMELINE

1524 Sailing under the French flag, Italian Giovanni da Verrazano is the first European to enter what's now New York Harbor.

1609 Henry Hudson sails up the Hudson River, exploring for the Dutch East India Company.

1626 The Dutch settle in Nieuw Amsterdam and make it a fur-trading post; Peter Minuit, governor of Nieuw Amsterdam, buys Manhattan Island from the Algonquin Indians for trinkets worth 60 florins (about $24).

1664 English invaders take Nieuw Amsterdam from the Dutch (wooden-legged Peter Stuyvesant is the Dutch governor).

1673 The Dutch take back Manhattan.

1674 Under the Treaty of Westminster, the Dutch finally give Nieuw Amsterdam to the English, who rename it New York after James, duke of York.

1776 American colonists topple the statue of King George on Bowling Green on July 9, but by year's end New York becomes a British

Post–World War II & Today

While most of the country prospered after World War II, New York, with those Moses-built highways and a newly forming car culture, endured an exodus to the suburbs. By 1958, the Dodgers had left Brooklyn and the Giants had left the Polo Grounds in upper Manhattan. This economic slide climaxed in the late 1970s with the city's declaration of bankruptcy.

As Wall Street rallied during the Reagan years of the 1980s, New York's fortunes also improved. In the 1990s, with Rudolph Giuliani—whom they haven't named anything after yet—as the mayor, and then followed by the current mayor, Michael Bloomberg, the city rode a wave of prosperity that left it safer, cleaner, and more populated. The flip side of this boom was that Manhattan became more homogenized. Witness the Disney-fication of Times Square—the ultimate symbol of New York's homogenization—and the growing gap between the rich and the poor.

Everything changed on September 11, 2001, when terrorists flew planes into the Twin Towers of the World Trade Center. But New York's grit and verve showed itself once more, as the city immediately began to rebound emotionally from that terrible tragedy. The financial aftermaths of the attacks were also short-lived, and the city has experienced an unprecedented building boom in the first decade of the 21st century.

Wall Street became the scourge of Main Street during the financial recession that walloped the nation in 2008 and was ongoing at press time. The recession claimed major Wall Street firms like Lehman Brothers and Bear Stearns. The venerable investment firm Goldman Sachs agreed to a $550-million settlement for its role in the financial fallout, but at press time, many of the firm's employees were being awarded fat, pre-recession-size bonuses—an indication that the top of New York's economic food chain, at least, is on the rebound.

NEW YORK CITY'S ARCHITECTURE

New York City contains a wealth of architectural styles, from modest row houses to ornate churches to soaring skyscrapers. Constructed over 300 years, these buildings

stronghold for the rest of the American Revolution.	**1820** New York City is the nation's largest city, with a population of 124,000.
1783 Victorious Gen. George Washington bids farewell to his troops at Fraunces Tavern in Lower Manhattan.	**1853** The World's Fair is held in New York's Bryant Park.
1789 Washington is inaugurated as the first president at Federal Hall in New York City, the first capital of the new United States.	**1858–73** Central Park is laid out by Frederick Law Olmsted and Calvert Vaux.
1790 Philadelphia deposes New York City as the nation's capital.	**1883** The Brooklyn Bridge is completed, linking Manhattan and Brooklyn.
	1885–86 The Statue of Liberty is erected in New York Harbor.
1792 The first U.S. stock exchange is founded in New York City, making it the country's financial capital.	**1892** Ellis Island opens, begins processing more than a million immigrants yearly.

continues

represent the changing tastes of the city's residents from Colonial times to the present. A brief look at the city's most popular styles provides a unique perspective on the city's past, present, and future.

Georgian (1700–76)

This style reflects Renaissance ideas made popular in England, and later in the United States, through the publication of books on 16th-century Italian architects. In the United States, the style was seen as an appropriate expression of the relative prosperity and security of the colonies. It was a sharp contrast to the unadorned Colonial style that preceded it.

St. Paul's Chapel, on Broadway between Vesey and Fulton streets (1764–66, Thomas McBean), the only pre-Revolutionary building remaining in Manhattan, is an almost perfect example of the Georgian style, with a pediment, colossal columns, Palladian window, quoins, and balustrade above the roofline (see illustration). Although it's a 20th-century reconstruction of a formal English house built here in 1719, **Fraunces Tavern,** 54 Pearl St., is another fine example of the style.

Federal (1780–1820)

Federal was the first truly American architectural style. Federal was popular with successful merchants throughout the cities and towns of the eastern seaboard. Its connection to the prosperous empires of Rome and Greece was seen as an appropriate reference for the young United States.

In New York, the Federal style was popular for row houses built after the 1811 creation of the city's grid pattern of avenues and streets.

In the **West Village,** near and along Bedford Street between Christopher and Morton streets, are more original Federal-style houses than anywhere else in Manhattan. House nos. 4 through 10 (1825–34) on Grove Street, just off Bedford, present one of the most authentic groups of late Federal–style houses in America.

1904 The first subway departs from City Hall.

1911 The Triangle Shirtwaist factory fire downtown kills 148 garment workers, among them children as young as 12 and 13. The fire led to legislation protecting worker safety and eventually to the banning of children from the labor force.

1920 Babe Ruth joins the New York Yankees.

1923 Yankee Stadium opens.

1929 The stock market crashes on October 29, sending not only Wall Street but also the entire nation into an economic tailspin that results in the Great Depression.

1931 The Empire State Building opens and is the tallest building in the world.

1939 The New York World's Fair opens in Flushing Meadows, Queens.

1947 The Brooklyn Dodgers sign Jackie Robinson, the first African American to play in the Major Leagues.

1957 Elvis Presley performs live in New York on the *Ed Sullivan Show.*

1969 The Gay Rights movement begins with the Stonewall Rebellion in Greenwich Village.

Greek Revival (1820–60)

The Greek Revolution in the 1820s, in which Greece won its independence from the Turks, recalled to American intellectuals the democracy of ancient Greece and its elegant architecture, created around 400 B.C. At the same time, the War of 1812 diminished American affection for the British influence, including the still-dominant Federal style. The style was so popular it came to be known as the National Style, and was used for numerous state capitols, as well as the U.S. Capitol in Washington, D.C.

Perhaps the city's finest Greek Revival building is **Federal Hall National Memorial** (1834–42), at 26 Wall St., where George Washington took his presidential oath in 1789 (see illustration). It has a Greek temple front, with Doric columns and a simple pediment, resting on a high base, called a plinth, with a steep flight of steps.

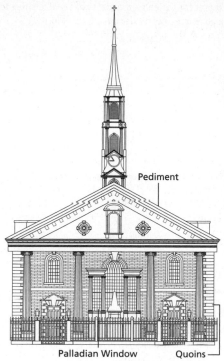

Pediment

Palladian Window   Quoins

St. Paul's Chapel

1990   David Dinkins becomes the first African-American mayor of New York City.

2000   The New York Yankees beat the New York Mets in the first Subway Series in 44 years. New York's population exceeds eight million.

2001   Terrorists use hijacked planes to crash into the Twin Towers of the World Trade Center, bringing the towers down and killing more than 3,000 people.

2003   Smoking is banned in all restaurants and bars.

2005   Throughout February, tourists from around the world stroll through Christo and Jeanne-Claude's *The Gates*, a joyous art installation that fills Central Park with strategically placed saffron-colored flags.

2006   Construction begins on the controversial Freedom Tower, to be built at the site of the World Trade Center.

2007–08   The bursting of the housing bubble and the subsequent liquidity shortfalls (fueled by toxic

continues

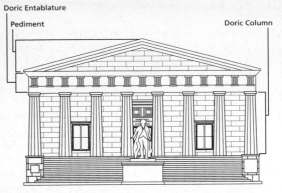

Doric Entablature

Pediment

Doric Column

Federal Hall National Memorial

Gothic Revival (1830–60)

The term *Gothic Revival* refers to a literary and aesthetic movement of the 1830s and 1840s that occurred in England and later in the United States. The revival style was used for everything from timber cottages to stone castles and churches. Some structures had only one or two Gothic features, most commonly a steeply pitched roof or pointed arches, whereas other buildings, usually churches, were accurate copies of English Gothic structures.

Trinity Church, at Broadway and Wall Street (Richard Upjohn, 1846), is one of the most celebrated, authentic Gothic Revival structures in the United States. Here you see all the features of a Gothic church: a steeple, battlements, pointed arches, Gothic tracery, stained-glass windows, flying buttresses (an external bracing system for supporting a roof or vault), and medieval sculptures. This was the tallest building in the area until the late 1860s.

Italianate (1840–80)

The architecture of Italy served as the inspiration for this building style. Its adaptability made it immensely popular in the 1850s. In New York, the style was used for urban row houses and commercial buildings. The development of cast iron at this time permitted the mass production of decorative features that few could have

credit-default swaps and other complex derivatives) trigger an economic free-fall, with housing prices and the stock market plummeting, big Wall Street banking/investment firms like Lehman Brothers imploding, and the federal government coming to the rescue with institutional bailouts.

2008 The last season for old Yankee Stadium; the new stadium opens in 2009.

2009 The southern section of the High Line urban park, a repurposed elevated freight line, opens in June.

2009 The New York Yankees win the World Series in their first year at the new stadium.

2009 Michael Bloomberg wins reelection as mayor of New York City after successfully campaigning to overturn the city's term-limits law.

afforded in carved stone. This led to the creation of cast-iron districts in nearly every American city, including New York.

New York's **SoHo–Cast Iron Historic District** has 26 blocks jammed with cast-iron facades, many in the Italianate manner. The single richest section is **Greene Street** between Houston and Canal streets. Stroll along here and take in building after building of sculptural facades.

Early Skyscraper (1880–1920)

The invention of the skyscraper can be traced directly to the use of cast iron in the 1840s, as seen in New York's SoHo. Experimentation with cast and wrought iron eventually allowed buildings to rise higher. (Previously, buildings were restricted by the height supportable by their load-bearing walls.) Important technical innovations—involving safety elevators, electricity, fireproofing, foundations, plumbing, and telecommunications—combined with advances in skeletal construction to create a new building type, the skyscraper. These buildings were spacious, cost-effective, efficient, and quickly erected—in short, the perfect architectural solution for America's growing downtowns.

Solving the technical problems of the skyscraper did not resolve how the building should look.

New York's early skyscrapers relied heavily on historical decoration. A good early example in the Beaux Arts mode is the **American Surety Company**, at 100 Broadway (Bruce Price, 1895). The triangular **Flatiron Building**, at Fifth Avenue and 23rd Street (Daniel H. Burnham & Co., 1902), has strong tripartite divisions and Renaissance Revival detail. And, finally, the later **Woolworth Building** (Cass Gilbert, 1913), on Broadway at Park Place, dubbed the "Cathedral of Commerce," is a neo-Gothic skyscraper with flying buttresses, spires, sculptured gargoyles, and pointed arches.

Beaux Arts (1890–1920)

This style takes its name from the Ecole des Beaux-Arts in Paris, where a number of prominent American architects (including **Richard Morris Hunt** [1827–95], **John Mervin Carrère** [1858–1911], and **Thomas Hastings** [1860–1929], to name only a few) received their training, beginning around the mid–19th century. These architects adopted the academic design principles of the Ecole, which emphasized the study of Greek and Roman structures, composition, and symmetry, and the creation of elaborate presentation drawings. Because of the idealized origins and grandiose use of classical forms, the Beaux Arts in America was seen as the ideal style for expressing civic pride.

New York has several exuberant Beaux Arts buildings, exhibiting the style's key features. The **New York Public Library**, at Fifth Avenue and 42nd Street (Carrère & Hastings, 1911), is perhaps the best example. Others of note are **Grand Central Terminal**, at 42nd Street and Park Avenue (Reed & Stem and Warren & Wetmore, 1903–13), and the **U.S. Customs House** (Cass Gilbert, 1907), on Bowling Green between State and Whitehall streets.

International Style (1920–45)

In 1932, the Museum of Modern Art hosted its first architecture exhibit, titled simply "Modern Architecture." Displays included images of International Style buildings from around the world, many designed by architects from Germany's Bauhaus, a progressive design school. The structures shared a stark simplicity and functionalism, a definite break from historically based, decorative styles.

The International Style was popularized in the U.S. through the teachings and designs of **Ludwig Mies van der Rohe** (1886–1969), a German émigré based in Chicago. Interpretations of the "Miesian" International Style were built in most U.S. cities, including New York, as late as 1980.

Two famous examples of this style are the **Seagram Building,** at 375 Park Ave. (Ludwig Mies van der Rohe, 1958), and **Lever House,** 390 Park Ave., between 53rd and 54th streets (Skidmore, Owings & Merrill, 1952). The latter is credited for popularizing the use of plazas and glass curtain walls.

Another well-known example is the Secretariat building in the **United Nations** complex, at First Avenue and 46th Street (1947–53), designed by an international committee of architects.

Art Deco (1925–40)

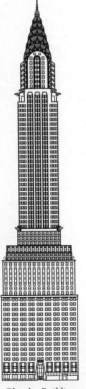

Chrysler Building

Art Deco is a decorative style that took its name from a Paris exposition in 1925. The jazzy style embodied the idea of modernity. One of the first widely accepted styles not based on historic precedents, it influenced all areas of design from jewelry and household goods to cars, trains, and ocean liners.

Art Deco buildings are characterized by a linear, hard edge, or angular composition, often with a vertical emphasis and highlighted with stylized decoration. The New York zoning law of 1916, which required setbacks in buildings above a certain height to ensure that light and air could reach the street, gave the style its distinctive profile.

Despite the effects of the Depression, several major Art Deco structures were built in New York in the 1930s, often providing crucial jobs. **Rockefeller Center** (Raymond Hood, 1932–40), a complex that sprawls from 48th to 50th streets, between Fifth and Sixth avenues, includes 30 Rockefeller Plaza, a tour de force of Art Deco style, with a soaring, vertical shaft and aluminum details. The **Chrysler Building,** Lexington Avenue at 42nd Street (William Van Alen, 1930), is a towering tribute to the automobile (see illustration). The Chrysler's needle-like spire with zigzag patterns in glass and metal is a distinctive feature on the city's skyline. The famous **Empire State Building,** Fifth Avenue at 34th Street (Shreve, Lamb & Harmon, 1931), contains a black- and silver-toned lobby among its many Art Deco features.

Postmodern (1975–90)

After years of steel-and-glass office towers in the International Style, Postmodernism burst on the scene in the 1970s with the reintroduction of historical precedents in architecture. With many feeling that the office towers of the previous style were too cold, Postmodernists began to incorporate classical details and recognizable forms into their designs—often applied in outrageous proportions.

The **Sony Building,** at 550 Madison Ave. (Philip Johnson/John Burgee, 1984), brings the distinctive shape of a Chippendale cabinet to the New York skyline. The **Morgan Bank Headquarters,** 60 Wall St. (Kevin Roche, John Dinkeloo & Associates, 1988), resembles a classical column, with modern interpretations of a base, shaft, and capital. The base of the column mirrors the style of the facade of the 19th-century building across the street.

The new building boom at the beginning of the 21st century has brought edifices designed by such modern architectural giants as Frank Gehry, who designed the **IAC Building** on West 18th Street with the look of billowing curtains, and Renzo Piano, who designed the 52-story headquarters of the *New York Times* at 620 Eighth Ave. at 42nd Street, which opened in November 2007 (and was climbed by not one but two "human spiders" on the same day in June 2008!).

SHOW & TELL: GETTING THE KIDS INTERESTED IN NYC

Several corny old songs come in handy as memory guides for New York City geography: Start with "I'll take Manhattan / The Bronx and Staten Island too" to teach your kids about the city's five boroughs, the other two being Brooklyn and Queens. Then there's "New York, New York, a wonderful town / The Bronx is up and the Battery's down / The people ride in a hole in the ground." Discuss the subway lines—rendered in different colors on the map—and talk about the neighborhoods and sights they pass through. New York's subways have been cleaned up incredibly since the early 1980s, and it's perfectly safe to take your kids for rides on these underground trains.

Current TV shows tend to present New York either as a hangout for navel-gazing singles or as a gritty battlefield for cops. For a more fun image of Manhattan, try two of my favorite New York kids' movies, *Ghostbusters* and *Splash. Crocodile Dundee* is a lighthearted look at how an outsider might view New York. *The Muppets Take Manhattan* captures the city in its own wacky, cartoony spirit. *Stuart Little* and *Home Alone II* show kids adventuring in NYC; the Olsen twins' *New York Minute* is a tweens' fantasy of NYC escapades. For a kids'-eye view of grown-up New York, try the Tom Hanks classic *Big* or its more recent girl equivalent, *13 Going on 30.* Older kids interested in downtown lifestyle might like *Desperately Seeking Susan* or Adam Sandler's *Big Daddy.* Digging deep into the classics vaults, you could get *Miracle on 34th Street,* the musical *On the Town,* or the priceless *Breakfast at Tiffany's.* For particular neighborhoods, *You've Got Mail* is a love letter to the Upper West Side; *Crossing Delancey* captures the Lower East Side; and *Everybody Says I Love You* (along with most other Woody Allen films) serenades the Upper East Side. For outer-borough views, consult *Moonstruck* or *Saturday Night Fever* (Brooklyn) or *Raising Helen* (Queens).

New York City's skyline is a famous sight—prime your youngsters for that first glimpse of it. Buildings to identify include the Empire State Building, with its tall antenna tower up which the original King Kong climbed; the Chrysler Building's chrome-tipped Art Deco spire, looking for all the world like a spectacular hood ornament; the riverside United Nations, a vertical plane of sheer glass anchored by the dome of the General Assembly; the slant-roofed white Citibank Building; and the Chippendale-style crest on the Sony Building. The Statue of Liberty is another indelible New York landmark to show your kids pictures of ahead of time. Yet another is Rockefeller Plaza, where a giant gilded statue overlooks an ice-skating rink in winter and an outdoor cafe in summer—and where the even-more-giant Rockefeller Center Christmas tree sparkles during the holiday season.

Older kids may have strong associations with New York's battery of sports teams—depending on the season, watch some innings of Yankees or Mets baseball; a Jets or Giants football game; a Rangers, Devils, or Islanders hockey match; or a Knicks or Nets basketball game.

TOP kids' books SET IN NEW YORK CITY

Picture Books

○ *The Adventures of Taxi Dog,* by Debra and Sal Barracca (Dial; ages 2–6). This, or any of the Barraccas' books about Maxi the Taxi dog, is a lovable look at the city from the seat of a yellow cab.

○ *Tar Beach,* by Faith Ringgold (Crown; ages 2–5). This charming book recounts evocative memories of a Harlem childhood and hot summer nights up on the roof.

○ *The Escape of Marvin the Ape,* by Caralyn and Mark Buehner (Dial; ages 3–6). This book portrays a fugitive gorilla happily losing himself in New York City's parks, museums, stores, and ballparks.

○ *The Little Red Lighthouse and the Great Gray Bridge,* by Hildegarde H. Swift and Lynd Ward (Harcourt Brace; ages 4–7). A Hudson River lighthouse feels superseded by the new George Washington Bridge, until one dark and stormy night. . . . Kids can still see both landmarks today.

○ *Eloise,* by Kay Thompson (Simon & Schuster; ages 4–8). This irrepressible 6-year-old growing up in the Plaza Hotel definitely has an exotic view of life. Perfect for the precocious.

Chapter Books

○ *The Cricket in Times Square,* by George Selden (Farrar, Straus and Giroux or Yearling paperback; ages 6–10). A Connecticut cricket winds up in the Times Square subway station and becomes the toast of Manhattan.

○ *Stuart Little,* by E. B. White (Harper & Row; ages 7–10). The Little family's mouse-size young son has adventures in and around Central Park.

○ *All of a Kind Family,* by Sydney Taylor (Dell Yearling; ages 7–10). This portrait of a Jewish family living on the Lower East Side is a window into turn-of-the-20th-century New York.

○ *The Saturdays,* by Elizabeth Enright (Puffin Books; ages 7–10). Four siblings pool their resources to explore New York City on weekends; it's set in the 1940s but is not as dated as it may seem.

○ *Harriet the Spy,* by Louise Fitzhugh (HarperTrophy; ages 8–11). Spunky sixth grader Harriet M. Welch keeps tabs on her East Side friends and neighbors.

○ *From the Mixed-Up Files of Mrs. Basil E. Frankweiler,* by E. L. Konigsburg (Simon & Schuster or Aladdin paperback; ages 8–12). A 12-year-old Connecticut girl and her younger brother hole up in the Metropolitan Museum and become involved in an art mystery.

○ *Gossip Girls,* by Cecily von Ziegesar (Little Brown; ages 13 and up). This is a paperback series depicting the lives and loves of Upper East Side private-school brats; trashy and a little risqué, it's like *Sex and the City* for teens.

PLANNING A FAMILY TRIP TO NEW YORK CITY

N ew York City is much more kid-friendly than most visitors anticipate—the trick lies in planning your trip to take advantage of it. Timing is everything, as is fortifying yourself with all the printed information you can snare.

For additional help in planning your trip and more on-the-ground resources (including the best ways to get around town), turn to chapter 4.

VISITOR INFORMATION

Before you leave home, head to the official NYC & Company tourism website, **www.nycgo.com**, for the latest on, well, everything—top attractions, events, suggested itineraries, tours, and TV show tapings, plus basic tips—and download the official visitor guide as well as city, park, and bike maps. To request a free copy of the *Official Visitor Guide*, call ⓒ **800/NYCVISIT** [692-8474] or 212/397-8222.

The **Times Square Alliance** (www.timessquarenyc.org) is a terrific source for information about Broadway theater, Midtown hotels and restaurants, and special events. For upcoming **events in city parks,** visit www.nycgovparks.org; for **Central Park events,** go to www.centralpark.com.

You can also get a good sense of all that's going on in the city by checking out **Time Out New York Kids** (www.timeout.com/newyork/kids), which has up-to-date, detailed listings of cultural events kids would enjoy, as does the website **www.urbanbaby.com**. We also like **Macaroni Kid** (www.national.macaronikid.com), an exhaustive listing of the goings-on in New York, reported by parent/publishers; you can sign up for the weekly online newsletter from the correspondents from the Upper East Side, the Upper West Side, or Downtown—all report on goings-on all over town.

For visitor-center and information-desk locations once you arrive, see "Visitor Information," in chapter 4.

FOR U.K. VISITORS The **NYCVB Visitor Information Center** is at 36 Southwark Bridge Rd., London, SE1 9EU (ⓒ **020/7202-6367**). You can order the *Official Visitor Guide* by sending an A5-size self-addressed envelope and 72p postage to the above address. For New York–bound travelers in London, the center also offers free one-on-one travel-planning assistance.

WHEN TO GO

New York buzzes every day, with pretty much everything open year-round. All school vacation seasons—late December, spring vacation, and summer—tend to be busy times; lots of museums schedule special programs then, because New York schoolchildren are looking for something to do, too. December is particularly jampacked, with lots of annual holiday entertainment (the *Nutcracker,* the Big Apple Circus, the Radio City Christmas Spectacular). Fall is traditionally the prime season for culture, with new plays opening on Broadway and classical-music venues booked solid, but even in summer, music series at Lincoln Center and star-studded limited-run plays fill the boards. Spring and summer weekends really bustle, with street fairs all over town and what seems like an endless succession of parades, one for every ethnic group in the city, filing down Fifth Avenue. Following are suggestions on the best times to visit the Big Apple when it comes to weather, crowds, and budgetary considerations.

WEATHER   Many consider those hot and muggy mid-July and mid-August days, when temperatures can go up to as high as 100°F (38°C) with 90% humidity, as New York's worst weather. But don't get put off by this—summer has its compensations, such as wonderful free open-air concerts and other events, as we've mentioned. But if you are at all temperature sensitive, and you plan to spend a lot of your visit outdoors, your odds of getting comfortable weather are better in June or September.

Another period when you might not like to stroll around the city is during January or February, when temperatures are commonly in the 20s (below 0°C) and those concrete canyons turn into wind tunnels. The city looks gorgeous for about a day after a snowfall, but the streets soon become a slushy mess. Again, you never know—temperatures have regularly been in the 30s and mild 40s (single digits Celsius) during the past few "global warmed" winters. If you hit the weather jackpot, you could have a bargain bonanza (see "Money & Costs," later in this chapter).

Fall and spring are the best times in New York. From April to June and September to November, temperatures are mild and pleasant, and the light is beautiful. With the leaves changing in Central Park and just the hint of crispness in the air, October is a fabulous time to be here—but expect to pay for the privilege.

If you want to know what to pack just before you go, check the Weather Channel's online 10-day forecast at **www.weather.com**. You can also get the local weather by calling ℭ **212/976-1212.**

New York's Average Temperature & Rainfall

	JAN	FEB	MAR	APR	MAY	JUNE	JULY	AUG	SEPT	OCT	NOV	DEC
Daily Temp. (°F)	32	34	42	53	63	72	77	76	68	58	48	37
Daily Temp. (°C)	0	1	6	12	17	22	25	24	20	14	9	3
Days of Precipitation	11	10	11	11	11	10	11	10	8	8	9	10

SEASONAL GUIDELINES   The global recession has forced many hoteliers to offer special packages to keep rooms filled, but in general lodging in the city remains pricey. If money is a big concern, you might want to follow these rough seasonal guidelines.

New York Metropolitan Area

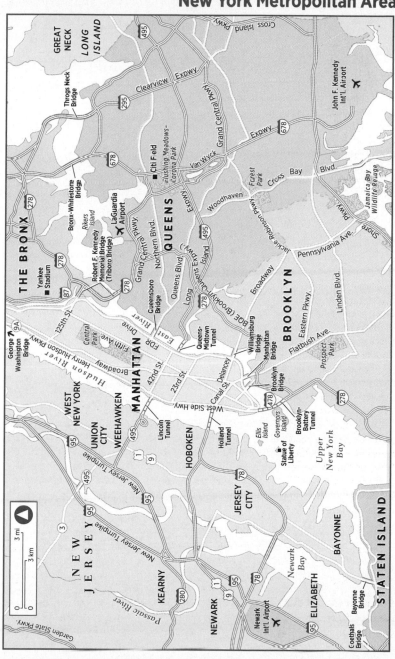

Bargain hunters might want to visit during the post-holidays winter, between the first of the year and early April. Sure, you might have to bear some cold weather, but that's when hotels are suffering from the post-holiday blues, and rooms often go for a relative song—a song in this case meaning a room with a private bathroom for as little as $150. AAA cardholders can do even better in many cases (generally a 5%–10% savings if the hotel offers a AAA discount). However, be aware that the occasional convention or event, such as February's annual Fashion Week, can sometimes throw a wrench in your winter savings plans.

Spring and fall are traditionally the busiest and most expensive seasons after holiday time. Don't expect hotels to be handing you deals, but you may be able to negotiate a decent rate.

The city is drawing more families these days, and they usually visit in the summer. Still, the prospect of heat and humidity keeps some people away, making July and the first half of August a cheaper time to visit than later in the year; good hotel deals are often available.

During the Christmas season, expect to pay top dollar for everything. The first 2 weeks of December—the shopping weeks—are the worst when it comes to scoring an affordable hotel room; that's when shoppers from around the world converge on the town to catch the holiday spirit and spend, spend, spend. But Thanksgiving can be a great time to come, believe it or not: Business travelers have gone home, and the holiday shoppers haven't yet arrived. It's a little-known secret that most hotels away from the Thanksgiving Day Parade route have empty rooms, and they're usually willing to make great deals to fill them.

Also note that hotels are slightly less crowded on weekends, when business travelers clear out of town; many even offer weekend package rates.

Kids' Favorite New York City Events

The following information is always subject to change. Be sure to confirm information before you make plans around a specific event. Call the venue or visit the NYC & Company tourism website **www.nycgo.com** before you leave home; or pick up a copy of *Time Out New York* once you arrive in the city for the latest details.

JANUARY

New York National Boat Show. Slip on your Top-Siders and head to the **Jacob K. Javits Convention Center,** which promises a leviathan fleet of boats and marine products from the world's leading manufacturers. Call ℂ **212/984-7000** or visit **www. nyboatshow.com** or www.javitscenter.com. Third week in January.

Restaurant Week. Twice a year some of the best restaurants in town offer three-course prix-fixe meals at *almost* affordable prices. At lunch, the deal is $24.07 (as in 24/7), while dinner is $35. It's a great way to sample the menu at some of New York's most heralded restaurants (and not break the bank doing it), especially with older kids with more adventurous palates. Book your

tables at **www.nycgo.com/restaurantweek**. Late January.

FEBRUARY

Black History Month is observed with some very good programs for kids at museums around town. Throughout February.

Chinese New Year. Every year, Chinatown rings in its own New Year (based on a lunar calendar) with 2 weeks of celebrations, including parades with dragon and lion dancers, plus vivid costumes of all kinds. The parade usually winds throughout Chinatown along Mott, Canal, and Bayard streets, and along East Broadway. Go to **www.explore chinatown.com** or **www.betterchinatown. com**. Chinese New Year falls on January 23 in 2012, and it's the Year of the Dragon.

New York International Children's Film Festival. This fun festival showing the latest in film for kids 3 to 18 is screened at venues around town. The NYICFF Awards Ceremony is held in March, and young viewers get to vote to award festival prizes for certain portions of the program. In addition, the festival hosts special screenings of kids' films (new and old) all year long. Go to **www.gkids.com**.

Westminster Kennel Club Dog Show. The ultimate purebred-pooch fest. Some 30,000 dog fanciers from all over the globe congregate at **Madison Square Garden** for the 133rd "World Series of Dogdom." All 2,500 dogs are American Kennel Club Champions of Record, competing for Best in Show. Check the website **www.westminsterkennelclub.org** for further info. Tickets are available after January 1 via **Ticketmaster** (*(C)* **212/307-7171;** www.ticketmaster.com). February 14 and 15, 2011.

MARCH

The **St. Patrick's Day parade** rolls down Fifth Avenue with more than 150,000 marchers—it's the world's largest civilian parade. The parade usually starts at 11am, but go early if you want a good spot. Go to **www.saintpatricksdayparade.com/nyc/newyorkcity.htm** for more information. March 17.

The **Ringling Bros. and Barnum & Bailey Circus** begins its annual month-long run at Madison Square Garden. For dates and ticket information, check out the website **www.ringling.com** or contact Madison Square Garden (*(C)* **212/465-MSG1** [465-6741]; www.thegarden.com). Late March to mid-April.

APRIL

The annual **Central Park Easter egg hunt** is held on Easter weekend near the Bandshell, with activities, giveaways, and visiting celebrities.

The **Easter Parade** is a stroll down Fifth Avenue that anyone can join—the bigger the bonnet, the better. The parade generally runs from about 10am to 3 or 4pm. Call *(C)* **212/484-1222.** Easter Sunday.

MAY

Bike New York: TD Bank Five Boro Bike Tour. The largest mass-participation cycling event in the United States attracts about 30,000 cyclists from all over the world. After a 42-mile ride through the five boroughs, finalists are greeted with a traditional New York–style celebration of food and music. Call *(C)* **212/932-BIKE** (932-2453) or visit **www.bikenewyork.org.** First or second Sunday in May.

Ninth Avenue International Food Festival. Street fairs are part of the New York landscape each summer, but this is one of the best. You can spend the day sampling Italian sausages, clams and oysters on the half-shell, homemade pirogi, spicy curries, and other ethnic dishes. Street musicians, bands, and vendors add to the festive atmosphere stretching along Ninth Avenue from 37th to 57th streets. Call *(C)* **212/484-1222.** Early to mid-May.

The Brooklyn Botanic Garden's annual **Cherry Blossom Festival** takes a cue from Japanese tradition in celebrating the flowering pink trees around its pond. Call *(C)* **718/623-7200** or visit **www.bbg.org.** Early May.

Fleet Week welcomes a host of U.S. and foreign naval ships to the Hudson River piers around Memorial Day weekend, highlighted by a parade of ships. Call *(C)* **212/484-1222.** Late May.

JUNE

Museum Mile Festival. Fifth Avenue from 82nd to 106th streets is closed to cars from 6 to 9pm as 20,000-plus strollers enjoy live music from Broadway tunes to string quartets, street entertainers from juggling to giant puppets, and free admission to nine Museum Mile institutions, including the Metropolitan Museum of Art and the Guggenheim. Call *(C)* **212/606-2296** or check **www.museummilefestival.org** or any of the participating institutions for details. Usually the second Tuesday in June.

SummerStage. A summer-long festival of outdoor performances in Central Park, featuring world music, pop, folk, and jazz artists ranging from Fiona Apple to the New York Grand Opera (always performing Verdi) to the Chinese Golden Dragon Acrobats. Performances are mostly free, but certain events require purchased tickets (usually around

$35). Call ☎ **212/360-2756** or visit **www. summerstage.org**. June through August.

JULY

Independence Day Harbor Festival and Fourth of July Fireworks Spectacular. Start the day amid the crowds at the Great July Fourth Festival in lower Manhattan, and then catch Macy's fireworks extravaganza (one of the country's most fantastic) over the East River (the best vantage point is from FDR Drive, which closes to traffic several hours before sunset). Call ☎ **212/ 484-1222** or Macy's Visitor Center at 212/ 494-3827. July 4.

Lincoln Center Festival. This festival celebrates the best of the performing arts from all over—theater, ballet, contemporary dance, opera, nouveau circus performances, even puppet and media-based art. Recent editions have featured performances by Ornette Coleman, the Royal Opera, the Royal Ballet, and the New York Philharmonic. Schedules are available in mid-March, and tickets go on sale in May or early June. Visit **http://new.lincolncenter. org/live**. Throughout July.

Midsummer Night's Swing. Dancers head to the **Lincoln Center's Josie Robertson Plaza** for evenings of big-band swing, salsa, and tango under the stars to the sounds of top-flight bands. Dance lessons are offered with purchase of a ticket. Visit **http://new. lincolncenter.org/live**. July and August.

AUGUST

The **Lincoln Center Out-of-Doors Festival** turns the plaza around the arts complex into one big street fair, with crafts and food stalls and loads of free performances. Visit **http://new.lincolncenter.org/live** for this year's schedule. Throughout August.

The **U.S. Open Tennis Championships** are played in Flushing Meadows, Queens, for 2 weeks starting just before Labor Day. If at all possible, be here for **Arthur Ashe Kids' Day,** which kicks off the tournament with appearances by the pros, music, and interactive games and clinics ($10–$20). Tickets for both go on sale in May or early June and often sell out immediately; call ☎ **866/OPEN-TIX** (673-6849) or 718/760-6200 well in advance;

visit **www.usopen.org** for additional information. Late August to early September.

SEPTEMBER

The **Feast of San Gennaro** fills the streets of Little Italy with carnival booths and Italian food stands for 11 days around the saint's day, September 19. Call ☎ **212/768-9320** or visit **www.sangennaro.org** for details.

OCTOBER

Feast of St. Francis. Animals from dogs to goldfish to elephants are blessed as thousands of *Homo sapiens* look on at the **Cathedral of St. John the Divine.** It's a magical experience. A festive fair follows the blessing and music events. It's a good idea to buy tickets in advance. For tickets, call the cathedral's box office at ☎ **212/ 662-2133** or visit www.stjohndivine.org. First Sunday in October.

Ice-Skating. Show off your skating style in the limelight at the diminutive **Rockefeller Center rink** (☎ 212/332-7654; www. rockefellercenter.com), open from mid-October to mid-March or early April (you'll skate under the magnificent Christmas tree for the month of Dec). In Central Park, spacious **Wollman Rink** has views of the park and the Central Park South skyline; it's on the east side of the park between 62nd and 63rd streets (☎ **212/439-6900;** www. wollmanskatingrink.com). **Lasker Rink** lies midpark between 106th and 108th streets (☎ **917/492-3857**). Both Central Park skating rinks usually close in early April.

The **Big Apple Circus** settles in for its annual 3-month run at Lincoln Center's Damrosch Park. Call ☎ **212/307-4100** or check out **www.bigapplecircus.org**. Mid-October through mid-January.

The **Greenwich Village Halloween Parade** marches up lower Sixth Avenue with sass and style. Call the Village Voice Parade hot line at ☎ **212/475-3333,** ext. 14044, or visit **www.halloween-nyc.com**. October 31.

NOVEMBER

The **Radio City Christmas Spectacular** at Radio City Music Hall ushers in the holiday season early, beginning a 2-month run. Call ☎ 212/247-4777 or visit **www.radiocity christmas.com/newyork** for exact dates;

buy tickets at the box office or via Ticket-master's Radio City Hotline at ℂ **212/307-1000** or www.ticketmaster.com.

The **Holiday Train Show** at the New York Botanical Garden in the Bronx is a spectacular holiday treat, featuring vintage trains running past replicas of New York landmarks—extraordinary miniatures made out of plant materials. Visit **www.nybg.org** for details. Late November through mid-January.

The Chocolate Show. This burgeoning 4-day event devoted to chocolate takes place each year about 2 weeks before Thanksgiving and is open to the public. The event features booths representing more than 50 of the world's best chocolate makers, tastings, demonstrations, and activities for children. For info, call **866/CHOC-NYC** (246-2692) or 212/889-5112 or visit **www.chocolateshow.com**.

The **Macy's Thanksgiving Day Parade** runs from 77th Street and Central Park West down to Broadway and 34th Street; sidewalk viewing along the route is first-come, first-served. The night before, it's great fun to watch the parade's mighty balloons being inflated on 77th and 81st streets, around the Museum of Natural History; go early—it gets to be a mob scene by 8pm. Call Macy's Visitor Center at ℂ **212/494-4495.**

DECEMBER

The **Christmas Tree Lighting** at Rockefeller Center is accompanied by an ice-skating show and a huge crowd. The tree stays lit around the clock until after the New Year. Contact ℂ **212/332-6868** or www.rockefellercenter.com for this year's date.

The *Nutcracker* ballet, performed by the New York City Ballet every year at Lincoln Center, is a perpetual delight. Call ℂ **212/870-5570** or visit www.nycballet.com.

The Lighting of the Giant Hanukkah Menorah at Fifth Avenue and 59th Street is performed on the world's largest menorah (32 ft. high) each evening during Hanukkah.

New Year's Eve is celebrated famously in Times Square; although this is hardly an event for kids (or for parents who aren't crazy about lunatic crowds), several other events around town capitalize on the holiday. Contact www.timessquarenyc.org for details. December 31 to January 1.

ENTRY REQUIREMENTS

Virtually every air traveler entering the U.S. is required to show a passport. All persons, including U.S. citizens, traveling by air between the United States and Canada, Mexico, Central and South America, the Caribbean, and Bermuda are required to present a valid passport. *Note:* U.S. and Canadian citizens entering the U. S. at land and sea ports of entry from within the western hemisphere must now also present a passport or other documents compliant with the Western Hemisphere Travel Initiative (WHTI; see www.getyouhome.gov for details). Children 15 and under may continue entering with only a U.S. birth certificate, or other proof of U.S. citizenship.

For information on how to obtain a passport (for both U.S. citizens and international visitors), go to **"Passports"** in chapter 13 (**"Fast Facts"**).

Visas

The U.S. State Department has a **Visa Waiver Program (VWP)** allowing citizens of the following countries to enter the United States without a visa for stays of up to 90 days: Andorra, Australia, Austria, Belgium, Brunei, Czech Republic, Denmark, Estonia, Finland, France, Germany, Hungary, Iceland, Ireland, Italy, Japan, Latvia, Liechtenstein, Lithuania, Luxembourg, Malta, Monaco, the Netherlands, New Zealand, Norway, Portugal, San Marino, Singapore, Slovakia, Slovenia, South Korea, Spain, Sweden, Switzerland, and the United Kingdom. (*Note:* This list was accurate at press time; for the most up-to-date list of countries in the VWP, consult http://travel.state.gov/visa.) Even though a visa isn't necessary, in an effort to help U.S. officials check travelers against terror watch lists before they arrive at U.S. borders, visitors from VWP countries must register online through the Electronic System for Travel Authorization (ESTA) before boarding a plane or a boat to the U.S. Travelers must complete an electronic application providing basic personal and travel eligibility information. The Department of Homeland Security recommends filling out the form at least 3 days before traveling. Authorizations will be valid for up to 2 years or until the traveler's passport expires, whichever comes first. Currently, there is no fee for the online application. **Note:** Any passport issued on or after October 26, 2006, by a VWP country must be an **e-Passport** for VWP travelers to be eligible to enter the U.S. without a visa. Citizens of these nations also need to present a round-trip air or cruise ticket upon arrival. E-Passports contain computer chips capable of storing biometric information, such as the required digital photograph of the holder. If your passport doesn't have this feature, you can still travel without a visa if the valid passport was issued before October 26, 2005, and includes a machine-readable zone; or if the valid passport was issued between October 26, 2005, and October 25, 2006, and includes a digital photograph. For more information, go to **http://travel.state.gov/visa**. Canadian citizens may enter the United States without visas, but will need to show passports and proof of residence.

Citizens of all other countries must have (1) a valid passport that expires at least 6 months later than the scheduled end of their visit to the U.S.; and (2) a tourist visa.

For specifics on how to get a visa, go to **"Visas"** in **"Fast Facts,"** in the appendix.

Medical Requirements

Unless you're arriving from an area known to be suffering from an epidemic (particularly cholera or yellow fever), inoculations or vaccinations are not required for entry into the United States.

Customs
WHAT YOU CAN BRING INTO THE U.S.

Every visitor 21 years of age or older may bring in, free of duty, the following: (1) 1 U.S. quart of alcohol; (2) 200 cigarettes, 50 cigars (but not from Cuba), or 3 pounds of smoking tobacco; and (3) $100 worth of gifts. These exemptions are offered to travelers who spend at least 72 hours in the United States and who have not claimed them within the preceding 6 months. It is forbidden to bring into the country almost any meat products (including canned, fresh, and dried meat products such as bouillon, soup mixes, and so forth). Generally, condiments including vinegars, oils, pickled goods, spices, coffee, tea, and some cheeses and baked goods are permitted. Avoid rice products, as rice can often harbor insects. Bringing fruits and vegetables is prohibited since they may harbor pests or disease. International visitors may carry in or out up to $10,000 in U.S. or foreign currency with no formalities; larger sums must be declared to U.S. Customs on entering or leaving, which includes filing form CM 4790. For details regarding U.S. Customs and Border Protection, consult your nearest U.S. embassy or consulate, or **U.S. Customs** (www.customs.gov).

WHAT YOU CAN TAKE HOME FROM NEW YORK

U.S. Citizens: U.S. Customs & Border Protection (CBP), 1300 Pennsylvania Ave. NW, Washington, DC 20229 (© **877/287-8667;** www.cbp.gov).

Canadian Citizens: Canada Border Services Agency, Ottawa, Ontario, K1A 0L8 (© **800/461-9999** in Canada, or 204/983-3500; www.cbsa-asfc.gc.ca).

U.K. Citizens: HM Customs & Excise, Crownhill Court, Tailyour Road, Plymouth, PL6 5BZ (© **0845/010-9000;** from outside the U.K., 020/8929-0152; www. hmce.gov.uk).

Australian Citizens: Australian Customs Service, Customs House, 5 Constitution Ave., Canberra City, ACT 2601 (© **1300/363-263;** from outside Australia, 612/6275-6666; www.customs.gov.au).

New Zealand Citizens: New Zealand Customs, The Customhouse, 17–21 Whitmore St., Box 2218, Wellington, 6140 (© **04/473-6099** or 0800/428-786; www.customs.govt.nz).

WHAT TO PACK

It's important to remember that this is preeminently a walking city. There's almost always a bit of a walk from the subway to wherever you're going, and even if you intend to cab it everywhere, you'll have to sprint for a taxi or two or trudge a few blocks when no cabs are in sight—which will happen. So bring your most **comfortable walking shoes,** whether sneakers, hiking shoes, cushioned sandals, or some sort of sturdy hybrid. Lots of shoe companies, among them Rockport, Merrell, Ecco, Mephisto, and Hush Puppies, make good-looking shoes with cushioned soles that can double as walking shoes and dining-out shoes, so you can make a seamless transition from street to restaurant without having to schlep back to your hotel.

Walking a lot also makes **strollers** a must for any young children who can't hike at least a mile without complaining. Strollers can be a hassle, though, when getting in and out of cabs or up and down subway stairs; a stroller that folds easily makes life simpler. If you have an infant, a **soft carrier** is an even better idea.

July and August can be miserably hot and sticky, conditions worsened by the fact that subway platforms are like saunas, thanks to the heat thrown off by the subway trains' air-conditioning (subway cars are glacially cool, by the way). **Short-sleeved T-shirts** and **shorts** are best—the roomier, the better. **Sun hats** are a great idea for the kids.

January and February are cold. **Warm gloves, hats,** and **scarves** are advisable if you arrive from November to March (sometimes Apr). If it does snow, the streets are plowed swiftly, and sidewalks get shoveled fast: It takes a really big blizzard to stop Manhattan in its tracks. But plowed banks of snow can stand for weeks, getting filthier and filthier. **Waterproof boots** are a good idea in winter, just in case, because lake-size puddles form at curbs—too big for kids to jump over.

If you're bringing an infant, call ahead to your hotel to check what baby equipment it can provide—besides a crib, it may help to have a highchair in your room. You may want to pack a few **electrical-outlet covers** so you can childproof your room when you arrive. Of course, you can buy diapers, wipes, formula, and no-tears shampoo here, but it might be handier to bring your own **bottles, sippy cups, feeding dish, infant spoon,** and **changing pads.**

Accidents do happen, so bring **extra changes of clothes** for your children; for infants and for toddlers who haven't mastered the fine art of using the potty, make that two or three changes of clothes for each day. You'll also want a **tote bag** full of toys and books. Older kids may want to carry their own **backpacks** with books, colored markers and pads, a deck of cards, hand-held electronic games, a personal CD player, or whatever keeps them happy.

Few restaurants have real dress codes; it is the rare spot that requires men to wear jackets and ties out to dinner. Bring along a **dressy outfit** (a jacket and tie for men;

boys may be able to get by without the tie) only if you plan to attend a dressy affair. That doesn't mean you should wear jeans or T-shirts out to dinner; bring "casual dressy" outfits that you can wear sightseeing and dining out.

GETTING THERE

Getting to New York City

BY PLANE

Three major airports serve New York City: **John F. Kennedy International Airport** (℃ **718/244-4444**) in Queens, about 15 miles (1 hr. driving time) from midtown Manhattan; **LaGuardia Airport** (℃ **718/533-3400**), also in Queens, about 8 miles (30 min.) from Midtown; and **Newark International Airport** (℃ **973/961-6000**) in nearby New Jersey, about 16 miles (45 min.) from Midtown. Information about all three airports is available online at **www.panynj.gov/airports**.

Even though LaGuardia is the closest airport to Manhattan, it has a bad reputation for delays and terminal chaos, in both ticket-desk lines and baggage claim. You may want to use JFK or Newark instead. (JFK has the best reputation for timeliness, such as it is, among New York–area airports.)

Almost every major domestic carrier serves at least one of the New York–area airports; most serve two or all three. Among them are **American** (℃ 800/433-7300; www.aa.com), **Continental** (℃ 800/525-3273; www.continental.com), **Delta** (℃ 800/221-1212; www.delta.com), **United** (℃ 800/864-8331; www.united.com), and **US Airways** (℃ 800/428-4322; www.usairways.com).

In recent years, there has been rapid growth in the number of start-up, no-frills airlines serving New York (and 2008–10 brought the demise of some of them, so definitely check and see whether the following are still flying when you are planning your trip). You might check out Atlanta-based **AirTran** (℃ 800/AIRTRAN [247-8726]; www.airtran.com), Denver-based **Frontier** (℃ 800/432-1359; www.flyfrontier.com), or Detroit-based **Spirit Airlines** (℃ 800/772-7117; www.spiritair.com). The JFK-based cheap-chic airline **JetBlue ★** (℃ 800/JETBLUE [538-2583]; www.jetblue.com) has taken New York by storm with its low fares and service to cities throughout the nation. The budget Canadian carrier **WestJet** (℃ 888/937-8538; www.westjet.com) makes regular flights from Toronto into Newark. The nation's leading discount airline, **Southwest** (℃ 800/435-9792; www.iflyswa.com), flies out of LaGuardia and MacArthur (Islip) Airport on Long Island, 50 miles east of Manhattan.

For a more complete list of the major airlines that fly to New York City, go to "Airline Websites" in chapter 13.

 Choosing Your NYC-Area Airport

It's more convenient to fly into Newark than JFK if your destination is Manhattan, and fares to Newark are often cheaper than those to the other airports. Newark is particularly convenient if your hotel is in Midtown West or downtown.

Taxi fare into Manhattan from Newark is roughly equivalent to the fare from JFK—both now have **AirTrains** in place (see "Getting into Town from the Airport," below), but the AirTrain to Newark from Manhattan is quicker.

GETTING INTO TOWN FROM THE AIRPORT

With young kids in tow, it's best to take a **cab** from the airport into the city. All three airports have orderly taxi stands where you line up until it's your turn for the uniformed dispatcher to help you into a licensed cab (only yellow cabs are licensed to pick up passengers from JFK and LaGuardia; New Jersey cab companies work from Newark).

Generally, travel time between the airports and Midtown by taxi or car is 45 to 60 minutes for JFK, 20 to 35 minutes for LaGuardia, and 35 to 50 minutes for Newark. Always allow extra time, especially during rush hour and peak holiday travel times.

If your kids are older, you don't have loads of luggage, and you want to save a little money, take a bus or shuttle into town—or, if you're coming from JFK, take the **Air Train** (see below).

For transportation information for all three airports (JFK, LaGuardia, and Newark), call the Port Authority's **Air-Ride** (© **800/247-7433**), which offers 24-hour recorded details on bus and shuttle companies and car services registered with the New York and New Jersey Port Authority. Similar information is available at **www.panynj.gov/airports**.

The Port Authority runs staffed Ground Transportation Information counters on the baggage-claim level at each airport where you can get information and book various kinds of transport. Most transportation companies also have courtesy phones near the baggage-claim area.

Following are the details on all your ground transportation options to and from the area airports.

TAXIS Despite significant rate hikes the past few years, taxis are still a quick and convenient way to travel to and from the airports. They're available at designated taxi stands outside the terminals, with uniformed dispatchers on hand during peak hours at JFK and LaGuardia, around the clock at Newark. Follow the GROUND TRANSPORTATION or TAXI signs. There may be a long line, but it generally moves pretty quickly. Fares, whether fixed or metered, do not include bridge and tunnel tolls ($4–$6) or a tip for the cab driver (15%–20% is customary). They do include all passengers in the cab and luggage—never pay more than the metered or flat rate, except for tolls and a tip (a $1 peak-time surcharge from 4–6pm and a 50¢ surcharge from 8pm–6am also applies on New York yellow cabs). Taxis have a limit of four passengers, so if there are more in your group, you'll have to take more than one cab. Of course, if you have a little one you can hold in your lap, the cab driver will probably let you take more than four people in one cab. For more on taxis, see "Getting Around," in chapter 4. The taxi fees from each airport are currently as follows:

o **From JFK:** A flat rate of $45 to Manhattan (plus tolls and tip) is charged. The meter will not be turned on and the surcharge will not be added. The flat rate does not apply on trips from Manhattan to the airport.

o **From LaGuardia:** It's $24 to $30, metered, plus tolls and tip.

o **From Newark:** The dispatcher for New Jersey taxis gives you a slip of paper with a flat rate ranging from $30 to $38 (toll and tip extra), depending on where you're going in Manhattan, so be precise about your destination. New York yellow cabs aren't permitted to pick up passengers at Newark. The yellow-cab fare from Manhattan to Newark is the meter amount plus $15 and tolls (about $50–$70, perhaps a few dollars more with tip). During rush hours (6–9am and 4–6pm) and Saturday and Sunday noon–8pm, an additional $5 surcharge (except to Staten Island) is added to trips into the city. Jersey taxis aren't permitted to take passengers from Manhattan to Newark.

PRIVATE CAR & LIMOUSINE SERVICES Private car and limousine companies provide convenient 24-hour door-to-door airport transfers for roughly the cost of a taxi. The advantage they offer over taking a taxi is that you can arrange your pickup in advance and avoid the hassles of the taxi line. Call at least 24 hours in advance (even earlier on holidays), and a driver will meet you near baggage claim (or at your hotel for a return trip). You'll probably be asked to leave a credit card number to guarantee your ride. You'll likely be offered the choice of indoor or curbside pickup; indoor pickup is more expensive but makes it easier to hook up with your driver (who usually waits in baggage claim bearing a sign with your name on it). You can save a few dollars if you arrange for an outside pickup; call the dispatcher as soon as you clear baggage claim and then take your luggage out to the designated waiting area, where you'll wait for the driver to come around, which can take anywhere from 10 minutes to a half-hour. Besides the wait, the other disadvantage of this option is that curbside can be chaos during prime deplaning hours.

Vehicles range from sedans to vans to limousines and tend to be clean and comfortable. Prices vary slightly by company and the size of car reserved, but expect a rate roughly equivalent to taxi fare if you request a basic sedan and have only one stop; toll and tip policies are the same. (**Note:** Car services are not subject to the flat-rate rule that taxis have for rides to and from JFK.) Ask when booking what the fare will be and if you can use your credit card to pay for the ride so there are no surprises at drop-off time. There may be waiting charges tacked on if the driver has to wait an excessive amount of time due to flight delays when picking you up, but the car companies will usually check on your flight to get an accurate landing time.

Reliable companies include **Carmel** (℡ **800/922-7635** or 212/666-6666), **Allstate** (℡ **800/453-4099** or 212/333-3333), and **Dial 7** (℡ **800/222-9888** or 212/777-7777). (Keep in mind, though, that these services are only as good as the individual drivers—and sometimes there's a lemon in the bunch. If you have a problem, report it immediately to the main office.)

For a bit more luxury and service, one good option is **Luxor Limo** (℡ **866/990-4111;** www.luxorlimo.com), where the cars are spacious and the drivers as reliable as you will find and with rates not much higher than the above companies.

These car services are good for rush hour (no ticking meters in rush-hour traffic), but if you're arriving at a quieter time of day, taxis work just fine.

PRIVATE BUSES & SHUTTLES Buses and shuttle services provide a comfortable and less expensive (but usually more time-consuming) option for airport transfers than do taxis and car services.

SuperShuttle serves all three airports; **New York Airport Service** serves JFK and LaGuardia; **Olympia Trails** and **Express Shuttle USA** serve Newark. These services are a good option for getting to and from Newark during peak travel times because the drivers usually take lesser-known streets that make the ride much quicker than if you go with a taxi or car, which will virtually always stick to the traffic-clogged main route.

The familiar blue vans of **SuperShuttle** (℡ **800/258-3826;** www.supershuttle. com) serve all three area airports, providing door-to-door service to Manhattan and points on Long Island every 15 to 30 minutes around the clock. As with Express Shuttle, you don't need to reserve your airport-to-Manhattan ride; just go to the ground-transportation desk or use the courtesy phone in baggage claim and ask for SuperShuttle. Hotel pickups for your return trip require 24 to 48 hours' notice; you can make your reservations online. Fares run $15 to $22 per person, depending on the airport, with discounts available for additional persons in the same party.

New York Airport Service (☎ **718/875-8200**; www.nyairportservice.com) buses travel from JFK and LaGuardia to the Port Authority Bus Terminal (42nd St. and Eighth Ave.), to Grand Central Terminal (Park Ave. btwn 41st and 42nd sts.), and to select Midtown hotels between 27th and 59th streets, plus the Jamaica LIRR Station in Queens, where you can pick up a train for Long Island. Follow the GROUND TRANSPORTATION signs to the curbside pickup or look for the uniformed agent. Buses depart the airport every 20 to 70 minutes (depending on your departure point and destination) between 6am and midnight. Buses to JFK and LaGuardia depart the Port Authority and Grand Central Terminal on the Park Avenue side every 15 to 30 minutes, depending on the time of day and the day of the week. To request direct shuttle service from your hotel, call the above number at least 24 hours in advance. One-way fare for JFK is $15, $27 round-trip; to LaGuardia it's $12 one-way and $21 round-trip.

Olympia Airport Express (☎ **800/8-NEWARK** [863-9275] or **212/964-6233**; www.coachusa.com/olympia) provides service every 15 to 30 minutes (depending on

---

If You're Flying into MacArthur Airport on Southwest

Southwest Airlines is one of several carriers flying into New York via Long Island's MacArthur Airport, 50 miles east of Manhattan. (The others are Delta, Spirit, Northwest, and US Airways.) If you're on one of these flights (because the price was *soooo* low), here are your options for getting into the city:

Colonial Transportation (☎ 631/589-3500; www.colonialtransportation.com), **Classic Transportation** (☎ 631/567-5100; www.classictrans.com), and **Legends** (☎ 888/LEGENDS [534-3637] or 888/888-8884; www.legendslimousine.com) will pick you up at Islip Airport and deliver you to Manhattan via private sedan, but expect to pay about $125 plus tolls and tip for door-to-door service (which kind of defeats the purpose of flying a budget airline). Be sure to arrange for it at least 24 hours in advance.

For a fraction of the cost, you can catch a ride aboard a **Hampton Jitney** coach (☎ 631/283-4600; www.hampton jitney.com) to various drop-off points on Midtown's east side. The cost is $29 per person, plus a $12 taxi fare from the terminal to the Hampton Jitney stop.

Hampton Jitney can explain the details and arrange for taxi transport.

Colonial Transportation (☎ 631/589-3500; www.colonialtransportation.com) also offers regular shuttle service that traverses the 3 miles from the airport to the Ronkonkoma Long Island Rail Road station, where you can pick up an LIRR train to Manhattan. The shuttle fare is $5 per person, $1 for each additional family member accompanying a full-fare customer. From Ronkonkoma, it's about a 1½-hour train ride to Manhattan's Penn Station; the one-way fare is $13 at peak hours, $9.50 off-peak (half-fare for seniors 65 or older and kids 5–11). You can also catch the Suffolk County Transit bus no. S-57 between the airport and the station Monday to Saturday for $1.50. Trains usually leave Ronkonkoma once or twice every hour, depending on the day and time. For more information, call ☎ 718/217-LIRR (217-5477) or visit www.mta.nyc.ny.us/lirr.

For additional options and the latest information, call ☎ 631/467-3210 or visit www.macarthurairport.com.

If you're traveling to a borough other than Manhattan, call **ETS Air Service** (✆ 718/221-5341) for shared door-to-door service. For Long Island service, call **Classic Transportation** (✆ 631/567-5100; www.classictrans.com) for car service. For service to Westchester County or Connecticut, contact **Connecticut Limousine** (✆ 800/472-5466 or 203/878-2222; www.ctlimo.com) or **Prime Time Shuttle of Connecticut** (✆ 866/2-TheAir; www.primetimeshuttle.com).

If you're traveling to points in New Jersey from Newark Airport, call **Olympic Airporter** (✆ 800/822-9797 or 732/938-6666; www.olympic-limo.com) for Ocean, Monmouth, Middlesex, and Mercer counties, plus Bucks County, Pennsylvania; or **State Shuttle** (✆ 800/427-3207 or 973/729-0030; www.stateshuttle.com) for destinations throughout New Jersey.

Additionally, **New York Airport Service** express buses (✆ 718/875-8200; www.nyairportservice.com) serve the entire New York metropolitan region from JFK and LaGuardia, offering connections to the Long Island Rail Road; the Metro-North Railroad to Westchester County, upstate New York, and Connecticut; and New York's Port Authority terminal, where you can pick up buses to points throughout New Jersey.

the time of day) from Newark Airport to Penn Station (the pickup point is the northwest corner of 34th St. and Eighth Ave., and the drop-off point is the southwest corner), the Port Authority Bus Terminal (on 42nd St. btwn Eighth and Ninth aves.), and Grand Central Terminal (on 41st St. btwn Park and Lexington aves.). Passengers to and from the Grand Central Terminal location can connect to Olympia's Midtown shuttle vans, which service select Midtown hotels. Call for the exact schedule for your return trip to the airport. The one-way fare runs $15, $25 round-trip; seniors and passengers with disabilities ride for $6.

SUBWAYS & PUBLIC BUSES   For the most part, your best bet is to stay away from the MTA when traveling to and from the airport—especially if you have small kids in tow. You might save a few dollars, but subways and buses that currently serve the airports involve multiple transfers, and you'll have to drag your luggage with you. Spare yourself the drama.

The only exception to this rule is the subway service to and from JFK, which connects with the AirTrain (see below). The subway *can* be more reliable than taking a car or taxi at the height of rush hour, but *a few words of warning:* This isn't the right option for you if have very young children in tow or you're bringing more than a single piece of luggage, since there's a good amount of walking and some stairs involved in the trip, and you'll have nowhere to put all those bags on the subway train. And *do not* use this method if you're traveling to or from the airport late at night or super early in the morning—it's not the safest or fastest way then. For complete subway information, see chapter 4.

AIRTRAIN   A few years back, a new rail link revolutionized the process of connecting by public transportation to New York–area airports: JFK and now Newark International Airport, in New Jersey. *A word of warning for both AirTrains:* Yes, you'll save money, but if you have a bevy of small children, mobility issues, or mountains of luggage, skip the AirTrain. You'll find it easier to rely on a taxi, car service, or shuttle service that can offer you door-to-door transfers.

AirTrain Newark now connects Newark-Liberty International Airport with Manhattan via a speedy monorail/rail link. Even though you have to make a connection, the system is fast, pleasant, affordable, and easy to use. Each arrivals terminal at Newark Airport has a station for the AirTrain, so just follow the signs once you collect your bags. All AirTrains head to **Newark International Airport Station,** where you transfer to a **NJ Transit** train. NJ Transit will deliver you to New York Penn Station at 33rd Street and Seventh Avenue, where you can get a cab or transfer to the subway or bus. The one-way AirTrain fare is $11 (children 4 and under ride free). NJ Transit tickets can be purchased from vending machines at both the air terminal and the train station (no ticket is required to board the AirTrain).

Note that travelers heading to points beyond the city can also pick up Amtrak and other NJ Transit trains at Newark International Airport Station to their final destinations.

A few bumpy years after opening in 2003, **AirTrain JFK** is beginning to operate more efficiently. Though you can't beat the price—only $5 (plus $2.25 subway fare if you take a subway to the AirTrain), $13 if you take the Long Island Rail Road—you won't save much on time getting to the airport. And, of course, children 4 and under ride free. From midtown Manhattan, the ride can take anywhere from 40 minutes to an hour, depending on your connections. Only a few lines connect with the AirTrain: the A, E, J, and Z; the E, J, Z to Jamaica Station and the Sutphin Boulevard–Archer Avenue Station; and the A to Howard Beach/JFK Airport Station. The MTA is working hard to clear up the confusion, and though they are contemplating adding connections to the AirTrain in lower Manhattan sometime in the next decade, there's not much they can do now to speed up the trip.

For more information on AirTrain Newark, call © **888/EWR-INFO** (397-4636) or go online to www.panynj.gov/airports/ewr-airtrain.html. For connection details, click on the links on the AirTrain website or contact **NJ Transit** (© **800/626-RIDE** [626-7433]; www.njtransit.com) or **Amtrak** (© **800/USA-RAIL** [872-7245]; www.amtrak.com).

For more information on AirTrain JFK, go online to www.panynj.gov/airports/jfk-airtrain.html. For connection details, click on the links on the AirTrain website or the MTA site, **http://mta.info/mta/airtrain.htm**.

BY CAR

From the **New Jersey Turnpike** (I-95) and points west, there are three Hudson River crossings to the city's West Side: the **Holland Tunnel** (Lower Manhattan), the **Lincoln Tunnel** (Midtown), and the **George Washington Bridge** (Upper Manhattan). From **upstate New York,** take the **New York State Thruway** (I-87), which crosses the Hudson River on the Tappan Zee Bridge and becomes the **Major Deegan Expressway** (I-87) through the Bronx. For the East Side, continue to the Triborough Bridge and then down the FDR Drive. For the West Side, take the Cross Bronx Expressway (I-95) to the Henry Hudson Parkway or the Taconic State Parkway to the Saw Mill River Parkway to the Henry Hudson Parkway south.

From **New England,** the **New England Thruway** (I-95) connects with the **Bruckner Expressway** (I-278), which leads to the Triborough Bridge and the FDR Drive on the East Side. For the West Side, take the Bruckner to the Cross Bronx Expressway (I-95) to the Henry Hudson Parkway south.

Note that you'll have to pay tolls along some of these roads and at most crossings. If your state has an **E-ZPass** program (**www.ezpass.com**), as most states in the Northeast do, your pass will allow you to go through the designated E-ZPass lanes.

Once you arrive in Manhattan, park your car in a garage (expect to pay $20–$45 per day) and leave it there. Don't use your car for traveling within the city. Public transportation, taxis, and walking will easily get you where you want to go without the headaches of parking, gridlock, and dodging crazy cabbies.

BY TRAIN

Train travel can be great fun for kids. **Amtrak** (© **800/USA-RAIL** [872-7245]; www.amtrak.com) runs frequent service to New York City's **Penn Station,** on Seventh Avenue between 31st and 33rd streets, where you can get a taxi, subway, or bus to your hotel. To get the best rates, book early (as much as 6 months in advance) and travel on weekends.

If you're traveling to New York from a city along Amtrak's Northeast Corridor—such as Boston, Philadelphia, Baltimore, or Washington, D.C.—Amtrak may be your best travel bet, particularly on the high-speed Acela trains. The Acela express trains cut travel time from D.C. down to 2½ hours, and travel time from Boston to a lightning-quick 3 hours.

FLYING WITH KIDS

If you plan carefully, you can make it fun to fly with your kids—and, equally important, ensure a positive travel experience for your fellow passengers:

- **Reserve a seat in the bulkhead row** if you have babies or toddlers. You'll have more legroom and your children will be able to play on the floor underfoot.
- **Book the window and aisle seats,** on the chance that no one will book the middle seat (if someone has done so, politely ask whether he or she minds moving once you're on the plane). Check at the gate to see if any empty rows are still available. That way, your child will have more room to move in and around his seat and be less tempted to walk in the aisle. Reserving the aisle seat for you or your spouse also protects your child from jostling passersby.
- **Pack items for your kids in your carry-on luggage,** such as books, snacks, and toys (oh, okay, go ahead and pack that DVD player). Be sure to bring self-contained compact toys with few pieces. Be aware that electronic games can interfere with the aircraft navigational system, and their noisiness may annoy your adult neighbors. Small coloring books and crayons work well, as do card games like Go Fish.
- **Have a long talk with your children** before you depart for your trip, explaining to them what to expect at takeoff, at landing, and during the flight. Explain to your kids the importance of good behavior in the air—how their own safety can depend upon their being quiet and staying in their seats during the trip.
- **Pay extra attention to the safety instructions** before takeoff. Consult the safety chart behind the seat in front of you, and show it to your children. Be sure you know how to operate the oxygen masks, as you'll be expected to secure yours first and then help your children with theirs. Locate the emergency exits before takeoff, and plot out an evacuation strategy for you and your children, just in case.
- **Be sure your child's seatbelt remains fastened properly.** Sudden turbulence is a danger to a child who is not buckled into his or her own seat restraint. This will also make it harder for your children to wander off.
- **Bring milk with you on the plane**—few airlines carry milk (other than concentrate for coffee) anymore. The TSA allows formula, breast milk, and juice in containers larger than 3 ounces, but you must declare the liquid at the security checkpoint before you board the plane. (Carry only as much milk as you think you

will need on the flight.) If you're carrying regular milk, it's a good idea to use 3-ounce bottles, the maximum-size container the TSA allows onboard—anything larger is prohibited.

○ **Always accompany children to the lavatory.**
○ Some airlines **serve children's meals first.** When you board, ask a flight attendant if this is possible, especially if your children are very young or seated toward the back of the plane.

Getting Around

For everything you need to know to get around the city safely and efficiently, go to chapter 4.

MONEY & COSTS
Keeping Costs Low

New York is a notoriously expensive destination to visit, but there are definitely ways to keep expenses under control. The first is to aggressively look for **hotel discounts,** through a travel agent or on the Internet. Many Midtown hotels offer excellent weekend or summer packages. Once you arrive, use **public transportation** instead of taxis as often as possible; subways are wonderfully fast and safe, and buses, though prone to traffic slowdowns, are a great way to tour the city. Oh, and **walking**—probably the best way to see the city—is free! Use the **TKTS booth** or other theater discount schemes to get half-price tickets to Broadway shows; even though the season's hottest seats may be excluded, you're bound to get into something memorable. And make **smart restaurant choices;** theme restaurants may be exciting for kids, but you'll pay double the price for a mediocre hamburger there. Sample New York's great neighborhood bistros, coffee shops, and ethnic restaurants instead, and if there's no children's menu per se, don't be shy about asking to have your children share one adult-size entree—that is, if you can get two siblings to agree on an entree. Find **a hotel with self-catering capabilities**—a kitchen or kitchenette—so you can save on meals by having breakfast in, for example (bagels from the local deli, plus fresh orange juice). Or dine in like a real New Yorker—**call for takeout food!**

WHAT THINGS COST IN NEW YORK CITY	U.S. $
Taxi from the airport to Manhattan	25.00–70.00
Double room, moderate	250.00
Double room, inexpensive	150.00
Three-course dinner for one without wine, moderate	20.00–25.00
Bottle of Brooklyn Lager beer	2.00–3.00
Bottle of Coca-Cola	1.00–1.50
Cup of coffee	1.00–1.50
1 gallon/1 liter of premium gas	2.95/1.87
Admission to most museums	8.00–20.00

ATMS

In most Manhattan neighborhoods, you can find a bank with **ATMs** (automated teller machines) every couple of blocks. Many small stores and delis have ATMs with varying fees to withdraw money from your bank account or credit card—but we'd steer clear of these in general; thieves have been known to prey on these machines to access users' cards and PIN numbers.

STAYING HEALTHY

New York City has no less healthy an environment than that of any other large city: The climate is temperate, public hygiene is relatively good, and the water supply is highly drinkable (in fact, in blind taste tests, New York tap water often scores higher than bottled waters). Although most visitors don't think of New York as an outdoor destination, if you plan to be in the parks a good deal during warm weather, insect repellent is advised, as mosquito- and tick-borne illnesses like the West Nile virus and Lyme disease can be contracted here almost as readily as anywhere in the Northeast.

If you or your child suffers from conditions like epilepsy, diabetes, or heart problems, wear a **MedicAlert identification tag** (© 888/633-4298; www.medicalert. org), which will immediately alert doctors to your condition and give them access to your records through MedicAlert's 24-hour hot line.

WHAT TO DO IF YOU GET SICK AWAY FROM HOME

There is one great advantage to getting sick in the city that never sleeps: Drugstores and hospital emergency rooms are open 24 hours a day, should you need them, and the quality of medical care is very high. (Go to the "Fast Facts" section in chapter 13 for the one nearest you, as well as **emergency numbers.**)

If you get sick, ask your hotel concierge to recommend a local doctor—even his or her own. This will probably yield a better recommendation than any toll-free telephone number would.

The **NYU Downtown Hospital** offers physician referrals at © 888/698-3362 or 212/312-5000. You can also try the emergency room at a local hospital. Many hospitals also have walk-in clinics for emergency cases that are not life-threatening; you may not get immediate attention, but you won't pay the high price of an emergency room visit. **DOCS at New York Healthcare,** 55 E. 34th St., between Park and Madison avenues (© 800/673-3627 or 212/252-6001), for nonemergency illnesses, is affiliated with Beth Israel Medical Center and is open Monday through Thursday from 8am to 8pm, Friday from 8am to 7pm, Saturday from 9am to 3pm, and Sunday from 9am to 2pm. We list hospitals and emergency numbers under "Fast Facts," in chapter 13.

Bring an extra supply of any **prescription medications** you or your child may be taking, and carry them in their original containers, with pharmacy labels—otherwise, they may not make it through airport security. Divide them between carry-on and checked luggage so that if you lose a bag, you won't be left in the lurch. It's also a good idea to contact your pediatrician before you leave to get a written prescription for any medicines you might lose or run out of and to obtain a reference for a New York City pediatrician in case of a sudden illness. Failing that, your hotel's front desk should be able to put you in touch with a local doctor if illness flares up during your New York City stay. To be on the safe side, bring a supply of any over-the-counter medication your child often needs—why waste vacation time looking for the one brand of diaper ointment that works on your baby's bottom?

Avoiding "Economy Class Syndrome"

Deep vein thrombosis, or as it's known in the world of flying, "economy-class syndrome," is a blood clot that develops in a deep vein. It's a potentially deadly condition that can be caused by sitting in cramped conditions—such as an airplane cabin—for too long. During a flight (especially a long-haul flight), get up, walk around, and stretch your legs every 60 to 90 minutes to keep your blood flowing. Other preventive measures include frequent flexing of the legs while sitting, drinking lots of water, and avoiding alcohol and sleeping pills. If you have a history of deep vein thrombosis, heart disease, or another condition that puts you at high risk, some experts recommend wearing compression stockings or taking anticoagulants when you fly; always ask your physician about the best course for you. Symptoms of deep vein thrombosis include leg pain or swelling, or even shortness of breath.

If you have dental problems on the road, a service known as **1-800-DENTIST** (© **800/336-8478**) will provide the name of a local dentist.

CRIME & SAFETY
Staying Safe

The FBI consistently rates New York City as one of the safest large cities in the United States, but it is still a large city and crime most definitely exists. Here are a few tips for staying safe in New York:

- Trust your instincts, because they're usually right.
- You'll rarely be hassled, but it's always best to walk with a sense of purpose and self-confidence. Don't stop in the middle of the sidewalk to pull out and peruse your map.
- Anywhere in the city, if you find yourself on a deserted street that feels unsafe, it probably is; leave as quickly as possible.
- If you do find yourself accosted by someone with or without a weapon, remember to keep your anger in check and that the most reasonable response (maddening though it may be) is to not resist.

SUBWAY SAFETY TIPS In general, the subways are very safe, especially in Manhattan. There are panhandlers and questionable characters like anywhere else in the city, but subway crime has gone down to 1960s levels. Still, stay alert and trust your instincts. Always keep a hand on your personal belongings.

When using the subway, **don't wait for trains near the edge of the platform** or on extreme ends of a station. During non–rush hours, wait for the train in view of the token-booth clerk or under the yellow DURING OFF HOURS TRAINS STOP HERE signs, and ride in the train operator's or conductor's car (usually in the center of the train; you'll see his or her head stick out of the window when the doors open). Choose crowded cars over empty ones—there's safety in numbers.

Avoid subways late at night, and splurge on a cab after about 10 or 11pm—it's money well spent to avoid a long wait on a deserted platform. Or take the bus.

SPECIALIZED TRAVEL RESOURCES

Family Travel

To locate accommodations, restaurants, and attractions that are particularly kid-friendly, refer to the "Kids" icon throughout this guide.

Good bets for the most timely information include the "Weekend" section of Friday's *New York Times,* which has a section, "Spare Change," that includes the week's best kid-friendly activities; the weekly *New York* magazine (www.nymag.com), which has a full calendar of children's events in its listings section; the weekly *Time Out New York* (www.timeout.com/newyork), which also has a weekly kids' section with a bit of an alternative bent; and the monthly *Time Out New York Kids* (www.timeout.com/newyork/kids), which has an exhaustive listings of kids' activities, kid-friendly restaurants, children's shops, and much, much more. The first place to look for **babysitting** is in your hotel (better yet, ask about babysitting when you reserve). Many hotels have babysitting services or will provide you with lists of reliable sitters. If this doesn't pan out, call the **Baby Sitters' Guild** (© **212/682-0227;** www.babysittersguild.com). The sitters are licensed, insured, and bonded, and can even take your child on outings.

Travelers with Disabilities

Most disabilities shouldn't stop anyone from traveling in the U.S. Thanks to provisions in the Americans with Disabilities Act (ADA), most public places are required to comply with disability-friendly regulations. Almost all public establishments (including hotels, restaurants, museums, and so on, but not including certain National Historic Landmarks) and at least some modes of public transportation provide accessible entrances and other facilities for those with disabilities.

New York is more accessible to travelers with disabilities than ever before. The city's bus system is wheelchair-friendly, and most of the major sightseeing attractions are easily accessible. Even so, **always call first** to be sure that the places you want to go to are fully accessible.

Most hotels are ADA-compliant, with suitable rooms for wheelchair-bound travelers as well as those with other disabilities. But before you book, **ask specific questions based on your needs.**

Many city hotels are in older buildings that have had to be modified to meet requirements; still, elevators and bathrooms can be on the small side, and other impediments may exist. If you have mobility issues, you'll probably do best to book one of the city's newer hotels, which tend to be more spacious. At **www.access-able.com**, you'll find links to New York's best accessible accommodations (click on "World Destinations"). Some Broadway theaters and other performance venues provide total wheelchair accessibility; others provide partial accessibility. Many also offer lower-priced tickets for theatergoers with disabilities and their companions, though you'll need to check individual policies and reserve in advance.

Hospital Audiences, Inc. (© **212/575-7676;** www.hospitalaudiences.org) arranges attendance and provides details about accessibility at cultural institutions as well as cultural events adapted for people with disabilities. Services include the invaluable **HAI Hot Line** (© **212/575-7676**), which offers accessibility information for hotels, restaurants, attractions, cultural venues, and much more. This nonprofit organization also publishes *Access for All,* a guidebook on accessibility, available free of charge on the website, www.hospitalaudiences.org.

Another terrific source for travelers with disabilities who are coming to New York City is **Big Apple Greeter** (✆ **212/669-8159;** www.bigapplegreeter.org). All of its employees are extremely well versed in accessibility issues. They can provide a resource list of city agencies that serve those with disabilities, and sometimes have special discounts available for theater and music performances. Big Apple Greeter even offers one-to-one tours that pair volunteers with visitors with disabilities; they can even introduce you to the public transportation system if you like. Reserve at least a week ahead.

SuperShuttle (✆ **800/BLUE-VAN** [258-3826] or 212/258-3826; www.supershuttle.com) operates minibuses with lifts from Newark airports to Midtown hotels by reservation; arrange pickup 3 or 4 days in advance. **Olympia Trails** (✆ **877/894-9155;** www.coachusa.com/olympia) provides service from Newark Airport, with half-price fares for travelers with disabilities (be sure to prepurchase your tickets to guarantee the discount fare, as drivers can't sell discounted tickets). Not all buses are appropriately equipped, so call ahead for the schedule of accessible buses (press "0" to reach a real person).

Taxis are required to carry people who have folding wheelchairs and service dogs.

Public buses are an inexpensive and easy way to get around New York. All buses' back doors are supposed to be equipped with wheelchair lifts (though the city has had complaints that not all are in working order). Buses also "kneel," lowering their front steps for people who have difficulty boarding. Passengers with disabilities pay half-price fares ($1). The **subway** isn't fully wheelchair accessible, but a list of about 30 accessible subway stations and a guide to wheelchair-accessible subway itineraries is on the MTA website. Call ✆ **718/596-8585** for bus and subway transit info or go online to www.mta.nyc.ny.us/nyct and click on the wheelchair symbol.

You're better off not trying to rent your own car to get around the city. But if you consider it the best mode of transportation for you, **Wheelchair Getaways** (✆ **800/642-2042** or 800/344-5005; www.wheelchairgetaways.com) rents specialized vans with wheelchair lifts and other features for travelers with disabilities throughout the New York metropolitan area.

GLBT Travelers

Gay and lesbian culture is as much a part of New York's basic identity as yellow cabs, high-rises, and Broadway theater. Indeed, in a city with one of the world's largest, loudest, and most powerful GLBT populations, homosexuality is squarely in the mainstream. So city hotels tend to be neutral on the issue, and gay couples with kids shouldn't have a problem.

All over Manhattan, but especially in neighborhoods like the **West Village** (particularly Christopher St., famous the world over as the main drag of New York gaymale life) and **Chelsea** (especially Eighth Ave. from 16th to 23rd sts., and W. 17th to 19th sts. from Fifth to Eighth aves.), shops, services, and restaurants have a lesbian and gay flavor.

The **Lesbian, Gay, Bisexual & Transgender Community Center,** familiarly known as "The Center," is at 208 W. 13th St., between Seventh and Eighth avenues (✆ **212/620-7310;** www.gaycenter.org). The center is the meeting place for more than 400 lesbian, gay, and bisexual organizations. You can check the online events calendar, which lists hundreds of happenings—lectures, dances, concerts, readings, films—or call for the latest. Their site offers links to gay-friendly hotels and guest-houses in and around New York, plus tons of other information; the staff is also friendly and helpful in person or over the phone.

Other good sources for lesbian and gay events are the free weekly newspaper *Gay City News* (www.gaycitynews.com) and the magazines *Next* (www.nextmagazine.com) and *GONYC* (www.gomag.com), which is lesbian-oriented. You'll also find lots of information on their websites.

The weekly *Time Out New York* (http://newyork.timeout.com) has a terrific gay and lesbian section. The Center (see above) publishes a monthly guide listing many events (also listed on its website).

In addition, there are lesbian and gay musical events, such as performances by the **New York City Gay Men's Chorus** (📞 212/344-1777; www.nycgmc.org); health programs sponsored by the **Gay Men's Health Crisis** (**GMHC**; 📞 800/AIDS-NYC [243-7692] or hotline 212/367-1000; www.gmhc.org); the **Gay & Lesbian National Hot Line** (📞 888/TheGLNH [843-4564]; www.glnh.org), offering peer counseling and information on upcoming events; and many other organizations.

Senior Travel

Members of **AARP**, 601 E St. NW, Washington, DC 20049 (📞 888/687-2277; www.aarp.org), get discounts on hotels, airfares, and car rentals. AARP offers members a wide range of benefits, including *AARP: The Magazine* and a newsletter. Anyone over 50 can join.

New York subway and bus fares are half-price ($1) for people 65 and older. Many museums and sights (and some theaters and performance halls) offer discounted admittance and tickets to seniors, so don't be shy about asking. Always bring an ID card, especially if you've kept your youthful glow.

Many hotels offer senior discounts; **Choice Hotels** (which include Comfort Inns), for example, gives 10% off their published rates to anyone over 50, provided you book your room through their nationwide toll-free reservations number (that is, not directly with the hotels or through a travel agent). For a complete list of Choice Hotels, visit **www.hotelchoice.com**.

Many reliable agencies and organizations target the 50-plus market. **Road Scholar** (📞 800/454-5768; www.roadscholar.org) arranges worldwide study programs (including some in New York City) for those age 55 and over.

Student Travel

Check out the **International Student Travel Confederation (ISTC;** www.istc.org) website for comprehensive travel services information and details on how to get an **International Student Identity Card (ISIC),** which qualifies students for substantial savings on rail passes, plane tickets, entrance fees, and more. It also provides students with basic health and life insurance and a 24-hour help line. The card is valid for a maximum of 18 months. You can apply for the card online or in person at **STA Travel** (📞 800/781-4040 in North America; 📞 132 782 in Australia; 📞 0871 2 300 040 in the U.K.; www.statravel.com), the biggest student travel agency in the world; check out the website to locate STA Travel offices worldwide. If you're no longer a student but are still under 26, you can get an **International Youth Travel Card (IYTC),** which entitles you to some discounts, from the same people. **Travel CUTS** (📞 800/592-2887; www.travelcuts.com) offers similar services for both Canadians and U.S. residents. Irish students may prefer to turn to **USIT**

(☎ **01/602-1904;** www.usit.ie), an Ireland-based specialist in student, youth, and independent travel.

STAYING CONNECTED

Telephones

Generally, hotel surcharges on long-distance and local calls are astronomical, so you're better off using your **cellphone.** Many convenience stores and drugstores sell **prepaid calling cards** in denominations up to $50; for international visitors these can be the least expensive way to call home. Many public pay phones at airports now accept American Express, MasterCard, and Visa credit cards. **Local calls** made from pay phones cost either 25¢ or 50¢ (no pennies, please).

That said, there aren't as many pay phones on the streets of New York City as there used to be because of the prevalence of cellphones, and the ones that are there are often out of order.

For details on making calls to and from New York City, go to "Fast Facts," in chapter 13.

Cellphones

Just because your cellphone works at home doesn't mean it'll work everywhere in the U.S. (thanks to our nation's fragmented cellphone system). It's a good bet that your phone will work in major cities, but take a look at your wireless company's coverage map on its website before heading out. If you need to stay in touch at a destination where you know your phone won't work, **rent** a phone that does from **InTouch USA** (☎ **800/872-7626;** www.intouchglobal.com) or a rental-car location, but beware that you'll pay something like $1 a minute or more for airtime.

If you're not from the U.S., you'll be appalled at the poor reach of the **GSM (Global System for Mobile Communications) wireless network,** which is used by much of the rest of the world. Your phone will probably work in most major U.S. cities; it definitely won't work in many rural areas. To see where GSM phones work in the U.S., check out www.t-mobile.com/coverage. And you may or may not be able to send SMS (text messaging) home.

Voice over Internet Protocol (VoIP)

If you have Web access while traveling, consider a broadband-based telephone service (in technical terms, **Voice over Internet Protocol,** or **VoIP**) such as Skype (www.skype.com) or Vonage (www.vonage.com), which will allow you to make free international calls from your laptop or in a cybercafe. Neither service requires the people you're calling to also have that service (though there are fees if they do not). Check the websites for details.

Internet & E-mail

WITH YOUR OWN COMPUTER

Most hotels, cafes, coffeehouses, and airports in NYC have Wi-Fi (wireless fidelity). These "hotspots" offer high-speed Wi-Fi access for free or charge a fee for usage. Most laptops sold today have built-in wireless capability. You should have no trouble finding Wi-Fi hotspots throughout the city, including coverage in many hotels (although you wouldn't believe how many of the toniest hotels nickel-and-dime guests by charging daily rates on Wi-Fi usage in the rooms!).

For dial-up access, most business-class hotels in the U.S. offer dataports for laptop modems.

WITHOUT YOUR OWN COMPUTER

Most major airports have **Internet kiosks** or Wi-Fi areas that provide basic Web access for a per-minute/hour/day fee that's usually much higher than cybercafe prices.

For help locating cybercafes and other establishments where you can go for Internet access, see the box "Where to Check Your E-mail in the City That Never Sleeps," below.

WHERE TO check your e-mail IN THE CITY THAT NEVER SLEEPS

If your hotel doesn't offer free access to its business center or a terminal in the lobby to check your e-mail (and many do), where can you go to check it if you don't have a computer with you?

All branches of the **New York Public Library** (www.nypl.org) feature computers that offer free access to the Internet, electronic databases, library catalogs, and Microsoft Office. They are also supposed to offer Wi-Fi, but we've found that having it listed on their website and actually having it operative can be two different things.

More free access is available at the **Times Square Visitors Center,** 1560 Broadway, between 46th and 47th streets (℃ **212/768-1560;** daily 8am–8pm); you can use computer terminals to send e-mails courtesy of Yahoo!, and you can even send an electronic postcard with a photo of yourself home to Mom.

FedEx Office (www.fedex.com) charges 30¢ per minute ($15 per hour) and there are dozens of locations around town. In addition, an increasing number of delis and copy shops frequently stick an INTERNET sign in the window, and you can log on in a unit wedged into a corner next to the ATM for a couple bucks, while you drink your genuine New York City deli coffee.

GETTING TO KNOW NEW YORK CITY

A t first glance, New York can be a very intimidating town, especially when you have a flock of youngsters under your wing. Take time from the outset to get a grasp of the city layout and the best navigating methods.

ORIENTATION
Visitor information

Before you leave home, head to the official NYC & Company tourism website, **www.nycgo.com**, for the latest on, well, everything—top attractions, events, suggested itineraries, tours and TV show tapings, plus basic tips—and download the official visitor guide as well as city, park, and bike maps. To request a copy of the official NYC guide, call ℭ **800/ NYCVISIT** (692-8474) or 212/397-8222. Once you've hit the city, you can find official New York City information centers scattered around Manhattan; the main one is the **NYC Official Visitor Information Center** at 810 Seventh Ave. between 52nd and 53rd streets (ℭ **212/484-1222;** open Mon–Fri 8:30am–6pm and Sat–Sun 9am–5pm). There are also kiosks in **Times Square** (run by the Times Square Alliance, below; Seventh Ave. btw. 46th and 47th sts.); **Harlem** (The Studio Museum in Harlem, 144 W. 125th St.); **City Hall Park** (Broadway and Park Row, downtown); and **Chinatown** (at the triangle where Canal, Walker, and Baxter sts. meet). Stop by to load up with maps, brochures, and sightseeing suggestions, along with "twofers" for savings on Broadway and Off-Broadway plays.

The **Times Square Alliance** (www.timessquarenyc.org) is a terrific source for information about Broadway theater, Midtown hotels and restaurants, and special events; it operates the **Times Square Visitor Center** (Seventh Ave. btw. 46th and 47th sts.; Mon–Fri 9am–7pm and Sat–Sun 8am–8pm). For listings of **Lincoln Center** events, visit its website at www.lincolncenter.org. For upcoming **events in city parks,** visit www.nycgovparks.org; for **Central Park events,** go to www.centralpark.com.

A street BY ANY OTHER NAME

When the street sign says . . .	It's the same as . . .
Amsterdam Avenue	Tenth Avenue (above 59th St.)
Avenue of the Americas	Sixth Avenue
Central Park North	West 110th Street (btw. Fifth Ave. and Central Park West)
Central Park South	59th Street (btw. Fifth and Eighth aves.)
Central Park West	Eighth Avenue (from 59th to 110th sts.)
Columbus Avenue	Ninth Avenue (above 59th St.)
Fashion Avenue	Seventh Avenue (from 34th to 42nd sts.)
Park Avenue	Fourth Avenue (above 14th St.)
St. Mark's Place	8th Street (from Third Ave. to Ave. A)
West End Avenue	Eleventh Avenue (from 59th to 107th sts.)

City Layout

Major Arteries in Manhattan   The limited-access FDR Drive runs along Manhattan's East River shore, from the Brooklyn Battery Tunnel (which links to Brooklyn) north to the Triborough Bridge (which links to Queens and to I-95. It was officially renamed the Robert F. Kennedy Memorial Bridge in 2008). The West Side Highway goes from Battery Park up along the Hudson, eventually becoming the limited-access Henry Hudson Parkway, running all the way to Manhattan's northern tip and on through the Bronx (Riverdale), where it becomes the Saw Mill Parkway.

Broadway is Manhattan's spine, beginning at Battery Park and angling north all the way through Washington Heights (from there on, as U.S. 9, it continues all the way to Albany). Since Manhattan's axis is skewed to the northeast, Broadway—which runs due north—seems to run at an angle, and every time it crosses a major avenue in the Manhattan grid, there's a significant traffic junction: **Union Square** at 14th Street, **Madison Square** at 23rd Street, **Herald Square** at 34th Street, **Times Square** at 42nd Street, **Columbus Circle** at 59th Street, **Lincoln Square** at 66th Street, **Verdi Square** at 72nd Street, and **Straus Park** at 106th Street. Above 59th Street, where Central Park divides Manhattan, Broadway is the West Side's main drag.

The other big avenues in the grid are one-way, with the exception of the Upper West Side's **Central Park West** and the East Side's **Park Avenue.** The avenues that run uptown (north) are **First Avenue, Third Avenue, Madison Avenue, Sixth Avenue** (also called **Avenue of the Americas**), **Eighth Avenue,** and **Tenth Avenue** (called **Amsterdam Ave.** above 59th St.). To go downtown (south), take **Second Avenue, Lexington Avenue, Fifth Avenue, Seventh Avenue, Ninth Avenue** (called **Columbus Ave.** above 59th St.), or **Eleventh Avenue** (called **West End Ave.** from 59th to 107th sts.).

In the older areas of town, below 8th Street, the grid doesn't apply, and you'll need a map to navigate. **Hudson Street** is a major northbound thoroughfare on the West

Manhattan Neighborhoods

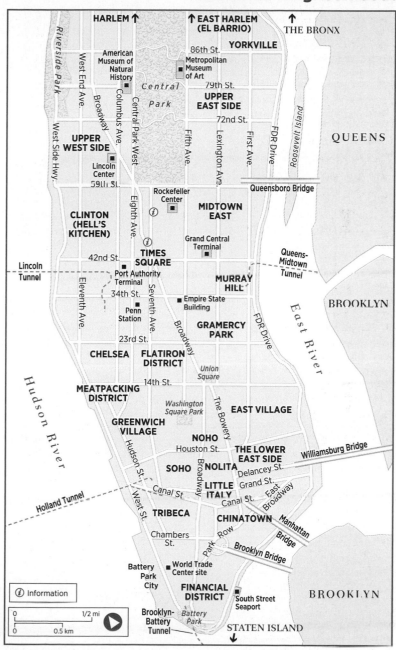

HARLEM ↑

↑ EAST HARLEM (EL BARRIO)

↑

THE BRONX

YORKVILLE

86th St.

Riverside Park

West End Ave.

American Museum of Natural History

Metropolitan Museum of Art

Central Park

79th St.

UPPER EAST SIDE

72nd St.

QUEENS

Columbus Ave.

Broadway

Central Park West

Fifth Ave.

Lexington Ave.

First Ave.

FDR Drive

Roosevelt Island

West Side Hwy.

UPPER WEST SIDE

Lincoln Center

59th St.

Queensboro Bridge

Eighth Ave.

Rockefeller Center

MIDTOWN EAST

CLINTON (HELL'S KITCHEN)

Grand Central Terminal

Queens-Midtown Tunnel

Lincoln Tunnel

42nd St.

TIMES SQUARE

Port Authority Terminal

MURRAY HILL

BROOKLYN

Eleventh Ave.

34th St.

Penn Station

Empire State Building

Seventh Ave.

Broadway

GRAMERCY PARK

FDR Drive

East River

23rd St.

CHELSEA

FLATIRON DISTRICT

Union Square

MEATPACKING DISTRICT

14th St.

Washington Square Park

EAST VILLAGE

Hudson River

GREENWICH VILLAGE

The Bowery

NOHO

Houston St.

THE LOWER EAST SIDE

Williamsburg Bridge

Hudson St.

SOHO

NOLITA

Broadway

Delancey St.

Holland Tunnel

Canal St.

LITTLE ITALY

Grand St.

Canal St.

East Broadway

West St.

TRIBECA

CHINATOWN

Manhattan Bridge

Chambers St.

Park Row

Brooklyn Bridge

Battery Park City

World Trade Center site

ⓘ Information

FINANCIAL DISTRICT

South Street Seaport

BROOKLYN

0   1/2 mi

0   0.5 km

Brooklyn-Battery Tunnel

Battery Park

STATEN ISLAND

↓

Cross streets are listed for every destination in this book, but be sure to ask for the cross street (or avenue) if you're ever calling for an address.

When you give a taxi driver an address, always specify the cross streets. New Yorkers, even most cab drivers, probably wouldn't know where to find 994 Second Ave., but they do know where to find 51st and Second. If you're heading to the restaurant La Bonne Soup, for example, tell them that it's on 55th Street between Fifth and Sixth avenues. The exact number (in this case, no. 48) is given only as a further precision.

Side; on the East Side it's **Fourth Avenue** (the southern section of Park Ave.), which is created when the **Bowery** splits into Third and Fourth avenues.

Most cross streets in the grid are one-way; generally, in Manhattan even-numbered streets are eastbound and odd-numbered streets are westbound. The following major cross streets, however, are two-way: **Canal Street,** which cuts across the island from the Manhattan Bridge to the Holland Tunnel; **Houston Street** (pronounced "*How-stun*"), which funnels traffic from the Williamsburg Bridge to the Holland Tunnel; and **14th Street, 23rd Street, 34th Street, 42nd Street, 57th Street, 59th Street** (aka Central Park South), **72nd Street, 79th Street, 86th Street, 96th Street,** and **110th Street** (aka Central Park North). Above the park, **125th Street** is Harlem's major two-way commercial street.

Central Park bisects Manhattan between 59th Street and 110th Street, dividing the Upper East Side from the Upper West Side. To cross Central Park **from the Upper East Side,** your choices are 66th Street, 72nd Street (open weekday rush hours only), 79th Street, 85th Street, and 97th Street. If you're going east **from the Upper West Side,** your options are 65th Street, 81st Street, 86th Street, and 96th Street. All other car entrances to the park feed into the circular drive, open only during weekday rush hours.

MAJOR ARTERIES IN THE OUTER BOROUGHS The **Grand Central Parkway** leads from the Triborough Bridge to LaGuardia Airport, in northern Queens, and on to Long Island. The **Long Island Expressway (I-495)** goes from the Queens Midtown Tunnel across Queens, through Forest Hills and Flushing, and out to Long Island. **Northern Boulevard** is one of Queens's major commercial thoroughfares.

The **Brooklyn-Queens Expressway**—known as the BQE—runs north-south, linking Brooklyn and Queens; you can get on it from the Grand Central Parkway, from the 59th Street Bridge (also called the Queensboro Bridge), from the Queens-Midtown Tunnel, and from the three Brooklyn-Manhattan bridges: the Williamsburg, the Manhattan, and the Brooklyn. At the southern end of Brooklyn, the BQE links with the **Verrazano Bridge** (toll $9 westbound only) from Staten Island, then (as the **Belt Parkway**) swings around the coast past Coney Island and the Rockaways, feeding into **Southern Parkway,** which heads out to Long Island. Radiating out from Brooklyn Heights, **Atlantic Avenue, Flatbush Avenue,** and (starting near Prospect Park) **Ocean Parkway** fan out across Brooklyn.

The **Cross-Bronx Expressway (I-95)** is the major highway cutting across the Bronx; the **Bronx River Parkway** runs up through Bronx Park, where you'll find the Bronx Zoo and the Botanical Garden.

Manhattan Neighborhoods in Brief

Manhattan was settled from its southern tip northward, so the oldest area is **Lower Manhattan,** roughly everything south of Canal Street. Within this, the **Financial District,** concentrated around Wall Street and lower Broadway, has pretty much obscured traces of the early colonial settlement with its battery of skyscrapers, but you'll still find a few venerable churches tucked away, and many of the skyscrapers themselves are early-20th-century landmarks. The only really historic quarter left is on the East River waterfront at **South Street Seaport.** Southwest of the Seaport, you'll find **City Hall,** other municipal buildings, and an imposing set of courthouses clustered around **Foley Square.** Over on the Hudson side of the narrow island is open green space at Battery Park and the planned community of **Battery Park City,** which has a lovely riverside promenade. **Ground Zero,** the site of the World Trade Center tragedy, lies just inland from Battery Park City. The nickname **TriBeCa** derives from *Tri*angle *Be*low *Ca*nal Street, but the label is used for only the northwestern chunk of that triangle, a cool neighborhood of spacious, uncrowded streets and converted industrial lofts dotted with kid-friendly restaurants, parks, and shops.

Above South Street Seaport and the courts, **Chinatown** occupies the East River side of the below-Canal area, but it burst its boundaries long ago to spill north of Canal Street, engulfing the old tenements of **Little Italy,** which still clings to Mulberry Street as its main drag. East of Little Italy lies the **Lower East Side,** for years the Jewish immigrant district, more recently a hot spot for young urban bohemians. To the west of Little Italy, a derelict 19th-century industrial zone was converted in the 1970s to the lofts and boutiques of artsy **SoHo** (*So*uth of *Ho*uston St.—pronounced, by the way, "*How*-stun," never "*Hew*-stun").

Above Houston Street you enter the Villages—**Greenwich Village,** from Broadway west to the Hudson River; and the **East Village,** from Broadway on east across Avenues A, B, C, and D. Greenwich Village still has a certain bohemian cachet, and its quiet side streets, with their vintage architecture, make a fine place to ramble. The East Village is funkier and grittier, just the place to bring teenagers who think their parents are so uncool they don't want to be seen with them. (Just walk five paces behind, okay?) Teens may also want to hang out in the New York University area, which sprawls around the Village's focal point, Washington Square Park, or in the now-chic northwest corner of the West Village, still called the Meatpacking District for its (ever-dwindling) butchers' trade.

Above 14th Street the Manhattan grid falls into place, and the city starts to get more buttoned-down. Between 14th and 30th streets, **Chelsea** occupies the area from Sixth Avenue west. This is a hot area for art galleries, fashion-industry types, and gays; at its far west end, the Chelsea Piers sports complex on the river is a major draw for families. East of Sixth Avenue is what's called the **Flatiron District** (named after the famous Flatiron Building at 23rd St. and Broadway), a trendy area for restaurants and nightlife, and the quiet older neighborhoods around **Gramercy Park,** the city's only

Free New York City Tours

If you'd like to tour a specific neighborhood with an expert guide, call **Big Apple Greeter** (© 212/669-8159; www.bigapplegreeter.org) at least 1 week ahead of your arrival. This nonprofit organization has specially trained volunteers who take visitors around town for a free 2- to 4-hour tour of a particular neighborhood. And they say New York isn't friendly!

private park. North of Gramercy lays **Murray Hill,** a largely residential neighborhood.

Midtown is the major business district, sprawling across the island from about 34th Street to 59th Street. Big department stores and big international brands march up Fifth Avenue, with a handful of museums set on side streets; the **Theater District** clusters around revamped and high-amped **Times Square** (42nd St. and Broadway)—with its high-wattage neon billboards, Times Square is a jaw-dropping sight (and for the most part PG-rated). By far the greatest number of Manhattan hotels is in Midtown, and many restaurants as well. But with its crowded sidewalks full of working New Yorkers, it's not necessarily a place where families can easily maneuver. Come here to shop and to gawk at the tall buildings; but venture along the side streets, and you'll get a better idea of how New York families experience the city.

The **Upper West Side** occupies the part of Manhattan directly west of Central Park— here you'll find great museums for kids, lots of kid-friendly restaurants, toy stores, and playgrounds in both Central and Riverside parks. The **Upper East Side,** everything east of Central Park, is a quixotic mix of elegant old-money apartments and ugly concrete high-rises. It's rich in pricey children's clothing shops (many on Madison Ave.) and top museums, especially along the park on Fifth Avenue. You'll see packs of uniformed kids from the neighborhood's tony private schools gathering in pizza parlors and Gaps.

Above Central Park to the west is **Morningside Heights,** dominated by Columbia University and two magnificent churches— Riverside Church and the Cathedral of St. John the Divine. East of Morningside Park, **Harlem** takes over the island north of Central Park. Many tourists visit Harlem as part of a guided tour, though you can certainly check it out on your own. However, your kids' interest in the social-history aspects of a Harlem guided tour may lag if they're under 10. Unless you're visiting The Cloisters (the Metropolitan Museum's medieval-art branch in Fort Tryon Park), there's not much reason for you to tour **Washington Heights,** which lies above Harlem.

The Outer Boroughs in Brief

New York City's other four boroughs surround the island of Manhattan. To the north and east lies the **Bronx,** which only partly deserves its bad rap as a crime-infested slum. Parts of the Bronx are rotten indeed, but the Bronx also includes suburban Riverdale, along the Hudson, and the middle-class Fordham area, anchored by Fordham University and Bronx Park (where the Bronx Zoo and the New York Botanical Garden are). Arthur Avenue is home to a small but choice Little Italy enclave of wonderful restaurants, food markets, and Italian pastry shops. The New York Yankees aren't called the Bronx Bombers for nothing: Yankee Stadium is at 161st Street in the Bronx; the subway takes you directly to the stadium.

The landmass directly east of Manhattan (the western end of Long Island) contains the two most populous boroughs: Brooklyn and Queens. Immortalized (rightly or wrongly) as Archie Bunker territory, **Queens** is the city's great middle-class borough, where hardworking immigrant groups have colonized various neighborhoods from Astoria to Flushing. Directly across the river from Manhattan, Long Island City and Williamsburg are havens for young artists, and Forest Hills in the middle of Queens is a manicured residential area. Farther-out areas of Queens, like St. Albans, Little Neck, and Douglaston, are basically suburban neighborhoods.

A rewarding destination in itself, **Brooklyn** has in Prospect Park one of the city's most glorious outdoor spaces, some of the city's best restaurants, good museums, and lovely residential areas, notably brownstone-lined Brooklyn Heights, right across the Brooklyn Bridge from Manhattan, and nearby gentrified row house neighborhoods such as Cobble Hill, Carroll Gardens, Fort Greene, and

MANHATTAN'S bridges & tunnels

Manhattan's an island—to get on or off it, you have to go over or under the water. Going clockwise around the island, starting from the northern tip, you can take the **Henry Hudson Bridge** (on the Henry Hudson Pkwy.; $3 toll), the **Triborough Bridge** ($5.50 toll), the **59th Street/Queensboro Bridge** (no toll), or the **Queens-Midtown Tunnel** (part of I-495; $5.50 toll). A trio of toll-free bridges into Brooklyn—the **Williamsburg,** the **Manhattan,** and the **Brooklyn**—all connect handily with the Brooklyn-Queens Expressway, as does the **Brooklyn Battery Tunnel** ($5.50 toll) at the island's southern tip. Two big tunnels cross the Hudson on Manhattan's west side—the **Holland Tunnel** ($8 toll only into Manhattan), which funnels into Canal or Houston Street; and the **Lincoln Tunnel** ($8 toll only into Manhattan), which funnels into 40th Street—and the **George Washington Bridge** (part of I-95; $8 toll only into Manhattan) crosses above the water up at 175th Street.

Drivers can zip through bridge and tunnel tollbooths much faster—and at discounted toll fares—if they have **E-ZPass,** a small device that drivers can post on their windshields to have tolls electronically deducted from a credit card account. Certain lanes at toll stations are designated for E-ZPass users only. To set up an account, call ℅ **800/333-TOLL** (333-8655) or go online at **www.e-zpassny.com.** Note that E-ZPass devices are also compatible with the New Jersey, Pennsylvania, and Massachusetts turnpikes; the New York State Thruway; Delaware River bridges; and the Atlantic City Expressway.

Park Slope (the last has the advantage of bordering Prospect Park, Central Park's Brooklyn cousin). Facing Staten Island across the Narrows, Bay Ridge is a vast middle-class enclave; Brighton Beach, on Brooklyn's southern shore, is a former Jewish area now heavily colonized by immigrant Russians. But other Brooklyn neighborhoods, like Bedford-Stuyvesant, Brownsville, and East New York, aren't for the uninitiated.

That leaves **Staten Island,** the most suburban of the boroughs, the one that's always threatening to secede from the city—which actually makes sense, because Staten Island is geographically part of New Jersey. Staten Island's attractions for visitors—the restored historic village at Richmond Town, a zoo, a children's museum, a couple of historic houses—don't lure many New Yorkers across the water, which suits most Staten Islanders just fine. Still, the Staten Island Ferry ride is one of those classic New York things to do, a pleasant way to spend an hour or so crossing the harbor—and it's free.

GETTING AROUND

Manhattan's transportation systems are showing their age. Yes, it's miraculous that so many people can gather on this little island and move around it, but it's also true that teeth-gnashing gridlock is a way of life, trains often get delayed, and subway tunnels are uncomfortably crowded at rush hours. For the most part, however, you can get where you're going pretty quickly—if you use the subway. Buses lumber along in traffic (good way to sightsee!), and taxi rides creep along on busy thoroughfares. Even though the New York City subway system is, to put it mildly, inelegant—it's ear-deafeningly creaky, smelly, and crowded—it's a remarkably safe, swift way to move around the city.

Between traffic gridlock and subway delays, sometimes you just can't get there from here—unless you **walk.** New York is one of the great walking cities of the world, and walking can sometimes be the fastest way to navigate the island. During rush hours, you'll easily beat car traffic while on foot, as taxis and buses stop and groan at gridlocked corners. You'll also see a lot more by walking than you will if you ride beneath the street in the subway or fly by in a cab. So pack your most comfortable shoes and hit the pavement—it's the best, cheapest, and most appealing way to experience the city.

By Subway

It's more than a century old and carries more passengers than all the other mass-transit rail system in the U.S. combined. But the NYC subway system just keeps chugging along; the trains themselves are spiffier and subway crime is at an all-time low. Rush-hour crowds can still be pushy, and derelicts, panhandlers, and pop-up entertainers still disturb riders' peace from time to time. Trains don't run as often as they should, either, especially in light of recent budget cuts that eliminated a number of subway lines. But the subway is truly a viable, fast alternative, especially for long daytime rides, when you'll save time as well as money by gliding under the streets instead of getting mired in city traffic.

The **Metropolitan Transit Authority** (© **718/330-1234;** www.mta.nyc.ny.us) operates the city's buses and subways, which run 24 hours. Even mildly adventurous visitors should feel comfortable underground from 7am to 8pm—however, the morning and evening rush hours (generally 8–9:30am and 5–6:30pm weekdays) make the trains so crowded you'd be better off not traveling then, especially with a family to squeeze in. Currently the **fare** is $2.25, and for your money you can ride as long and far as you like, changing lines at any of more than 50 transfer points. Children under 44 inches tall ride free; in practice, kids under 6 can just duck under the turnstile bar, and no one challenges them. (In some neighborhoods, even 12-year-olds can duck under the turnstile and no one will blink.)

New Yorkers use multiride **MetroCards,** with magnetic strips that automatically deduct one fare every time you slip them through a groove in a turnstile; each time you run your card through a turnstile, your remaining balance is displayed. Metro-Cards can be bought in various denominations from $3 to $80 and can be refilled at fare booths or at vending machines in many stations. Up to four passengers traveling together can use the same MetroCard—just slide it through the turnstile once for each rider.

Bonuses of 20% are offered for buying MetroCards of $10 or more; unlimited-ride passes are also available, costing $89 for 30 days, $27 for 7 days, and $8.25 for a 1-day Fun Pass (expires at 3am the following day). All of these except the 1-day pass are available at fare booths and vending machines; the Fun Pass can be bought only in the vending machines or at newsstands and shops around town (look for blue-and-yellow MetroCards Sold Here signs). **Only one catch:** Unlimited-ride passes can't be reused at the same subway station or bus stop for 18 minutes, so to take advantage of the discounts, you'll have to buy each member of your family a separate card.

MetroCards allow riders **free transfers** to and from city buses. If you're coming from a city bus, just slide your card through the subway turnstile's groove, and the machine should indicate that this is a transfer. Note that transfers do expire after a certain amount of time; sometimes you'll be pleasantly surprised when you reenter the system half an hour after one ride to find that your second ride registers as a transfer, but don't count on it. MetroCards also work on the city's PATH trains to New Jersey.

Maps are posted inside stations (usually out by the token booths, so you can make sure where you're going before you enter) and in most cars. Near the token booths, many stations now also feature detailed street maps of the immediate area, so you can get oriented before you hit the street.

By Bus

There are two ways to pay your $2.25 bus fare: with a **MetroCard** (the same one you use for the subway) or $2.25 in exact change (no pennies). You can't buy Metro-Cards onboard, however; you have to get them at a subway station. Children under 44 inches tall ride free (there's a line near the driver's seat against which to measure your child), but in practice kids under 6 are usually allowed to ride free, regardless of height.

To transfer for free to a second bus, dip your MetroCard into the farebox slot; if you've just come from the subway or another bus, the machine will register this as a

art DOWN UNDER

Many Manhattan subway stations were renovated in the 1990s, and more will be in the new century. The tile walls along waiting platforms often feature work by local artists or symbols appropriate for that particular neighborhood. Some of our favorites: the fossils and critters crawling over the walls of the **West 81st Street** stop on the B, C lines (beneath the American Museum of Natural History); the artwork by local schoolchildren at the **West 86th Street** stop on the 1, 9 line and at the **Columbus Circle** station (A, B, C, D, 1, 9 trains); the scenes from famous operas and ballets at **West 66th Street/Lincoln Center** station on the 1, 9 line; the fanciful cartoon characters peeking out from the floors and ceilings of the **14th Street** stop on the A, C, E lines; the sea creatures slithering over the **Houston Street** station (1, 9 line); and the scurrying beavers at the **Astor Place** stop on the 6 line (obscure reference: Astor Place is named after 19th-c. tycoon John Jacob Astor, whose fortune originally came from beaver furs).

transfer (reading "XFER OK" or "2 XFERS OK" if two passengers are using the same card). Transfers expire after a certain amount of time, but you probably can slip into a shop between buses and still have your second ride count as a transfer. **Note:** If more than one passenger is using the same MetroCard, when you are transferring to a second bus or train, *dip only once for the transfer.* (Dip a second time, and an additional fare will be deducted.)

If you're using coins, request a transfer card from the driver of the first bus *when you pay your fare.*

Each bus's destination is displayed above its front windshield; routes are posted at most bus stops. Look for blue-and-red bus-stop signs along sidewalks; at transfer points, a glassed-in shelter often accompanies them. Within Manhattan, bus stops are stationed every 2 or 3 blocks along avenues or major crosstown streets. Once you're riding a bus, if you wish to get off at the next stop, press any one of several electronic strips posted around the bus. A sign at the front of the bus should light up, reading STOP REQUESTED, and the driver will then pull over at the next stop.

If you're trying to get around the Lower Manhattan area around Battery Park City, Wall Street, and the South Street Seaport, you should also know about the free **Downtown Connection** bus service organized by the Downtown Alliance (© 212/566-6700; www.downtownny.com). Running about every 10 to 15 minutes between 10am and 7:30pm, these buses travel from the northern end of Battery Park City around Manhattan's southern tip to South Street Seaport, making 16 stops en route. For a downloadable bus-route map, go to the website and click on "Downtown Connection."

By Taxi

The only taxis authorized to pick up passengers hailing them on the street are **yellow cabs,** which have an official Taxi and Limousine Commission medallion screwed onto the hood. So-called gypsy cabs, working for car services, sometimes stop illegally for passengers on the street; but because they have no meter, you'll have to negotiate your own fare with the driver, and you'll have no legal recourse if there's a problem. To know whether a yellow taxi is available, look for the lit-up center sign on the roof of the cab; off-duty cabs (side sections of the roof sign lit) may pick up passengers at their own discretion.

Taxi meters calculate the fare: currently $2.50 when you get in, plus 40¢ for each one-fifth of a mile or 120 seconds of waiting time in traffic. The meter should "click" every 4 blocks in normal traffic or once every crosstown block. There's an extra 50¢ charge from 8pm to 6am, a $1 surcharge for peak weekday service (Mon–Fri 4–8pm), and a New York State tax surcharge of 50¢ per trip, and passengers pay any bridge or tunnel tolls. A 15% to 20% tip is expected, unless the service is bad. For complaints or inquiries about lost property, dial © 311 or go online at **www.nyc.gov/taxi**.

Technically, a taxi doesn't have to take more than four passengers (with adults, this is possible only if one sits in the front seat next to the driver). But if your kids are small, most cabbies will let you all squeeze in, which is good news for families of five. All New York yellow cabs are supposed to have working seat belts. If your kids are car-seat-size, technically you could haul around a car seat and strap it in every time you get in a cab, but the only person I've ever known to do this did it only once, when cabbing her newborn home from the hospital. Always strap a child in with his or her own seatbelt, or, barring that, just hold him or her in your lap while you're strapped in (ER docs say that strapping a child inside your seatbelt while he's in your lap can cause the child more injury in the event of an accident).

By Ferry

The free **Staten Island Ferry** (© 718/727-2508) at Battery Park remains the best way to enjoy views of the Manhattan skyline, New York Harbor, and the Statue of Liberty. To reach the South Ferry terminal, take the R, W train to Whitehall Street or the 1, 9 to South Ferry. If you don't have any business on Staten Island, simply disembark from the ferry, go through the turnstiles, and turn around for the return trip.

The **New York Waterway Ferry System** (© 800/53-FERRY [533-3779]; www. nywaterway.com) runs a number of commuter ferries. Most cost $3 to $5 one-way; they link New Jersey (from Jersey City, Weehawken, Hoboken, or Liberty Harbor) to Midtown (W. 39th St.) and Downtown (the World Financial Center in Battery Park City or Pier 11 at Wall St.).

New York Water Taxi offers two seasonal weekend hop on, hop off water-taxi experiences on the New York waterways (© 201/742-1969; www.harborexperience. com). The "NY HarborWay Ferry" shuttles between South Street Seaport and Fulton Ferry Landing (at the southern tip of Brooklyn Bridge Park). A round-trip ticket is $3–$10; a round-trip family fare (two adults, two children) is $6–$15. The "Statue of Liberty Downtown Express" is a 90-minute loop that takes you from midtown to downtown Manhattan or Fulton Ferry Landing (Brooklyn). The fare: $25 adults, $15 children (Sat and Sun only). You can purchase tickets on the boat or online. New York Water Taxi also runs harbor cruises.

By Car

First of all, I do not recommend driving in the city—it's the least efficient way to get around town. But if you must drive, keep in mind that car-rental rates at the airports are often lower than those in Midtown. All the big national chains operate several locations, including at all three major airports: **Avis** (© 800/331-1212; www.avis.com), **Budget** (© 800/527-0700; www.budget.com), **Dollar** (© 800/ 800-3665; www.dollar.com), **Enterprise** (© 800/261-7331; www.enterprise. com), **Hertz** (© 800/654-3131; www.hertz.com), and **National** (© 800/227-7368; www.nationalcar.com).

If you're visiting from abroad and plan to rent a car in the United States, you probably won't need the services of an additional automobile organization. If you're planning to buy or borrow a car, automobile-association membership is recommended. **AAA, the American Automobile Association** (© 800/222-4357; http://travel. aaa.com), is the country's largest auto club and supplies its members with maps, insurance, and, most important, emergency road service. *Note:* Foreign driver's licenses are usually recognized in the U.S., but you should get an international one if your home license is not in English.

PARKING On the streets, look for parking signs stating what days or hours you can park curbside. In Midtown and other spots where police feel it's vital to keep traffic flowing, your illegally parked car will be towed in minutes, so don't even think of violating parking laws. In residential neighborhoods, "alternate side of the street parking" means that everybody's expected to shift their cars to the opposite curb once a day. Officers are required to complete any parking ticket they start to fill out, so pleading will do no good. If your car does get towed, call the **Borough Tow**

Pound at ✆ **212/971-0770** to find out where it is; you'll have to pay $185 in cash to retrieve it.

Space is so tight in New York that some residents are willing to pay over $400 a month for parking-garage spaces. Public garages dot Manhattan streets every 2 blocks or so, with rates averaging about $12 to $15 for less than 2 hours, $20 to $30 for half a day, and $40 overnight. Better-known commercial parking-garage operators include **Rapid Park, Manhattan Parking,** and **GMC.** Prices are sometimes lower at night or on weekends in business districts and during the day in residential areas; outdoor lots are less expensive, when you can find them. Few hotels offer parking. Some Midtown hotels provide valet parking at about $35 per night, often with the requirement that guests not take their cars from the garage between arrival and final departure. The city government's website at **www.nyc.gov** provides maps of licensed parking facilities, as well as information about how to obtain the **NYC Parking Card** (✆ **718/786-7042**), which gives you access to certain municipal metered parking. Otherwise, street metered parking (MUNI Meter) costs 50¢ for 12 minutes—*if* you can find a free space, which isn't easy.

DRIVING RULES Every passenger is supposed to wear a seat belt, and all kids 5 and under should be in car seats of some kind. Except for major crosstown streets and a few north-south avenues (Broadway, Park Ave.), most of Manhattan's streets are one-way, so sometimes you'll have to circle around a couple of blocks to get to a specific address. Right turns on red are *not* legal, and left turns are prohibited in some major intersections (watch for signs). Several major avenues have designated bus lanes (marked on the pavement), which are off-limits to cars during rush hours. Keep in mind that using a **hand-held cellphone while driving** is illegal in New York City (offenders face a fine of $130).

Midtown Manhattan streets are prone to the phenomenon known as *gridlock.* Beware of edging into an intersection in slow-moving traffic—if you don't manage to get through the intersection before the light changes, you can get stranded in the path of oncoming cross-traffic. If a police officer's watching, you may be ticketed for "blocking the box."

PLANNING YOUR OUTINGS

Everything is relatively close together in Manhattan, but if you're traveling by cab, traffic jams can make even a few blocks' travel take half an hour; waiting for frequent changes of buses or subways can add up to lots of wasted time; and plodding long distances on foot could tire out the kids (or you) before you get to the sights you want to see. Instead, plan carefully and you may be able to spend the entire day within a few blocks' radius, wasting little time on street travel. If you do have to hop from one part of town to another, don't underestimate travel time—snarled traffic or sluggish subways or buses can make a 40-block journey seem to take forever.

Prime areas for families are the **Upper West Side,** with the American Museum of Natural History and the Children's Museum of Manhattan; **SoHo,** with the Children's Museum of the Arts and the Fire Museum; **Midtown,** where you'll find the Sony

A Museum Note

One thing to take into account is museum closing days—many are closed on Monday. For a list of those that will be open, see "Rainy Days & Mondays," in chapter 7.

Wonder Technology Lab, Rockefeller Center, the Empire State Building, and the Museum of Modern Art; **Lower Manhattan,** with South Street Seaport; and the Upper East Side stretch of Fifth Avenue known as **Museum Mile.** If you're going to **Brooklyn** to see the Botanic Garden or Prospect Park Zoo, take in the Transit Museum and Brooklyn Heights on the same day. The same ferry goes to both the **Statue of Liberty** and **Ellis Island,** so it's a natural to do both the same day—but after waiting in all those lines, you probably won't have time to do much else that day. The **Bronx Zoo** and the **New York Botanical Garden** are right next to each other, but it'd be pretty exhausting to do both sprawling venues in a day.

Finding a Restroom

If you've got a recently toilet-trained toddler in tow, better think ahead, because in Manhattan it's not easy to find a bathroom at sudden notice. The **Times Square subway station** does have four clean attended bathrooms, for which there's often a line; **Grand Central Terminal** has a few, but they're not what you'd call clean. Restrooms can be found in **Central Park** and **Riverside Park** (see chapter 9 for locations), as well as in **Bryant Park,** which is at 42nd Street and Sixth Avenue behind the **New York Public Library;** the library itself has nice large bathrooms. Another option may be to use the bathrooms at various skyscrapers' shopping atriums, notably those at the **Sony Building** (56th St. and Madison Ave.), **Trump Tower** (56th St. and Fifth Ave.), the **Citicorp Building** (btw. Lexington and Third aves. and 53rd and 54th sts.), and the **Time-Warner Center** at Columbus Circle (59th St. and Columbus Ave.). **Barnes & Noble** bookstores, which are all around the city (see chapter 10), have decent bathrooms available. And here's one good thing about the number of **Starbucks** coffee shops dotting Manhattan: Nobody seems to mind if you stroll in just to use the bathroom. Major hotel lobbies are other good bets, although some of them require guest-room card keys for entry. In a pinch, if your child looks very distressed, you should be able to talk sympathetic waiters or store owners into letting you use their facilities.

Best advice: Always use the potty at your hotel before you leave, and stop in the restroom before you leave any museum or restaurant.

FAMILY-FRIENDLY ACCOMMODATIONS

O ne big problem families have had with New York hotels is that most are in Midtown, between 30th and 59th streets—just about the least desirable part of town for parents to stay in with their children. There's traffic, there's noise, there's hardly any greenery, and there's little resident population to fill the sidewalks at night. Besides, Midtown's tourist attractions—the Theater District, Fifth Avenue and Madison Avenue shopping, gourmet restaurants—don't matter so much when you've got kids in tow. Of course, Midtown does have some superb hotels whose facilities and service level more than compensate for the location; there are also decent moderately priced hotels that cater well to families. But the list of hotels we recommend is deliberately skewed to include more choices in other neighborhoods. If you can, why not stay near Central Park or the American Museum of Natural History or the Metropolitan Museum of Art? Lower-Manhattan hotels are close to South Street Seaport, the Statue of Liberty/Ellis Island ferry, and Hudson River Park, and they often have incredible weekend discount packages.

Which brings us to the other big problem: **cost.** Manhattan hotels sit on some very expensive real estate, pay staff wages in a top urban job market, and, because they're often the flagships of various lodging chains, definitely tilt toward the high end of the luxury spectrum. New York City has one of the highest average room rates in the country, and hotels here don't have to discount to fill their beds—citywide occupancy rates regularly hover in the 90% range and up. Many hotels are designed to target business travelers and conventioneers, whose expense accounts presumably cover those hotel bills—so why court cost-conscious families? (Never mind that more and more business travelers and conventioneers are bringing their families along, turning a business trip into a family vacation as well.)

If a **swimming pool** is important to you and your kids, we warn you now: Few Manhattan hotels have them, and some that do have pools sell memberships to adult New Yorkers, who may resent having a bunch of kids doing cannonballs in the deep end when they're trying to get some laps in on their lunch hour. We've listed nearly every hotel that does have a pool but tried to give you an idea of how welcoming those pools really are for families.

5

One thing a family can always use when traveling is a **kitchenette**—if you can throw together meals (or get takeout) in your room, you can easily save $100 a day, not to mention keep your children happy by not requiring them to use their restaurant manners three times a day. Suite hotels in general get our vote whenever they include some kind of kitchen facilities; they're also great with younger kids because you can put toddlers to bed at 8pm and retreat to the other room for a room-service dinner, a movie on cable TV, whatever. Seems a shame to spend your evening this way when you're in Manhattan, but for a couple of evenings of a 1-week stay, it can be just the ticket to de-stress after a long day.

Also look for hotels that offer **complimentary breakfast;** this is another money saver and a good way to fill up before hitting the streets.

On this built-up island, there just isn't the range of properties you'd find even in other expensive markets like London and Paris. You've got fleabags, you've got palaces—and not a whole lot in between. But face it: In between is where most families need to be. We've concentrated on ferreting out midrange hotels that are at least decent, if not always charming and atmospheric. When we do include some of the high-priced four-stars, it's because they offer something families especially value—not necessarily stunning decor, hushed privacy, and meticulous valet service (three things that don't mix well with small children anyway), but a pool, a kids' program, or a family-friendly location.

WHEN IS HIGH SEASON? Some hotels report that their slow time is January to early March; others say that July and August are their slow times. Just about all hotels, however, are booked *way* in advance from Thanksgiving to mid-December. When a big convention hits town, it can be impossible to find a room for love or money. Moral of the story: Call for reservations as soon as you know you're coming to New York to make sure you won't get shut out. But the other side of the coin is also true—call at the last minute, and you may get lucky even at one of the most popular properties.

Because New York attracts lots of business visitors as well as tourists, some hotels, especially those in Midtown or downtown, are more likely to have rooms free on weekends. Always ask about weekend packages if that's when you plan to check in.

> ### Best Hotel Bets
>
> See chapter 1 for a list of my hotel favorites—the most family-friendly, the best views, and more.

RESERVATION SERVICES **Quikbook** (© 800/789-9887; www.quikbook. com) will book you into any of more than 80 hotels, including all the Affinia Group suite hotels, the Doubletree Guest Suites, the Crowne Plazas, and Le Parker Meridien; there's no charge, and they can often get you discounts of 25% to 40%. The nationwide **Central Reservation Service** (© 800/873-4683; www.crshotels. com) also offers a discount, quoted as 10% to 40%, when they help you book rooms in New York. **Hotels.com** (© 800/246-8357; www.hotels.com) offers discount hotel booking in several large cities across the country, including New York.

A NOTE ABOUT HOTEL SERVICES Certain services are so standard in Manhattan hotels that we haven't noted them in individual reviews. Because tall buildings here interfere badly with TV reception, every hotel that offers in-room

TVs—and that's virtually all of them—offers **digital cable TV,** which means you'll have a range of channels to surf. Most hotels also have on-demand television options, pay-per-view, or some other **in-room movie service** feeding into the TVs. In the past couple of years, **Wi-Fi** has become standard in most hotels; a number of accommodations charge a daily fee to use it in your room—another tacky way to tack on extra fees, if you ask us—or offer it on a terminal in the lobby, but it's generally available somewhere for free on-site. **Dry-cleaning** and **laundry services** are usually available.

Just about every concierge or front desk has a list of **babysitters** they've used, usually provided by one of the city's many bonded child-care agencies. Rates can be steep—from $15 to $20 per hour, with additional fees for more children, plus cab fare to get home afterward ($15–$20). What you'll get will be professional babysitters, many of them from Europe, Asia, or South America, as well as North America. They'll come to your hotel room and take care of your children there.

Parking at just about all these Manhattan hotels, whether the hotel has its own garage or merely gives you a discount at nearby garages (the latter being more usual), is based on a per-night rate that assumes you won't be taking your car in or out during the day. Once you start moving the car, you'll have to pay more. Just another reason not to use your car while you're visiting.

A NOTE ABOUT PRICES I've categorized hotels according to a fairly basic rate for a family of four. In some hotels, that'll be the price for a double room with two double beds. In others, it may require a connecting pair of double rooms (though hardly any hotels will guarantee you'll get two rooms that connect—they're covering themselves in case the folks next door don't check out as expected—but in general, if you request connectors, you'll get them). In some hotels we've had to base things on the assumption that a small suite will be the best family deal. At any rate, we call a hotel **inexpensive** if that fictional family of four can stay for less than $225 a night; **moderate** if their bill will run $225 to $300; **expensive,** $300 to $400; and **very expensive,** over $400. (Those terms are, of course, relative to the Manhattan lodging price structure in general—and remember, that's for four people.) Quoted rates don't include the 14.25% New York City hotel tax, the occupancy tax, which is around $3.50 per room per night.

These are based on "rack rates," the hotel's standard rates for peak times. Corporate discounts and package deals can bring them in at as much as $100 lower a night, so we've also noted which hotels regularly offer good discounts. Some hotels regularly offer summer packages, while others are likely to activate package deals at the last minute, when occupancy rates appear to be falling short of projected levels. (Yield management is the name of the game.) Even if you've already secured a room at rack rates in a lower-priced hotel, just before you arrive, you might call a couple of pricier places to see if any special deals have kicked in. You could get a premium room for less, if you're lucky.

THE UPPER WEST SIDE
Expensive

Excelsior Hotel ★★ This longtime neighborhood hotel—perfectly situated right across the street from the city's top family attraction, the American Museum of Natural History—has been transformed from a bargain lodging into a smart upscale hotel, with a French Provincial motif in soothing greens and soft rosy browns. The bathroom fixtures are up-to-date, with nice country-French tile accents. The rooms are good-sized—a family of four could fit into one of the double-doubles (double room with two double beds), though a one-bedroom suite, with its queen-size pullout couch in the smallish sitting room, would give even more privacy (one-bedroom suites have one queen-size or two double beds; two-bedroom suites have all queen-size beds). The small but handsome wood-paneled lobby has an ornate plasterwork ceiling, much like many of the grand old apartment houses around the corner up Central Park West. Unfortunately, there's no room service, but complimentary continental breakfast is available on-premises in a breakfast room.

The location is superb—facing the wooded side yard of the American Museum of Natural History, on a clean and relatively quiet West Side block of luxury apartment buildings. (Ask about the hotel's Natural History Museum package.) You're half a block from Central Park, and there are loads of good restaurants and stores nearby on Columbus Avenue. The Excelsior is popular, particularly on weekends—reserve a couple of months ahead, if you can.

The hotel restaurant shut its doors in April 2010; stay tuned for what may open in its place.

45 W. 81st St. (btw. Central Park West and Columbus Ave.), New York, NY 10024. ℂ **800/368-4575** or 212/362-9200. Fax 212/721-2994. www.excelsiorhotelny.com. 198 units. $239–$379 double; $329–$449 suite. Children 11 and under stay free in parent's room. Rollaway $20; crib free. AE, DC, DISC, MC, V. Parking garages nearby. Subway: B, C to 81st St./Museum of Natural History. **Amenities:** Concierge; conference room; fitness center; Wi-Fi ($3.95/half-hour; $9.95/day); library. *In room:* A/C, TV, Wi-Fi ($3.95/half hour; $9.95/day).

The Lucerne ★★ Just a block from the American Museum of Natural History, in an area rich with restaurants and shopping, the Lucerne has all the earmarks of a chic boutique hotel, but it still works well for families. It's set in a gorgeous 1904 landmark building of plum-colored brownstone with baroque ornamentation running riot around its columned entrance; the small lobby sparkles like a jewel, with marble floors, big potted plants, and deep settees. Glossy, traditional room decor features striped and floral fabrics, thick carpeting, and framed prints. The good-size marble-and-granite bathrooms gleam with top-of-the-line fixtures. For dramatic views, be sure to ask for a room that looks out onto the Hudson River.

Fire laws prohibit rollaways in the double rooms, so unless you've got only one infant, you'll need a suite; but the Lucerne has 42 of these, with either two queen-size beds or a king-size bed plus a queen foldout couch, and all the suites have kitchenette areas. You'll be happy (or not) to know that the in-room TV options include Nintendo games. The service level of this hotel lifts it above other neighborhood options, with a concierge in the lobby, a business center, and a pocket-size fitness center. They've even added a small but decadent in-house spa. Hotel guests get a 15% discount for breakfast at the downstairs **Nice Matin** restaurant, a popular neighborhood restaurant serving French-Mediterranean cuisine; it's open for breakfast, lunch, and dinner.

201 W. 79th St. (at Amsterdam Ave.), New York, NY 10024. ℂ **800/492-8122** or 212/875-1000. Fax 212/721-1179. www.thelucernehotel.com. 186 units. $270–$400 double; $315–$520 suite. Children 11 and under stay free in parent's room. Crib free. AE, DC, DISC, MC, V. Parking $30 (valet parking $45). Subway: 1 to 79th St. **Amenities:** Restaurant; concierge; fitness center; room service; spa. *In room:* A/C, TV w/Nintendo, fridge, Wi-Fi (free), microwave.

Uptown Accommodations

Affinia Gardens **12**
The Carlyle **11**
Comfort Inn Central Park West **8**
Days Hotel New York City-
  Broadway **2**
Excelsior Hotel **3**
Gracie Inn **10**
Hotel Beacon **7**
Hotel Newton **1**
Hotel Wales **9**
Loews Regency **13**
The Lucerne **4**
Milburn Hotel **6**
On the Ave Hotel **5**

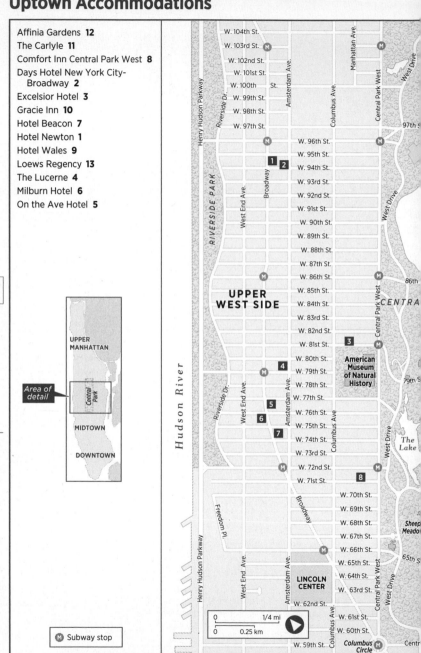

Yes, hotel prices are high in New York, and the costs climb even higher for families paying for extra people in the room or even extra rooms. Save big bucks, enjoy more space, and live among the locals by staying in a B&B or a short-stay apartment in New York. The city has plenty of reliable operators offering a range of lodgings, from elegant rooms in prewar apartment buildings to sunny, fully furnished apartments in historic brownstones. Fully equipped kitchens help save big on dining out. Prices can start as low as $90 a night. Check out **City Sonnet** (www.citysonnet.com; $125–$450 double) for both hosted and unhosted lodging in apartments and artists' lofts; or **Manhattan Getaways** (www.manhattangetaways.com; $125–$165 rooms; $165–$750 apts) for furnished rooms or private apartments. The New York page at **BedandBreakfast.com** (www.bedandbreakfast.com/manhattan-new-york.html) lists B&Bs, inns, guesthouses, and apartments for rent.

On the Ave Hotel ★   Definitely the hip choice on the Upper West Side. The trendy lobby looks very minimalist, with pale stone walls, a slick dark-wood floor, and a few scattered pieces of black leather furniture. It's been smartly designed upstairs as well, with a Zen-like simplicity—neutral carpet, gauze curtains, stainless steel sinks, a sleek panel of varnished wood morphing from headboard into canopy over the bed. Rooms, however, are smallish and contain only a king or queen bed, which means that a family will need to snag connecting rooms (of which there are about 30 in the hotel) or go for the penthouse suites, which have sitting areas and, often, balconies. This stylish hotel is very popular, especially with younger travelers; the location is convenient, with the American Museum of Natural History only 2 blocks away and Lincoln Center a 10-block stroll down Broadway. There's also a marvelous cityscape view accessible to all guests from a common-area balcony. In 2008, On the Ave welcomed the addition of **Fatty Crab,** an uptown branch of the celebrated downtown Malaysian restaurant. The hotel is also pet-friendly. Ask about the hotel's many seasonal packages.

2178 Broadway (entrance on 77th St.), New York, NY 10023. ✆ **800/509-7598** or 212/362-1100. Fax 212/787-9521. www.ontheave-nyc.com. 253 units. $179–$444 double; $269–$469 suite; $284–$569 penthouse suite. Children 11 and under stay free in parent's room. Rollaway $20. AE, DC, MC, V. Parking $37 in nearby garage. Subway: 1 to 79th St. **Amenities:** Restaurant; concierge; fitness center; Wi-Fi (free in lobby). *In room:* A/C, plasma TV, CD player, hair dryer, minibar, Wi-Fi ($14/day).

Moderate

Comfort Inn Central Park West   Despite the tony-sounding name, this budget-priced chain hotel isn't on classy Central Park West, but on a side street just off the park, in a narrow converted apartment building clad in gray stone. But it *is* near the park, and close to the American Natural History Museum, and within walking distance of Lincoln Center—a handy location that, given the price, is hard to beat. The small, modern lobby hasn't got much charm, nor do the rooms—floral bedspreads, bland traditional furniture with a shiny cherrywood finish, small standard bathrooms—and the doubles are too tight to accommodate more than three guests, once you've wedged in a crib. Still, at the right season these rooms are cheap enough that you can book two for your family and still be in the moderate range, and the free continental breakfast (limited as it is) is a very nice bonus (as is the free Wi-Fi; bless you, Comfort Inn). It's a decent choice for a short stay if you plan to be out on the town most of the time anyway. Note that Comfort Inn has some 15 locations all over Manhattan; go to **www.comfortinn.com** to find the right location for you.

31 W. 71st St. (btw. Central Park West and Columbus Ave.). ℭ **877/424-6423** or 212/721-4770. Fax 212/579-8544. www.comfortinn.com. 90 units. $179–$309 double. Children 11 and under stay free in parent's room. Rates include continental breakfast. AE, DC, DISC, MC, V. Parking $30–$40 nearby. Subway: 1, 2, 3 to 72nd St. **Amenities:** Concierge, fitness center. *In room:* A/C, TV, hair dryer, high-speed Internet access (free).

Hotel Beacon ★ Converted from an apartment building in the early 1990s, the Beacon offers just what we need more of in this city: clean, respectably furnished rooms with all the important amenities and none of the glitzy frills, in a neighborhood great for kids. Riverside Park is 2 blocks west and Central Park is 3 blocks east; the American Museum of Natural History and the Children's Museum of Manhattan are just a few blocks up the street, and Lincoln Center isn't far down Broadway. You'll find a quiet marble-clad lobby; wide, well-lit corridors; and good-size rooms freshly done up in a traditional decor (glossy dark Queen Anne–style furniture, muted rose and tan color schemes, and framed botanical prints on the walls). There's a fully equipped kitchenette with a microwave in every room; the marble bathrooms aren't large but look sparkling clean and have tidy little amenities baskets.

Even the doubles are big enough for a family, because they have a king bed or two double beds and enough space for a crib or rollaway. Suites add on a sitting room with a foldout couch. There's no room service, but a coffee shop is right on the corner. Though this is a busy stretch of Broadway, the windows are pretty well soundproofed (internal walls could use a little more soundproofing, unfortunately); since the 25-story hotel is one of the tallest buildings in the neighborhood, the upper-floor rooms facing west have nice views over Riverside Park and the Hudson. The Beacon

PURE Allergy-Friendly Rooms

Let's face it, you've got a lot of folks rotating through hotel rooms, and with asthma and allergy conditions on the rise, an increasing number of parents are seeking a clean option—and hotels are catching on. The PURE Allergy-Friendly Room ensures an environment that's 99.9% allergen free. Rooms given the PURE treatment offer hypoallergenic bedding, high-tech air purification, intensive surface cleaning, the Pure-Shield ™ (which repels microorganisms), and sanitized AC and heating. The PURE system even attacks viruses and bacteria, a real comfort to families traveling during the flu season. All of the hotels we've included in our guide are well maintained by solid housekeeping crews, but if you want to go that extra mile, the following New York hotels offer PURE rooms: **Doubletree Guest Suites** (p. 72), **Paramount Hotel** (p. 75), **Radisson Lexington Hotel** (p. 80). Check out **www.pureroom.com** for updates on new PURE-affiliated hotels.

—Ailsa Fox

gets a steady stream of business, so reserve as far in advance as possible, especially in June and October; weekdays tend to be less busy than weekends, so plan accordingly. Ask about theater packages.

2130 Broadway (at 75th St.), New York, NY 10023. © **800/572-4969** or 212/787-1100. Fax 212/724-0839. www.beaconhotel.com. 260 units. $205 double; $255 suite; $345 and up 2-bedroom suite. Children 12 and under stay free in parent's room. Rollaway $15; crib free. AE, DC, DISC, MC, V. Parking $31. Subway: 1, 2, 3 to 72nd St. **Amenities:** 24-hr. restaurant. *In room:* A/C, TV, hair dryer, kitchenette, MP3 docking station, Wi-Fi (free).

Inexpensive

Days Hotel New York City–Broadway Don't let the unglamorous upper-Broadway environs put you off: You're half a block from an express subway stop, where trains can whisk you to the Theater District in minutes, and with several good casual restaurants nearby (not to mention top playgrounds and sports facilities in both Riverside and Central parks), this neighborhood works very well for families.

The hotel itself is unexceptional, with tight corridors, a ho-hum chain-hotel decor, and window air-conditioners (not that there's any view to block). Bathrooms, though neatly modernized, are on the small side, but any way you look at it, a stay here puts you in the inexpensive rate category. All rooms with two beds have double beds. Junior suites have one queen bed and a pullout double-size sofa.

5

COOL pools

You'll get fabulous views year-round at the snazzy, glass-enclosed atrium pool at **Le Parker Meridien** (p. 73), which is 42 stories up, with panoramas of Central Park and the Midtown skyline. The enclosed pool at the **Millennium U.N. Plaza Hotel** (p. 80) may be only 27 stories up, but it's right on the East River, which means not only river views but also unobstructed skyline views south. What's more, the Millennium U.N. Plaza's pool features gorgeous tile work and a canopy overhead. Also in Midtown, the **Crowne Plaza Times Square** (p. 69) has a gleaming 50-foot indoor lap pool with a nice view, if that matters to you.

Farther west, the **Skyline Hotel** (p. 76) has a smallish enclosed rooftop pool of an earlier vintage, squirreled away in a hard-to-find upstairs nook; the plus here is big windows grabbing a bit of a Hudson River view. Hours are limited, however. The largest hotel pool in town is the blue Olympic-size one at the **Travel Inn** (p. 76), which is outdoors (hence open seasonally only), surrounded by wings of the hotel; a very pleasant patio area provides space for lounging poolside. The **Holiday Inn Midtown 57th Street** (p. 75) has a small outdoor rooftop pool, open Memorial Day through Labor Day.

Downtown, the new **Trump SoHo** (p. 84) has a pool and pool deck (and bocce court!), and the **Trump International Hotel & Tower** (p. 69) overlooking Central Park has a small heated pool. The outdoor rooftop pool at the **Hotel Gansevoort** (p. 82) in the Meatpacking District is a pretty spectacular spot (it morphs into an indoor heated pool in the winter), but family swim time is limited. Across the East River in Brooklyn, the **New York Marriott at the Brooklyn Bridge** (p. 87) has a 75-foot-long lap pool where kids can cavort after a day of sightseeing.

Lots of tour operators know about this place, so book well ahead. Weeknights are considerably cheaper than weekends, and summer means lower rates, though even then rooms book up fast. There's no room service, but there are plenty of nearby coffee shops. It's a sensible, no-fuss option for families who plan to be out and about most of the time anyway.

215 W. 94th St. (btw. Broadway and Amsterdam Ave.). ✆ **800/228-5151,** 800/834-2972, or 212/866-6400. Fax 212/866-1357. www.daysinn.com. 365 units. $135–$263 double. Children 11 and under stay free in parent's room. Rollaway $20; crib free. AE, DC, MC, V. Parking $30–$40 in nearby garages. Subway: 1, 2, 3 to 96th St. **Amenities:** Fitness center. *In room:* A/C, TV, fridge ($15 extra), hair dryer.

Hotel Newton   With a cheerful, eager-to-please staff and newly refurbished rooms, the Newton has moved up a notch from basic budget lodging to pleasant good-value hotel, with such newfangled amenities as Wi-Fi and flatscreen TVs. The lobby is bright and has a comfy seating area, whereas restful guest rooms are neatly done up in beige and rose hues with soft carpeting and functional wooden furniture. A deluxe room with two double beds would accommodate a family, but for a little more you could upgrade to the junior suite, which also has a sitting area and kitchenette. Bathrooms are small, but housekeeping keeps them sparkling. So what if the only views are of other buildings, the elevator is tiny, and the hallways are narrow; there's an express subway stop right outside the hotel door, the neighborhood is friendly and safe, and you weren't planning to spend all your time in your hotel room anyway, were you? The Key West Café downstairs is a shiny, up-to-date coffee shop with a huge menu, serving three meals a day, and the nearby area has loads of other family-friendly dining options.

2528 Broadway (btw. 94th and 95th sts.), New York, NY 10025. ✆ **800/643-5553** or 212/678-6500. Fax 212/678-6758. www.thehotelnewton.com. 105 units. $179–$235 double; $250 suite. Children 11 and under stay free in parent's room. Rollaway $28; crib free. AE, DC, MC, V. Parking $27. Subway: 1, 2, 3 to 96th St. **Amenities:** Restaurant; fitness center; room service; Wi-Fi ($1/5 min. in business center). *In room:* A/C, TV, kitchenettes in suites, Wi-Fi ($4.95/day).

The Milburn Hotel ★   The Milburn Hotel has a lot to offer at a great price. The hallways are narrow, but the rooms are decent-size (a few even have small outdoor terraces), with recently upgraded furnishings fastidiously maintained. Adding a crib or rollaway would make one of the doubles seriously snug; a family should probably go for a one-bedroom suite, which adds a living room with foldout couch. Kitchenettes have been smartly tucked into all rooms, with a microwave, minifridge, and tiny sink. Keeping kids happy in the room becomes easier with the in-room flatscreen TVs and DVD players. To complete the package, the front desk will provide PlayStations, children's books, and DVD selections for the whole family at no extra charge (upon request). Plus, the hotel has complimentary Wi-Fi in both the rooms and the public spaces.

The Milburn's entrance is just around the corner from Broadway, making it incredibly convenient for shopping and restaurants; though the Milburn has no restaurant, it offers a dining plan with discounts at good local restaurants. Considering you'll have a kitchenette, it's good to know that food shopping is especially great in this neighborhood, with the Fairway market and Citarella's fish store a couple blocks south, and H&H Bagels and Zabar's gourmet emporium a few blocks north. Riverside Park is only 2 blocks away, too. All told, an excellent deal.

242 W. 76th St. (btw. Broadway and West End Ave.), New York, NY 10023. © **800/833-9622** or 212/362-1006. Fax 212/721-5476. www.milburnhotel.com. 122 units. $159–$269 double; $199–$399 suite. Rollaway $15; crib free. Rates include continental breakfast Mon–Thurs. AE, DC, MC, V. Parking $25. Subway: 1 to 79th St.; 1, 2, 3 to 72nd St. **Amenities:** Fitness room; pool privileges nearby; room service. *In room:* A/C, TV/DVD, CD player, kitchenette, MP3 docking station, Wi-Fi (free).

THE UPPER EAST SIDE

Very Expensive

The Carlyle ★★★   The roster of celebrity guests includes everyone from Jack Nicholson to JFK, Brooke Astor to David Bowie, Harry Truman to Princess Diana. Many of the staff, from the bellmen to the concierges, make working at The Carlyle a lifetime career, delivering white-glove service that's rare indeed. Surprisingly enough, all this makes The Carlyle a great family hotel, if the prices aren't beyond your budget. The neighborhood is wonderfully quiet and well behaved, and the rooms are huge—even a double is big enough for a smaller family, with a crib or rollaway brought in.

Rooms are elegant and classically beautiful, with sumptuous chintzes and thick carpets draping the hotel's fine Deco bones. From its first decorator in the 1930s, Dorothy Draper, to more recent refurbishments by Thierry Despont and Cameron Barnett, The Carlyle has been furnished by Manhattan society's top residential designers. "Residential" is the key word—if a room has shelves, they'll be stocked with books; vases and china dishes and ormolu clocks are set out on the occasional tables; every sitting room and bedroom has its own entertainment center. More than a dozen rooms even have Steinway or Baldwin grand pianos. Suites have sleek modern kitchens, while even the double rooms at least have an alcove with a sink and well-stocked minibar. The bathrooms are big and gleaming, with Kiehl's toiletries, thick towels and terry-cloth robes, and makeup mirrors; most tubs have whirlpools.

The Carlyle's dining choices have always attracted locals, from the plush and intimate **Carlyle Restaurant** decorated in the style of an English manor (breakfast, lunch, and dinner, with a lavish Sun brunch) and the **Café Carlyle,** a renowned cabaret venue, to the **Gallery,** a Turkish-style red-velvet lobby area with a few small tables—just the place for breakfast coffee and afternoon tea, as well as post-theater snacks. But best of all for kids is the atmospheric **Bemelmans Bar,** with its fanciful murals painted by Austrian artist Ludwig Bemelmans, creator of the *Madeline* books ("In an old house in Paris that was covered in vines lived twelve little girls in two straight lines . . . "), where the charming **Madeline's Tea Party** is held on cool-weather weekends (p. 110). The hotel also offers another level of pampering with the newly opened **Sense Spa.** You can even have Fido walked while you see the sights.

The hotel is 35 stories tall, so if you're lucky enough to snag a room overlooking Central Park, you'll have a view to die for. Carlyle guests are near enough to the park to scamper right over and play, as well as being close to the Fifth Avenue museums and the glorious children's shops on upper Madison Avenue. For an added touch of swellegance, tuck your wee one into the Silver Cross Balmoral Pram (with the Carlyle Crest, of course), available for complimentary use during your stay, and explore the neighborhood.

35 E. 76th St. (at Madison Ave.), New York, NY 10021. ℂ **800/227-5737** or 212/744-1600. Fax 212/717-4682. www.thecarlyle.com. 188 units. $692–$1,400 double; $1,215–$6,000 suite. AE, DC, MC, V. Valet parking $50. Subway: 6 to 77th St. **Amenities:** Restaurant; cafe/cabaret; bar; lounge; babysitting; concierge; fitness center; room service; spa; pet services; secretarial services. *In room:* A/C, TV/DVD, CD player, fax, hair dryer, kitchen (in suites), minibar, MP3 docking station, Wi-Fi ($15/day).

Expensive

Affinia Gardens The all-suites Affinia Gardens attracts a lot of business from the cluster of hospitals around 68th Street and York Avenue, but this relatively residential neighborhood also makes sense for families on a short stay. From the small, stylish lobby, with its tranquil waterfall wall, the decor is spare, Zen-like, and contemporary—serene surroundings in which to crash after a long day. Request a junior suite with a pullout couch as well as a king or two double beds, or go for the one- or two-bedroom suites, which have separate bedrooms and sitting rooms, with sleeper sofas. In general, the staff seems helpful and friendly, accommodating whatever requests guests have. The hotel offers room service from one of four restaurants nearby (Italian, Chinese, burgers, and diner).

215 E. 64th St. (btw. Second and Third aves.), New York, NY 10021. ℂ **866/AFFINIA** (233-4642) or 212/355-1230. Fax 212/758-7858. www.affinia.com. 129 units. $399–$1,299 suite. Children 10 and under stay free in parent's room. Rollaway $20; crib free. AE, DC, DISC, MC, V. Valet parking $50. Subway: 4, 5, 6 to 59th St.; 6 to 68th St.; N, R, W to Lexington Ave./59th St. **Amenities:** Concierge; fitness center; room service; spa services; pillow menu. *In room:* A/C, TV, kitchenette, Wi-Fi ($15/day).

Hotel Wales ★ There's more than a touch of Edwardian Kensington to this charming century-old hotel in Carnegie Hill, a historic Upper East Side neighborhood full of tony private schools and well-off families. Only a block from Central Park and Museum Mile, the hotel is smack in the middle of upper Madison's strip of upscale children's shops. The lobby looks like the entry hall in a private mansion, with its marble staircase, carved wood banisters, dark wainscoting, and striped wallpaper, and the room decor is tastefully traditional—beautiful restored woodwork, original cabinets, and cedar-lined closets. The Pied Piper Room, where guests can help themselves to a granola-and-muffins breakfast, is a big comfy space with potted palms and Victorian settees where chamber music is played at teatime and on Sunday evening.

Rooms are very comfortable, with Belgian linens, handsome wood accents and armoires, and soft hues. Absolutely the only drawback to staying in this hotel is that the rooms are so small you can barely fit a crib in—better to go for a suite, which consists of a fair-size bedroom and an adjoining sitting area with a pullout sofa. (There are no connecting doubles.) The bathrooms are tiny yet outfitted with top-quality fixtures. Kids get a kick out of the hotel's Puss-in-Boots theme, discreetly carried out with framed prints on the walls and designs on the bath toiletries. Every room has a TV, and DVD players are available upon request. **Paola's Restaurant** is now located in the Hotel Wales, as is the separately owned **Sarabeth's Restaurant,** rightly popular for its delicious brunch.

1295 Madison Ave. (at 92nd St.), New York, NY 10128. ℂ **212/876-6000.** Fax 212/876-7139. www.hotelwalesnyc.com. 88 units. $270–$399 double; $370–$699 suite. Extra person $20. Rollaway $20; crib free. Rates include continental breakfast. AE, DC, DISC, MC, V. Valet parking $52. Subway: 6 to 96th St. **Amenities:** 2 restaurants; breakfast room; concierge; fitness room; room service. *In room:* A/C, TV, fridge on request, Wi-Fi ($13/day).

Loews Regency ★★   This place has star power, with famous folks wandering in and out on a regular basis. But the Regency staff likes to sprinkle stardust on everyone who stays here, including children. This is one of the most kid-friendly hotels in town, in fact. Kids are given welcome gifts, and the hotel even has its own kids' concierge to set up tours and recommend places to see. In the summer, the hotel has lemonade in the lobby; in the winter, hot chocolate. Bring your dog along with you, too—Fido will get a menu of treats, a water bowl, and a mat to soak up the slop. Rooms are big and roomy, with supremely comfy beds. The hotel has a gracious elegance that's not stuffy and a winning staff. Be sure to ask about the Family Fun Package when making your reservation.

540 Park Ave. (at 61st St.), New York, NY 10128. ℂ **866/563-9792** or 212/759-4100. Fax 212/826-5674. www.loewshotels.com. 353 units. $399–$589 double; $669–$1,139 suite. Children 17 and under stay free in parent's room. Rollaway $25; crib free. AE, DC, MC, V. Valet parking $56. Subway: N, R, 4, 5, 6 to 59th St. **Amenities:** 2 restaurants; lounge/cabaret; concierge; fitness room; 24-hr. room service. *In room:* A/C, flatscreen TV, CD player, hair dryer, minibar, Wi-Fi ($15/day).

Inexpensive

Gracie Inn 🎁   If only New York had more places like the Gracie Inn! First off, there's the neighborhood: the Upper East Side, on a side street near the East River, not far from Carl Schurz Park—the part of the East Side where middle-class families live and shop and go to school. Then there are the thoughtful service and quiet un-hotel-like atmosphere, which make this a welcome retreat from Manhattan bustle—the sort of bed-and-breakfast boutique hotel you can find all over Europe but rarely in the States. The inn even offers a soothing afternoon tea service to welcome you back from a long day out in the city.

Once you get past the unprepossessing exterior and minuscule lobby, the five-story town house (with elevator) has individually decorated suites. Antiques, stenciled wallpapers, rag rugs, hardwood floors, and lace curtains go for a country-inn look that's never too frilly or precious; fresh flowers are set out in the rooms, and plump snowy duvets are on the beds. Every suite has a tidy little kitchen with all utensils, and a continental breakfast is brought to your room each morning. Cribs or rollaways could fit handily even in the studios, though a one- or two-bedroom suite would be better for a family, especially the penthouse duplex (kids will have a blast running up and down the snug wooden staircase). With skylights, a greenhouse wall, and weathered wood terraces, the penthouse suites get loads of sun, but even rooms on the lower floors are fairly light. Don't expect to walk to the subway—York Avenue is a long way east from the subway line—but buses and taxis are easy to find, and the neighborhood has plenty of good, reasonably priced restaurants.

502 E. 81st St. (btw. York and East End aves.), New York, NY 10028. ℂ **212/628-1700.** Fax 212/628-6420. www.gracieinnhotel.com. 13 units. $199 studio suite; $229 1-bedroom suite; $359 penthouse. Discounts offered for weekly and monthly stays. Rollaway or crib free. Rates include continental breakfast. AE, DC, DISC, MC, V. Parking garages nearby. Subway: 6 to 77th St. *In room:* A/C, TV/DVD, CD player, hair dryer, kitchenette, Wi-Fi (free).

MIDTOWN WEST

Very Expensive

The Plaza ★   After a $400-million, 2-year renovation, the Plaza, like so many other hotels nowadays, is part condo and part hotel. There are now 282 guest rooms ranging from a roomy 482-square-foot guest room to suites of almost 1,500 square feet, some with terraces, and all rooms and suites feature white-glove butler service. Little girls will go mad for the **Eloise Suite** (starts at $995) ★, where they can bounce around like crazy on the plush Eloise-themed bed, pink-candy-striped walls, and zebra-print carpet. Designed by celebrity fashion icon Betsey Johnson, the room is all things Eloise, right down to the tiny Eloise and Weenie dolls. Kids will love the just-opened **Plaza Food Hall,** the newest Todd English creation, which consists of eight different culinary stations for eat-in/takeout and cooking demonstrations, as well as vendors for flowers, specialty foods, and home goods. The world-famous **Palm Court** is open once again for high (expensive) tea, and the **Oak Room** and **Oak Bar** for cocktails and dinner.

Fifth Ave. at Central Park South, New York, NY 10019. ✆ **888/850-0909** or 212/759-3000. Fax 212/759-3001. www.fairmont.com/theplaza. 282 units. $695–$1,145 double; $925–$6,000 suite. Rollaway $75; crib free. AE, DC, DISC, MC, V. Valet parking $65. Subway: F to 57th St; N, R, Q to 5th Ave./59th St. **Amenities:** 2 restaurants; food court; 2 bar/lounges; concierge; fitness center; room service and butler service; spa. *In room:* AC, TV, hair dryer, minibar, safe, Wi-Fi ($15/day).

Trump International Hotel & Tower ★   The $30-million renovation of this Phillip Johnson landmark was completed in summer 2010, with the emphasis on super-duper luxe. It can be chillingly expensive, yes, but the kids' amenities are top-notch, and a stay here plays into the fantasy of living the swellegant life. We've been New Yorkers for more than 20 years, and we've never seen Central Park views like the ones from the hotel's top floors. Is the crystal chandelier (specially requested by Donald) overkill? Perhaps, but the more gauche elements of the Trump brand have been wrestled to the ground and tamed. And those views! The Trump properties are family affairs, with Ivanka's hand in the tastefully elegant decor and the Donald pushing for 55-inch TVs and Blu-ray players. All suites have fully stocked kitchens with Sub-Zero appliances and lots of cabinet space and closets for longer stays. Security is excellent: You need a key just to ride in the elevator. The children's program, Trump Kids, is a canny, all-out assault to capture the family trade. At check-in, kids get a complimentary Trump gift bag, with a Trump stuffed elephant, coloring books, crayons, and more. Available for their recreational pleasure are Wii, PlayStation, and Xbox; MP3 players with kid-friendly music; and board games. Little moguls can even have personalized Trump Kids Biz cards printed up! Kids are welcome to use the narrow, 55-foot indoor heated lap pool. At no extra charge, the Trump Baby Attaché will baby-proof the room before you arrive, prestock it with supplies—formula, diapers, baby monitor, humidifier, even a Diaper Genie—and provide a rocking chair, playpen, and crib (and a signature Trump bib, yours to keep). The spa offers special tween and teen treatments. The acclaimed restaurant **Jean Georges** is on-site; it's connected to the sun-filled, family-friendly **Nougatine,** which has all-day kids' menus and an outdoor terrace. Ask and you shall receive chocolate-covered animals crackers and, at bedtime, milk and cookies.

One Central Park West, New York, NY 10023. ✆ **888/448-7867** or 212/299-1000. www.trumpintl.com. 167 units. $825–$875 double; $995–$2,400 suite. Children 11 and under stay free in parent's room. AE, DC, DISC, MC, V. Parking $50–$60/day. Subway: 1, 2, A, B, C, D to Columbus Circle. **Amenities:** 2 restaurants; bar; babysitting; concierge; fitness center; heated pool; room service; spa; Wi-Fi (free in lobby). *In room:* A/C, TV, Blu-ray DVD, CD player, fridge, hair dryer, MP3 docking station, Wi-Fi ($15/day).

Expensive

Crowne Plaza Times Square Manhattan ★   In the spiffed-up Times Square, the spiffed-up 46-story Crowne Plaza is nicely positioned to be a major player. With

Midtown Accommodations

Affinia Dumont **24**
Affinia 50 Suite Hotel **17**
Beekman Tower Hotel **18**
Crowne Plaza Times Square
    Manhattan **6**
Doubletree Guest Suites
    Times Square **6**
Eastgate Tower **22**
Flatotel **5**
Four Seasons **11**
Holiday Inn Midtown
    57th Street **2**
The Kimberly **16**
Le Parker Meridien **12**
Millennium U.N. Plaza
    Hotel **21**
Novotel New York
    Times Square **4**
The Paramount Hotel
    New York **9**
The Plaza **13**
Radisson Lexington
    New York **19**
Renaissance New York Hotel
    Times Square **7**
Roger Smith Hotel **20**
Shelburne Murray Hill
    Suites **23**
Skyline Hotel **3**
Southgate Tower **11**
Travel Inn **10**
Trump International Hotel
    & Tower **1**
Waldorf=Astoria **15**

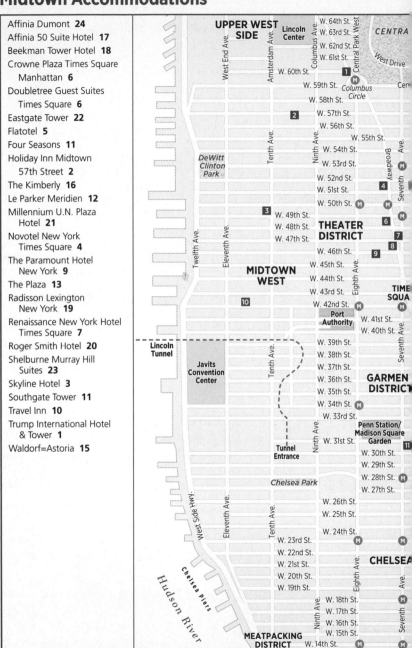

a reception area one floor up from Broadway (security is thorough but not oppressive) and tight soundproofing, you can feel removed from the tumult but not bunkered in—many windows overlook the razzmatazz, including some around the pool and at the end of every corridor. The guest floors begin on the 16th story (several floors of offices are in between the lobby and the guest rooms), giving many rooms great skyline or river views. Yet this contemporary 770-unit hotel sticks firmly to the middle of the road, in style as well as rates. Its lobby has some marble and brass and plush touches, but it's not overbearing; the room decor is traditional and corporate, with greens and browns and lots of table lamps; the restaurants are generally casual, with a breakfast buffet (or if you really want to get going fast in the morning, pick up coffee, juice, and muffins to go from the lobby bar).

Families have several layout options: a double room with two double beds; connecting doubles; a smallish sitting room with your choice of one or two bedrooms connecting; or a large sitting room (complete with a minibar/serving area and dining table) with your choice of one or two bedrooms connecting. Along with pullout sofas, the Crowne Plaza has some pull-down Murphy beds, which kids might enjoy, and in-room video games to keep them occupied. Some extra amenities (terry bathrobes, a jar of hard candies) are offered on Crowne Plaza Club floors, but it might be worth it if only because you can get continental breakfast free in the lounge, a huge windowed parlor with dynamite views; once the corporate travelers have cleared out at 9am or so, the room is virtually empty. The health club is an obvious attraction for families, though there are some caveats: The fitness center is run by the New York Sports Club, whose members get priority over hotel guests weekdays at lunchtime and after work. The 50-foot lap pool, however, is open to guests at all times; if you want to make sure there's room, call ahead to reserve a lane.

1605 Broadway (btw. 48th and 49th sts.), New York, NY 10019. ℂ **800/2-CROWNE** (227-6963), 800/980-6429, or 212/977-4000. Fax 212/333-7393. www.crowneplaza.com. 770 units. $319–$529 double; $749–$1,399 suite. Children 18 and under stay free in parent's room. Rollaway $30; crib free. AE, DC, DISC, MC, V. Valet parking $39–$49. Subway: 1 to 50th St.; N, R, W to 49th St. **Amenities:** 1 restaurant; bar; babysitting; concierge; fitness center w/classes; indoor pool; room service; Wi-Fi ($11/30 min. in business center); ATM. *In room:* A/C, TV, minibar, Wi-Fi ($$20/day).

Doubletree Guest Suites Times Square ★

The all-suites Doubletree more than makes up for what might be an off-putting location, smack-dab on Times Square with newly renovated guest suites. The suite concept is a natural for families anyway, because you automatically get sleeping space for four or six, depending on whether you request a king-size bed or two doubles in the bedroom (there's a foldout sofa in the sitting room). All suites have kitchenettes with a microwave, a stocked minibar, and TVs in both rooms.

Now let's get to the really unusual ways the Doubletree provides for families: There's no charge for cribs, playpens, and strollers, and you can request that the cable movie service be shut off if you're worried your kids will go wild with the remote.

The amusement-park-sized Toys "R" Us is just across the street, and the TKTS booth is steps away for half-price Broadway tickets. Not to mention that the very glitter, lights, and noise that is Times Square lies just outside your door (you and your kids may disagree on whether this is actually a good thing). Security is good, though not forbidding: There's a ground-floor foyer with monitored elevators leading up to the guest lobby, and a separate bank of elevators goes up to guest-room floors. After 11pm, guests have to show their key card to be admitted into the guest-room elevators. At 45 stories, the Doubletree does have some high-floor rooms with Midtown views; but what's more important about the height is that it means there are lots of rooms, so more families can take advantage of this great deal.

The **Center Stage Café** has whimsical wall murals carrying out its Broadway theater theme—face one way, and you'll feel like an audience watching the stage; face the other, and you'll feel like performers looking up at the audience in the painted balcony. The restaurant serves a breakfast buffet, lunch, and dinner and has a kids' menu, naturally. The decor of the newly opened **Ginger's Restaurant** is based on the Broadway musicals of the Roaring Twenties. A new lobby lounge and a state-of-the-art fitness center are also great perks.

1568 Broadway (at 47th St. and Seventh Ave.), New York, NY 10036. (℃) **800/222-8733** or 212/719-1600. Fax 212/921-5212. http://doubletree1.hilton.com. 460 units. $299–$559 suite; $1,199–$1,650 2-bedroom suite. Children 17 and under stay free in parent's room. Crib free. AE, DC, DISC, MC, V. Valet parking $35–$40. Subway: 1 to 50th St.; N, R, W to 49th St.; B, D, F, V to 47th–50th sts./Rockefeller Center. **Amenities:** 2 restaurants; lounge; concierge; fitness center; room service; Wi-Fi (free in lobby and public areas). *In room:* A/C, TV, fridge, hair dryer, kitchenette, minibar, Wi-Fi ($13/day).

Le Parker Meridien ★★ The 731-room property looks chic enough, with a marble-columned lobby and Zen-like guest rooms—but Le Parker Meridien does a superlative job of making families feel welcome. On arrival, kids are given the hotel's own hand-drawn coloring book; the elevators play continual cartoons and classic silent slapstick comedies; and kids can borrow a Razor scooter from the front desk to whiz around the neighborhood. Not only does the concierge know what's on for kids, but guests can also consult an online concierge even before arrival to scope out kid-friendly activities. Naturally, items like highchairs, night lights, bottle warmers, and safety plugs are available on request.

With its splendid glass-enclosed atrium pool, sun deck, ⅛-mile rooftop jogging track, and top-notch health club, this family-owned hotel is a super choice for any athletic family. The 57th Street location is close to Midtown attractions, yet only 2 blocks from Central Park; several rooms on the 42-story hotel's upper floors—say, from 20 on up—offer green park views. The artfully uncluttered guest rooms are clad in cherry and cedar wood and are spacious by Manhattan standards. Rooms and suites have either king-size beds or twins, and rollaway cots are rented out for extra kids. The Tower Suites aren't a bad deal, with a king-size bed in one room, a pullout couch in the other, a bathroom, a kitchenette, and an awesome skyline view on upper floors. The suites have full kitchenettes with pots, plates, and condiments available upon request. But best of all is the rotating blond-wood entertainment console—which, naturally, has video games on tap as well as movies.

Norma's serves gargantuan gourmet breakfasts, all the way through lunchtime, and **Knave** is an atmospheric bar. But face it, the restaurant that kids will dig the most here is the no-name **burger den** hidden off the lobby, which serves nothing but dang good burgers, cheeseburgers, and fries. Look for a neon burger hung discreetly near the concierge desk, and follow.

118 W. 57th St. (btw. Sixth and Seventh aves.), New York, NY 10019. (℃) **800/543-4300** or 212/245-5000. Fax 212/307-1776. www.parkermeridien.com. 731 units. $369-$529 double; $489 and up suite. Weekend packages available. Rollaway or crib $30. AE, DC, DISC, MC, V. Valet parking $50. Subway: N, Q, R, W to 57th St./Seventh Ave. **Amenities:** 2 restaurants; bar; concierge; fitness center; indoor pool; room service; spa; Wi-Fi ($10/hr in lobby); jogging track; squash and racquetball courts. *In room:* A/C, TV/DVD, CD player, hair dryer, kitchenette in suites, minibar, Wi-Fi ($16/day).

Renaissance New York Hotel Times Square ★　Sleek and corporate-looking as it is, the 26-floor Renaissance isn't the kind of hotel families automatically gravitate to, but those who do wind up here should be very pleasantly surprised. First, you're right in the thick of the Times Square action, but in a good way—the famous Coca-Cola sign hangs on the hotel's south wall; the TKTS discount ticket booth is a few steps away; many rooms look out onto one or another of the fabled supersigns; and the hotel restaurant, with windows on three sides, offers the best panoramic view of the Times Square intersection. (You couldn't ask for a better ringside seat on New Year's Eve.) Yet the riffraff get screened out by the ground-floor security lobby (the guest lobby is up on the third floor), and double-paned windows do an amazing job of keeping out traffic noise.

Inside, everything is mahogany and brass and marble and truly handsome. Families can fit nicely into the doubles, which are roomier than most Midtown doubles—go with a king-size-bedded room with a rollaway or a room that has two double beds (rooms with two doubles won't accommodate a rollaway). Suites consist of a king-size-bedded sleeping room and a sitting room with a pullout couch. Minibars are set under a marble countertop, which makes a handy place for fixing snacks or lunches. The hotel isn't too buttoned down to have a sense of fun: Instead of pillow mints, you get apples at turndown (because you're in the Big Apple, get it?), and there are board games at the front desk to while away the time. The hotel's new restaurant, **Two Times Square,** serves contemporary American cuisine (from Fatty Crab chef Zak Pellacio) and is open for breakfast, lunch, and dinner.

714 Seventh Ave. (btw. 47th and 48th sts.), New York, NY 10036. ℂ **888/236-2427** or 212/765-7676. Fax 212/765-1962. www.marriott.com. 310 units. $429–$709 double. Children 15 and under stay free in parent's room. Rollaway or crib free. AE, DC, DISC, MC, V. Valet parking $54. Subway: N, R, W to 49th St.; B, D, F, V to 47th–50th sts./Rockefeller Center; 1 to 50th St. **Amenities:** Restaurant; breakfast room; lounge; concierge; fitness center; room service; Wi-Fi (free in lobby). *In room:* A/C, flatscreen TV, hair dryer, minibar, Wi-Fi ($17/day includes all calls in continental U.S.).

Moderate

Flatotel ★　Just down the street from the Novotel (see below), this spiffy midtown choice has a great location, within walking distance of all of Midtown's attractions and shopping, with Broadway theaters and Times Square just to the west, and Rockefeller Center, Radio City Music Hall, and the Museum of Modern Art to the east. But equally important: Flatotel's rooms offer space to burn (deluxe one-bedroom suites are 1,100 sq. ft.!), and all 47 suites have kitchens—even the junior suites (the equivalent of a Manhattan studio apartment). Some one-bedroom suites even have 1½ bathrooms. The decor is warm and comfortable, and the higher floors have terrific city views, always a kid-pleaser. All of which is to say that this is an excellent family choice.

132 W. 52nd St. (btw. Sixth and Seventh aves.), New York, NY 10019. ℂ **800/352-6835** or 212/887-9400. Fax 212/887-9795. www.flatotel.com. 288 units. From $399 double; from $549 suite. Children 11 and under stay free in parent's room. AE, DC, DISC, MC, V. Parking $30. Subway: B, D, E to Seventh Ave.; 1, 9 to 50th St.; N, R to 49th St. **Amenities:** Restaurant; bar; babysitting; concierge; fitness center; room service. *In room:* A/C, TV, CD player, fridge, hair dryer, kitchen (in some suites), Wi-Fi (free).

Novotel New York Times Square ★　At this warm, well-run hotel, the prices are fantastic for a stay in a prime location. What makes it even more appealing to families is that two children 15 and under get free breakfast at the on-site **Café**

Nicole (and stay free in their parent's room), and the "family rooms" nicely fit two adults and two children. The Novotel also has a children's play space and welcome gifts—all in all, it's a winning choice for families. The room decor is perfectly fine, bland but comfortable, with a vaguely Scandinavian blond-wood minimalism and nice firm mattresses with good linens.

226 W. 52nd St. (at Broadway), New York, NY 10019. (C) **800/668-6835** or 212/315-0100. Fax 212/765-5365. www.novotel.com. 480 units. $266–$518 double. 2 children 15 and under stay free in parent's room and get free breakfast. AE, DC, DISC, MC, V. Parking $30. Subway: 1, 9 to 50th St.; C, E to 50th St.; N, R to 49th St. **Amenities:** Restaurant; babysitting; children's play space; concierge; fitness center; room service; Wi-Fi (free in lobby); ATM. *In room:* A/C, TV/DVD, hair dryer, minibar, Wi-Fi ($10).

Paramount Hotel New York ★   The aggressively cool "pop nouveau" Philippe Starck decor seems almost dated now, but it's still fun to step into the minimalist gray lobby with its asymmetrical rug, cartoonishly shaped armchairs, and free-standing stairway of brushed stainless steel. Young singles who look like *Gossip Girl* extras stare meaningfully at each other at the **Library Bar.** Heading upstairs, you may be disoriented by the deeply colored lighting inside the elevators. The spartan white rooms would almost resemble a doctor's office if not for the whimsical black-and-white checkerboard carpets, the stylized furnishings, and giant Vermeer reproductions in gilt-framed headboards; the bathrooms have an inverted cone of brushed stainless steel for a sink. Beds are pillowed in soft Egyptian cotton linens and down comforters—all in white, of course (some rooms have been recently renovated; you can select these online or ask when you call for a reservation).

Truth to tell, though, it's stunning, and most kids really get into its self-consciously stagy decor. One big drawback is size—some double rooms do have two double beds, but that doesn't leave a whole lot of space. Suites go fast, so book early. The west–of–Times Square location is close to Broadway theaters and Eighth Avenue's mixed bag of restaurants. All in all, this is a super place for a few nights' stay.

235 W. 46th St. (btw. Broadway and Eighth Ave.), New York, NY 10036. (C) **866/760-3174** or 212/764-5500. Fax 212/354-5237. www.nycparamount.com. 597 units. $309–$443 double; $449–$629 suite. Rollaway $25; crib free. AE, DC, DISC, MC, V. Parking $45. Subway: A, C, E to 42nd St./Port Authority; C, E to 50th St.; N, Q, R, S, W, 1, 2, 3, 7 to 42nd St./Times Square. **Amenities:** Restaurants; coffee bar; 2 bars; concierge; fitness center; room service. *In room:* A/C, flatscreen TV, hair dryer, minibar, Wi-Fi ($14/day).

Inexpensive

Holiday Inn Midtown 57th Street ⚓   This reassuring 18-floor motor inn in a residential area of Midtown's far west fringe is a very workable option for families, and a 2008 renovation means the decor has been refreshed and everything's in good working order. If you're driving into Manhattan, the low parking rate for the attached garage may appeal to you, especially because this property is close to the West Side Highway. And if your kids can't survive a vacation without a pool handy, the outdoor rooftop pool (open in summer only) may be a draw. Yes, it's a bit of a walk from here to Midtown attractions, but the relative quiet and calm may make all the difference, and the immediate neighborhood has lots of casual, locals-only restaurants that'll welcome you and your kids. But then again, kids eat free in the hotel restaurants (the **Gotham Café** for breakfast, lunch, and dinner)—a great deal in a city where practically nothing comes free.

The paneled front-desk area is low-key and pleasant, with a lobby bar (the restaurant and breakfast room are down a hallway). Although the guest room layouts are chain-motel-predictable, with large windows looking out at nothing particularly scenic, the double rooms are of decent size by Manhattan standards—they hold two double beds comfortably, which means a whole family may be able to fit in. There are a number of connecting doubles, if your family wants more space to spread out. Those who are interested in swimming might try to snag a room in the south tower, where the pool is.

440 W. 57th St. (btw. Ninth and Tenth aves.), New York, NY 10019. ✆ **888/465-4329** or 212/581-8100. Fax 212/581-7739. www.holidayinn.com. 597 units. $187–$261 double. Rollaway $15; crib free. AE, DC, DISC, MC, V. Valet parking $25. Subway: A, B, C, D, 1 to 59th St./Columbus Circle. **Amenities:** Restaurant; bar; concierge; fitness center; outdoor pool; room service. *In room:* A/C, TV, minibar, Wi-Fi (free).

Skyline Hotel 🦺 With the transformation of the gritty Hell's Kitchen neighborhood into respectable Clinton, the Tenth Avenue location of the Skyline is no longer a drawback. And the place has been nicely renovated in green-and-rust tones, including the 231 guest rooms, all of which now boast flatscreen TVs and mini-fridges. Most rooms are large enough to hold two double beds, which means that families may be able to get by with one room; junior and one-bedroom suites comfortably sleep six. We're talking bargain here (parking is just $10 a day), and many European travelers have already found it; so book well ahead. The large indoor pool is on the penthouse floor and has lots of surrounding windows, but there's a catch: It's open mornings and evenings only except for Saturday and Sunday, when it also opens from noon to 9pm. For these prices, however, people are happy to work around such minor inconveniences.

Off the lobby, the hotel restaurant serves only breakfast, but there were rumblings at press time about a new on-site restaurant. There's a wealth of fun restaurants just a block away on Ninth Avenue, however. Yes, it's a trek from here to most sights, but it's generally easy to hail a cab outside the hotel door. Now that it's no longer scary to walk this far west on 49th or 50th streets, the Skyline makes a lot of sense if you're trying to save a buck or two.

725 Tenth Ave. (btw. 49th and 50th sts.), New York, NY 10019. ✆ **800/433-1982** or 212/586-3400. Fax 212/582-4604. www.skylinehotelny.com. 231 units. $169–$309 double. Rollaway $20; crib free. AE, DC, DISC, MC, V. Parking $10 (no in/out during stay). Subway: A, C, E to 50th St. **Amenities:** Restaurant (breakfast only); lounge; concierge; indoor pool. *In room:* A/C, TV, Nintendo, hair dryer, minifridge, Wi-Fi ($9.95/day).

Travel Inn ★ 🦺 One of New York's very best deals is this bright, clean, sprucely decorated motor inn way at the end of 42nd Street—beyond Theater Row and not far from the Circle Line boat tours. One reason to stay here is that you get free parking; of course, what you save in parking you could easily spend in taxi fare. The Travel Inn remains very busy—there are many times when it's sold out months and months in advance—partly because it's handy for the nearby Javits Convention Center, partly because it has a pool—with a lifeguard on duty!—and, well, did we mention that the parking is *free?*

If you don't mind the concrete surrounds (the hotel certainly seems secure enough), you could save a whole lot by staying here. A family could fit comfortably in these rooms, which have two double beds, a desk, a dresser, and upholstered chairs. The decor is standard hotel-room traditional but very nicely kept; the bathrooms are spotless. And as befits a true motor inn, there's a big lap pool (open May–Oct), set in a spacious tiled area with lots of lounge chairs and room to stroll around. A number of rooms overlook the pool area from balconied walkways—request one of these, as opposed to the ones overlooking the street. The fitness room with weights and exercise machines is small but serviceable. The attached **Theater Row Diner** offers 24-hour room service, and a host of other area restaurants are happy to deliver as well.

515 W. 42nd St. (btw. Tenth and Eleventh aves.), New York, NY 10036. © **800/869-4630** or 212/695-7171. Fax 212/967-5025. www.thetravelinnhotel.com. 160 units. $160–$250 double. Rollaway $15; crib free. AE, DC, DISC, MC, V. Free parking. Subway: A, C, E to 42nd St./Port Authority. Bus: M42. **Amenities:** Coffee shop; fitness room; outdoor pool; room service. *In room:* A/C, TV, fridge (in some), Wi-Fi ($6/day).

MIDTOWN EAST
Very Expensive

Four Seasons ★★　Now owned by Ty Warner of Beanie Baby fame, this handsome 52-story hotel designed by I. M. Pei sets high standards for service, upscale chic, and high prices. The tortoiseshell onyx skylight and soaring octagonal limestone columns in the cathedral-like foyer instill a sense of awe, and everything from there on is hushed and knowingly subtle. Smartly dressed guests wander through the lobby toting designer shopping bags; the attentiveness of the staff is wonderful, without a trace of fawning or condescension. This hotel manages to be decorous without being uptight (and kid radar can register uptightness a mile away). The guest rooms are outfitted with understated but sleek modern furnishings, beautifully streamlined stuff Frank Lloyd Wright would approve of. The marble bathrooms are huge and superbly appointed, with roomy adjacent dressing areas.

The room layouts aren't particularly handy for families: A maximum of one extra bed is allowed per room (crib or rollaway), and only a few adjoining doubles can be set off by shutting a common door to the corridor. If connecting rooms are booked up, larger families will have to go for one of the 63 suites, which knocks you up and over the $1,000 range. Some of the suites are on the higher floors, 31 and above, which gives many of them stunning Central Park views. But the Four Seasons chain is known for valuing its young guests; special amenities for kids include a welcome gift, well-focused kids' menu, kid-size bathrobes, baby toiletries, and a collection of books, toys, coloring books, and DVDs to borrow. You can also borrow a stroller at no extra charge.

57 E. 57th St. (btw. Madison and Park aves.), New York, NY 10022. © **800/819-5053** or 212/758-5700. Fax 212/758-5711. www.fourseasons.com. 368 units. $655–$1,550 double; $650–$1,950 suite. Extra person $50. Rollaway or crib free for 18 and under. AE, DC, DISC, MC, V. Parking $60. Subway: 4, 5, 6 to 59th St. **Amenities:** 2 restaurants; 4 lounges; concierge; fitness center; room service; spa; Wi-Fi (free in lobby and public spaces). *In room:* A/C, TV/DVD, CD player, fridge, hair dryer, minibar, Wi-Fi ($13/day).

Expensive

Beekman Tower Hotel ★　In many respects, the circa-1928 Beekman Tower offers the best of all worlds. You're fairly convenient to Midtown but in the posh residential East 50s, where peace and quiet reign. You have all the roominess of a small apartment but with lots of hotel services. You get some super views but don't have to pay through the nose for them.

This orange-brick Deco tower rising on a slope just north of the United Nations is known to New Yorkers for the **Top of the Tower** (breakfast and dinner only), a pleasant and unpretentious restaurant and lounge with a stunning view of the skyline and East River. What New Yorkers don't seem to know is what a great deal this all-suites hotel is. Its smallest suite, the studio, will work only for a small family—it has a queen- or full-size bed and a small sofa (not all of them fold out)—but there's plenty of room for a crib or rollaway, and it has a kitchenette. The one-bedroom suites are perfectly fine, with a foldout couch in the spacious living room and a separate bedroom with a king- or queen-size bed. And they have full kitchens—a four-burner stove; a full refrigerator; a big sink; a microwave; pots and pans; and, incredibly enough, a dishwasher. With clean, up-to-date appliances and a grocery-shopping service, these are kitchens people really can use. Ask for a "C-line suite" and you'll also get a dynamite East River view (some even have terraces). The traditional room decor is easy to live with; deluxe suites also have VCRs, in-room fax machines, and, on top floors, balconies. July and August are particularly good times to snag a room; significant discounts may be offered all times of year, so inquire when you book.

3 Mitchell Place (First Ave. at 49th St.), New York, NY 10017. © **866/298-4806** or 212/355-7300. Fax 212/753-9366. www.thebeekmanhotel.com. 176 units. $369 studio suite; $305–$459 1-bedroom suite; $599 and up 2-bedroom suite. Rollaway $20; crib free. AE, DISC, MC, V. Valet parking $50. Subway: E, V to Lexington Ave./53rd St.; 6 to 51st St. **Amenities:** Restaurant; bar; concierge; fitness center; limited room service. *In room:* A/C, TV, kitchenette, Wi-Fi ($13/day).

The Kimberly ★ 🏢　More people ought to know about this plush smaller hotel on a spruce Midtown East block heading toward the town houses of Turtle Bay. The small lobby, full of shiny marble and gilt rococo furnishings, has pizazz but not a high snobbery quotient, thanks to a friendly, unpretentious veteran staff. Because the 30-story building was designed in the mid-1980s as an apartment building (it was turned into a hotel immediately), the rooms are all newly renovated, and they're all big—even the standard doubles don't feel crowded when they have two double beds in them (a great setup for families on a short visit). The closets are sizable, as are the nicely appointed bathrooms. Most units in the hotel are suites; the one-bedroom suites could sleep six, with two double beds in the bedroom and a pullout couch in the sitting room. The look is one of comfortable elegance, with quality furniture in dark woods, pillowy featherbedding, and Italian linens. All suites have galley kitchens with cooking burners, pots and pans, and full-size refrigerators. The Kimberly Luxury Suites, on the 22nd and 23rd floors, are sumptuous one- and two-bedroom suites or doubles with antique-reproduction furniture and 42-inch plasma TVs. Almost every room has a balcony, where you can sit and have breakfast or cocktails while watching the Manhattan ad execs, lawyers, and publishing types scurry to or from their offices far below. Though there's no pool on-site, guests get free use of the New York Health & Racquet Club's pool, where there's a Saturday-morning swim session just for families. Even better: On Sundays, the Kimberly offers a 4-hour family brunch cruise on the *Kimberly Yacht* ($25 per person); the 75-foot yacht sails from May to September. One caveat: The hotel is now right next door to Nikki Midtown, an offshoot of the international Nikki Beach nightclub franchise; you may want to ask for a room on a higher floor to avoid any noise or commotion.

145 E. 50th St. (btw. Lexington and Third aves.), New York, NY 10022. © **800/683-0400** or 212/702-1600. Fax 212/486 6015. www.kimberlyhotel.com. 192 units. $379–$444 1-bedroom suite; $669–$779 2-bedroom suite. Children 17 and under stay free in parent's room. Weekend rates and summer packages available. Rollaway or crib free. AE, DC, DISC, MC, V. Valet parking $30. Subway: 6 to 51st St.; E, V to Lexington Ave./53rd St.; 6 to 51st St. **Amenities:** Concierge; fitness room; complimentary access to New York Health & Racquet Club; room service. *In room:* A/C, TV, fax, fridge, hair dryer, kitchenette (in suites), MP3 docking station, Wi-Fi ($13/day).

Waldorf Astoria ★★   My Aunt Mabel always said that the only place she'd ever go camping was at the Waldorf Astoria. It was an icon of luxury then, and it's an icon of luxury now. The Waldorf gets regular spit-and-polish renovations, with plenty of money and taste devoted to maintaining its character. The wide, stately corridors, the vintage Deco door fixtures, the white-gloved bellmen, the luxe shopping arcade, and that knockout lobby all trumpet Grand Hotel, and there's a certain thrill about being here. Enter from the Park Avenue side and you'll cross a stunning round mosaic under an immense crystal chandelier; in the main lobby, the four-sided free-standing Waldorf clock, covered with bronze relief figures, should fascinate your children.

Upstairs, the wide, plush-carpeted corridors seem to run on forever. The room decor is pleasant, if unremarkable—a sort of traditional English-country-house look. The standard double rooms are plenty spacious; request a room with two double beds if you've got more than one kid. A minisuite, combining one king-size-bedded room with a sitting room, might work better, though not all have foldout couches; some suites have kitchenettes, so ask for one if that's important. There's also a number of connecting doubles you can request. The staff seems unfailingly gracious, though in such a large hotel you won't get the personal service you might at a smaller place. Do inquire about special discounts, because they pop up year-round (ask about the Real Deal Family Package). There are 244 rooms in the Waldorf Towers, with a separate entrance. The duke and duchess of Windsor and John F. Kennedy are among the guests who've resided here; it's also a favorite of Bill Clinton. Staying in the pricier Towers, which have more distinctive antique-laden decor, snags you some extra amenities, like complimentary continental breakfast and hors d'oeuvres in a lounge on the 26th floor.

The Waldorf's restaurants may no longer be major players in the New York restaurant universe, but they're consistently excellent: **Oscar's,** the ornate **Peacock Alley,** and the clubby steak-and-seafood **Bull and Bear.**

301 Park Ave. (btw. 49th and 50th sts.), New York, NY 10022. ☎ **800/WALDORF** (925-3673), 800/
HILTONS (445-8667), or 212/355-3000. Fax 212/872-7272. www.waldorfnewyork.com. 1,413 units.
$339–$429 double; from $449 suite. Children 17 and under stay free in parent's room. Rollaway $25–
$50 per stay; Pack 'n Play playards free. DC, DISC, MC, V. Parking $45. Subway: 6 to 51st St. **Amenities:**
3 restaurants; 3 bars; babysitting; concierge; fitness center w/steam rooms (day-use fee $14); room
service; spa. *In room:* A/C, TV, hair dryer, minibar, Wi-Fi ($16/day).

Moderate

Millennium U.N. Plaza Hotel ★   The Millennium U.N. Plaza's neighborhood
hardly qualifies as Midtown—across from the United Nations, it's deliciously quiet
and residential. When you combine that with the peerless views (all rooms are on
the 28th floor or above, overlooking the East River or the skyline, uptown or downtown), the premium prices start to make sense. The clientele is heavily international,
with foreign businesspeople as well as some United Nations visitors. Although it's a
sleek corporate-style hotel, families may well be attracted not only by the neighborhood but also by the fact that it has a great pool—what may be the prettiest pool in
town, with a haremlike canopy hanging overhead and dynamite views from windows
on two sides.

There are two towers to choose from, connected by a disconcertingly slick lobby:
the original East Tower, built in 1976, and the newer West Tower, built in 1980.
While the East Tower is on the same elevator bank as the pool and has a more contemporary decor (think blond wood, opaque glass, and neutral fabrics), the West
Tower makes up for it with floor-to-ceiling windows and warm-toned furnishings that
feel homelike (homelike, that is, if you're a wealthy international diplomat). The east
wing's sleek minimalist design carries into the bathrooms, which feel a bit bigger than
those in the west wing. The wall hangings are framed museum-quality international
textile pieces. Double rooms have only a king-size bed or two twins (two kids could
fit in one of these European-size twins), and fire laws permit only one rollaway. Most
families go for a junior suite or duplex one-bedroom suite, or spring for a spacious
two-bedroom suite.

1 United Nations Plaza (44th St. and First Ave.), New York, NY 10017. ☎ **866/866-8086** or 212/758-
1234. Fax 212/702-5051. www.millenniumhotels.com. 427 units. $299–$379 double; $429 and up suite.
Weekend packages available. Rollaway $35; crib free. AE, DC, DISC, MC, V. Valet parking $35–$40.
Subway: S, 4, 5, 6, 7 to 42nd St./Grand Central. **Amenities:** Restaurant; babysitting; concierge; fitness
center; indoor pool; room service; indoor tennis court; Wi-Fi ($13/day in lobby and public spaces).
In room: A/C, TV, hair dryer, high-speed Internet access, minibar, Wi-Fi ($13/day).

Radisson Lexington Hotel New York ★   This handsome 1920s vintage property along Lexington's Midtown hotel strip looks and feels like an upscale boutique
hotel, especially after a 2008 $20-million renovation. But at 27 stories and 700-plus
rooms, it's much larger than it feels. Look and listen, and you'll notice it has a sophisticated international clientele (not surprising in the U.N. vicinity). The architecture
is a heady blend of Art Deco and Gothic elements: Kids will enjoy spotting the terra-
cotta figures on the facade, the griffins and dragons prancing over the vaulted ceiling
of the Lexington Avenue entryway, and the birds and lizards etched onto the elevator's
brass doors. But from the spiffy porte-cochere above the 48th Street entrance to the
two-story mahogany-paneled lobby with textured fabrics and brushed-nickel fixtures,
the Radisson Lexington has been smartly renovated for a contemporary look without
sacrificing the property's charm.

The guest-room decor shows quiet verve, with a Deco palette of muted earth tones and granite-top work desks. Bathrooms have been tidily modernized, with gray marble floors and modern white fixtures. Amenities like full-length mirrors, large desks, and high-speed Internet access bespeak the Radisson's attention to traveling executives. What families may appreciate more, though, is room size: The one-bedroom suites are positively rambling, with a huge bedroom and sitting room (some even have little terraces where you can step outside and study the skyscrapers all around). Business-class rooms are large doubles with either two double beds or a king bed and foldout couches; the great thing about these is that they have two bathrooms. Deluxe rooms have a king, a queen, or two single beds, but there's plenty of room for a rollaway. The whole place seems well run, with thoughtful, friendly service; it's dignified enough to be restful, but not at all stuffy.

Breakfast, lunch, and dinner are served in **Raffles,** a cheery dinerlike corner coffee shop; the hotel's upscale restaurant is **Dynasty,** a lovely gourmet Chinese restaurant that does a brisk lunch and dinner business with nonguests as well as guests.

511 Lexington Ave. (at 48th St.), New York, NY 10017. (C) **800/448-4471** or 212/755-4400. Fax 212/308-0194. www.lexingtonhotelnyc.com. 705 units. $209–$384 double; $289–$1,009 suite. Rollaway $25; crib free. AE, DC, DISC, MC, V. Parking nearby $40 for 24 hr. Subway: 6 to 51st St.; S, 4, 5, 6, 7 to 42nd St./Grand Central. **Amenities:** 2 restaurants; Starbucks; nightclub; babysitting; concierge; fitness center; room service; Wi-Fi (free in lobby). *In room:* A/C, TV, hair dryer, minibar upon request, Wi-Fi ($9.95/day).

Roger Smith Hotel 🗡 The Roger Smith is decidedly quirky, which may be why so many musicians and artists and Europeans choose to stay here. The small oval lobby is a minigallery in itself, with paintings, sculptures, and polished wainscoting (there's more art next door in an actual art gallery run by Roger Smith). Upstairs, however, the look is more like a country inn, with individually decorated rooms featuring such items as four-poster or iron beds, stocked bookshelves, and chintz upholstery and bedspreads. Lots of hotels boast of a homey feeling, but the rooms here really do qualify. There are a variety of room layouts, including some connecting rooms and a junior suite that has a double bed and a foldout couch in the same room. All doubles and suites can accommodate two adults and two children. Bathrooms are somehow homelike as well, not lavish but trim and up-to-date. For the price of a double at the Waldorf or The Plaza, here you can get a suite that includes not only a pullout couch in the sitting room and a double bed in the bedroom, but also a second cozy bedroom with a twin bed. Nickel-and-diming is blessedly kept to a minimum here: Wi-Fi is complimentary throughout the hotel—hooray!—as are all local and 800 calls. Charmingly, each room has its own little book library.

Though none of the rooms has a full kitchen, all suites have pantries with a refrigerator and coffeemaker. **Lily's,** a spunky little bistro with gaudy murals, serves an interesting Continental menu for breakfast, lunch, and dinner (closed weekends). This lively, fun hotel does a pretty brisk business, but its slowest months are July and August—peak family travel time—so cross your fingers and call ahead if you're visiting New York in the summer.

501 Lexington Ave. (at 47th St.), New York, NY 10017. (C) **800/445-0277** or 212/755-1400. Fax 212/758-4061. www.rogersmithhotel.com. 133 units. $249–$299 double; $279–$399 suite. Extra person $20. Children 11 and under stay free in parent's room. Rollaway or crib free. AE, DC, DISC, MC, V. Valet parking $35. Subway: S, 4, 5, 6, 7 to 42nd St./Grand Central. **Amenities:** Restaurant; concierge; health club access ($25/day); room service. *In room:* A/C, TV, fridge, hair dryer, MP3 docking station (in deluxe suites only), Wi-Fi (free).

THE MEATPACKING DISTRICT & GREENWICH VILLAGE

Expensive

Hotel Gansevoort ★ For many in the Meatpacking District, the construction of this slick hipster hotel represented the beginning of the end of a funky, slightly rough-at-the-edges neighborhood. Since then, there have indeed been many changes to the district, a cobblestoned slice of old New York in the Village's wild west—designer shops, hip restaurants, star salons, even the looming shadow of the hipper-than-hip Standard hotel. But the Gansevoort seems to have staying power and is surprisingly accessible, especially when it comes to kids. First off, the hotel has a fabulous rooftop pool, with floats and underwater lighting and music—but keep in mind that hours are limited for families. All children receive an overflowing lunchbox of treats and juice boxes upon arrival. Kids have access to board games, Xbox, or Nintendo's Wii free of charge and get milk and cookies at turndown. For babies, there's a basket full of baby powder, shampoo, soap, lotion, and a washcloth. Adults should be very happy here, too, with chic rooms highlighted by delicious feather beds, Egyptian cotton linens, and state-of-the-art amenities. Just across the street is Pastis (see chapter 6), and you're close to the Pier 51 Waterpark and Chelsea Piers. *Note:* Ask for a room as far from the noisy hotel bars as possible.

18 Ninth Ave. (at 13th St.). © **877/426-7386** or 212/206-6700. Fax 212/255-5758. www.hotel gansevoort.com. 187 units. Doubles $445–$605 (duplex penthouse $5,000). AE, MC, V. Subway: A, C, E to 14th; L to 8th Ave. **Amenities:** Restaurant; 2 bars; babysitting; rooftop pool; spa. *In room:* A/C, LCD TV, CD players, hair dryer, MP3 docking stations, Wi-Fi (free).

Moderate

Washington Square Hotel ★ 🍴 With its fantastic location in a leafy neighborhood at the corner of Washington Square Park, the focal point of Greenwich Village—Bob Dylan and Joan Baez lived here when it was the Hotel Earle in the folkie 1960s—the Washington Square Hotel would probably do well even if it weren't so nice. The good news is that this small hotel is a winner on its own account: clean, cheery, tastefully furnished—and very reasonably priced. Book a room here as soon as you know you're coming to New York, because lots of people have found out about this gem and it's nearly always full, especially on weekends.

The smallish rooms are just big enough to accommodate a crib or rollaway, but a family should spring for a quad room, which has two double beds; request no. 902, the largest, which is in front with a superb view of leafy Washington Square Park. (Any front room on the fifth through ninth floors has good park views.) If you need connecting doubles, request room nos. 219 and 220, which share a bathroom. All other rooms have their own small but spruce white-tiled bathrooms; the bedrooms sport a snazzy Art Deco look, with rose-colored walls, frosted-glass light fixtures, mahogany and pink granite accents, black leather headboards, and comfy pillow-top mattresses.

At the back of the Parisian-looking little lobby, with its wrought-iron gate and marble staircase, there's an atmospheric little bar; the attached **NorthSquare** restaurant draws locals on its own merits. There's no room service, but this part of

Downtown Accommodations

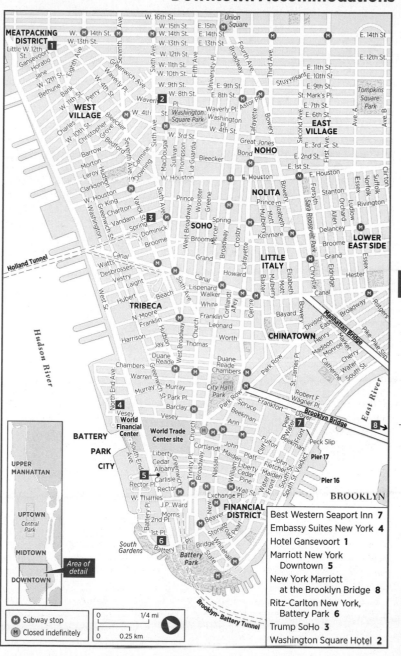

Best Western Seaport Inn **7**
Embassy Suites New York **4**
Hotel Gansevoort **1**
Marriott New York
  Downtown **5**
New York Marriott
  at the Brooklyn Bridge **8**
Ritz-Carlton New York,
  Battery Park **6**
Trump SoHo **3**
Washington Square Hotel **2**

Ⓜ Subway stop
Ⓜ Closed indefinitely

the Village is crawling with restaurants in all price ranges that stay open all hours, and walking around here is a pleasure at night.

103 Waverly Place (btw. Sixth Ave. and MacDougal St.), New York, NY 10011. © **800/222-0418** or 212/777-9515. Fax 212/979-8373. www.washingtonsquarehotel.com. 150 units. $213–$370 double. Crib free. Rates include continental breakfast. AE, MC, V. Parking nearby $40. Subway: A, B, C, D, E, F, V to W. 4th St. **Amenities:** Restaurant/lounge; lobby bar; small fitness room. *In room:* A/C, TV, hair dryer, Wi-Fi (free).

SOHO & LOWER MANHATTAN
Very Expensive

Ritz-Carlton New York, Battery Park ★   Facing out onto New York Harbor, this luxury high-rise has without a doubt the best views of any Manhattan hotel. It opened in January 2002, a much-heralded emblem of downtown's triumphant rebound after the World Trade Center attacks. A majority of rooms face the harbor, and each of the Statue of Liberty view rooms and suites has its own telescope so you can zoom in on each spike in Lady Liberty's crown. Anchoring the lower end of Battery Park City (like a bookend to balance the Embassy Suites a few blocks north), the Ritz-Carlton is convenient to downtown attractions such as the Ellis Island/Statue of Liberty ferry, the Museum of Jewish Heritage (right behind the hotel), the new Skyscraper Museum (in the Ritz-Carlton building), and the National Museum of the American Indian (2 blocks away). The beautifully landscaped South Cove portion of Battery Park City is the hotel's backyard.

The hotel recently invested $10 million on a renovation of all guest rooms. Signature details are lots of wood paneling; a discreet Art Deco–inspired lobby; heartwarming tones of gold, ocher, and green; and artworks specially commissioned from living New York artists—that and big windows everywhere, to drink in those wide-open harbor views. Even the standard double rooms are large enough for a family; request one with two double beds, or take advantage of a pullout sofa or rollaway bed. Suites don't necessarily add bed space so much as they add entertaining space (and a super home-theater system, which would indeed be great for parents relaxing in the room after the kids have gone to sleep). Weeknights are busy here, so weekend visitors may be able to net some serious rate discounts.

The Ritz-Carlton has a well-deserved reputation as a kid-friendly hotel chain. Every youngster who visits gets a Ritz-Carlton teddy bear turndown (the bear is yours to keep!), and you can call for the hotel's bath butler to draw a perfectly calibrated bubble bath (complete with rubber ducky). Meals are served downstairs in the **2 West Steakhouse,** which has a well-tailored kids' menu.

2 West St. (at Battery Place), New York, NY 10004. © **800/241-3333** or 212/344-0800. Fax 212/344-3804. www.ritzcarlton.com. 298 units. $365–$570 double; $565 and up for suites. Children 12 and under stay free in parent's room. Weekend packages available. AE, DC, DISC, MC, V. Parking $60. Subway: 4, 5 to Bowling Green. **Amenities:** Restaurant; bar; lounge; babysitting; concierge; fitness center room service; spa; Wi-Fi ($13/day in lobby). *In room:* A/C, TV, hair dryer, minibar, Wi-Fi ($13/day), bathrobes, scale.

Trump SoHo ★   The Trump SoHo towers over everything around it, its sleek and sparkling ceramic-glass facade rising 46 stories. Newly opened in spring 2010, the hotel is located in a nondescript commercial district dubbed "Hudson Square" by local business folk. The hotel itself looms above a car-choked stretch of Varick Street that sees traffic slowly funneling into the Holland Tunnel every day at rush hour. But it's also only 1 block from SoHo, 2 blocks from TriBeCa, and 3 blocks from the beauteous Hudson River Park. Inside the hotel, the vibe is cool and hushed, with flatteringly low lighting, earth-brown tones, and deep pile rugs on a composite floor. The concept is condo hotel, with 391 privately owned hotel rooms for rent; a sun-splashed Northern Italian restaurant, **Quattro;** a lovely spa; and—families, listen up—a 4-foot-deep outdoor pool, pool deck, and bocce court. Each floor has only 12 rooms, so you've got space to sprawl, and floor-to-ceiling windows show off the truly **unparalleled views ★★★** of the Hudson River and New Jersey—from north-facing bathroom windows you can even see all the way uptown as Fifth Avenue snakes up to Central Park. Rooms are comfortably chic, with Fendi Casa furnishings and Turkish-marble bathrooms. The Trump Kids club gives little guests lots of extra goodies, including a complimentary Trump Kids bag at check-in, filled with a stuffed elephant, coloring books, and crayons. Plus, just hand any kid the Control 4 clicker—which controls the cool drapes, lights, TV—for hours of entertainment.

246 Spring St. (at Varick St.), New York, NY 10013. ✆ **877/828-7080** or 212/842-5500. www.trumpsoho.com. 391 units. $599–$659 double; $799–$859 suite. Weekend and summer packages available. Rollaway or crib free. AE, DISC, MC, V. Valet parking $65–$73/day. Subway: 6 to Spring St. **Amenities:** Restaurant; lounge; library bar; babysitting; concierge; fitness center; pool; room service; spa; Wi-Fi (free in lobby). *In room:* A/C, TV, minibar, Wi-Fi ($13/day).

Expensive

Embassy Suites New York ★ This classy Hilton property in Battery Park City, with views of the harbor on one side and of the downtown skyline on the other, is a great deal for families on weekends, when the rates fall well into the moderate category. (On weekdays, they may slide up into very expensive.) Every suite has a private bedroom (with one king or two double beds) and a separate living room with foldout couch. Bathrooms are roomy, with tubs, and there's always a table big enough for paperwork or art projects, not to mention room-service meals. The place has a with-it sort of buzz, from the curvy bright yellow wall behind the reception desk, to the soaring atrium dominated by an 11-story purple-and-blue Sol LeWitt abstract painting, to the sleek room decor, all neutral tones and textured fabrics and striking art prints commissioned expressly for the hotel. A complimentary breakfast buffet is served each morning, always a huge plus for families. Even better: Every suite has a PlayStation.

The Embassy Suites building also contains an 11-screen Regal Cinema movie theater. The location is prime: The well-outfitted New York Sports Club is a handy on-site add-on for hotel guests, and there are many family-friendly restaurants in the area—the tuned-in concierge will point you in the right direction. The excellent playgrounds of Hudson River Park are only steps from the hotel, as is the gorgeous riverside promenade of Battery Park City. Right outside the hotel's door is one of the coolest memorials ever: the **Irish Hunger Memorial,** a tilting acre of Irish sod complete with a ruined crofter's cottage. You're within decent walking distance of the Museum of Jewish Heritage, the National Museum of the American Indian, the Skyscraper Museum, and the ferry to Ellis Island and the Statue of Liberty, and you're across West Street from the former World Trade Center site.

Just across the Hudson River, directly facing Manhattan's West Village, are the vintage burgs of Hoboken and Jersey City, classic Jersey towns where scads of young urban professionals on a career track in NYC have smartly taken up residence. The zippy commute on the PATH train under the Hudson River often takes less time than traveling from lower Manhattan to uptown—it's a mere 10 minutes to downtown Hoboken from the Christopher Street PATH station (and it's cheaper than subway fare). A handful of top chain hotels have landed on this side of the Hudson. You can stay in comfort and style at reduced rates with fantastic views of Manhattan spread out before you (it's considerably quieter, too). The stylish **W Hoboken** (225 River St.; ✆ **201/253-2400; www.starwood hotels.com**) sits on the Hoboken waterfront just 4 pleasant blocks from the PATH station; pets are welcome, too. In Jersey City, the **Hyatt Regency Jersey City** (2 Exchange Place; ✆ **201/469-1234; www.jerseycity.hyatt.com**) has sparkling Manhattan and river views and a pool.

102 North End Ave. (btw. Murray and Vesey sts.), New York, NY 10282. ✆ **800/EMBASSY** (362-2779) or 212/945-0100. Fax 212/945-3012. www.embassynewyork.com. 463 units. $329–$569 suite. Children 17 and under stay free in parent's room; restrictions on rollaways in some rooms. Crib free. Rate includes full breakfast and cocktail reception. AE, DC, DISC, MC, V. Valet parking $55. Subway: A, C, E, 1, 2, 3 to Chambers St. **Amenities:** Concierge; fitness center; room service. *In room:* A/C, TV/VCR, CD player, minibar, Wi-Fi ($9.95), microwave.

Marriott New York Downtown ★ A good downtown choice for families, the 38-floor Marriott Financial Center has wonderful skyline and harbor views. And a recent renovation has given the 490 doubles (and seven suites) a fresh new look, with marble bathrooms and the Marriott's Revive beds swathed in down comforters.

The small lobby's traditional marble-and-mahogany look is pleasantly unintimidating, almost cozy. Though guest rooms here don't give you the same kind of space to stretch out in as the Embassy Suites, the double rooms with two double beds are roomy enough to take a crib or rollaway, and there are plenty of connecting doubles. The executive suite is a decent option for families (book directly through the hotel). Rooms have large windows to drink in those views. The on-site restaurant, **85 West Sports Bar & Grill,** serves light grill food for breakfast, lunch, and dinner, and there's a **Starbucks** on-site. If you're going to be in Manhattan for the weekend, ask if weekend packages are in effect—they could save you nearly $100 a night over the weekday rates, plus throw in a complimentary breakfast. Summer packages plunge even lower. You'll be right across from Battery Park City, within walking distance of the Statue of Liberty/Ellis Island ferry, and not far from South Street Seaport—and have a very comfy hotel room to boot.

85 West St. (at Albany St.), New York, NY 10006. ✆ **800/228-9290** or 212/385-4900. Fax 212/227-8136. www.marriott.com. 497 units. $369–$529 double; $549 and up suite. Weekend and summer packages available. Rollaway or crib free. AE, DC, DISC, MC, V. Valet parking $55–$65. Subway: E to World Trade Center/Chambers St.; R to Rector St. **Amenities:** Restaurant; Starbucks; concierge; fitness center; room service; Wi-Fi (free in lobby); ATM. *In room:* A/C, TV, minibar, Wi-Fi ($13/day).

Moderate

Best Western Seaport Inn   This spunky little hotel in a converted 19th-century red-brick building has an offbeat location—on a cobbled street just north of the Fulton Fish Market, a couple of blocks up from South Street Seaport, in the lee of the Brooklyn Bridge's Manhattan entrance ramps (a delightful *trompe l'oeil* mural on a brick building just east of the hotel shows you what the view through the bridge's arches would look like if the building weren't in the way). Walk through the front door to find a country-style decor and a cheerful staff. Rooms have double beds, queens, or kings. The bathrooms are up-to-date and dazzlingly clean. While you don't get kitchenettes, there's an unstocked minifridge in every room. The newly upgraded Terrace Rooms have big terraces with a table and chairs and partial views of the East River and Seaport. The complimentary continental breakfast is a nice plus, as are the fresh-baked cookies offered every afternoon and the board games on hand at the front desk for kids to borrow. Wi-Fi is complimentary throughout the hotel.

The immediate area has been transformed lately by a spate of residential co-op buildings, bringing in its wake more foot traffic and street-level businesses. Pace University is a block away, and there's no trouble getting cabs at night if you walk a block to Pearl Street. Though the inn has no restaurant and no room service, local restaurants deliver, and Chinatown is as close as the Seaport for nighttime forays. For what you save on frills, you can easily afford to spend a little money on cabs by staying here.

33 Peck Slip (btw. Front and Water sts.), New York, NY 10038. (© **800/HOTEL-NY** [468-3569] or 212/766-6600. Fax 212/766-6615. www.seaportinn.com. 72 units. $289–$389 double. Children 17 and under stay free in parent's room. Rollaway $25; crib free. Rates include deluxe continental breakfast and afternoon tea. AE, DC, DISC, MC, V. Parking $20 nearby. Subway: 4, 5, 6 to City Hall; J, M, Z to Chambers St. **Amenities:** Concierge; fitness room. *In room:* A/C, TV, fridge, hair dryer, Wi-Fi (free).

BROOKLYN

As the *New York Times* reported in summer 2010, Brooklyn is undergoing a hotel boom. In addition to the Marriott (see below), the borough now has three Best Westerns, one Sheraton, and a growing contingency of boutique hotels, such as the **Nu Hotel** (© **718/852-8585;** www.nuhotelbrooklyn.com) in Boerum Hill (close to some of the city's best restaurants on Smith St.); **the Hotel Le Bleu** (© **718/625-1500;** www.hotellebleu.com) in Park Slope; and **Hotel Le Jolie** (© **718/625-2100;** www.hotellejolie.com), just over the East River in Williamsburg—plus, it's estimated that some 40 additional properties are in the works. These Brooklyn lodgings represent good value for longer-stay travelers; the *New York Times* reported that room rates at Brooklyn hotels were some 15% lower than that for comparable rooms in Manhattan.

Moderate

New York Marriott at the Brooklyn Bridge   Brooklyn Heights is said to be America's first suburb, and many Manhattanites still have the notion that Brooklyn is not quite "New York." But anyone who's spent time there knows better. In addition to having its own attractions (including a top-notch children's museum), Brooklyn is very much part of New York City, not to mention wonderfully convenient to downtown Manhattan—the Wall Street area, Battery Park, and the Statue of Liberty ferry are only one subway stop away. Located in downtown Brooklyn, near picturesque Brooklyn Heights, the Marriott is also a mere 7-minute subway ride from trendy SoHo, 1 block from the TKTS discounted Broadway ticket booth, and, of particular interest to families, only a few blocks away from the famous Brooklyn Bridge, with its pedestrian walkway where energetic kids can run off steam while their parents enjoy breathtaking views. Another plus for families is the 75-foot lap pool; several kids were swimming happily the day we visited. Don't be put off by the location on Adams Street, a busy, nondescript thoroughfare feeding the Brooklyn Bridge; the hotel itself is spacious, comfortable, attractive, and well organized without being the least bit uptight or intimidating.

Kids will love the domed ceiling that soars above the entryway and mezzanine lobby, a stunning mural of the sky behind a white trellised gazebo. As you sweep up to the lobby on the escalator between huge potted plants, for a split second you feel as if you're flying. Otherwise, there's a businessy feel to the place, with its network of conference rooms off the main lobby. Guest rooms are pleasant enough, with standard hotel antique reproduction furniture, but high ceilings make rooms feel spacious. There are some connecting rooms, and the doubles themselves have two double beds and just enough extra space to fit a crib or cot. Room decor is reasonably cheery, with red, gold, and green patterned bedspreads and soft green carpeting.

The **Archives** restaurant off the lobby lounge takes its name from the Brooklyn memorabilia it proudly exhibits (on loan from the Brooklyn Historical Society); it serves breakfast and lunch (the adjoining lounge is open for dinner). Kids will also enjoy some of the reasonably priced family restaurants on nearby Montague Street in Brooklyn Heights, a 5-minute walk from the hotel.

333 Adams St., Brooklyn, NY 11201. © **888/436-3759** or 718/246-7000. Fax 718/246-0563. www. marriott.com. 665 units. $399–$449 double; $599 and up suite. Rollaway or crib free. AE, DC, DISC, MC, V. Parking $18–$28. Subway: A, C, F to Jay St./Borough Hall; 2, 3, 4, 5 to Borough Hall; M, R to Court St. **Amenities:** Restaurant; bar; concierge; health club/fitness center; indoor pool; room service, Wi-Fi (free in lobby). *In room:* A/C, TV, minibar, Wi-Fi ($15/day).

FAMILY-
FRIENDLY
DINING

One of the great pleasures of being in New York is dining out in one of the city's many world-renowned restaurants. You don't have to be a longtime resident to make the most of the culinary opportunities, either: Visitors are giving locals stiff competition for seats—and that includes vacationing families. In fact, statistics from NYC & Company (the city's official tourism bureau) show that more families visit New York City than any other group. And what, you may ask, is tops on visitors' to-do lists? For domestic travelers, eating out wins out over sightseeing, museum-going, and shopping. For international visitors, dining out is topped only by shopping.

These days, families are a huge part of the city's restaurant scene. From an early age, New York kids are indoctrinated into this dazzling culinary stew—and more and more restaurants are finding ways to welcome children. Plus, the city is filled with solid midrange choices—Italian trattorie, French bistros, and all-American neighborhood favorites—that welcome children with open arms. Keep in mind, too, that the city's kitchens are used to meeting the exacting standards of picky eaters and won't blink at special requests for plain pasta with butter or crustless sandwiches. So don't think that just because you have kids in tow in one of the world's top culinary capitals you have to spend your mealtimes in a purgatory of chicken fingers and french fries. Do as the locals do: Bring the kids along on your gastronomic adventures. But first, some common-sense caveats.

No, we do not expect you to breeze into Le Bernardin on a Friday night with a passel of toddlers. This is a bad idea on many levels. To begin with, not many adults who've reserved a table for a leisurely (and not inexpensive) 2- or 3-hour dining experience in a fine restaurant will be thrilled to share their dining space with boisterous children. Then there's the weekend factor. New York City is a major restaurant town, and you can bet that the most popular restaurants will be swamped with serious diners on Friday and Saturday nights. If you're going to try to dine in a nice or somewhat trendy restaurant, reserve a table on a **less-busy night** (Sundays are always fun). Keep in mind that **summer** is a great, family-friendly time to try out (and actually snag a reservation at) some of the city's hottest restaurants (the natives have gone to the beach).

And unless your kids are gold-star graduates of the Emily Post school of mealtime manners, **eat early,** not at the height of the dinner service.

PEGGY POST: THE FINER POINTS OF dining out with kids

It's a question that etiquette expert **Peggy Post** (Emily Post's great-grand-daughter-in-law) is asked all the time: *At what age can we take our kids out to a restaurant?* "By all means, take your children out to dinner," Post says. "It's great to get kids used to going out." Post suggests using the following guidelines when dining out to ensure that everyone has a positive experience—and you've put consideration for other diners at the forefront and diminished the potential for ruining someone else's special night.

o **Pick the right place for your family.** Always ask the reservations person if the restaurant is kid-friendly. Many restaurants have kids' menus, kids' diversions, even dining sections for families. Others may not have kid-specific bells and whistles, but welcome kids nonetheless.

o **Assess your child's preparedness.** At what age can you take a child to a nice restaurant? Some kids are really well-behaved early on; others are unpredictable—there's no black and white. But for the most part, very young children don't sit still naturally for long, so try to select a place where the meals don't go on forever. Toddlers can be unpredictable, and sometimes the experience is simply too much pressure for them, and you—not to mention other patrons, whose dining experience can be easily ruined by an unruly or ill-mannered child.

o **Prep your children.** Teach them about sitting still and using their "inside" voices. Bring "quiet toys" to keep kids occupied, crayons and coloring books, say, or books. Before going, tell the child that she'll be given a menu and is expected to stay at the table until the meal ends. Maybe bring some favorite snacks to eat.

o **Be efficient.** Order as soon as possible and ask if the waiter can bring an appetizer or bread right away to keep the child occupied. And make sure you figure out what the child wants *before* the server comes to the table.

o **Be aware of other patrons.** A child kicking the back of someone's chair does not endear himself to anyone. Make sure your child stays put and is not running around—it drives people crazy and is a hazard to the staff. If your child makes a mess, do the best you can to help the waitstaff clean up. You don't have to crawl under the table to pick up crumbs, but do help pitch in where it makes sense.

o **Take a break.** If your child is getting restless, leave the dining area for a minute. Walk around outside or in an area away from other diners so you aren't driving anyone crazy or getting in the way of the waitstaff.

o **Don't linger over dessert and coffee.** Start getting the check as you're finishing the meal.

o **Have your wits about you.**

o **Be ready to make an exit if you have to.**

Kids are most welcomed before the restaurant is packed with patrons. Better yet: Take the brood out for **weekend brunch,** which has become prime family time in some of the city's grooviest grown-up spots.

Of course, one way to circumvent the previous caveats is to choose a restaurant with **sidewalk seating.** The open-air arrangement minimizes the impact of noisy children on other diners, provides endless distraction, and makes messes seem less important. A restaurant with other **divertissements,** such as eye-popping decor, big picture windows, even a jukebox, not only provides a distraction but can prove to be a memorable experience for all.

If your children are squeamish or picky eaters, **play it safe:** Don't choose a place that is too exotic or thoroughly unfamiliar. If they're happy, you'll be happy.

If your kids are not ready for prime time and you still want to dine well, **call room service or order takeout.** Most NYC hotels are fortunate to have highly rated restaurants, and you can easily enjoy superlative meals in the comfort of your hotel room.

Finally, remember that **some restaurants are simply not suitable for kids 12 and under.** This is a generalization, I know, but something to keep in mind when choosing a place to eat.

HOURS & RESERVATIONS   Most Manhattan restaurants serve continuously—you can generally order dinner as early as 5pm if that's what you're used to, though most New Yorkers eat around 7 or 8pm. Again, if you have small children in tow, it's a good idea to dine earlier rather than later.

If you're dining anywhere in the Theater District (the W. 40s) or near Lincoln Center (the W. 60s), you'll be competing with lots of other people trying to finish dinner before an 8pm curtain time; unless you're trying to make that curtain, too, delay your arrival until 7:30pm or so, when most of these restaurants are ready to draw a sigh of relief and relax. Similarly, Midtown and Lower Manhattan restaurants can be very busy from 11:30am to 2:30pm.

I've noted in this chapter if a given restaurant doesn't take **reservations** or if reservations are generally necessary to ensure a table. If there's no notation about reservations, you have a fair chance of being seated even if you haven't called ahead, but making a reservation is always smart.

DRESS CODES   Although a few posh Manhattan restaurants still cling to formal dress codes, requiring men to wear a jacket and tie, none of the restaurants listed here do. Many New Yorkers do like to dress it up a bit for a night out, but "casual-chic" is the general buzzword for restaurant dining.

THE (HOMEGROWN) CHAIN GANG   New York is the proud progenitor of several homegrown minichains, many of which offer terrific, locally sourced food in family-friendly settings. Look for our top recommendations throughout this chapter in boxes called "The (Homegrown) Chain Gang."

FOOD ZONES   Certain streets or neighborhoods have evolved into mini food meccas—dense concentrations of smart, casual little eateries and innovative takeout joints packed into a city block or two. These are great spots to break up a brutal day of sightseeing with delicious lunch choices for the whole family—where you're in and out with a minimum of fuss. Look for our top recommendations throughout this chapter in boxes called "Food Zones."

A Note About Prices

The following reviews include a range of specific menu prices as often as possible; the restaurants are categorized as expensive, moderate, or inexpensive, based on rough estimates of what it would cost to feed a family of four—two parents and two children, assuming that one of the kids is young enough to be satisfied with either a kids' meal or a half portion or just an appetizer. If this mythical family would have to spend $80 or more for dinner (excluding any bar tab), I've classed that restaurant as **expensive**; between $60 and $80, **moderate;** under $60, **inexpensive.**

A NOTE ABOUT FAST FOOD The reality of eating out with small children is that fast-food joints are sometimes a blessing. Most of those in high-traffic areas of Manhattan are spanking clean and recently renovated; somehow, there's always a McDonald's or a Burger King or a Sbarro just where you need one. There's also a McDonald's delivery service operating in Manhattan (how New Yorkers do love to phone out for their food!): Call © **212/337-3278** to get your Happy Meals and Big Macs brought to your door.

A NOTE ABOUT BROOKLYN Brooklyn is undergoing a restaurant renaissance, with numerous small, artisanal restaurants serving some of the best food in the city—and many welcome children with open arms. Unfortunately, for reasons of space, this book does not include Brooklyn restaurants. For information about dining out in Brooklyn, check out *Time Out New York*'s restaurant listings when you get to town.

RESTAURANTS BY CUISINE

AMERICAN

American Girl Cafe ★★ (Midtown, $$$ p. 110)

The Barking Dog ★ (Upper East Side, $$, p. 106)

Blue Ribbon Bakery ★★ (Greenwich Village, $$$, p. 124)

Blue Smoke ★★ (Gramercy Park, $$, p. 121)

Boat Basin Café ★ (Upper West Side, $, p. 105)

Bubby's ★★ (TriBeCa, $, p. 137)

Chat 'n' Chew ★ (Flatiron District, $, p. 122)

City Bakery ★★ (Chelsea, $$, p. 121)

Fetch Bar & Grill ★ (Upper East Side, $$, p. 107)

Good Enough to Eat ★ (Upper West Side, $$, p. 103)

Hard Rock Cafe (Midtown, $$, p. 115)

Henry's ★ (Upper West Side, $$, p. 103)

Jekyll & Hyde Club (Midtown, $$$, p. 113)

Knickerbocker Bar & Grill ★★ (Greenwich Village, $$$, p. 124)

Landmarc ★ (TriBeCa, $$$, p. 136)

Luke's Bar and Grill ★★ (Upper East Side, $$, p. 107)

Mickey Mantle's (Midtown, $$, p. 117)

Odeon ★★ (TriBeCa, $$$, p. 136)

Peanut Butter & Co. (Greenwich Village, $, p. 126)

Planet Hollywood (Midtown, $$, p. 117)

Popover Café (Upper West Side, $$, p. 103)

Prime Burger ★ (Midtown, $, p. 118)

Sarabeth's Central Park South ★★ (Midtown, $$, p. 117)

The Smith ★ (East Village, $$, p. 127)

Sweetiepie ★ (Greenwich Village, $$, p. 126)

Virgil's Real Barbecue ★ (Midtown, $$, p. 118)

BAGELS

H&H Bagels (Upper West Side, $, p. 102)

H&H Bagels East (Upper East Side, $, p. 102)

Ess-a-Bagel (Murray Hill and Midtown East, $, p. 102)

Kossar's Bialys (Lower East Side, $, p. 102)

BARBECUE

Blue Smoke ★★ (Gramercy Park, $$, p. 121)

Brother Jimmy's Bait Shack (Upper East Side, $, p. 108)

Brother Jimmy's BBQ (Upper West Side and Upper East Side, $, p. 105 and p. 108)

Hill Country ★★ (Flatiron District, $$, p. 122)

Rodeo Bar (Flatiron District, $, p. 123)

Virgil's Real Barbecue ★ (Midtown, $$, p. 118)

BRITISH

Alice's Tea Cup ★★ (Upper West Side and Upper East Side, $, p. 104 and 108)

BURGERS

BLT Burger (Greenwich Village, $, p. 119)

Brgr (Chelsea, $, p. 119)

Corner Bistro (Greenwich Village, $, p. 119)

Hard Rock Cafe (Midtown, $$, p. 115)

Luke's Bar and Grill ★★ (Upper East Side, $$, p. 107)

Prime Burger ★ (Midtown, $, p. 118)

Sassy's Sliders (Upper East Side, $, p. 110)

Shake Shack (Madison Park, $, p. 119)

Stand (Greenwich Village, $, p. 119)

CHINESE

Big Wong ★ (Chinatown, $, p. 135)

Chinatown Brasserie ★ (NoHo, $$$, p. 133)

Golden Unicorn (Chinatown, $$, p. 134)

Jing Fong (Chinatown, $, p. 135)

Lili's Noodle Shop & Grill (Upper East Side, $, p. 109)

Oriental Garden ★ (Chinatown, $$, p. 134)

Peking Duck House ★★ (Chinatown, $$$, p. 134)

Ping's ★ (Chinatown, $$, p. 135)

CONTINENTAL

Madeline's Tea Party at the Carlyle Hotel ★★ (Upper East Side, $$, p. 110)

Schiller's Liquor Bar ★ (Lower East Side, $$, p. 127)

DELI

Artie's Delicatessen ★ (Upper West Side, $, p. 104)

Barney Greengrass ★★ (Upper West Side, $$, p. 101)

Carnegie Deli (Midtown, $$, p. 115)

Stage Deli ★ (Midtown, $, p. 119)

DESSERTS

Alice's Tea Cup ★★ (Upper West Side and Upper East Side, $, p. 104 and 108)

Baked by Melissa (Union Square, $, p. 109)

Buttercup Bake Shop (Midtown, $, p. 109)

Caffe Dante (Greenwich Village, $, p. 127)

Caffé Roma ★ (Little Italy, $, p. 133)

Ciao Bella (Nolita/Little Italy, $, p. 132)

Crumbs (Upper West Side, Downtown, and Upper East Side, $, p. 109)

Cupcake Cafe (Midtown, $, p. 109)

Restaurants by Cuisine

FAMILY-FRIENDLY DINING

Alice's Tea Cup **16**, **34**
Artie's Delicatessen **8**
Barking Dog Luncheonette **19**, **33**
Barney Greengrass **6**
Barron's Pizza **18**
Bella Luna **4**
Boat Basin Café **7**
Brother Jimmy's **11**, **20**, **32**
Carmine's **3**
Fetch Bar & Grill **21**
Gabriela's **2**
Good Enough to Eat **9**
Gray's Papaya **15**
Henry's **1**
H&H Bagels **10**
H&H Midtown Bagels East **29**
John's Pizzeria Eastside **35**
Lexington Candy Shop **27**
Lili's Noodle Shop & Grill **26**
Luke's Bar and Grill **30**
New Pizza Town **14**
Papaya King **24**
Popover Café **5**
Sambucca **22**
Sassy's Sliders **23**
Serendipity 3 **36**
Shake Shack **13**, **22**
T & R Pizzeria **12**
Tony's di Napoli **28**
Two Little Red Hens **25**

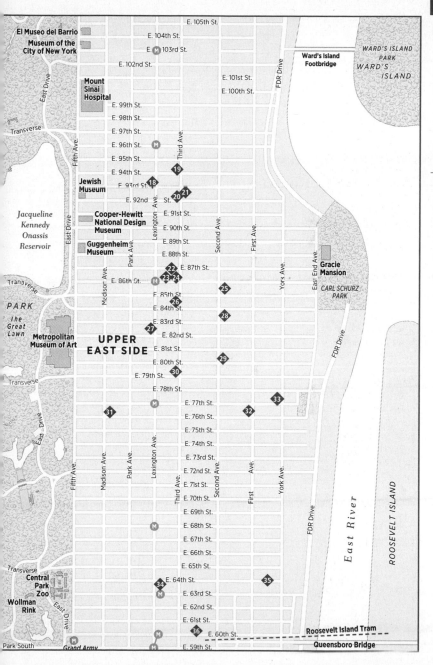

Restaurants by Cuisine

FAMILY-FRIENDLY DINING

American Girl Café **26**

Angelo's Coal Oven Pizza **17, 22**

Barking Dog **32**

Benihana **20**

Blue Smoke **34**

Brgr **12**

Buttercup Bake Shop **25**

Carmine's **9**

Carnegie Deli **3**

Chat'n' Chew **42**

Chelsea Market **14**

The City Bakery **40**

Cupcake Café **11**

Ellen's Stardust Diner **5**

F&B **13**

The Grand Central Dining Concourse **29**

The Great American Health Bar **19**

Hard Rock Café **1**

Hill Country **33**

Jekyll & Hyde Club **18**

John's Times Square **8**

Kosher Delight **30**

La Bonne Soupe **21**

Mesa Grill **41**

Mickey Mantle's **16**

Pete's Tavern **38**

Planet Hollywood **7**

Prime Burger **23**

Rock Center Café **31**

Rodeo Bar **35**

Ruby Foo's **6**

Sarabeth's Central Park South **15**

Shake Shack **36**

Stage Deli **4**

Tony's di Napoli **27**

Virgil's Real Barbecue **28**

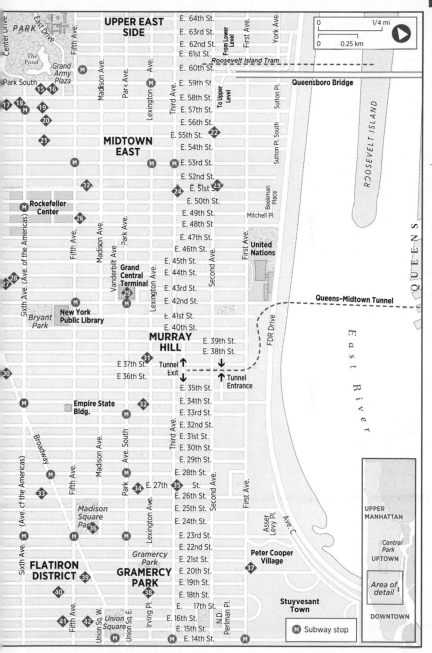

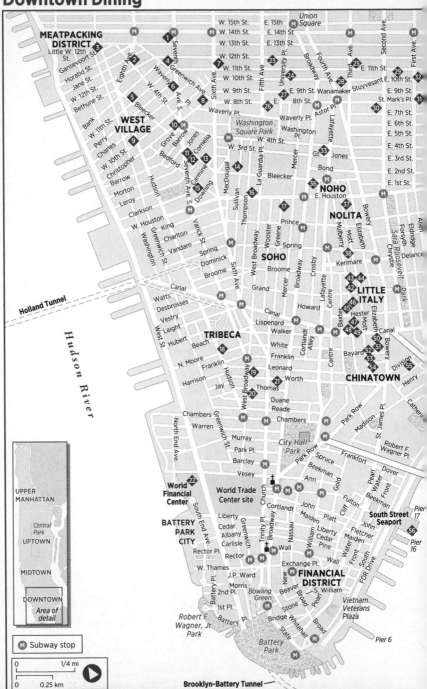

MEATPACKING DISTRICT

WEST VILLAGE

Washington Square Park

MEATPACKING DISTRICT
Little W. 12th St.
Gansevoort St.
Horatio St.
Jane St.
W. 12th St.
Bethune St.
Bank
W. 11th St.
Perry
Charles
W. 10th St.
Christopher
Barrow
Morton
Leroy
Clarkson
W. Houston
King
Charlton
Vandam
Spring
Dominick
Broome
Canal
Watts
Desbrosses
Vestry
Laight
Hubert
Beach
N. Moore
Franklin
Harrison
Jay
Chambers
Warren

Holland Tunnel

Hudson River

TRIBECA

SOHO

NOHO

NOLITA

LITTLE ITALY

CHINATOWN

Union Square

Washington Square Park

UPPER MANHATTAN

Central Park

UPTOWN

MIDTOWN

DOWNTOWN
Area of detail

World Financial Center

World Trade Center site

BATTERY PARK CITY

FINANCIAL DISTRICT

South Street Seaport

Battery Park

Bowling Green

Vietnam Veterans Plaza

Robert F. Wagner, Jr. Park

Brooklyn-Battery Tunnel

Ⓜ Subway stop

0   1/4 mi
0   0.25 km

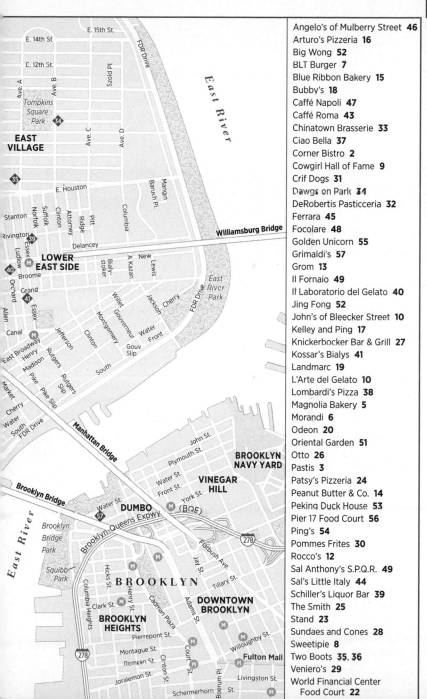

E. 15th St.

E. 14th St.

E. 12th St.

Szold Pl.

FDR Drive

Ave. A

Ave. B

Ave. C

Ave. D

East River

Tompkins
Square
Park 🔢

**EAST
VILLAGE**

🔢

E. Houston

Stanton

Norfolk

Suffolk

Clinton

Attorney

Ridge

Pitt

Mangin

Baruch Pl.

Columbia

Williamsburg Bridge

Rivington

Essex

Ludlow

Delancey

**LOWER
EAST SIDE**

Broome

Orchard

Grand

Allen

Essex

Bialy-
stoker

A Kazan

New

Lewis

Willet

Jackson

Cherry

*East
River
Park*

FDR Drive

Canal

Jefferson

Gouverneur

Montgomery

Clinton

Water

Front

East Broadway

Henry

Madison

Rutgers

Gouv
Slip

Pike

Pike Slip

Rutgers Slip

South

Market

Cherry

Water

South

FDR Drive

Manhattan Bridge

John St.

Plymouth St.

**BROOKLYN
NAVY YARD**

Water St.

Front St.

York St.

**VINEGAR
HILL**

Brooklyn Bridge

Water St.

DUMBO

🔢

(BQE)

Brooklyn-Queens Expwy.

278

East River

*Brooklyn
Bridge
Park*

Squibb
Park

Columbia Heights

Hicks St.

Henry St.

BROOKLYN

Cadman Plaza

Jay St.

Flatbush Ave.

Tillary St.

Adams St.

**DOWNTOWN
BROOKLYN**

Clark St.

**BROOKLYN
HEIGHTS**

Pierrepont St.

Willoughby St.

278

Montague St.

Remsen St.

Court St.

Clinton St.

Fulton Mall

Joralemon St.

Boerum Pl.

Livingston St.

Schermerhorn St.

Angelo's of Mulberry Street **46**
Arturo's Pizzeria **16**
Big Wong **52**
BLT Burger **7**
Blue Ribbon Bakery **15**
Bubby's **18**
Caffé Napoli **47**
Caffé Roma **43**
Chinatown Brasserie **33**
Ciao Bella **37**
Corner Bistro **2**
Cowgirl Hall of Fame **9**
Crif Dogs **31**
Dawgs on Park **34**
DeRobertis Pasticceria **32**
Ferrara **45**
Focolare **48**
Golden Unicorn **55**
Grimaldi's **57**
Grom **13**
Il Fornaio **49**
Il Laboratorio del Gelato **40**
Jing Fong **52**
John's of Bleecker Street **10**
Kelley and Ping **17**
Knickerbocker Bar & Grill **27**
Kossar's Bialys **41**
Landmarc **19**
L'Arte del Gelato **10**
Lombardi's Pizza **38**
Magnolia Bakery **5**
Morandi **6**
Odeon **20**
Oriental Garden **51**
Otto **26**
Pastis **3**
Patsy's Pizzeria **24**
Peanut Butter & Co. **14**
Peking Duck House **53**
Pier 17 Food Court **56**
Ping's **54**
Pommes Frites **30**
Rocco's **12**
Sal Anthony's S.P.Q.R. **49**
Sal's Little Italy **44**
Schiller's Liquor Bar **39**
The Smith **25**
Stand **23**
Sundaes and Cones **28**
Sweetiepie **8**
Two Boots **35, 36**
Veniero's **29**
World Financial Center
   Food Court **22**

DeRobertis Pasticceria (East Village, $$, p. 130)

Ferrara (Little Italy, $, p. 133)

Grom (Greenwich Village, $, p. 127)

Il Laboratorio del Gelato (Lower East Side, $, p. 129)

L'Arte del Gelato (Greenwich Village, $, p. 127)

Magnolia Bakery (Greenwich Village, $, p. 109)

Serendipity 3 ★ (Upper East Side, $$, p. 107)

Tribeca Treats (TriBeCa, $, p. 109)

Two Little Red Hens (Upper East Side, $, p. 109)

Veniero's (East Village, $$, p. 130)

DINER

Ellen's Stardust Diner ★ (Midtown, $$, p. 115)

Lexington Candy Shop ★★ (Upper East Side, $, p. 108)

Prime Burger ★ (Midtown, $, p. 118)

Serendipity 3 ★ (Upper East Side, $$, p. 107)

FRENCH

La Bonne Soupe ★ (Midtown, $$, p. 116)

Pastis ★★ (Meatpacking District, $$$, p. 130)

Pommes Frites (East Village, $, p. 128)

HOT DOGS

Crif Dogs (East Village, $, p. 128)

Dawgs on Park (East Village, $, p. 128)

F&B (Chelsea, $, p. 128)

Gray's Papaya (Upper West Side, $, p. 128)

Papaya King (Upper East Side, $, p. 128)

INDIAN

Mitali East (East Village, $, p. 113)

ITALIAN

Angelo's Coal Oven Pizza ★ (Midtown, $, p. 120)

Angelo's of Mulberry Street (Little Italy, $$, p. 131)

Arturo's Pizzeria (Greenwich Village, $$, p. 125)

Bella Luna ★ (Upper West Side, $$, p. 101)

Caffé Napoli (Little Italy, $$, p. 131)

Carmine's ★ (Upper West Side and Midtown, $$, p. 102 and 115)

Focolare ★ (Little Italy, $$, p. 131)

Il Fornaio (Little Italy, $, p. 131)

John's of Bleecker Street ★★ (Greenwich Village, $, p. 126)

John's Times Square ★★ (Midtown, $, p. 120)

Morandi ★★ (Greenwich Village, $$$, p. 124)

Patsy's Pizzeria (Greenwich Village, $, p. 106)

Pete's Tavern ★ (Gramercy Park, $, p. 122)

Rock Center Café ★ (Midtown, $$$, p. 114)

Sal Anthony's S.P.Q.R. (Little Italy, $$$, p. 130)

Sambuca ★ (Upper West Side, $$, p. 104)

Tony's di Napoli (Upper East Side and Midtown, $$$, p. 106 and 114#)

Two Boots ★ (East Village, $, p. 128)

V & T Pizzeria & Restaurant (Upper West Side, $, p. 105)

JAPANESE

Benihana ★★ (Midtown, $$$, p. 111)

KOSHER

Great American Health Bar (Midtown, $, p. 129)

Kosher Delight (Midtown, $, p. 129)

MEXICAN

Gabriela's ★ (Upper West Side, $$, p. 103)

MIDDLE EASTERN

Kalustyan's (Midtown, $, p. 113)

PAN-ASIAN

Ruby Foo's ★ (Midtown, $$$, p. 114)

PIZZA

Angelo's Coal Oven Pizza ★ (Midtown, $, p. 120)

Arturo's Pizzeria (Greenwich Village, $$, p. 125)

Barron's Pizza (Upper East Side, $, p. 110)

Famous Ray's Pizza of Greenwich Village (Greenwich Village, $, p. 118)

Farinella ★★ (TriBeCa/Chinatown, $, p. 137)

Grimaldi's (Brooklyn, $, p. 137)

Il Fornaio (Little Italy, $, p. 131)

John's of Bleecker Street ★★ (Greenwich Village, $, p. 126)

John's Pizzeria Eastside ★★ (Upper East Side, $, p. 110)

John's Times Square ★★ (Midtown, $, p. 120)

Lombardi's Pizza ★ (Little Italy, $, p. 132)

New Pizza Town (Upper West Side, $, p. 105)

Otto ★ (Greenwich Village, $$, p. 125)

Patsy's Pizzeria (Greenwich Village, $, p. 106)

Sal's Little Italy (Little Italy, $, p. 132)

T & R Pizzeria (Upper West Side, $, p. 105)

Two Boots ★ (East Village $, p. 128)

V & T Pizzeria & Restaurant (Upper West Side, $, p. 105)

SOUTHERN

Brother Jimmy's Bait Shack (Upper East Side, $, p. 108)

Brother Jimmy's BBQ (Upper West Side and Upper East Side, $, p. 105 and p. 108)

Cowgirl Hall of Fame ★ (Greenwich Village, $$, p. 125)

SOUTHWESTERN

Mesa Grill ★ (Union Square, $$$, p. 121)

TEX-MEX

Cowgirl Hall of Fame (Greenwich Village, $$, p. 125)

Rodeo Bar (Flatiron District, $, p. 123)

THE UPPER WEST SIDE

Moderate

Barney Greengrass ★★ 🎒 DELI   As authentic as **Artie's** (p. 104) is contrived, Barney Greengrass has been a West Side institution since 1908, and it looks like it hasn't been redecorated in half a century—the vintage dairy cases, chipped Formica tabletops, stained brownish wallpaper, and fluorescent lighting are an aggressive statement of the fact that the food's so good, you come here anyway. The fish here is so silky, so meltingly tender, that it converted me for life (problem is, nobody else's lox is ever gonna live up to this standard). The service is famously laconic, even gruff, but food arrives quickly. Sodas come in cans; the plates are plain white institutional china—who cares? Your kids may not get the time warp charm of this place, but if they're at all inclined to try classic deli food—lox, chopped liver, cold borscht, chopped herring, whitefish salad, with omelets and bagels as safe alternatives—they'll love it. It's especially good for breakfast, but on weekends you may have to wait in line.

541 Amsterdam Ave. (at 86th St.). ✆ **212/724-4707.** www.barneygreengrass.com. No reservations. Egg dishes $5.50–$19; sandwiches $6.75–$18; smoked fish platters $25–$45. AE, MC, V during the week; no credit cards on weekends. Tues–Fri 8:30am–4pm; Sat–Sun 8:30am–5pm. Subway: 1 to 86th St.

Bella Luna ★ ITALIAN   This sunny restaurant with art-hung yellow walls looks like it'd be strictly for grown-ups, but from day one the place has been extremely easygoing about young diners, always happy to bring them a small portion of plain pasta. The Tuscan-style pasta dishes are truly delicious, as are the veal and fish

THE BEST OF THE bagels

Why is it that bagels in other cities just don't taste as good as New York bagels? There can't be such a mystery, after all, to baking what's essentially a chewy bread doughnut. And bagels are such a great kid-pleasing food—some New Yorkers even use them to pacify teething infants—that we'd hardly know what to do without them.

In my opinion, the premier outlet is **H&H Bagels** (www.hhbagels.com; call ✆ **800/NY-BAGEL** [692-2435] for shipping anywhere), which has two 24-hour retail shops in Manhattan: (1) 2239 Broadway, at 80th Street (✆ **212/595-8000**), and (2) 639 W. 46th St., between Eleventh Avenue and the West Side Highway (✆ **212/765-7200**). Besides selling hot bagels to the public, H&H supplies bagels to delis and grocery stores all around the city, so look for signs boasting WE HAVE H&H BAGELS. The problem with H&H is that it has no seating and doesn't serve bagels with any spread (in local parlance, a "schmear"), though you can buy separate little tubs of cream cheese, chopped liver, egg salad, herring in cream sauce, whatever. At least the store has finally installed a coffee machine so you can get a cup of coffee to go. **H&H Midtown Bagels East,** 1551 Second Ave., near 80th Street (✆ **212/717-7312;** www.hhmidtown bagelseast.com), is a former branch that had to litigate for the right to keep using the name; it too has wonderfully chewy bagels, with the added convenience of a deli counter where countermen can cut and dress your bagels. I know many people who'd award the crown to **Ess-a-Bagel,** 359 First Ave., at 21st Street (✆ **212/260-2252;** www.ess-a-bagel.com), and 831 Third Ave., at 51st Street (✆ **212/980-1010**), a full-service bagel deli where you can sit down and eat. But if you really want to get authentic, you might journey down to the Lower East Side to try **Kossar's Bialys,** 367 Grand St., between Essex and Norfolk streets (✆ **212/473-4810**).

—Holly Hughes

dishes, the bruschetta, and the mixed antipasto starter (practically a meal in itself); the kids often fill up on the crusty, dense bread. Prices are gentle on the wallet, too.

584 Columbus Ave. (btwn 88th and 89th sts.). ✆ **212/877-2267.** www.bellalunanyc.com. Highchairs, boosters. Reservations recommended. Main courses $11–$20. AE, MC, V. Daily noon-10:30pm (11pm Fri-Sat); Sun 4-10pm. Subway: B, C, 1 to 86th St.

Carmine's ★ ITALIAN   The original location of this popular northern Italian eatery (see also p. 115) is still tough to get into, so be sure to make a reservation. That said, this lively, hearty restaurant is fun, with a decor that's a 1960s throwback (dark-wood trim, chrome bar stools) and the aroma of garlic hanging in the air. The menu features superbly executed standards like shrimp scampi, rigatoni with sausage, chicken Marsala, veal scaloppine, and big, thick steaks. The dining room can be noisy, but it's a cheerful rumble so conversation isn't impossible. Portions are served family-style and are legendarily huge, so order accordingly—insist on your children splitting a dish with you, even if they're big eaters. We always over-order, though; the menu's so tempting, we just can't help it.

2450 Broadway (btwn 90th and 91st sts.). ✆ **212/362-2200.** www.carminesnyc.com. Highchairs, boosters. Reservations recommended. Family-style main courses (serve 2-4 people) $25-$42 (more for porterhouse steaks and lobsters). AE, DC, MC, V. Sun-Thurs 11:30am-11pm; Fri-Sat 11:30am-midnight. Subway: 1 to 86th St.

Gabriela's ★ MEXICAN Gabriela's serves up astonishingly good regional dishes that go well beyond rote Mexican combo platters. The roast chicken is a marvel, succulent and delicately spiced; quesadillas are light, crisp, and flavorful; and you can't go wrong with any of the spicy casseroles and soups. As for kids, there are simple tacos (served without hot red sauce—hooray!), accompanied by rice and beans, as well as a number of fruit drinks, fruit shakes, and exotic Mexican soft drinks. The staff is cordial and accommodating; the softly lit stucco walls have a golden glow that's very relaxing, even when the restaurant is packed to the gills, as it usually is. It's a popular place for weekend brunch.

688 Columbus Ave. (btwn 93rd and 94th sts.). ℭ 212/961-9600. www.gabrielas.com. Subway: B, C, 1, 2, 3 to 96th St. Highchairs, boosters. Reservations recommended. Main courses $15–$22. AE, DISC, MC, V. Mon–Thurs 11:30am–11pm; Fri 11:30am–midnight; Sat 11am–midnight; Sun 11am–11pm.

Good Enough to Eat ★ AMERICAN Serving "good, old-fashioned American" comfort food since 1981, this charming little restaurant grew out of a bakery, so you can bet the pies and cakes are excellent. Tables are small, with weathered wood pickets around to strike a rustic note; cut flowers add another farmhouse touch. Breakfasts are to die for: How about apple pancakes, banana-walnut pancakes, or Peter Paul pancakes (Belgium chocolate and coconut)? Though the menu focuses on old-fashioned American dishes like mac 'n' cheese, meatloaf, and a classic turkey dinner (with homemade cornbread), chef/owner Carrie Levin trained at the Russian Tea Room and the Four Seasons, and is perfectly capable of turning out stunning daily fish specials, lemon Parmesan chicken breast, and a vegetable Napoleon that's memorable indeed. Its kids' menu, "designed and tested by kids," has pasta, burger bites, chicken fingers, and mac 'n' cheese—a hit parade of children's faves.

483 Amsterdam Ave. (btwn 83rd and 84th sts.). ℭ 212/496-0163. www.goodenoughtoeat.com. Kids' menu. No reservations. Main courses $15–$25; kids' menu $5–$7.50. AE, MC, V. Mon–Thurs 8am–10:30pm; Fri 8am–11pm; Sat 9am–4pm and 5:30–11pm; Sun 9am–4pm and 5:30–10pm. Subway: 1 to 86th St.

Henry's ★ AMERICAN This popular spot features solid versions of all-American standards in a handsome dining room that was patterned after the Gamble House, a major Arts and Crafts landmark in Pasadena, California. The woody inside is roomy, and an outdoor cafe offers even more space. It's a family favorite for Upper West Siders and Columbia University profs, and don't think they don't know it—you and your kids will be warmly welcomed and well taken care of. The usual kid-friendly dishes—pasta, burgers, fries—are all here.

2745 Broadway (at 105th St.). ℭ 212/866-0600. www.henrysnyc.com. Highchairs, boosters. Reservations recommended. Main courses $14–$26. AE, DC, DISC, MC, V. Mon–Thurs noon–11pm; Fri noon–midnight; Sat 11am–4pm and 5pm–midnight; Sun 11am–4pm and 5–11pm. Subway: 1, 9 to 103rd St.

Popover Café AMERICAN This pleasantly upscale cafe's signature teddy bears lined up in the front windows have always deluded folks into thinking it's a restaurant for kids—but it's not particularly so, and the staff has been burned enough by unsupervised brats that they've added a note on children's manners to their menu. With an unpretentiously handsome decor (red plaid banquettes, cadet-blue walls, granite-speckled Formica tabletops), it serves the West Side equivalent of the East Side ladies-who-lunch crowd, wholesome chic types who appreciate sprout-bedecked salads and soul-warming soups accompanied by a light-as-air baked popover. The owner seems somewhat to have accepted the family fate, serving milk in a lidded paper cup and adding a kids' menu of sorts—yet a grilled cheese cooked on hearty home-baked peasant bread isn't necessarily as good as one made with Wonder Bread if you're 4 years old. Avoid weekend brunch, when the lines can be ridiculous.

551 Amsterdam Ave. (at 87th St.). ✆ **212/595-8555.** www.popovercafe.com. Kids' menu, highchairs, boosters. No reservations. Main courses $9.95–$28; kids' menu $3.95–$6.95. AE, MC, V. Mon–Fri 8am–10pm; Sat–Sun 8:30am–10pm. Subway: B, C, 1 to 86th St.

Sambuca ★ ITALIAN   This 22-year-old business is a great place for family birthday celebrations; the waiters are very friendly, you can color on the paper tablecloths, and the food consists of straightforward Italian classics, served in robust portions (gluten-free dishes are also available). Dishes are served in both regular and family-style portions. If you order family-style, don't over-order—a family of five can choose a couple of entrees and still leave a lot of food on the platters. The chicken piccata is a real winner, as is the penne with eggplant and mozzarella. The kids' menu includes spaghetti several different ways, ravioli, and good old chicken fingers. The dining room is pleasantly soft-hued and contemporary, with sponged orange walls, iron sconces, and Tuscan painted pottery on wall brackets. Very casual, but you still get that special dining-out feeling.

20 W. 72nd St. (btwn Columbus Ave. and Central Park West). ✆ **212/787-5656.** www.sambucanyc.com. Kids' menu, highchairs, boosters. Reservations recommended. Main courses $15–$37 (family-size portions); kids' menu $13. AE, DC, DISC, MC, V. Mon–Thurs 5–10pm; Fri–Sat 5–11pm; Sun 3–10pm. Subway: B, C, 1, 2, 3 to 72nd St.

Inexpensive

Alice's Tea Cup ★★ 📖 BRITISH/DESSERTS   Little girls adore this unique little spot snuggled into a West Side brownstone, with its shabby-chic jumble of second-hand furniture and mismatched china. Lewis Carroll quotes are stenciled on the walls, and the gift shop in front is full of treasures. While it's perfect for tea parties—the menu of teas is encyclopedic, brownies and cookies arrive freshly baked and buttery, and crumbly scones are served with clotted cream and preserves—Alice's is brilliant for lunch or dinner too, serving around-the-world favorites like cucumber sandwiches, curried chicken salad, and croque-monsieur. Eating here is a special treat indeed.

102 W. 73rd St. (btwn Columbus and Amsterdam aves.). ✆ **212/799-3006.** www.alicesteacup.com. Kids' menu, highchairs. Salads and sandwiches $8–$14; kids' dishes $7–$8; high tea $37. AE, DISC, MC, V. Daily 8am–8pm. Subway: B, C, 1, 2, 3 to 72nd St.

Artie's Delicatessen ★ DELI   Pastrami is a cornerstone of the huge menu, though the scrumptious meatloaf is even better. Pickles come standard with table service as does the crisp, tangy coleslaw. Teenagers will love the hot chicken wings. Hot dogs, potato pancakes, and grilled-cheese sandwiches are other kid-friendly choices. Service is quick and friendly, and the white-tiled setting is always noisy enough that no one minds if kids add to the din. Okay, so it's only a decade old, as opposed to burnished veterans like the Carnegie Deli or Barney Greengrass; Artie's still has good classic deli food (at reasonable prices), at least a couple of old-timer waiters, and a sort of go-figure nonchalance that's very kid-friendly and very New York.

2290 Broadway (at 83rd St.). ✆ **212/579-5959.** www.arties.com. Kids' menu, highchairs, boosters. No reservations. Sandwiches and burgers $8.95–$15; main courses $13–$18; kids' menu $7–$8. AE, DISC, MC, V. Sun–Thurs 9am–11:30pm; Fri–Sat 9am–1am. Subway: 1 to 86th or 79th St.

Boat Basin Café ★ AMERICAN   A stroke of genius, to put an outdoor restaurant here overlooking the houseboat marina in lower Riverside Park. Not only are the views west over the Hudson spectacular (time it right, and you'll get a sunset show to die for), but the vaulted limestone arches of this open-air structure give it a kind of European charm. And the food is better than what you'd expect at an outdoor cafe, with good grilled burgers and zestfully seasoned salads and sandwiches. (You can also order grilled salmon and barbecued chicken or ribs.) The trappings are supercasual: checked vinyl tablecloths, sturdy plastic chairs, folding tables, and fries heaped in a plastic basket on wax paper. It can get crazy busy around happy hour, and the service can dawdle, but kids don't seem to mind; they're busy counting boats on the river.

W. 79th St. at the Hudson River, in Riverside Park. ⓒ **212/496-5542.** www.boatbasincafe.com. Kids' menu. No reservations. Burgers, hot dogs, and sandwiches $3–$17; main courses $16–$26; kids' menu $2.75–$3.50. AE, DC, MC, V. Late Mar to end of Oct. Mon–Wed noon–11pm; Thurs–Fri noon–11:30pm; Sat 11am–11:30pm; Sun 11am–10pm. Subway: 1 to 79th St.

Brother Jimmy's BBQ BARBECUE/SOUTHERN   As the evening wears on, this low-lit, cluttered joint becomes a noisy, beery frat party, especially on nights when UNC and Duke square off in basketball. But the seven Brother Jimmy's restaurants definitely like kids and prove it by letting the under-12 set eat free (two free kids' meals per each paid adult entree)—a great deal in today's economy. And the barbecue is not bad, with meaty, spicy ribs, pulled pork, and chicken cooked slowly over hickory wood and slathered with a tangy sauce. Add a little cornbread, candied yams, corn on the cob, and black-eyed peas, and it's a welcome break from pizza and burgers.

428 Amsterdam Ave. (btwn 80th and 81st sts.). ⓒ **212/501-7515.** www.brotherjimmys.com. Kids' menu, highchairs, boosters. Reservations accepted for groups of 8 or more only. Main courses $13–$22; salads and sandwiches $6.95–$11. AE, DC, DISC, MC, V. Mon–Wed 4pm–midnight; Thurs–Fri 5pm–1am; Sat noon–1am; Sun noon–11pm; Wed–Sun noon–midnight during summer months. Subway: B, C, 1, 9 to 79th St.

Pizza

New Pizza Town PIZZA   Here's a neighborhood storefront that offers a very decent cheese slice for $2.50. No fancy airs or graces, just a good slice to go.

2196 Broadway (btwn 77th and 78th sts.). ⓒ **212/769-2323.** No reservations. Pizzas $12–$16. MC, V. Mon–Tues 10:30am–midnight; Wed 10am–1am; Thurs–Sat 11am–3am; Sun 10am–11pm. Subway: 9 to 79th St.

T & R Pizzeria PIZZA   Need a slice of pizza near the Natural History Museum? This dependable storefront pizzeria has good pizza by the slice or the pie, as well as calzones, lasagna, eggplant parm, and more.

403 Amsterdam Ave. (btwn 79th and 80th sts.). ⓒ **212/787-4093.** No reservations. Pizzas $12–$16. No credit cards. Mon–Wed 11am–midnight; Thurs–Sat 11am–3am; Sun 11am–11pm. Subway: to 79th St.

V & T Pizzeria & Restaurant ITALIAN/PIZZA   With its brick walls, painted murals, low lighting, and red-checkered tablecloths, V & T looks just like the campus pizza joint it is, the campuses in question being nearby Columbia and Barnard. The pizzas are fabulous, with thin crusts, runny cheese, and robust tomato sauce; other southern Italian dishes, like lasagna and baked ziti, are heartwarmingly good, too. Not much on ambience, but then, you don't get a lot of attitude, either.

1024 Amsterdam Ave. (btwn 110th and 111th sts.). ⓒ **212/663-1708.** www.vtpizzeriarestaurant.com. Highchairs. Main courses $8–$31; pizza $11–$19; kids' menu (dining-in only) $6–$8. AE, DC, DISC, MC, V. Sun–Mon 11:30am–11pm; Tues–Sat 11:30am–midnight. Subway: 1 to 110th St.

Patsy Lanciani opened his first pizzeria in East Harlem in the 1930s. Expanding beyond its original East Harlem location, the chain branches of **Patsy's Pizzeria** (www.patsyspizzeriany.com) have discarded the married-to-the-mob ambience in favor of wood paneling and potted plants and marble-topped tables, perfect for serving up savory brick-oven pizzas, crisp salads, and satisfying pastas. Patsy's has six locations in the city, including an Upper West Side branch a few blocks from the American Museum of Natural History (61 W. 74th St.) and in the NYU vicinity (67 University Place). www.patsyspizzeriany.com.

THE UPPER EAST SIDE

Expensive

Tony's di Napoli ITALIAN   Hearty southern Italian food is served family-style at this genial Upper East Side neighborhood spot, which opens onto a big sidewalk cafe in fair weather. Polaroids of satisfied customers in the front window and black-and-white head shots of race-car drivers on the yellowed plaster walls give it the look of a vintage family-owned red-sauce joint, though in fact it's part of the Dallas BBQ restaurant empire. Sunday lunch is the most popular time for families (Tony's doesn't serve lunch on weekdays), but you'll find kids sprinkled around the boisterous dining room on weeknights too. The family-style menu is strong on pasta dishes, with several chicken and veal offerings as well, plus a two-person steak for dedicated carnivores. If your family can't agree on dishes, half portions can be ordered for individuals, as well as kid-size portions of pasta (there's no separate kids' menu). Though I prefer the similar food at Carmine's (p. 102 and 115), the scene here is less frenetic, and the prices are certainly reasonable, considering that you can get away with $20 a head, including wine for adults. Note that there isn't room to park strollers beside tables.

1606 Second Ave. (btwn 83rd and 84th sts.). ✆ **212/861-8686.** www.tonysnyc.com. Highchairs, boosters. Reservations recommended. Main courses (serve 2–4 people) $18–$50. AE, DC, DISC, MC, V. Mon-Fri 5pm–midnight; Sat-Sun 2pm–midnight. Subway: 4, 5, 6 to 86th St.

Moderate

The Barking Dog ★ AMERICAN   Convenient to the 92nd Street Y and Carl Schurz Park, this retro diner serving American comfort food welcomes diners with wood-trimmed booths and parchment-shaded lamps at every table. The dog motif amuses most kids: Posters, cookie jars, and even bulldog hood ornaments from Mack trucks put dogs all around the room, and there's a dog bar outside, a blue-tiled corner trough with a polished spigot. But what really makes this place work for families is that it serves breakfast until 4pm—kids can feast on waffles or blueberry pancakes while parents get a chance to eat something suitably grown-up, like a salad of field greens with goat-cheese croutons or a grilled filet of salmon sandwich. For dinner, there's a good fried chicken with real mashed potatoes, baked ham, pot roast, and a homey meatloaf, as well as more sophisticated stuff like the pan-roasted breast of chicken with piquant Mediterranean-flavored ragout. Old-fashioned ice-cream sodas and sundaes are served from a vintage soda fountain. It has a new location inside the Affinia Dumont Midtown East.

(1) 1678 Third Ave. (at 94th St.). *Ⓒ* **212/831-1800.** Subway: 6 to 96th St. (2) 1453 York Ave. (at 77th St.).
Ⓒ **212/861-3600.** (3) Affinia Dumont hotel, 150 E. 34th St. (at Lexington Ave.). *Ⓒ* **212/871-3900.**
Subway: 6 to 77th St. Boosters, sassy seats. No reservations. Main courses $13–$22; sandwiches and
salads $6–$13. AE, DC, DISC, MC, V. Daily 7am–11pm.

Fetch Bar & Grill ★ AMERICAN   A welcoming environment and friendly staff go
a long way to make this neighborhood favorite work for kids; what really seals the deal
is the dog theme, with snapshots of beloved family pups covering every inch of the
warm yellow walls (hence the restaurant's name). The ever-popular burgers and fries,
delicious salads, omelets, soups, and pastas give you a decent range of options, with
grilled fish and roast chicken added at dinner. Anyone up for Philly cheesesteak egg
rolls?

1649 Third Ave. (btwn 92nd and 93rd sts.). *Ⓒ* **212/289-2700.** www.fetchbarandgrill.com. Kids' menu,
highchairs, boosters. Reservations recommended. Main courses $9–$19; kids' menu $6–$7. AE, DC,
DISC, MC, V. Mon–Fri 11am–3pm and 5–11pm (to midnight Fri); Sat–Sun 10am–3pm and 5pm–midnight.
Subway: 4, 5, 6 to 96th St.

Luke's Bar and Grill ★★ AMERICAN/BURGERS   This is a very civilized place
where children are included as a matter of course. Lots of brick and wood give it a
warm, clubby look that's also somehow young and casual; there's definitely an active
bar scene here, but it never overwhelms the pleasant, relaxing restaurant. Luke's
burgers are wonderful, firm and yet juicy, with an ever-so-slightly charred outside, and
the salads are big, fresh, and well conceived. Or you can go for the grilled-cheese
sandwich, roast chicken, or one of the pasta dishes. There's no attitude on the part of
the waiters: They seem genuinely happy to serve youngsters, even babies. If only
more restaurants were like this.

1394 Third Ave. (btwn 79th and 80th sts.). *Ⓒ* **212/249-7070.** www.lukesbarandgrill.com. Boosters,
sassy seats. Reservations accepted. Main courses $7.95–$28. No credit cards. Mon–Fri 11:30am–1am; Sat
10am–2am; Sun 10am–midnight. Subway: 6 to 77th St.

Serendipity 3 ★ DESSERTS/DINER   This cheery restaurant with its snugly
deep booths and Tiffany-style lamps has an interesting and eclectic menu, with good
burgers and such down-home faves as country meatloaf, chicken potpie, and barbecue chicken. It also offers parent pleasers like charbroiled Norwegian salmon and
curried shrimp almandine. But it's best known far and wide among the under-12 set

---

The (Homegrown) Chain Gang: Shake Shack

Muscling into Midtown and points
north, this high-quality burger joint is
spreading its insanely popular menu of
drive-in favorites to the rest of Manhattan. In addition to its flagship shack in
Madison Park (see later in this chapter),
the **Shake Shack** (www.shakeshacknyc.
com) now has locations on the **Upper
East Side** (154 E. 86th St., btwn Lexington and Third aves.; *Ⓒ* **646/237-5035**),
the **Upper West Side** (366 Columbus
Ave., at 77th St.; *Ⓒ* **646/747-8770**),

Citi Field (New York Mets stadium;
Flushing, Queens), and **Midtown** (691
Eighth Ave., at 44th St.; *Ⓒ* **646/435-
0135**). The Midtown location takes the
"shack" concept and turns it on its
head; this is a whopping half-block-
long eating establishment. It's all good
news for families: The Shake Shacks are
among the most child-friendly restaurants in town, with kid-pleasing burgers, fries, hot dogs, shakes, and frozen
custard.

as a source for huge, wickedly rich desserts; fountain sodas; and ice-cream sundaes. The Outrageous Banana Split is priced at $20 and worth every penny. Because space is tight, strollers and carriages cannot be accommodated within the restaurant. And it can get packed on the weekends.

225 E. 60th St. (btw. Second and Third aves.). ☎ 212/838-3531. www.serendipity3.com. Boosters. Reservations accepted for full meals only. Main courses $14–$23. AE, DC, DISC, MC, V. Sun–Thurs 11:30am–midnight; Fri 11:30am–1am; Sat 11:30am–2am. Subway: 4, 5, 6 to 59th St.

Inexpensive

Alice's Tea Cup ★★ BRITISH/DESSERTS   Chapter II of the popular West Side tearoom has the same boho assortment of castoff furniture and china, and the same delightful menu of sandwiches, omelets, salads, and pastries, with fuller selections available for dinner. The after-school snack menu attracts lots of private-school girls and their nannies.

156 E. 64th St. (at Lexington Ave.). ☎ 212/486-9200. www.alicesteacup.com. Kids' menu, highchairs. AE, DISC, MC, V. Salads and sandwiches $8–$14; kids' dishes $7–$8; high tea $37. Daily 8am–8pm. Subway: 6 to 68th St.

Brother Jimmy's Bait Shack BARBECUE/SOUTHERN   The rowdy roadhouse charm of Brother Jimmy's always appeals to kids. Blackened catfish and peel-and-eat shrimp are featured on a menu otherwise heavy on barbecued chicken, ribs, and pork. The kitchen doesn't stint on the spices, and beer flows plentifully. But kids are welcomed warmly, with a kids-eat-free policy that can't be beat anywhere else in town (two under-12s per parent, as long as the adult buys an entree rather than a sandwich). A variety of nightly "events" like All-U-Can-Eat-Ribs Sundays make every evening a party here.

1644 Third Ave. (at 92nd St.). ☎ 212/426-2020. www.brotherjimmys.com. Kids' menu, highchairs, boosters. Reservations accepted for groups of 8 or more only. Main courses $13–$22; salads and sandwiches $6.95–$11. AE, DC, DISC, MC, V. Mon–Wed 4pm–midnight; Thurs–Fri 5pm–1am; Sat noon–1am; Sun noon–11pm; Wed–Sun noon–midnight during summer months. Subway: 6 to 96th St.

Brother Jimmy's BBQ BARBECUE/SOUTHERN   With a jumble of frat-party paraphernalia littering the walls, low-lit Brother Jimmy's brings hickory-smoked Carolina barbecue—both Northern and Southern versions—to New York City. Thick 'n' meaty ribs, brisket, and chicken are served up in hefty dinners that also include cornbread and a choice of country sides; if your kids aren't into collard greens (yeah, right), you can satisfy them with creamed corn, french fries, or macaroni and cheese. As with the Upper West Side location (p. 105), it may be best to get here early, before the frat party swings into high gear.

1485 Second Ave. (btwn 77th and 78th sts.). ☎ 212/288-0999. www.brotherjimmys.com. Kids' menu, highchairs, boosters. Reservations accepted for groups of 8 or more only. Main courses $13–$22; salads and sandwiches $6.95–$11. AE, DC, DISC, MC, V. Mon–Wed 4pm–midnight; Thurs–Fri 5pm–1am; Sat noon–1am; Sun noon–11pm; Wed–Sun noon–midnight during summer months. Subway: 6 to 77th St.

Lexington Candy Shop ★★ 🍴 DINER   Walking through the door of the Lexington Candy Shop is like passing through a time warp: Inside is a perfectly preserved old luncheonette that's been around since 1925 and looks it. There's a counter with chrome-rimmed stools, along with a handful of wooden booths, where you can down creamy milkshakes and malteds, fresh lemonade, buttery grilled-cheese sandwiches, BLTs, outstanding cheeseburgers, pancakes, and crinkle fries. For the adults, there's fresh shrimp salad and hearty club sandwiches—as well as a classic New York City

THE cupcake CRAZE

Whether it's the crowns of buttercream frosting, the charm of a cake that fits neatly in your palm, or simply a touchstone from your childhood, cupcakes are more popular than ever in New York. Scattered throughout the city, bakeries that feature shiny glass cases full of these beloved treats have multiplied, with some small shops drawing not only neighborhood crowds but also citywide fame.

Perhaps the most famous of all is **Magnolia Bakery,** located at 401 Bleecker St. (at W. 11th St.; ϕ **212/462-2572**), its original store a homey little '50s-style shop (with screened door, natch) in Greenwich Village; *Sex and the City* tour buses stop here for cupcake breaks with alarming frequency. For sheer beauty (and industrial-strength buttercream), the **Cupcake Cafe**—located on the outskirts of midtown (545 Ninth Ave., at 40th St.; ϕ **212/465-1530;** www.cupcakecafe-nyc.com; as well as inside one of the city's best children's bookstores, Books of Wonder, 18 W. 18th St.; ϕ **212/465-1530**)—makes flower-bedecked cakes of purple violets, pink roses, and yellow sunflowers. Many a downtown children's party has been graced with the fashionable little cakes from **Tribeca Treats** (94 Reade St., btwn Church St. and W. Broadway; ϕ **212/571-0500;** www.tribecatreats.com), whose inventive flavors-of-the-day range from black velvet to s'mores. Speaking of little, the cupcakes at **Baked by Melissa** (7 E. 14th St, btwn Fifth Ave. and University Place; www.bakedbymelissa.com) have been shrunk to sassy little bite-size nuggets; pop 'em like M&Ms and feel good about yourself. Farther north, **Two Little Red Hens** on the Upper East Side (1652 Second Ave., at 85th St.; ϕ **212/452-0476**) is a local favorite, with frosting you can really sink your teeth into. **Crumbs** (www.crumbs.com) now has 12 Manhattan locations; their cupcakes are big and decadent. And in the middle of it all, the **Buttercup Bake Shop,** a descendant of Magnolia (973 Second Ave., at 51st St.; ϕ **212/350-4144**), offers a challenge to even the most determined sweet tooth. Both cake and frosting are overwhelmingly sweet—combined, they could send you into sugar shock.

egg cream. Best of all, the staff seems to positively perk up when they see kids coming. The front window is crammed full of stuffed animals for sale, which guarantees that children never pass by without stopping.

1226 Lexington Ave. (at 83rd St.). ϕ **212/288-0057.** www.lexingtoncandyshop.net. Boosters, sassy seats. Main courses $5.75–$12. AE, DC, DISC, MC, V. Mon–Sat 7am–7pm; Sun 9am–6pm. Subway: 4, 5, 6 to 86th St.

Lili's Noodle Shop & Grill CHINESE   The food in this classic noodle-shop/rotisserie is delicately spiced and not too greasy, a feat considering how fatty barbecue-roasted pork and chicken can be. The noodle dishes, even plain lo mein, are good; the soups come in enormous bowls and can be a challenge to finish, but the broth is light and flavorful, filled with fresh noodles and vegetables. Light varnished woods and streamlined shapes give the decor a smart, modern feel, and the service is efficient, casual, and friendly.

1500 Third Ave. (btwn 84th and 85th sts.). ϕ **212/639-1313.** Highchairs, boosters. Main courses $8.95–$20. AE, DC, DISC, MC, V. Daily 11am–11pm. Subway: 4, 5, 6 to 86th St.

Sassy's Sliders 🍴 BURGERS   If New York City has drained you dry—your wallet, that is—this is the place for you. The decor is very 1950s—wall tiles, Formica tables, and linoleum, all in Fiestaware colors—and so is the fast-food concept: 2-inch hamburgers steamed with onions, so small and moist they slide whole down your throat, hence the name "sliders." If you're thinking White Castle (which also specializes in. miniburgers), think again: Sassy's Sliders are much better, and with other choices like grilled chicken, ground turkey, and veggie burgers, this nifty little spot should satisfy everyone in the family. The hamburger slider ($1.09) is a perfect-size burger for a small kid anyway, and at these low prices, you may be able to feed the whole gang for, gulp, less than $20. Hey, you can panhandle for that kinda dough in no time! Most of its business is takeout and delivery, but there are a few tables inside.

1530 Third Ave. (at 86th St.). ✆ 212/828-6900. www.sassyssliders.com. No reservations. Burgers $1.09. AE. Mon–Tues 11:30am–10pm; Wed–Thurs 11:30am–11pm; Fri 11am–midnight; Sat 11:30am–midnight; Sun 11:30am–10pm. Subway: 4, 5, 6 to 86th St.

Pizza

Barron's Pizza 🎒 PIZZA   We stumbled into this pizzeria one Sunday noontime and had some of the best pie of our lives—tangy sauce, fresh mozzarella, crisp chewy crust—along with friendly counter service. The decor is a little different from your standard storefront pizza shop, with mosaic tile designs and wrought-iron cafe chairs. This is the sort of place you might not seek out without a recommendation, so take it from me: It's well above average. We go back whenever we're in the neighborhood.

1428 Lexington Ave. (at 93rd St.). ✆ 212/410-6600. Slice $2.25; plain pie $14–$16. No credit cards. Daily 9am–10pm. Subway: 6 to 96th St.

John's Pizzeria Eastside ★★ PIZZA   The great Village pizzeria chain (p. 120 and 126 later in this chapter) has opened this East Side branch for thin-crust, brick-oven pies, substantial green salads, and a few well-executed pasta dishes. The menu's limited, but every dish on it is delectable.

408 E. 64th St. (btwn First and York aves.). ✆ 212/935-2895. www.johnspizzerianyc.com. Reservations accepted for groups of 5 or more only. Pizzas $12–$18, toppings $2–$4.75; pastas $8.95–$14. AE, DISC, MC, V. Daily 11:30am–11pm. Subway: 4, 5, 6 to 59th St.

Afternoon Tea

Madeline's Tea Party at the Carlyle Hotel ★★ CONTINENTAL   Beneath the charming murals by Ludwig Bemelmans (the creator of the *Madeline* children's books) in the luxe surroundings of Bemelmans Bar, this tony East Side hotel (p. 66) offers a storybook **Madeline's Tea Party** every Saturday around late October and through the winter season (two seatings: 10am and 12:30pm). Finger sandwiches and delicate little pastries accompany finely brewed tea and other beverages, not to mention a singalong.

In the Carlyle Hotel, 35 E. 76th St. (at Madison Ave.). ✆ 212/570-7192. www.thecarlyle.com. AE, DC, DISC, MC, V. Full tea $40 adults and kids. Sat seatings 10am and 12:30pm. Subway: 6 to 77th St.

MIDTOWN

Expensive

American Girl Cafe ★★ AMERICAN   Girls would have begged to come to American Girl Place's house restaurant anyway, but parents will be gratified to

The (Homegrown) Chain Gang: Hale and Hearty Soups

Hale and Hearty may be the lone survivor of the soup craze that hit New York soon after the infamous *Seinfeld* "Soup Nazi" episode appeared. (Remember Soup Nutsy? Daily Soup?) It outlasted the competition for a number of reasons, foremost of which: It makes really good soup. It's hard to believe that soup made in a fairly industrial manner can still taste this fresh and savory (how do they keep the potatoes from getting mushy?). Standouts include mulligatawny; sweet corn chowder; and white bean and escarole. Kid-pleasing faves include macaroni and cheese with beef and hearty chicken noodle; the Roman tomato with pastini is toddler caviar. Hale and Hearty shops are set up largely as takeouts, but most offer nice areas to sit down, as well as big pitchers of fresh water with lemon slices to quench your thirst. Hale and Hearty has 21 shops all over Manhattan, including the food courts at Chelsea Market, Rockefeller Center, and the Grand Central Dining Concourse. Go to www.haleandhearty.com to find a location near you.

discover that the food is actually good. Advance reservations are essential, up to 6 months ahead in busy seasons, but it never hurts to stop by the front desk as you enter the store just to see if there are any free slots. Prix-fixe pricing simplifies everything, as does the small, well-chosen menu. As soon as you sit down, you're offered warm, gooey cinnamon buns (don't bypass these). At lunch and dinner there's one choice of appetizer (an arrangement of crudités, dips, cheeses, and breads that's already on the table when you arrive), and everybody gets the same dessert, a yummy little chocolate mousse in a flowerpot. Special touches make all the difference, as with the kids' pizza, decorated with veggies to look like tick-tack-toe, or the miniature hamburgers and hot dogs with the side of creamy mac 'n' cheese. Best of all, there are special doll seats where girls can prop their American Girl dolls while they eat (the dolls get their own tea sets, and you wouldn't believe how many girls carefully feed their dolls). If you haven't brought a doll, they'll kindly lend you one for the meal. The waitstaff is unfailingly patient and kind, and the decor is sophisticated yet girly. The experience will make your daughter's day, and—surprise, surprise—yours too.

609 Fifth Ave. (at 49th St.). ℂ **877/AG-PLACE** (247-5223). www.americangirl.com. Highchairs, boosters. Reservations required. Brunch $19; lunch $24; tea $20; dinner $26. AE, DISC, MC, V. Subway: E, V to Fifth Ave./53rd St.

Benihana ★★ JAPANESE   Watching the Benihana chefs at work with their flying knives, slicing and dicing the meat, seafood, and vegetables they'll grill on the teppanyaki right at your table, is endlessly fascinating to kids. (Best trick: the onion transformed into a smoking volcano, or the shrimp tail flipped into the top of the chef's hat.) As far as Japanese food goes, this doesn't require as adventurous a palate as, say, sushi does, so it's a great choice for kids. For adults, the grilled food constitutes a hearty, healthy meal (and, we admit, a guilty pleasure). Yes, the operation is clearly tourist-oriented, and some of the chefs look slightly bored—but is the experience any less authentic than a Southern roadhouse or Mexican cantina plopped down on the streets of Manhattan? What with the teahouse decor, dramatic lighting, and

You can sample a different culture every day you're in the city simply by turning a corner. That's because Manhattan is blessed with a number of ethnic enclaves that bring color and flavor to the streets of the city (and don't even get us started on Queens). In all of them, you can find wonderful places to eat. In addition, you can sample Brazilian specialties like *feijoada* (bean and meat stew) in restaurants pocketing **Little Brazil** on West 45th and 46th streets between Fifth and Sixth avenues.

○ **Chinatown.** Whether you choose one of the big, Hong Kong–style banquet restaurants or a modest dumpling house, your family will be welcomed in Chinatown. This is one of the country's largest Chinatowns, a sprawling enclave of restaurants and businesses that has bled into neighboring Little Italy and the Lower East Side. The food is good, cheap, and plentiful—and it's great fun for kids to be in a place that feels and sounds so utterly exotic. Yes, the streets and sidewalks are crowded with people, but the bustle of commerce is palpable. It's easily one of our favorite places in the city. For suggestions on where to eat, see the "Chinatown" listings, later in this chapter.

○ **Little Italy.** Some locals wouldn't dream of dining in Little Italy—which has certainly gotten little

but is not so genuinely Italian anymore—but we think it's a fun place for lunch or a family dinner, especially on warm-weather weekends when Mulberry Street becomes a strolling pedestrian mall and Frankie Sinatra croons from every storefront. Some places stray a little too close to theme-park Italian, but the pasta is red-sauce hearty and piled high on the plate, and kids eat up the show. For suggestions on where to eat, see the "Little Italy" listings, later in this chapter.

○ **Koreatown.** Close to Macy's and the Empire State Building, Koreatown is located in the low 30s between Sixth and Madison avenues, but its locus is 32nd Street between Fifth Avenue and Broadway. Turn a corner and you're in another world: Neon signs and billboards in Korean tout restaurants, snack shops, and late-night karaoke lounges. Korean barbecue restaurants are fun and delicious; basically, marinated meat is cooked on a grill right at your table. The waterfall in the two-story **Kum Gang San,** at 49 W. 32nd St. (ⓒ **212/967-0909;** www.kumgangsan.net), should be enough to draw kids, but come for reliably good barbecue and Korean favorites like *bimbimbap* and rice-flour pancakes filled with scallions and seafood.

food-flying floor show, kids feel they're getting an exotic experience, and it's great, cornball fun for everyone. Just try to take your eyes off the cook at work. . .

47 W. 56th St. (btwn Fifth and Sixth aves.). ⓒ 212/581-0930. www.benihana.com. Boosters. Reservations recommended. Lunch $9.50–$15; dinner $15–$46. AE, DC, DISC, MC, V. Mon–Fri 11:30am–2:30pm; Mon–Thurs 5–10pm; Fri 5–11pm; Sat noon–11pm; Sun noon–10pm. Subway: E, V to Fifth Ave./53rd St.; F to 57th St.; N, Q, R, W to 57th St./Seventh Ave.

o **Little Tokyo.** In the East Village, along and around 9th Street between Second and Third avenues, Japanese restaurants, stores, and sake bars have flourished. I like to buy Japanese snacks (like tasty shrimp chips) at the **Sunrise Mart** (4 Stuyvesant St., near Third Ave.; *(C)* **212/598-3040**) Japanese grocery store. For soul-warming ramen-noodle soup, head over to 10th Street between First and Second avenues to **Rai Rai Ken** (214 E. 10th St.; *(C)* **212/477-7030**); it's really little more than a cozy soup counter with 14 stools, but find your kids a seat and watch them slurp. The owners have opened a Japanese curry shop, **Curry-Ya,** next door (214 E. 10th St.; *(C)* **866/602-8779**), which serves nine kinds of Japanese curry.

o **Little India.** Two areas in Manhattan qualify as Little India enclaves. Little India in the East Village, along 6th Street between First and Second avenues, is just 1 block long, but its numerous Bengali restaurants compete side by side for diners' attention. These restaurants have several things in common: They're cheap, the food is decent, and they have atmosphere to burn, with colorful Indian fabrics draping the walls, dramatic lighting, and a background of seductive sitar or raga music. As you would expect, kids eat it up. One of the most dependable choices is **Mitali East** (334 E. 6th St.; *(C)* **212/533-2508**), a cozy downstairs spot where a water fountain splashes at the back of the dining room. Reliable choices include the spicy curries, *murgha tikka* (boneless chicken pieces cooked in a tandoori oven), *biryanis* (meats and vegetables mixed with rice), and masalas. The *papadoms* (thin, crisp lentil wafers) are downright addictive. The neighborhood of Murray Hill has a larger, more sprawling Little India, this one on and around Lexington Avenue from 26th to 29th streets, with restaurants, grocery stores, and sari shops. One of my favorite spots is **Kalustyan's** (123 Lexington Ave.; *(C)* **212/685-3451;** www.kalustyans. com), a Middle Eastern market that sells nuts, dried fruits, and spices out of big barrels and has a little cafe on the second floor selling homemade Indian and Middle Eastern specialties; it's famous for its delicious *mujadarra* (a traditional lentil-and-rice dish with caramelized onions, served as a salad or in pita bread).

Jekyll & Hyde Club AMERICAN   Other theme restaurants have staid display cases full of memorabilia; Jekyll & Hyde delivers a thrill-ride experience, from the crashing ceiling in the vestibule to the creepy artwork that stares back at you from the walls. The waiters all look decked out for Halloween, and there's a continual floor show of ghastly figures telling even ghastlier jokes—expect an extra $2.50 per person slapped onto your bill to cover the "entertainment." The food is somewhat beside the point, but for the record they serve burgers, popcorn shrimp, pizzas, pastas, baby back ribs, and more. The kitchen's general strategy seems to be to smother things with cheese if at all possible and to grill anything that's grillable.

1409 Sixth Ave. (btwn 57th and 58th sts.). © **212/541-9505.** www.jekyllandhydeclub.com. Kids' menu. Reservations accepted for groups of 15 or more only. Main courses $14–$32; kids' menu $13. AE. Mon-Thurs 11:30am–11pm; Fri 11:30am–1am; Sat 11am–1am; Sun 11:30am–11pm. Subway: F, N, Q, R, W to 57th St./Seventh Ave.

Rock Center Café ★ ITALIAN   If it weren't in the very heart of Midtown, this restaurant might have cause to be snooty about children, with its sleek, mahogany-trimmed contemporary decor and upscale New American menu. But as they say in the real estate biz, location is everything, and this location couldn't be more of a tour-ist magnet: set right on the lower plaza of Rockefeller Plaza, where you can watch the ice skaters in winter and sit out under Prometheus in summer. It's an awfully pleasant place to rest your weary bones. (And you can ride a tiny glass-enclosed elevator down from sidewalk level to the restaurant.) Where tourists flock, there are bound to be children, and the Rock Center Café has shrewdly decided to make the most of them with a decent children's menu—a petite filet mignon, handmade penne pasta, chicken tenders, and a grilled-cheese sandwich.

20 W. 50th St. (at Rockefeller Center). © **212/332-7620.** www.patinagroup.com. Kids' menu, high-chairs. Reservations recommended, especially for lunch. Lunch $20–$34; dinner $21–$38; kids' menus $12–$18. AE, DC, MC, V. Mon–Fri 7:30–10:30am, 11:30am–3pm, and 5–10pm; Sat 11am–3pm and 4–10pm; Sun 10am–3pm and 4–9pm. Subway: B, D, F, V to 47th–50th sts./Rockefeller Center.

Ruby Foo's ★ PAN-ASIAN   The red-lacquer Suzy Wong–style decor of this bi-level rice palace is eye-popping, and the menu hits all the high notes of Asian cuisine, from dim sum to sushi to maki rolls to Thai curries. Compared to more authentic Chinese, Japanese, or Thai restaurants, the food is only competent, but the stunning setting makes up for it—you'll feel like you're inside a jewel-toned lacquered box, with Chinese lanterns glowing overhead, your linen napkin crisply folded into a fan, chopsticks set before you in a gleaming metal stand. Don't expect to get in without a reservation, and don't expect the service to be speedy. The restaurant does, however, offer a coloring sheet and crayons to keep the kids busy. The kids' menu is irresistible, with Ruby's Noodles (chicken, steamed broccoli, and udon noodles), shrimp dump-lings, and PB&J Pinwheels; they even have chicken fingers and a grilled-cheese sandwich for those kids who will not try the Asian cuisine.

1626 Broadway (at 49th St.). © **212/489-5600.** www.brguestrestaurants.com. Kids' menu, highchairs, boosters. Reservations recommended. Lunch and dinner $19–$39; kids' menu $5–$6.50. AE, DISC, MC, V. Daily 11:30am–5pm; Sun–Thurs 5–11pm; Fri 5–11:30pm; Sat 5pm–midnight. Subway: 1 to 50th St.

Tony's di Napoli ITALIAN   Heaping platters of satisfying Italian food are served family-style at this boisterous, good-natured Theater District branch of the Upper East Side favorite (p. 106). The menu offers lots of pasta choices, but also veal, chicken, fish, and Tuscan-style steaks; the waiters really bustle to get folks out in time for their theater curtain.

147 W. 43rd St. (btwn Sixth and Seventh aves.). © **212/221-0100.** www.tonysnyc.com. Highchairs, boosters. Reservations recommended. Main courses (serve 2–4 people) $18–$50. AE, DC, DISC, MC, V. Mon–Fri 5pm–midnight; Sat–Sun 2pm–midnight. Subway: B, D, F, V to 42nd St.; N, Q, R, S, W, 1, 2, 3, 7 to 42nd St./Times Square.

Moderate

Carmine's ★★ ITALIAN It's a party every night at Carmine's, a big, effervescent place that manages to give off a warm, old-fashioned vibe amid all the noise and sprawl. Family-style platters and ultraefficient service make this one of the city's top choices for families, and you see plenty of kids sucking up spaghetti with gusto. The clattering, casual atmosphere absorbs a lot of tantrums, and once you've got a table, service is prompt (if you can't move customers in and out quickly in the Theater District, you're done for). Crayons and coloring books are whisked to the table, too. It's Northern Italian, and lots of it—and the quality is amazing considering the volume of meals they prepare here. The linguine with shrimp in red sauce is light and delicious; the chicken scarpariello in wine sauce is a wonder of garlicky flavor; and salads are fresh and tasty. The original branch is on the Upper West Side (p. 102).

200 W. 44th St. (btwn Broadway and Eighth aves.). ✆ **212/221-3800.** www.carminesnyc.com. Highchairs, boosters. Reservations after 6pm accepted for groups of 6 or more only. Family-style main courses (serve 2-4 people) $25-$42 (more for porterhouse steaks and lobsters). AE, DC, DISC, MC, V. Mon 11:30am-11pm; Tues and Thurs-Fri 11:30am-midnight; Wed and Sat 11am-midnight; Sun 11am-11pm. Subway: N, Q, R, S, W, 1, 2, 3, 7 to 42nd St./Times Square.

Carnegie Deli DELI A classic delicatessen restaurant, straight out of Woody Allen's *Broadway Danny Rose,* the Carnegie Deli may borrow its name from nearby Carnegie Hall, but the atmosphere is anything but refined and stuffy. Every table has a little bowl of crisp dill pickles on it, and the sandwiches are piled so high you can hardly get your mouth around them—corned beef, pastrami, brisket, chopped liver, the works, with Russian dressing the condiment of choice. You can also get kosher dairy dishes like blintzes, pirogi, and matzo brei, or eastern European home cooking like chicken paprikash, Hungarian goulash, and stuffed cabbage. The menu is as huge as the servings. Ya wanna know what New York was like in the '40s and '50s? Come here; order an egg cream, borscht, or gefilte fish; and schmooze away.

854 Seventh Ave. (btwn 54th and 55th sts.). ✆ **212/757-2245.** www.carnegiedeli.com. Highchairs, boosters. No reservations. Breakfast $8-$13; sandwiches and main courses $16-$23. No credit cards. Daily 6:30am-4am. Subway: B, D, E to Seventh Ave.

Ellen's Stardust Diner ★ DINER Enter this *Happy Days*–style diner through what looks like a vintage red subway car, and you're in a nostalgic time warp—streamlined chrome trim, turquoise vinyl and Formica, vintage movie posters and ads, and a wall full of subway posters introducing a bevy of Miss Subways (owner Ellen Hart was herself voted Miss Subways in 1959). A model train zips around on an elevated track above diners' heads, and TV monitors show old black-and-white TV shows. The food—your basic grab bag of burgers and fries, salads, omelets, tacos, and club sandwiches—tastes decent and comes in good-size portions; Nick at Niters may get a kick out of the cutesy names for menu items, like Fred Mertz-arella Sticks or the Cesar Romero Salad. The waitstaff is supercongenial, and Wednesday through Saturday nights they even sing, as part of a slightly goofy dinner-hour floor show.

1650 Broadway (at 51st St.). ✆ **212/956-5151.** www.ellensstardustdiner.com. Kids' menu, highchairs, boosters. Reservations accepted only for groups of 10 or more. Breakfast $3-$10; lunch and dinner entrees $7-$24; kids' menu $9.50. AE, DISC, MC, V. Mon-Thurs 7am-midnight; Fri-Sat 7am-1am; Sun 7am-11pm. Subway: 1 to 50th St.

Hard Rock Cafe AMERICAN/BURGERS Right in the pulsing heart of Times Square, under a big revolving neon guitar, this brassy burger joint promotes its rock-'n'-roll theme with such stellar memorabilia as a pair of John Lennon's wire-rims with

The West 56th Street stretch between Fifth and Sixth avenues is particularly rich in places to grab a picnic lunch to eat in nearby Central Park or sit down for a relaxing meal. It's also close to many Midtown hotels, which makes this a convenient destination for evening meals or even takeout to eat in your room. If the street has a restaurant anchor, it's likely to be **Benihana** (see above). Otherwise, it's a veritable U.N of culinary choices: Terrific Chinese soup dumplings are the specialty at the midtown offshoot of **Joe's Shanghai** (24 W. 56th St.; ✆ 212/333-3868; www.joeshanghairestaurants.com), and the comforting and inexpensive Japanese ramen (noodle) soups are winter warmers at **Men Kui Tei** (60 W. 56th St.; ✆ 212/757-1642). Get tapas-style "modern Korean" at **Chom Chom** (40 W. 56th St.; ✆ 212/213-2299; www.chomchomny.com). For sushi, there's **Ise** (58 W. 56th St.; ✆ 212/707-8702). Sample the lunch buffet at the Indian brasserie **Bay Leaf** (15 W. 56th St.; ✆ 212/957-1818; www.bayleafnyc.com) or have a leisurely Northern Italian meal in the old-school environs of **Il Tinello** (16 W. 56th St.; ✆ 212/245-4388). Reliable **Hale and Hearty Soups** has a branch (with tables) at 55 W. 56th St. (✆ 212/245-9200). And if your kids are adventurous, snag a reservation at star chef David Chang's newest venture, **Ma Peche**, a Franco-Asian culinary stew in the Chambers Hotel (15 W. 56th St.; ✆ 212/757-5878).

a cracked lens, a red feather boa of Janis Joplin's, Jimi Hendrix's purple velvet suit, and a complete set of collarless suits worn by the Beatles on the *Ed Sullivan Show.* Various trippy 1960s slogans pepper the place, scripted in neon or proclaimed on posters, but the target audience isn't baby boomers nostalgic for Woodstock: It's teenagers, who regard the place as a museum of their parents' goofy past. Despite its lowbrow Disneyland-ish cachet, the Hard Rock is really not so bad; the burgers and milkshakes are perfectly fine, the prices aren't out of sight, and there's something infectious about the blaring rock soundtrack. And if you've got teenagers in tow, the fact that the place is packed with callow teenagers might even be a plus. (Unless, of course, your teenager is too sophisticated for the place already.)

1501 Broadway (btwn 43rd and 44th sts.). ✆ **212/343-3355.** www.hardrock.com. Reservations accepted for groups of 15 or more only. Main courses $7.95–$14. AE, DC, DISC, MC, V. Sun–Thurs 11am-12:30am; Fri-Sat 8-10am and 11am-1:30am; Sun 8-10am. Subway: N, Q, R, S, W, 1, 2, 3, 7 to 42nd St./Times Square.

La Bonne Soupe ★ 🍴 FRENCH   This is a cozy, charming bistro, French but not snooty, that truly welcomes *les enfants.* The quiches are splendid, as is the onion soup gratinée, and there are a few fine fondue dishes (talk about throwbacks). Omelets, salads, and filet mignon fill out the menu. The "junior menu" offers hamburger, cheeseburger, or chicken breast with french fries and dessert. There are two floors, the lower one softly lit and paneled, the cheery upper floor more like an Alpine chalet, checkered tablecloths and all. Service isn't speedy, but it's pleasant. This is a nice change of pace from the pounding, pulsating theme-restaurant experience.

48 W. 55th St. (btwn Fifth and Sixth aves.). ✆ **212/586-7650.** www.labonnesoupe.com. Kids' menu. Reservations recommended. Main courses $14–$26; kids' menu $11. AE, MC, V. Mon–Thurs 11:30am-11pm; Fri-Sat 11:30am-11:30pm; Sun 11:30am-10:30pm. Subway: F, N, Q, R, W to 57th St./Seventh Ave.

Mickey Mantle's AMERICAN   Young fans hungering for a brush with 21st-century athletic celebrity may not get the point of this sleek blond-wood sports shrine owned by the late, great baseball star Mickey Mantle: The autographed jerseys hanging on the walls belonged to Ted Williams, Hank Aaron, Stan Musial, Yogi Berra, and Joe DiMaggio, names from long-ago baseball cards, back in the days when they gave you bubble gum with your cards. Oh, yeah, there's a Shaquille O'Neal autographed basketball, but who's this Johnny Unitas whose name is scrawled on the football next to it? Of course, with 28 high-def LCD screens transmitting daily sports events, it's hard to live in the past. Still, the atmosphere is friendly and casual, and the menu has a sprinkling of grown-up dishes like grilled yellowfin tuna, New York strip, three-pepper-crusted chicken, and lobster ravioli with grilled shrimp. Most of the food is studiedly down-home, however, including Mick's own picks: chicken-fried steak, Texas barbecued ribs, and grilled sirloin chili with blue-corn tortillas. The Little League menu has the usual range of chicken fingers, grilled cheese, spaghetti, and burgers.

42 Central Park South (btwn Fifth and Sixth aves.). ⓒ **212/688-7777**. www.mickeymantles.com. Kids' menu, highchairs, boosters. Reservations recommended. Main courses $15–$32; kids' menu $9.95. AE, DC, DISC, MC, V. Sun–Thurs 11:30am–10pm; Fri–Sat 11:30am–11pm. Subway: N, R, W to Fifth Ave./59th St.

Planet Hollywood 🖐 AMERICAN   The Times Square location makes this movie-themed restaurant more convenient for tourists than when it was on 57th Street, but it has lost much of its pizazz. Large display cases in the high-ceilinged rooms feature a thinned-out collection of film memorabilia (with the nationwide proliferation of Planet Hollywoods, there must have been little to go around); what's left is mostly costumes and weapons from movies you've never heard of. Forget the classics: We're talking music videos and action movies (no surprise, considering that the founders were Bruce Willis, Sylvester Stallone, and Arnold Schwarzenegger). Service is lackluster, and the menu is squarely middle-of-the-road, with hamburgers, steaks, and grilled fish. On the plus side, the restaurant is big enough that you may not have to wait in line to get in, especially if you go before 8pm, and there's a kids' menu of standards like spaghetti and meatballs, chicken tenders, and pizza. The dramatic central room still has a bit of buzz, though the upstairs bar seems to be where it's happening.

1540 Broadway (at 45th St.). ⓒ **212/333-7827**. www.planethollywood.com. Kids' menu, highchairs, boosters. No reservations. Main courses $13–$29; kids' menu $8. AE, DC, DISC, MC, V. Sun–Thurs 8am–midnight; Fri–Sat 8am–1am. Subway: N, Q, R, S, W, 1, 2, 3, 7 to 42nd St./Times Square.

Sarabeth's Central Park South ★★ AMERICAN   This warm, handsome restaurant is a welcome break from the Midtown glut of theme eateries. It has more than a touch of smart Deco decor, with swanky zebra-pattern banquettes and chairs. It's part of the Sarabeth's Kitchen empire, which began in 1981 as a bakery and jam shop on the Upper West Side. It's open for breakfast, lunch, and dinner, and I recommend them all—the food here is delicious, made with fresh, seasonal ingredients, and comforting all at once. You and the kids will love the free-range-chicken potpie and the mini bacon-cheeseburgers. The Central Park Cobb salad here comes with lobster, crabmeat, and shrimp—zowie! And the breads, baked goods, and desserts, of course, are divine. Finish with a Sarabeth's cookie plate for the kids and a double chocolate pudding for yourself.

40 Central Park South (btwn Fifth and Sixth aves.). ⓒ **212/826-5959**. www.sarabethscps.com. Highchairs, boosters. Reservations recommended. Main courses $15–$27; prix-fixe menu $35. AE, MC, V. Mon–Sat 8am–11pm; Sun 8am–4pm and 5–10pm. Subway: N, R, W to Fifth Ave./59th St.

You may have noticed that an overwhelming number of pizza places in New York have the name Ray somewhere in the title: Famous Ray's, World Famous Ray's, Famous Original Ray's, Original Ray's, Ray's Famous, Ray's House of Pizza, Ray's Real Pizza. Most of these are trying to cash in on the success of Famous Ray's Pizza of Greenwich Village, where you'll often have to stand in line just to buy a slice to go. (Considering the equal popularity of the Village's John's of Bleecker Street, it could just as easily have been that every pizzeria in town was named John's.) Litigation has been useless in trying to convince these lesser Rays to change their names. Just for fun, ask your kids to keep a running log of Ray sightings as they ramble around the city—you may be surprised by how many they'll turn up.

Virgil's Real Barbecue ★ AMERICAN/BARBECUE   Your cutlery is wrapped in a maroon hand towel atop the plastic tablecloth, which tells you all you need to know about Virgil's—this is barbecue, and you're expected to get messy eating it. Along with the wood-smoked barbecued specialties, you get sides of down-home stuff like turnip greens, a slaw made with mustard greens, and buttery cornbread, as well as more mainstream choices like french fries and coleslaw for folks whose home isn't below the Mason-Dixon line. Kids who can't handle ribs are offered some safer choices, like grilled cheese and hot dogs. The decor is roadhouse chic, with polished wood paneling, ceiling fans, and a clutter of vintage livestock photos. Casual and friendly as it is, Virgil's has a postmodern self-consciousness—come on, that woodpile inside the front door is not there just to stoke the barbecue. But you might as well play along with the game when the food is this good and this hearty.

152 W. 44th St. (btwn Broadway and Sixth Ave.). ℂ **212/921-9494.** www.virgilsbbq.com. Kids' menu, highchairs, boosters. Reservations recommended. Main courses $17–$34; kids' menu $5.95. AE, DC, MC, V. Mon 11am–11pm; Tues–Fri 11:30am–midnight; Sat 9am–midnight; Sun 9am–11pm. Subway: N, Q, R, S, W, 1, 2, 3, 7 to 42nd St./Times Square.

Inexpensive

Prime Burger ★ 🍴 AMERICAN/BURGERS/DINER   Behind an unprepossessing Midtown coffee shop facade is this amazing slice of the 1950s (Truman Capote mentions it in *Breakfast at Tiffany's* under its former name, Hamburg Heaven). The decor is all chrome and Formica and fake wood paneling, with a long counter and spinning stools. Food is served on melamine plates, drinks come in plastic tumblers, and your order gets to your table unbelievably fast, all of which makes this great for young ones. But what kids may remember best are the seats at the front, which have wooden trays you swing in front of you in lieu of a table. The hand-formed hamburgers are small—maybe 5 inches in diameter—a welcome relief from most diners' too-big-to-finish wads of ground beef. French fries are crisp, tasty, and perfectly salted. The menu has many other offerings (chicken in a basket, BLTs, club sandwiches, grilled cheese, omelets, even retro choices like canned peaches with cottage cheese), but burgers—and the seats with the trays—are the main event.

5 E. 51st St. (btwn Madison and Fifth aves.). ℂ **212/759-4729.** www.primeburger.com. Kids' menu, highchairs, boosters. DISC, MC, V. Mon–Fri 6am–5pm; Sat 6am–7:30pm; closed Sun. Main courses $4.25–$13; kids' menu $5.95. Subway: 6 to 51st St.

Some say the city has gone meat mad, with steakhouses turning up on every other block and barbecue pits in every neighborhood. But it's the burger joints that are really cooking, with competition for the best patties a boon for burger lovers all over New York. Even top chefs like Daniel Boulud have come up with exquisite (and expensive) versions of the all-American burger at their upscale eateries—but I don't include those fancy joints here. Following are some of the tastiest, juiciest burgers (and kid-friendly burger venues) in the Big Apple.

o **BLT Burger,** 470 6th Ave., at 12th St. (☏ **212/243-8226;** www. bltburger.com). Superchef Laurent Tourondel has created BLT ("Bistro Laurent Tourondel") restaurants all over the city—BLT Fish, for one, and BLT Steak. This is his most casual, family-friendly spot, with succulent burgers. You can order the Classic (5 oz. of certified Black Angus beef), a Kobe beef version, or one made with Colorado lamb.

o **Brgr,** 287 Seventh Ave., at 26th St. (☏ **212/488-7550;** www.brgr. us). These burgers are made to order with top-quality ingredients and all-natural, humanely raised livestock, and it shows. A number of the toppings are even homemade.

o **Corner Bistro,** 331 W. 4th St., btwn Jane St. and Eighth Ave. (☏ **212/242-9502**). This place is a bar, the kind where people huddle in wooden booths and

initials have been carved into the tabletops. Which is precisely why some kids will think it's totally cool to come here; others will simply dig into the thick, juicy burgers and piles of fine fries. And if that's not enough, there's a pretty darn good jukebox.

o **Shake Shack,** Madison Square Park, at 23rd St. and Madison Ave. (☏ **212/889-6660;** www. shakeshacknyc.com). During the week, a long line of office workers snakes outside Danny Meyer's original "roadside food stand" in Madison Square Park. What are they waiting for? Terrific hamburgers, hot dogs, and milkshakes. Come on weekends or during off-hours and enjoy an alfresco picnic on a park bench—this is one of the city's nicest pockets of green. Shake Shack's new locations are: **Upper East Side** (154 E. 86th St., btwn Lexington and Third aves.; ☏ **646/237-5035**); the **Upper West Side** (366 Columbus Ave., at 77th St.; ☏ **646/747-8770**); **Citi Field** (New York Mets stadium; Flushing, Queens); and **Midtown** (691 Eighth Ave., at 44th St.; ☏ **646/435-0135**).

o **Stand,** 24 E. 12th St., University Place and Fifth Ave. (☏ **212/488-5900;** www.standburger.com). Not only can you get a regular-size classic burger here, but you also can order the mini version, a perfectly cooked, kid-size slider on a brioche roll for $4.

Stage Deli ★ DELI   Doggedly trying to compete with the **Carnegie Deli** up the street (p. 115), the Stage Deli promotes more of a theatrical connection; besides the requisite black-and-white glossies of stars plastered all over the place, near the door there's a large display case of Polaroids taken of more recent stars (I use the term loosely for folks like Pauly Shore and David Faustino, along with old reliables like Dom DeLuise—who, judging from the number of pictures posted in restaurants around town, must've eaten his way through the city). On many factors—the over-stuffed sandwiches, dill pickles on every table—the Stage Deli competes head-to-head with its rival, and there are some who even claim its corned beef is better; the cheesecake here is smooth as satin and of heroic proportions. The menu is more limited than Carnegie's, sticking mostly to sandwiches. On the whole, the Stage Deli is less atmospheric than the Carnegie, if vintage ambience is what you're after. Lunch and pre-theater hours are crazed, which may mean impatient service, something you don't need when you're with young kids.

834 Seventh Ave. (btwn 53rd and 54th sts.). ℂ 212/245-7850. www.stagedeli.com. Kids' menu, high-chairs. Reservations accepted only for parties of 8 or more. Sandwiches $10–$17; main courses $14–$22; kids' menu $6–$11. AE, DISC, MC, V. Daily 6am–2am. Subway: B, D, E to Seventh Ave.

Pizza

Angelo's Coal Oven Pizza ★ ITALIAN/PIZZA   Yet another claimant to the title of New York's most authentic pizza. With ties to the Patsy's dynasty, Angelo's (which is actually run by Angelo's nephew, John) is an upscale two-level pizzeria dishing up crisp thin-crust pies as well as calzones, salads, and pastas. The glossy decor features wood trim, green marble-topped tables, and parchment yellow walls; you can't get just a single slice of pizza here, but you can get a superb cannoli. I still wouldn't rate it as high as John's (see below), but it's an excellent choice for a Midtown meal. You can order pastas individual or family-style.

(1) 117 W. 57th St. (btwn Sixth and Seventh aves.). ℂ 212/333-4333. Subway: F, N, Q, R, W to 57th St./Seventh Ave.; B, D, E to Seventh Ave. (2) 1043 Second Ave. (at 55th St.). ℂ 212/521-3600. Subway: E, V to Lexington Ave./53rd St. (3) 1697 Broadway (at 53rd St.). ℂ 212/245-8811. Subway: E, V to Lexington Ave./53rd St. www.angelospizzany.com. Pizzas $15–$17; pasta courses (individual) $9.95–$17. AE, MC, V. Daily 11:30am–11pm.

John's Times Square ★★ ITALIAN/PIZZA   As good as all the John's Pizzeria branches are (p. 110 and 126), this one deserves special mention because it fills such a need in the Theater District for a quick, unpretentious, fabulous meal. The simple, white-walled space is stunning, too, a two-story dining room converted from a church, with a stained-glass dome in its upper reaches. Pizzas slide out of the brick ovens with incredibly thin, crisp crusts; the satisfying green salads are huge enough for two; and the stuffed homemade rolls are a special treat. They don't take reservations, so expect up to an hour's waiting time in the height of the pre-theater crush; but the food's worth it, and service is prompt enough to get you out before your curtain.

260 W. 44th St. (btwn Broadway and Eighth Ave.). ℂ 212/391-7560. Highchairs, boosters. No reservations. Pizzas $12–$18, toppings $2–$4.75; pastas $8.95–$14. AE, MC, V. Daily 11:30am–11:30pm. Subway: N, Q, R, S, W, 1, 2, 3, 7 to 42nd St./Times Square; A, C, E to 42nd St./Port Authority.

Food Court

The **Grand Central Dining Concourse** ★★ (Mon–Sat 7am–9pm; Sun 11am–6pm) is definitely a smart option, even if you're not taking a train into or out of the city. The globe-spanning assortment of vendors aren't the usual tired food-court chains but respected New York restaurants coaxed into this high-profile location, so expect to eat well. There's loads of seating under the cool marble arches, and a few of the participating restaurants, like **Two Boots** (pizza and Cajun food), **Zocalo** (trendy Mexican), and **Junior's** (classic deli), have sit-down table-service areas as well as carryout. I highly recommend it.

CHELSEA, THE FLATIRON DISTRICT & GRAMERCY PARK

Expensive

Mesa Grill ★ SOUTHWESTERN It's sprawling, colorful, and noisy—just the right environment for hungry and exuberant families. Mesa Grill has been a presence on lower Fifth Avenue for more than 20 years, and that's real staying power in a city that chews up and spits out restaurants for sport. The food is flavorful Southwestern, with lots of kid-pleasing dishes; the Mesa Burger comes with lightly spiced fries and the smoked shrimp tacos come with grilled tortillas. The high ceiling absorbs the buzzing chatter, and colorful seats camouflage spills—it's a fizzy, fun place to dine.

102 Fifth Ave. (btwn 15th and 16th sts.). ✆ **212/807-7400.** www.mesagrill.com. Highchairs, booster seats. Reservations recommended. Main courses $22–$39. AE, DISC, MC, V. Mon–Fri noon–2:30pm and 5:30–10:30pm (to 11pm Fri); Sat 11:30am–2:30pm and 5–11pm; Sun 11:30am–3pm and 5:30–10:30pm Subway. N, R, 4, 5, 6, L to 14th St/Union Square.

Moderate

Blue Smoke ★★ AMERICAN/BARBECUE Danny Meyer set out to make an authentic barbecue restaurant in New York City, and even devised a way to smoke his own barbecue on the premises, a near-impossible trick to pull off in a city of 1,001 permits. The result is a bustling, high-ceilinged space where the scent of barbecued meats is irresistible and big, wide booths are just right for families. It's a casual, sunny place with a menu that represents the best of regional American barbecue, with Memphis-style ribs, Texas beef ribs, Carolina pulled pork, and Kansas City spareribs. Children get the royal treatment here, and the kids' menu includes one entree (grilled salmon, grilled cheese, elbow pasta with butter or mac 'n' cheese, or Memphis baby backs), one side, dessert, and a drink—and for each kids' menu ordered, Blue Smoke will donate $1 to the nonprofit STREETS International, which provides aid and culinary training to street kids in developing countries.

116 E. 27th St. (btwn Park and Lexington aves.). ✆ **212/447-7733.** www.bluesmoke.com. Kids' menu, highchairs. Reservations recommended. Main courses $12–$37; kids' menu $9.50. Sun–Mon 11:30am–10pm; Tues–Thurs 11:30am–11pm; Fri–Sat 11:30–1am. Subway: 6 to 28th St.

The City Bakery ★★ AMERICAN How about a place that fuses our best and most endearing culinary impulses? Where you can dine on delicious food that is both comforting and healthful and environmentally sustainable, much of it plucked from the morning's greenmarket in Union Square? Where gigantic, hot-out-of-the-oven

---

The (Homegrown) Chain Gang: Craft & Company

You could hardly call chef Tom Colicchio's handful of Craft eateries a chain; they bear no kinship to industrial fast food. Among the city's most admired family-friendly dining options, Colicchio's award-winning flagship **Craft** (43 E. 19th St.; ✆ 212/780-0880), the more casual **Craftbar** (900 Broadway; ✆ 212/461-4300), and the even more casual sandwich shops **'wichcraft** (multiple locations; www.wichcraftnyc.com) provide impeccably sourced and reliably tasty seasonal food. All welcome families; Craft even has highchairs. For details, go to www.craftrestaurant.com.

chocolate chip cookies are not a guilty indulgence but an essential part of living, like air? Even better: This award-winning bakery/restaurant is one of the most kid-friendly lunch spots in town, with homemade fried chicken, syrup-soaked slabs of French toast, mac 'n' cheese, minipizzas, and an actual spinning wheel of chocolate. City Bakery is officially a "salad bar," but I bet you've never seen one like this one, piled high with bowls of homemade vegetables and pastas, cornmeal-crusted catfish, and lovingly fried chicken. I love the green beans dressed in mustard oil, curry leaf, and shaved coconut; the Old Bay chicken wings; the jasmine rice tossed with preserved Asian beans and Thai basil; and the pretzel croissants. On weekends the place is jumping with merry bands of kids, their Bugaboo strollers tucked neatly under the stairs.

3 W. 18th St. (btwn Fifth and Sixth aves.). ✆ **212/366-1414.** www.thecitybakery.com. Highchairs, toddlers' picnic table. No reservations. Salad bar $13/lb.; soups $4–$7; sandwiches $5–$10. AE, MC, V. Mon–Fri 7:30am–7pm; Sat 8am–7pm; Sun 10am–6pm. Subway: N, R, 4, 5, 6 to 14th St.

Hill Country ★★ BARBECUE   For us transplanted country folk, this place comes mighty close to feeling like home. It's got a spiffed-up Texas roadhouse feel, with lots of gleaming wood and splintered sunlight. It's family-friendly as all get-out, the kind of place where you can eat well and get messy in the process. Just grab the roll of paper towels adorning your table and give Junior a thorough mop-up before you leave. Did I mention that it's family-friendly? The brisket is justly admired, as are the smoked burgers. If kids don't go for barbecue, they can easily fill up on the substantial sides: Longhorn cheddar mac 'n' cheese, corn pudding, campfire beans, and cornbread. Hill Country offers economical weekly specials; families head to the trough for "Feed Your Family Sundays."

30 W. 26th St. (btwn Fifth and Sixth aves.). ✆ **212/255-4544.** www.hillcountryny.com. Highchairs, booster seats. Reservations recommended. Main courses $15–$30. AE, MC, V. Sun–Wed noon–10pm; Thurs–Sat noon–11pm; Sun 10am–6pm. Subway: N, R, 6 to 28th St.

Inexpensive

Chat 'n' Chew ★ AMERICAN   Here's another one of those places with (nudge, nudge) "down-home" decor—red-painted floors, dark-stained wood, farm implements and road signs on the walls—and yuck-it-up menu items like the Caesar Romero Salad, Uncle Red's Addiction (honey-dipped fried chicken), Not Your Mother's Meatloaf, and the Holy Cow (a 9-oz. hamburger). But, hey, the food is actually good and the staff warm and friendly. The fried catfish po' boy is especially moist and delicious, and the meatloaf comes with "skin on" smashed potatoes. Kids get offered a fairly standard menu of favorites, but the names will intrigue them: Flying Saucer Pancakes, for example, or Tarzan Sticks (chicken fingers).

10 E. 16th St. (btwn Fifth Ave. and Union Square W.). ✆ **212/243-1616.** www.chatnchewnewyorkcity. com. Kids' menu, highchairs, boosters. No reservations. Main courses $10–$16; kids' menu $5.95 at brunch, $6.95 at lunch and dinner. AE, MC, V. Mon–Fri 11am–midnight; Sat 10am–midnight; Sun 10am–11pm. Subway: N, R, W, 4, 5, 6 to 14th St.; L to Union Square.

Pete's Tavern ★ ITALIAN   If authenticity means something to you (and it does to us), then bypass those artificially concocted theme joints and discover a real slice of old New York. The restaurant has been a tavern since 1864, when it entertained such luminaries as O. Henry, who, in the first booth by the front doors, wrote the classic short story "Gift of the Magi"—a delicious story-time tale for kids if ever there was one. Pete's food is basic red-sauce Italian, and the bar can get a bit rowdy when the frat boys take over; but it's a grand place for kids—even if, as the salty manager said, "we got no balloons, no coloring books." There's no kids' menu, either, just gen-u-ine kids' food: spaghetti with meatballs, burgers, chicken wings, fried zucchini, and fries. It's stroller central during weekend brunches (10:30am–4pm).

129 E. 18th St. (at Irving Place). ✆ **212/473-7676.** www.petestavern.com. Highchairs. Reservations accepted. Dinner main courses $12–$25; lunch main courses $7–$23; brunch $9.95. AE, DISC, MC, V. Daily 11–2:30am. Subway: 4, 5, 6 to 14th St.

Rodeo Bar BARBECUE/TEX-MEX   Someone had a lot of fun decorating this bi-level space, with the feed-grain silo on the upper landing and the huge stuffed bison on a ledge above the bar. The weathered-wood walls are hung with old highway signs and lots of animal horns; Western music twangs, and a basket of taco chips arrives on your table in a flash. Children are a welcome part of the mix—on Monday night they even eat free. The menu is heavy on burgers, steaks, barbecue, fajitas, and burritos, but there are a fair number of vegetarian items and a short list of salads as well. French fries come piled high.

375 Third Ave. (at 27th St.). ✆ **212/683-6500.** www.rodeobar.com. Kids' menu, highchairs, boosters. Reservations accepted. Main courses $13–$20; kids' menu $7 (kids eat free Mon night). AE, DISC, MC, V. Daily 11am–4am. Subway: 6 to 28th St.

Food Court

Definitely the coolest place to eat in Chelsea is at **Chelsea Market ★★**, 75 Ninth Ave., between 15th and 16th streets (www.chelseamarket.com; Mon–Fri 7am–9pm; Sat–Sun 10am–8pm), a rambling series of food shops set in a rehabbed Nabisco factory. Older kids with a sense of style will appreciate the industrial-chic look, with scrubbed brick walls, exposed pipes, and utilitarian light fixtures; the focal point is a

Food Zone Union Square: East 17th Street

Sandwiched between Union Square, Broadway, and lower Fifth Avenue, this street is crammed with casual but cool restaurants and takeout joints. On a warm day, you can take your food over to Union Square, which has a big, leafy lawn with public tables and chairs and one of the city's most innovative playgrounds. You can get savory soups, salads, and sandwiches at both Café Medina (9 E. 17th St.; ✆ 212/242-2777) and Hale and Hearty Soups (11 E. 17th St.; ✆ 212/675-6611). Join the lines for made-to-order salads at Chop't (24 E. 17th St.; ✆ 646/336-5523; www.chopt salad.com). Artisanal hot dogs and sausages are on tap at Dogmatic (26 E. 17th St.; ✆ 212/414-0600). Adventurous kids can take a trip around the world with Malaysian and Thai specialties at Laut (15 E. 17th St.; ✆ 212/206-8989; www.lautnyc.com); takeout Japanese at Ennju (20 E. 17th St.; ✆ 646/336-7004); Cuban paella at Havana Central (22 E. 17th St.; ✆ 212/414-4999); and Middle Eastern baba ghanouj and hummus at tiny Rainbow Falafel (26 E. 17th St.; ✆ 212/691-8641). Healthy eaters will make a beeline for the additive-free sandwiches, salads, and soups at Pret à Manger (857 Broadway; ✆ 646/572-8010; www.pret.com/us), and just south around the corner are Heartland Brewery (hearty American food and artisanal beer; 35 Union Square W.; ✆ 212/645-3400) and Republic (pan-Asian noodles; 37 Union Square W.; ✆ 212/627-7172). Oh, and the Big Gay Ice Cream Truck (www.biggayicecream truck.com) is generally parked on the corner of 17th and Broadway for state-of-the-art sundaes and ice cream cones.

ripped-open water main gushing into a crumbling brick cavity in the floor. Among fish stores and produce stalls, you'll find top-quality takeout eateries like Hale and Hearty Soups, Amy's Bread, Sarabeth's Bakery, Buon Italia, Fat Witch Bakery, and the Lobster Place, all with tiny cafe tables nearby where you can enjoy the food.

GREENWICH VILLAGE

Expensive

Blue Ribbon Bakery ★★ AMERICAN   This neighborhood favorite is rarely anything but a sure thing when it comes to flavorful American-bistro food—the standards here are cooked to perfection. Blue Ribbon Bakery is part of the Blue Ribbon mini-empire, with Blue Ribbon Brasserie and Blue Ribbon Sushi nearby. All are worthy dining experiences, although the Bakery feels like the most kid-friendly of the bunch. It's set in a casual, candlelit space with glass windows surveying narrow Village streets. We were there on Friday date night, when the place was packed with couples and groups of young urban professionals—and smack-dab in the center was a table with small kids who were comfortable and happy and generally fawned over by the excellent waitstaff. The menu features plenty of dishes grown-ups will love (rack of lamb, duck confit, New Orleans–style barbecue shrimp), but it also manages to have kid-pleasing food on hand, such as fried chicken and hamburgers. You could make a dinner out of the extensive selection of small plates, and the excellent wine list is three pages deep. If you have a large group, ask for one of the rooms downstairs, an atmospheric enclave enveloped in 19th-century brick walls. The 135-year-old brick oven was discovered in the basement in 1995; it was beautifully restored, and the restaurant was basically built around it. The oven still cranks out homemade breads, crostini, and other baked delicacies.

35 Downing St. (at Bedford St.). © **212/337-0404.** www.blueribbonrestaurants.com. Highchairs. Reservations accepted for parties of 5 or more. Main courses $15–$37. AE, DC, DISC, MC, V. Mon–Thurs noon–midnight; Fri noon–2am; Sat 11:30am–2am; Sun 11:30am–midnight. Subway: A, B, C, D, E, F to W. 4th St.

Knickerbocker Bar & Grill ★★ AMERICAN/STEAKHOUSE   This cozy neighborhood throwback is always percolating and displays a sure hand with children; the kitchen is happy to whip up a plain buttered pasta for finicky eaters. Kids gravitate to the curvy leather banquettes that line the softly lit walls. The burgers are terrific, and grownups can sample one of downtown's top T-bone steaks ★ and inventive pastas, savory ribs, and other impeccably grilled butcher cuts. Be sure to bring the kids around Halloween, when the restaurant is spectacularly decorated.

33 University Place (at 9th St.). © **212/228-8490.** www.knickerbockerbarandgrill.com. High chairs, boosters. Main courses $16–$40. AE, DC, DISC, MC, V. Daily 11:45am–midnight (till 1am Tues–Thurs; till 2am Fri–Sat). Subway: N, R, W to 8th St./NYU; 6 to Astor Place.

Morandi ★★ ITALIAN   Eating at restaurateur Keith McNally's 2007 re-creation of a rustic Italian trattoria makes us really happy. It's a sunny spot, both inside and out, with a congenial staff, hearty regional Italian cooking, and the easygoing feel of an outdoor cafe on a Roman piazza. It's become a real neighborhood spot, with a sprinkling of actors, models, and moguls relaxing with their families and having a good time. Lunchtime is a fine time to come on a sun-dappled day; the evening becomes more of a scene, but really, this is one of those places that isn't trying so hard to scale the hip-o-meter—which makes it pretty cool in our book. We love the pesto pasta with green beans and potatoes, and the fried artichokes are first-rate. Kids of all ages are welcome here—dogs, too (outside only, of course)—and the tagliatelle Bolognese is a surefire winner for the little ones. It's now open for real Italian-style breakfasts—how about crepes with Nutella to start your day?

211 Waverly Place (at Charles St.). ✆ 212/627-7575. www.morandiny.com. Highchairs. Reservations recommended. Main courses $16–$29. AE, MC, V. Mon–Fri 8–11:30am and noon–midnight; Sat–Sun 10am–4pm; Sat 5:30–midnight; Sun 4:30–11pm. Subway: 1, 2, 3 to 14th St.; 1 to Christopher St.; A, B, C, D, E, F, V to W. 4th St.

Moderate

Arturo's Pizzeria ITALIAN/PIZZA   Crowded, dimly lit, and busy, this vintage hangout is right on the border between the Village and SoHo around Father Demo Square. It's a fun place to bring the family because it's the opposite of buttoned-down: It's a little raucous (some say lively), a little cramped (some say cozy), and old-school colorful, with corny still-life paintings a-kilter on the walls. Kids fit right in with the mix. Arturo's serves decent thin-crust pizzas; they're slung on your table fresh from a coal-fired oven, so hot the mozzarella could burn the roof of your mouth. You can get various pasta dishes too (go for the baked stuff like ziti and lasagna), but it's the pizzas you're here for. It's a casual sort of red-checkered-tablecloth place where drinks come in plastic tumblers and side salads come in plastic fake-wood bowls, which bodes well if you've got kids in tow. You may have to wait in line, though, and at particularly frantic mealtimes, it can be hard to get your waiter's attention. There's live jazz every night, which may make waiting easier. Arturo's is certainly as authentic as any place officially in Little Italy—and a good deal less touristy.

106 W. Houston St. (at Thompson St.). ✆ **212/677-3820.** Highchairs, boosters. Reservations not accepted on weekends. Pizzas $14 and up; main courses $16–$24. AE, MC, V. Mon–Sat 4pm–1am. Subway: 1 to Houston St.

Cowgirl Hall of Fame ★ SOUTHERN/TEX-MEX   Think the Old West motif of this West Village theme spot is corny? You're darn tootin' it's corny, and that's why kids get into it. Cowboy hats, boots, and lassos adorn the walls; steer horns poke from the mirrors and antlers from the chandeliers; younger customers are handed crayons to color a paper Indian headdress. Passable barbecue, hearty chili, and a mess of fried catfish are included in the menu roundup; kids' options feature some offbeat items such as corn dogs and Frito pie, along with the obligatory chicken fingers. You can sit outdoors in nice weather.

519 Hudson St. (at 10th St.). ✆ **212/633-1133.** www.cowgirlnyc.com. Kids' menu, highchairs, boosters. Reservations recommended. Lunch entrees $8.95–$15; dinner entrees $15–$20; kids' menu $4.50 $6.25. AE, MC, V. Mon–Fri 11am–11pm (to midnight Fri); Sat 10am–midnight; Sun 10am–11pm. Subway: 1 to Christopher St./Sheridan Square.

Otto ★ PIZZA   This sprawling, handsome space is always bubbling with chatter. It's a bustling place, with groups of friends and families happily munching on thin-crust pizza at big, round tables. Star chef Mario Batali and Company made an instant success of this space, which despite its sleek Deco bones never quite made it in its previous incarnations (remember One Fifth? Clementine?). Despite the prevalence of smart-looking young professionals, this is a great family restaurant (it was even named for the owners' combined eight children: *otto* is Italian for 8), with bubbling-hot pizzas, a sprinkling of simple pastas, *contorni* such as eggplant caponatina, Tuscan lentils, roasted beets, and fabulous handmade gelato to finish. The kitchen is happy to do a basic pasta with marinara sauce for children. The front of the restaurant is an *enoteca* designed to look like an Italian train station—it's a beaut.

One Fifth Ave. (entrance on 8th St.). ✆ **212/995-9559.** www.ottopizzeria.com. Highchairs, boosters. Reservations recommended. Pizza $7–$14; pasta $9; salad $8–$16. AE, DISC, MC, V. Daily 11:30am–midnight. A, B, C, D, E, F, V to W. 4th St.

Sweetiepie ★AMERICAN   Don't let the high-fructose decor turn you away. With padded pink banquettes, walls of mirrors, and a gilded birdcage in the window, Sweetiepie feels like an old-timey soda shop plumped up on estrogen. But wait: That's a real bar there, no? And it's actually quite comfy and nicely lighted, with energetic pastel wall murals. It's entirely whimsical, and kids love it. The thoughtful menu offers something for everyone, from mac 'n' cheese and spaghetti and meatballs to terrific salads and a smart cocktail list.

19 Greenwich Ave., btw. Christopher & 10th St. ✆ **212/337-3333.** www.sweetiepierestaurant.com. Highchairs and boosters. Reservations recommended. Main courses $15–$20. AE, MC, V. Daily noon–10pm (to 11pm Fri); Sat 10am–midnight; Sun 10am–10pm.

Inexpensive

John's of Bleecker Street ★★ ITALIAN/PIZZA   This is the kind of place that's often described as having no ambience, when in fact it has plenty—classic Village pizzeria ambience, with wooden booths, a faded mural of Olde Italy, a vintage tin ceiling, and an open view of the brick ovens where the pizzas are baked. Folks in the Village lament that John's doesn't sell pizza by the slice, but families should have no problem polishing off a whole pie. The crust is crunchy thin, with savory tomato sauce, bubbly melted mozzarella, and a host of fresh toppings to pick among (nothing too trendy, though)—the sausage and mushroom pizzas are particularly good. After eating at John's, you can say you've truly sampled New York pizza at its best. This branch takes no credit cards, but there's a cash machine in the back.

278 Bleecker St. (btwn Seventh Ave. and Morton St.). ✆ **212/243-1680.** www.johnsbrickovenpizza. com. No reservations. Pizzas $12–$14, toppings $2; pasta $8–$11. No credit cards. Mon–Sat 11:30am–midnight; Sun noon–midnight. Subway: to Christopher St./Sheridan Square.

Peanut Butter & Co. AMERICAN   Born of owner Lee Zalben's obsession, this is a quirky little store/restaurant that serves mostly, you guessed it, peanut butter. Peanut butter memorabilia decorates the golden-hued little cafe, and jars of the house brand are for sale, along with jam and Marshmallow Fluff and other suitable accompaniments. The menu's a hoot, with items like Ants on a Log (a celery stalk coated with peanut butter and raisins), your traditional Fluffernutter, and the Elvis (grilled peanut butter sandwich with bananas and honey—top it with bacon if you really want to eat like the King). If you must, you can also get a grilled cheese, a tuna-fish sandwich, or a baloney sandwich, you spoilsport you. But the peanut butter is superb, freshly ground from high-quality peanuts with just enough oil to make it spreadable. Every sandwich is served with potato chips and carrot sticks, and they'll even cut off the crusts for you. You should be drinking milk with your PB&J, but Welch's grape juice is also available, as are fountain treats such as egg creams and PB&J milkshakes. And for dessert, what else but peanut butter cookies or chocolate peanut butter pie?

240 Sullivan St. (btwn Bleecker and W. 3rd sts.). ✆ **212/677-3995.** www.ilovepeanutbutter.com. Kids' menu, highchairs, boosters. Sandwiches $5–$9. AE, DC, DISC, MC, V. Sun–Thurs 11am–9pm; Fri–Sat 11am–10pm. Subway: A, B, C, D, E, F, V to W. 4th St.

Sweet Stuff

ICE CREAM   The West Village has become ground zero for superb ice cream and gelato. Getting fevered press since its 2008 opening is **Grom** (233 Bleecker St., at Carmine St.; ✆ **212/206-1738;** www.grom.it/eng), the Turin-based Italian gelato shop whose product *New York* magazine described as having "the purest, cleanest, freshest flavors." See for yourself, or head down the street to another heralded gelato purveyor, **L'Arte del Gelato** (75 Seventh Ave. S., btwn Bleecker St. and W. 4th St.; ✆ **212/924-0803;** www.lartedelgelato.com), where gelato is made fresh daily.

PASTRIES & COOKIES   Fans of Italian pastries and cookies will find bliss on the traditional Italian strip of Bleecker Street between Sixth and Seventh avenues, where **Rocco's** (243 Bleecker St.; ✆ **212/242-6031;** www.roccospastry.com) still sells pignolia cookies, cannoli, and napoleons. Nearly a century old, **Caffe Dante** (79–81 MacDougal St., btwn Bleecker and Houston sts.; ✆ **866/681-0299;** www.caffe-dante.com) is a vintage Italian cafe where you can sit and rest your feet over strong espresso and Italian pastries.

THE EAST VILLAGE & THE LOWER EAST SIDE

Moderate

Schiller's Liquor Bar ★ CONTINENTAL   James Beard Award–winning restaurateur Keith McNally has done it again, creating an instant neighborhood favorite in this exactingly faithful re-creation of a French bistro. It's a neat trick, coming up with a place that is both hipster- and family-friendly; but, hey, how can you go wrong when you provide the public with warm, stylish surrounds, congenial service, and reliably excellent food? McNally has a knack, says *New York* magazine, for creating "fun, atmospheric places that grow old gracefully," and this is no exception. Hepcats abound in this old immigrant enclave, but Schiller's is a congenial, attitude-free zone where you can order satisfying renditions of roast chicken, steak frites, French onion soup, and Cobb salad. For kids, there are burgers, mac 'n' cheese, fish and chips, and homemade gnocchi.

131 Rivington St. (at Norfolk St.). ✆ **212/260-4555.** www.schillersny.com. Highchairs. Reservations recommended. Main courses $15–$29. AE, DISC, MC, V. Mon–Fri 11am–midnight; Sat–Sun 10am–5pm and 6pm–midnight. Late supper Mon–Thurs midnight–1am; Fri–Sat midnight–3am. Subway: F to Delancey St.; V to Second Ave.

The Smith ★ AMERICAN   Where, oh where did all these folks go before The Smith showed up on this nondescript block on Third Avenue? A solid hit since its opening in early 2008, The Smith cannily hit upon the right formula in a location that never quite gelled with other businesses. Now the spot is packed with diners, a lively, casual, and very congenial place to dine out, with surprisingly good food and a thoughtful menu of grown-up choices such as braised beef short ribs, roasted cod, and tuna tartare. Kids get crayons with which to doodle away almost before they sit down, and the menu is kiddie heaven, especially at breakfast or brunch—the pancakes are killer. At night Mom and Dad can sip a brew from the restaurant's smart selection (Duvel, Allagash White, Bluepoint Toasted Lager) or toast with a glass of good wine while the kids chow down on spaghetti and meatballs, mac 'n' cheese, or the house specialty, beer-battered string beans. Prices are reasonable too.

The ubiquity of the New York hot dog may be due to the century-old Coney Island frankfurter shrine of **Nathan's Famous,** 1310 Surf Ave., Brooklyn (✆ 718/946-2202), site of the annual world hot-dog-eating contest. But a recent crop of East Village hot dog emporiums have been standing Nathan's franks on their ends. **Dawgs on Park,** 178 E. 7th St., near Avenue B (✆ 212/598-0667), has a dog-centric theme, posting photos of customers' dogs; its signature offering is the deep-fried chili dog (beef, turkey, or tofu franks). Its rival is **Crif Dogs,** 113 St. Mark's Place, between First Avenue and Avenue A (✆ 212/614-2728), which has wacky slogans scrawled on the walls and offers over-the-top treats like a deep-fried bacon-wrapped hot dog topped with avocado and jalapeños. The frankfurters dished out at Chelsea's **F&B,** 269 W. 23rd St., between Seventh and Eighth avenues (✆ 646/486-4441), put a European spin on the standard hot dog; a few dollars will buy you beignets and *pommes frites* along with specialties like the Great Dane (a hot dog with rémoulade, roasted onions, and cucumber slices).

Uptown, your hot-doggery choices are more limited and less retro-chic. **Gray's Papaya,** 2090 Broadway, at 72nd Street (✆ 212/799-0243), may not tempt youngsters with its milky, sweet, refreshing papaya juice (there's also fruit punch and soda), but you can't complain about the plump, succulent hot dogs, which still cost about a buck—an absurdly quick and cheap meal, which you can eat stand-up at the counter or on the go as you walk on down the street. Gray's Papaya's Upper East Side counterpart is **Papaya King,** at the northwest corner of 86th Street and Third Avenue (✆ 212/369-0648).

55 Third Ave. (btwn 10th and 11th sts.). ✆ 212/420-9800. www.ctrnyc.com/THESMITH. Highchairs. Reservations recommended. Main courses $15–$29. AE, DISC, MC, V. Mon–Tues 8:30am–midnight; Wed–Thurs 8:30am–1am; Fri 8:30am–2am; Sat 10am–2am; Sun 10am–midnight. Subway: L to Third Ave.; 6 to Astor Place.

Inexpensive

Pommes Frites FRENCH   Not really a restaurant but a narrow storefront takeout joint with a bill of fare that's pretty straightforward: nothing but thin, crispy, Belgian-style french fries with all manner of sauces to dip them into. Considering that many children often eat nothing but fries anyway at sit-down restaurants, this isn't such a bad option for a lunchtime pit stop.

123 Second Ave. (at 9th St.). ✆ 212/674-1234. French fries $4–$7.50. No credit cards. Sun–Thurs 11am–1am; Fri–Sat 11am–3:30am. Subway: 6 to Astor Place.

Two Boots ★ ITALIAN/PIZZA   This dandy East Village restaurant couldn't be better for kids—in fact, it's one of the city's pioneers in serving kid-friendly food in a welcoming environment. To start, you've got witty junk-shop decor (strings of Christmas lights shaped like red chiles, old movie posters, and a pair of cowboy boots hanging on a pink wall); then when you're seated, the kids are handed coloring books. You know these people are used to dealing with kids when you see that the milk is served in plastic cups. The service can be pretty casual, but the waitresses relate to kids instantly, which always seems to make children behave better. For kids, probably the

EATING kosher

Even if you don't maintain a kosher diet, New York offers the best kosher family dining outside of Israel. The important thing to remember is that a kosher restaurant will be meat, dairy, or pareve (*pareve* means the food doesn't contain either meat or dairy products)—you won't find a cheeseburger or chicken parmigiana on any menu unless either the meat or the cheese is really an imitated product. This may sound restricting, but restaurants have learned to make do and become extremely creative in the process. **Note:** Because of the Sabbath, most kosher restaurants vary their hours on Friday and Saturday, depending on when sundown is on Friday night and when the Sabbath ends on Saturday night. (Some simply close all day Fri.) Call ahead to be sure when they'll be open if you plan to dine on Friday or Saturday.

If you're looking for a quick kosher bite, here are a couple of centrally located options: In Midtown, **Kosher Delight,** 1365 Broadway, at 36th Street (✆ 212/563-3366; www.kdexpress.com; meat), is the kosher answer to McDonald's and Burger King. Grilled burgers and chicken sandwiches are standard, but you can also choose from a small Chinese menu and Middle Eastern specialties like falafel. Kosher Delight also has free delivery to any location in Manhattan (although it's not guaranteed your food will arrive hot or within a reasonable amount of time). The **Great American Health Bar,** 35 W. 57th St., between Fifth and Sixth avenues (✆ 212/355-5177; www.greatamerican togo.com; dairy), proves that healthy food doesn't have to be boring and flavorless, offering a varied menu from salads to vegetarian chili to pastas. There are fresh-fruit health shakes blended with milk and yogurt, and kids may get a kick out of the pita pizza—tomato sauce, melted cheese, and vegetables baked on top of pita bread. Unlike most of these restaurants, the Health Bar is the only one of these restaurants that doesn't close Friday night.

most popular choice is the Pizza Face, an individual-sized pizza with vegetables arranged to form eyes, nose, and grin. For the adults, there's a range of salads, heroes, and Cajun-style po' boys. Two Boots now has six locations in the city, including in the Grand Central Dining Concourse.

(1) 37 Ave. A (at 2nd St.). ✆ **212/254-1919.** www.twoboots.com. Highchairs, boosters. Reservations accepted for groups of 6 or more only. Main courses $7.50–$13; pizzas $7.50–$24. AE, DISC, MC, V. Sun–Tues 11:30am–11pm; Wed–Thurs 11:30am–midnight; Fri–Sat 11:30am–2am. Subway: F, V to Lower East Side/Second Ave.

Sweet Stuff

ICE CREAM As the clinical-sounding name suggests, **Il Laboratorio del Gelato** (95 Orchard St., btwn Broome and Delancey sts.; ✆ 212/343-9922; www.laboratorio delgelato.com) takes its ice cream very seriously, and good thing—it's absolutely delicious, with creative flavors like apple cinnamon, bourbon pecan, and Thai chili chocolate. The sun-filled windows and creamy-white wainscoting give **Sundaes and Cones** (95. E. 10th St., btwn Third and Fourth aves.; ✆ 212/979-9398; www.sundaescones. com) an old-fashioned, summer-at-the-beach feel. The homemade ice cream comes in basic and not-so-basic flavors: Ready to try wasabi, red bean, or lychee?

ITALIAN PASTRIES   Two family-owned Italian pastry shops have held on in the East Village for a century, vestiges of an earlier immigrant community—and there's a reason they've survived. The better-known one is **Veniero's,** 342 E. 11th St., between First and Second avenues (② **212/674-7070;** www.venierospastry.com), a spiffed-up dessert cafe that's open until midnight to accommodate crowds of people craving after-dinner delights from cakes to cookies to cannoli, plus cappuccino and espresso that put Starbucks to shame. With kids, come in the afternoon, when you'll have no trouble getting a table. A more relaxed local crowd skips the lines at Veniero's and drifts over to **DeRobertis Pasticceria,** 176 First Ave., between 10th and 11th streets (② **212/674-7137**), which gives its around-the-corner neighbor a run for its money, serving creamy cannoli and cheesecake along with anise cookies and fruit tarts. The back room, with its pressed-tin ceiling and small marble tables, feels as authentic as any place in Little Italy. It shuts down completely for 2 weeks in July—hey, a family's got to take a vacation.

THE MEATPACKING DISTRICT
Expensive

Pastis ★★ FRENCH   Keith McNally's gorgeous re-creation of a Paris brasserie enjoys a picturesque setting on a cobblestone plaza in the Meatpacking District. Its serves terrific bistro fare: steak frites, croques, and salade niçoise. Kids are a big part of the scene, especially during the crowded weekend brunches. In the warm months, there's outdoor seating. The waitstaff is cheerful and attitude free, and kids get crayons to doodle with while they're munching on frites, hamburgers, pasta, or macaroni gratin.

9 Ninth Ave. ② **212/929-4844.** www.pastisny.com. Highchairs. Main courses $16–$35. AE, MC, V. Mon–Fri 8–11:15am and noon–midnight (to 2am Fri); Sat–Sun 10am–4:15pm and 6pm–3am; late-night suppers available after midnight. Subway: A, C, E to 14th St.

LITTLE ITALY & NOLITA

The tourist trade is the bread and butter of this little enclave, and some locals wouldn't be caught dead dining here, pooh-poohing the cookie-cutter pasta-and-red-sauce cuisine, the "O Solo Mio" blaring from storefronts, the Olde Italy decor, the flowery *"grazies"* and *"pregos."* That's a shame, because Little Italy is one of New York's most kid-friendly places to eat, and although the menus are formulaic, the food is generally good quality and sometimes even delicious. The pizzas are surprisingly good. For a kid, it makes for a great show—and hey, what's better than pizza and spaghetti for dinner? During the summer, Mulberry Street is closed off to traffic from Friday at 6pm to Sunday night. A bit of a turnoff: Getting the soft sell up and down Mulberry from maitre d's and restaurant touts trying to coax you into their restaurants.

Expensive

Sal Anthony's S.P.Q.R. ITALIAN   Lots of bustle and elbow room define this vast, high-ceilinged dining hall, where people on all sides are happily digging into Italian food: You can tuck your napkin into your collar here with no fear. Despite the brick walls and potted plants, the look is modern, not vintage trattoria. But what it lacks in coziness and atmosphere, it more than makes up for in efficiency, big portions, and party spirits; it seems there are always a few large tables occupied by extended families, bonding over fusilli and linguine. Pastas are good, as are the hearty meat dishes, especially the macho veal chop.

133 Mulberry St. (btwn Grand and Hester sts.). ☎ **212/925-3120.** www.spqrnyc.com. Highchairs, boosters. Reservations recommended. Three-course fixed-price dinner $30; dinner entrees $19–$37. AE, MC, V. Sun–Thurs noon–11pm; Fri–Sat noon–midnight. Subway: N, Q, R, W, 6 to Canal St.

Moderate

Angelo's of Mulberry Street ITALIAN   This Little Italy favorite, which has been around since 1902, turns out an incredibly long list of southern Italian pasta dishes with zestful flavor, most around $13. Don't be put off by the world-weary waitstaff; that's part of the entertainment. Make a reservation so you won't get stuck in the line of tourists waiting to get in, but don't be dissuaded by the place's lowbrow popularity—this is Little Italy, after all, where tourists flock to eat, and no restaurant here that's any good would be without a line. Order anything with garlic, or anything with tomato sauce. If your kids like their pasta plain, even they'll benefit from the fresh, homemade quality of the food.

146 Mulberry St. (btwn Grand and Hester sts.). ☎ **212/966-1277.** Sassy seats. Reservations recommended. Main courses $12–$17. AE, DC, MC, V. Tues–Thurs and Sun noon–11:30pm; Fri noon–12:30am; Sat noon–1am; closed Mon. Subway: N, Q, R, W, 6 to Canal St.

Caffé Napoli ITALIAN   For a leisurely dinner out with family, Caffé Napoli and its annex, **Trattoria Canta Napoli** (☎ **212/226-8705**), are recommended for their hearty Italian fare—and everyone seems to know it; this place is perpetually packed (good thing the restaurant stretches around the block). The food is upscale enough to feel like a treat, with seafood alongside the pasta dishes (Naples is a seaport, remember); specialties include the stuffed veal chop and the pasta malafemmina. The softly lit dining room has been tastefully decorated—Neapolitan pictures and artifacts are strewn about, but there's no attempt to make it look like the Old Country. Diners are encouraged to linger over their meals; waiters are attentive but not intrusive. And families are definitely welcome—they'll cheerfully do half portions of pasta for kids.

191 Hester St. (at Mulberry St.). ☎ **212/226-8705.** Highchairs. No reservations. Lunch prix fixe $8.50; dinner entrees $10–$34. AE, DC, DISC, MC, V. Daily 11am–2am. Subway: N, Q, R, W, 6 to Canal St.

Focolare ★ ITALIAN   The rustic, dark-wood decor of this handsome, intimate bistro has nothing to do with Olde Italy, garish murals, or rococo flourishes (offenders, you know who you are). It's got a homey stone fireplace. And the food is quality, from the Caesar salad to the pastas and pizzas. It's a pleasant respite from the Little Italy carnival—so does it really have to have its own aggressive tout out front pushing the goods like all the other joints?

115 Mulberry St. (at Canal St.). ☎ **212/993-5858.** Highchairs. Reservations recommended. Main courses $13–$31; pizza $12–$14. AE, MC, V. Sun–Thurs 11:30am–11pm; Fri–Sat 11:30am–midnight. Subway: N, Q, R, W, 6 to Canal St.

Inexpensive

Il Fornaio ITALIAN/PIZZA   The sign outside is explicit: KIDS WELCOME. And it goes without saying, no one will get too upset about spills or crying or food left on the plate in this unpretentious spot. It's small enough that you can't miss the shouted exchanges between waiters and cooks; but the pizza here has a long-standing reputation for excellence, so don't be surprised if you have to wait a few minutes for a table on a weekend. (And once you get in, don't be startled if you're hustled back out again fairly soon—not a bad thing if you're with kids.) Pizza, pasta, calzones, and muffalettas are on the lunch menu—who needs a chicken-fingers-and-burgers kids' menu? Pizza is not served at dinnertime, so settle in with a few pastas to feed the brood.

132A Mulberry St. (btwn Canal and Hester sts.). (C) **212/226-8306.** www.ilfornaionyc.com. Reservations recommended. Main courses $12–$22; pizzas $7–$18. AE, DC, DISC, MC, V. Daily 11:30am–10:30pm. Subway: N, Q, R, W, 6 to Canal St.

Pizza

Sometimes all you want is a quick bite of pizza to fuel you up and send you on your way. For a decent slice, check out **Frankie Cee's Pizza** at the **Italian Food Center** (186 Grand St., at Mulberry St.; (C) **212/925-2954;** cash only); tables are set up outside in nice weather.

Lombardi's Pizza ★ PIZZA Claiming to be a resurrection of New York's first pizza restaurant, which opened at 53 Spring St. in 1905—and where all the other pizza maestros learned their trade—Lombardi's is owned by a grandson of the original Gennaro Lombardi, and it does have an authentic coal oven, taken over from an old bakery. It's a bit north from the main Little Italy strip along Mulberry Street, but the look is nice and atmospheric, with the obligatory red-checkered tablecloths, brick walls, and white tiled floor. Its wonderful pizzas more than hold their own among the top contenders (John's, Patsy's, Angelo's), with lightly charred thin crusts and totally fresh ingredients. The clam pie is so good that it actually justifies the weird idea of putting seafood on a pizza. Don't expect to just pick up a slice: Sit your family down in a booth, and apply yourselves to consuming a whole pie.

32 Spring St. (btwn Mott and Mulberry sts.). (C) **212/941-7994.** www.firstpizza.com. Boosters. Reservations accepted for parties of 6 or more. Pizzas $16–$22. No credit cards. Sun–Thurs 11:30am–11pm; Fri–Sat 11:30am–midnight. Subway: 6 to Spring St.

Sal's Little Italy 📷 PIZZA/PASTA This cozy, modest spot is a little off the beaten track, but it always seems to be packed, and for good reason: The homemade pizzas are tasty and filling. Sal's has been making and serving pizza since 1975, when it was opened by a Neapolitan family in what was then the heart of Little Italy (it's now surrounded by boutiques and Chinese businesses). It serves not only pizzas (and 9-in. minipizzas), but also red-sauce pastas (including lasagna and ravioli), antipasti, and even hearty *secondi* such as shrimp parmigiana and *pollo Marsala*. The walls are filled with photos of the eclectic assortment of celebrities who've dined here, including Sarah Jessica Parker, Mario Batali, Victoria Gotti, and a few wise guys from the *Sopranos*.

369 Broome St. (at Mott St.). (C) **212/925-0440.** www.salslittleitaly.com. Reservations accepted for parties of 6 or more. Pizzas $6–$12; main courses $9.95–$15. AE, DISC, MC, V. Sun–Thurs noon–9:45pm; Fri–Sat noon–10:45pm. Subway: 6 to Spring St.

Sweet Stuff

ICE CREAM **Ciao Bella,** an award-winning premium ice cream found in stores all over the city, has a gelato shop at 285 Mott St., near Houston Street ((C) **212/431-3591;** www.ciaobellagelato.com) and a block from Old St. Patrick's Cathedral. (Once part of Little Italy, the neighborhood is now referred to as Nolita, but it's mere blocks from the restaurants of Little Italy proper.) The gelato is rich, creamy, and flavorful.

ITALIAN PASTRIES   In the heart of shrinking Little Italy, a pair of venerable pastry shops still convey the flavor of the old neighborhood. With its hexagonal-tile floors and tiny wrought-iron cafe tables, **Caffé Roma** ★, 385 Broome St., at the corner of Mulberry Street (© **212/226-8413**), is a great place to duck into for cannoli, those ricotta-filled roll-ups of sweet crisp pastry. Kids can drink frothy hot chocolate or chilled lemonade while parents indulge in cappuccino or espresso, made the classic way (no half-caf mocha double latte here). Follow Mulberry down to Grand Street, and you'll find the somewhat larger and brighter (and more crowded) **Ferrara,** 195 Grand St., between Mulberry and Mott streets (© **212/226-6150**), its refrigerated display cases crowded with mouthwatering pastries to go or to stay. If your kids want to sample Italian gelato (ice cream), this is a good place for that too.

SOHO & NOHO

Expensive

Chinatown Brasserie ★ CHINESE   This place is a treat for young and old alike. It's a big, glamorous space, staged to look like a vintage Chinese banquet hall, with ornate lamps, brasserie tables and chairs, and sexy lighting. Downstairs is a pond filled with koi fish, which never fails to mesmerize my toddler. It offers a slightly modern take on (largely) Cantonese favorites, with an emphasis on lighter and healthier (and pricier). It's kid-friendly Chinese, with few strange or exotic ingredients. Recommended dishes include pao pao beef, seasoned strips of beef sautéed with scallions and ginger; delicious roast pork tenderloin, thinly sliced; and kid-pleasing shrimp fried rice. The excellent dim sum is available all day long. Chinatown Brasserie is *not* the place to go on a Friday or Saturday night, when the scenesters take over. Better to come on a weekday evening or lunch or weekend brunch. Some families prefer low-key Sunday nights—evidenced by the strollers lining the front bar. There's a very nice outdoor space, where you can sit under wide umbrellas and watch the passing parade. I've put it under the "Expensive" category because the servings are so small you'll need to order a number of dishes, and it adds up.

380 Lafayette St. (at Great Jones St.). © **212/533-7000.** www.chinatownbrasserie.com. Highchairs, boosters. Reservations recommended. Main courses $14–$34; Peking duck $48. AE, DC, DISC, MC, V. Mon–Fri 11:30am–11pm (Fri to midnight); Sat 11am–midnight; Sun 11am–11pm. Subway: 6 to Bleecker St.

Inexpensive

Kelley and Ping ★ PAN-ASIAN   With its pressed-tin ceiling and wooden factory floor, Kelley & Ping looks very SoHo, but its friendliness to kids is unusual in this hyper-urban-chic neighborhood. It started out as an Asian grocery store but soon added an open kitchen in the center of the room; there are still stocks of bottled sauces and woks for sale along the walls. The noodles, stir-fries, and grilled meats (Vietnamese crispy duck, Thai grilled shrimp) go down well with children. There's a charming kids' menu: Who can resist a Bowl of Sunshine (golden broth with noodles and chicken) or Chicken Lollies (chicken skewers with peanut sauce)?

127 Greene St. (btwn Houston and Prince sts.). © **212/228-1212.** Kids' menu (dinner only), highchairs, boosters. Reservations accepted for parties of 6 or more. Lunch main courses $7.95–$11; dinner main courses $12–$18; kids' menu $3.75–$5. AE, MC, V. Daily 11:30am–5pm and 5:30–11pm. Subway: N, R to Prince St.; B, D, F to Broadway/Lafayette St.

CHINATOWN

In Chinatown, children not only are seen and heard, but also have a place at the restaurant table from an early age on. If you come to Chinatown for dim sum on a weekend, you will see generations of families sharing dishes at big, communal tables—it's both tradition and entertaining family pastime. So throughout Chinatown, and even in the very few white-tablecloth restaurants, children are welcomed, fawned over, and treated well.

Finding a place to eat in Chinatown isn't difficult—just stroll along Mott or Mulberry streets south of Canal Street, or along Bayard Street between Mott Street and the Bowery, and you'll pass dozens of decent restaurants with menus posted outside so you can check out what's on offer. They may not accept credit cards, and communicating with your waiter may require a little bit of menu-pointing and sign language; but as long as you order prudently, the food should be good. The following are some tried-and-true options.

Expensive

Peking Duck House ★★ CHINESE   This is one of the neighborhood's few upscale restaurants, with white linen tablecloths and a minimalist, monochromatic decor. The food is fresh and delectable, but the house specialty, Peking duck, is rightly the dish to order. This restaurant is pricier than most, and its service can be brusque; but every time we go we see groups of families enjoying a night out. There's also a Midtown location (236 E. 53rd St., btwn Second and Third aves.; ✆ **212/759-8260**).

28 Mott St. (near Pell St.). ✆ **212/227-1810.** www.pekingduckhousenyc.com. Main courses $7.50-$28; Peking duck $43. AE, MC, V. Sun-Thurs 11:30am-10pm; Fri-Sat 11:45am-11pm. Subway: J, M, N, R, Z, 6 to Canal St.

Moderate

Golden Unicorn CHINESE   This big, two-level Hong Kong–style banquet hall (with giant dragons as background decor) serves good, solid dim sum (some 100 types) from 10am to 4pm. I've also had good noodle dishes, such as the Singapore-style beef chow fun, here. Expect waits for tables on the weekends, with staff on walkie-talkies crisply keeping the crowds moving. The dining rooms are constantly refurbished, and everything looks spiffy and bright.

18 E. Broadway (at Catherine St.). ✆ **212/941-0951.** www.goldenunicornrestaurant.com. Main courses $9.95-$25; Peking duck $35. AE, DISC, MC, V. Mon-Fri 10am-11pm; Sat-Sun 9:30am-11pm. Subway: F to E. Broadway.

Oriental Garden ★ CHINESE   This is the smaller, quieter, much more understated neighbor of flashy Jing Fong (see below). It's actually a very pleasant place to have a leisurely lunch or dinner. But it's the food that gets consistently high marks. Even though the dim sum carts are considerably fewer and arrive at your table with less frequency than they do at the big dim sum palaces, Oriental Garden's dim sum delicacies are some of the freshest and tastiest in Chinatown. The seafood is fresh, and service is fast and no-nonsense.

14 Elizabeth St. (btwn Bayard and Canal St.). ✆ **212/619-0085.** Main courses $16-$29. AE. Mon-Fri 10am-11:30pm; Sat-Sun 9am-11:30pm. Subway: J, M, N, R, Z, 6 to Canal St.

Chinatown is famous for its dim sum palaces, where servers offer choice little delicacies from carts they wheel around the restaurant floor. It's a family ritual during the weekends. Eating dim sum is a novel experience that can be loads of fun for kids who are willing to sample new foods, though no item is really that far from standard Chinese dishes. During dim sum hours, the cart ladies start wheeling out hot, steaming carts laden with tiny dishes containing all kinds of delectable dumplings and skewers and rolls. You don't have to read a menu or speak Chinese with the cart ladies—just point to choose yourself a meal full of mouthwatering dishes. Great for sharing (and a smart economical choice), these offerings often include har gow (shrimp dumplings), pork buns, even chicken feet. Among our favorites: **Ping's (22 Mott St.; ℰ 212/602-9988; see below),** which has exceptionally fresh seafood, and **Oriental Garden (14 Elizabeth St.; ℰ 212/619-0085; see below),** a smaller, quieter place with consistently fresh and tasty food.

Ping's ★ CHINESE   Ping's is a somewhat scaled-down version of the often overwhelming Hong Kong–style banquet halls, but it crackles with activity the minute the dim sum carts start rolling through the aisles. It's one of the more attractive restaurants in Chinatown, and the dim sum is exemplary. Ping's excels in Cantonese-style seafood and noodle dishes, so you can't go wrong ordering either.

22 Mott St. (btwn Pell and Worth sts.). ℰ **212/602-9988.** Main courses $6.95–$25. MC, V. Daily 10:30am–midnight. Subway: J, M, N, R, Z, 6 to Canal St.

Inexpensive

Big Wong CHINESE   It certainly doesn't look like much, but this has long been a reliable spot for flavorful Cantonese food—one blogger called it the "King of Chinatown Cheap Eats." If you like congee (Chinese rice porridge), the version here is hard to beat, and the barbecued meats (you can see them hanging in the window) are crisply cooked. I thought the dim sum wasn't bad, either. If you're looking for good, basic, cheap Chinese, head to Big Wong.

67 Mott St. (near Bayard St.). ℰ **212/964-0540.** Main courses $4–$20. No credit cards. Daily 7am–10pm. Subway: J, M, N, R, Z, 6 to Canal St.

Jing Fong CHINESE   If you're looking to give the kids an eye-popping Chinatown experience, try this vast, chandeliered Hong Kong style dim sum parlor. A ride up a *lo-o-o-n-n-g* escalator delivers you into a bustling, gilded football-field-size dining emporium. The place can easily become a madhouse, but the steady stream of dim sum carts keeps the hot food coming. Is it the best dim sum in Chinatown? Not by a long shot, but for sheer theater, it's up there.

18 Elizabeth St. (near Canal St.). ℰ **212/964-5256.** Boosters. Reservations accepted for dinner only. Main courses $7–$24. AE, MC, V. Daily 10am–10pm; dim sum daily 10am–3:30pm. Subway: J, M, N, R, Z, 6 to Canal St.

Ditch the lackluster food choices at the South Street Seaport food court and head over to Stone Street and adjoining Coenties Slip for a memorable lunch break. This curving 18th-century alleyway has been repurposed as a car-free pedestrian street, where in the warm seasons you can dine at tables set up on the cobblestones sandwiched between centuries-old buildings. Cafes and taverns have followed, creating a dense conglomeration of fashionably laid-back eateries in a block-and-a-half of real estate. You can choose among **Stone Street Tavern** (52 Stone St.), **Adrienne's PizzaBar** (54 Stone St.), **Ulysses Folk House** (95 Pearl St., with seating on Stone St.), **Vintry Wine & Whiskey** (57 Stone St.), **Financier** (62 Stone St.), and the little **takeout joints** along Coenties Slip.

TRIBECA & LOWER MANHATTAN

Expensive

Landmarc ★ CONTEMPORARY FRENCH BISTRO   This is just one of those places that does things right, from the consistently delicious American bistro standards to the smart (and astonishingly well-priced) wine list to the easygoing, family-friendly atmosphere and creative kids' menu. The kids' choices feature generic stand-bys—grilled cheese sandwich, fish sticks, burgers, and pigs in a blanket—but also include a petite filet mignon, buttery orrechiette, and green-eggs-and-ham pesto. Grown-ups can enjoy salmon tartare, rock shrimp risotto, mussels (with four sauces to choose from), and any number of grilled meats, from pork chops to steaks to lamb chops. Every night has a pasta special, from hearty pasta Bolognese to rigatoni alla Genovese.

179 W. Broadway (at Leonard St.). ℂ **212/343-3883.** www.landmarc-restaurant.com. Kids' menu, highchairs. Reservations accepted only for parties of 6 or more. Main courses $15–$34; kids' menu $6–$17. AE, DC, DISC, MC, V. Mon–Fri noon–2am; Sat–Sun 9am–2am. Subway: 1 to Franklin St.

Odeon ★★ AMERICAN   The mellow Art Deco look of Odeon, with its wooden blinds and comfy banquettes, helped make it one of TriBeCa's first hot spots way back in the early 1980s. Standards have been kept up exceedingly well into the 21st century, and now it's a neighborhood fixture that welcomes families. It doesn't have theme nights; there are no TVs blaring sports events. The brasserie menu is inventive and constantly changing, but there's always simple classic food like burgers, roast chicken, steak frites, and pastas. This is also a good place to make a meal of two appetizers, with some excellent salads and a fine country pâté available. While there's no kids' menu, kids' options are available upon request. This is a place where grown-ups come to dine with their children. There's very little attitude and a lot of smart cooking going on here—no wonder Odeon has survived.

145 W. Broadway (at Thomas St.). ℂ **212/233-0507.** www.theodeonrestaurant.com. Highchairs. Reservations recommended. Brunch $9.50–$32; lunch $11–$32; dinner $15–$34. AE, MC, V. Mon–Wed 11:45am–2am; Thurs–Fri 11:45am–2am; Sat 10am–2am; Sun 10am–midnight. Subway: A, C, 1, 2, 3 to Chambers St.

Moderate/Inexpensive

Bubby's ★★ AMERICAN "Homey" is the word for this comforting TriBeCa restaurant, with its wooden chairs, whitewashed wainscoting, and kitschy clutter. The food is comforting as well, with sandwiches, burgers, pastas, and a great selection of pies—not to mention breakfast food served until 4pm, good to know if you've got kids who like scrambled eggs and French toast for lunch. There are also more upscale salads and chicken and fish dishes to please adults. It's the sort of place that understands that kids may like their spaghetti with butter and Parmesan instead of tomato sauce and that cooked carrots go down better if you drizzle maple syrup on top. The laid-back ambience somehow makes children willing to linger. The Saturday and Sunday brunch is very popular, and you may have to wait in line for a table. On Sundays, kids 7 and under eat free at dinner.

120 Hudson St. (at N. Moore St.). ✆ **212/219-0666.** www.bubbys.com. Kids' menu, highchairs, boosters. Reservations recommended; no reservations accepted for weekend brunch. Lunch $8–$24; dinner $15–$23, kids' menu $5–$8. DC, MC, V. Tues–Sun open 24 hr.; Mon 9am–midnight. Subway: 1 to Franklin St.; A, C, E to Canal St.

Pizza

Farinella Italian Bakery ★★ PIZZA It's little more than a storefront with a handful of tables, and it's situated on a nondescript street in the government office land just west of TriBeCa and east of Chinatown. But for our money this is the best pizza in the city, guided by a former hip-hop artist from Naples who learned to make Roman-style pizza in the Campo de' Fiori. Sold by the square slice ($2–$4) or, as in Roma, by the 4-foot-long *palam* or half-*palam* (a half-*palam* has about eight square slices), the pizza is feathery light, its brittle crust soulfully flavored with salt and good olive oil. Ingredients are as organically and locally sourced as possible. Vegetarians do well here; a favorite slice is the primavera: zucchini and mushrooms dotted with fresh mozzarella. Also emerging from the oven is hearty lasagna, soup, and other savory dishes. Farinella bakes big loaves of rustic bread—apricot walnut, chocolate, raisin walnut—that are seriously discounted after 4pm. You can grab a *palam* of pizza (pizza this ethereally light takes less than 10 minutes in the big Tagliavini oven)—and eat on the Federal Plaza just east, facing the columned courthouses of Foley Square. They are scheduled to open an Upper East Side location at 1132 Lexington Ave., between 78th and 79th sts.

90 Worth St. (btwn Church St. and Broadway). ✆ **212/608-3222.** www.farinellabakery.com. Boosters. No reservations. Pizzas $10–$38. AE, MC, V. Mon–Sat 7am–9:30pm. Subway: A, C to Chambers St.

Grimaldi's PIZZA Yet another contender for the title of Best Pizza in New York, Grimaldi's lays legitimate claim to honors in the coal-oven category, with gooey homemade mozzarella and chunky tomato sauce topping a wonderfully thin but not tough crust. Like its rivals Anthony's, John's, and Lombardi's, it doesn't serve slices, and there are often lines out the door on summer evenings waiting for a table. Persevere: The line moves quickly enough, and you'll have views of the Manhattan skyline to entertain yourselves while you wait. (Better yet, come in the late afternoon, when there's no crush.) Inside, just as you'd expect, the tables are covered in red-checkered cloths, and Sinatra and Pavarotti dominate the jukebox as well as the photos on the walls. If your kids are into pepperoni, be sure to order some on your pizza—Grimaldi's uses the best in town. Make a Grimaldi's pizza your kids' reward for walking over the Brooklyn Bridge (it sits right beneath the bridge, by the old Fulton ferry landing), and top it off with a post-pizza ice-cream cone down by the river at the Brooklyn Ice Cream Works.

19 Old Fulton St. (btwn Front and Water sts.), Brooklyn. © **718/858-4300.** Boosters. No reservations. Pizzas $12 and up. No credit cards. Sun–Thurs 11:30am–11pm; Fri–Sat 11:30am–midnight. Subway: A, C to High St.

Food Courts

On the top floor of the **Pier 17** pavilion at **South Street Seaport,** a big food court enjoys the kind of picture window river views normally reserved for the toniest restaurants. Unfortunately, the food is nothing to write home about, but it's certainly varied: pizza, Chinese, deli, seafood, and Japanese. The food court in the **World Financial Center** in Battery Park City features a cluster of sit-down, table-service restaurants; but the ambience is casual enough for kids, and there are takeout options.

EXPLORING NEW YORK CITY WITH YOUR KIDS

Yes, everyone knows that New York City is a world-class sightseeing destination. Yet visiting parents may be baffled at first—many of the top museums are not inherently suited for youngsters (the Frick Museum won't even admit anyone 9 and under), real estate is too tight for anything like a theme park, and though there are four children's museums—one in Manhattan, one in Brooklyn, one on Staten Island, and one out on Long Island (see chapter 12)—none of them is as central to local kids' lives as their counterparts in Boston, Chicago, San Francisco, or even Indianapolis. Many of its famous family attractions get so crowded, especially on weekends and school holidays, that tourists face waiting in long lines. (Tip: If you're visiting during the school year, hit the popular museums in the mornings, when the local kids are in school.)

But New York City's charms are inexhaustible, and as soon as you start thinking out of the tourist box, the city will open its best-kept secrets for you. My advice? For one thing, don't sell your children short: They may appreciate those smaller specialty museums, historic houses, and botanic gardens more than you'd expect. For another thing, don't be afraid to get on a subway and zip to the outer boroughs. Remember, kids love subway rides, and on weekends especially it's the way to go. Spend a day in **Brooklyn** in Prospect Park, dividing your time between the Wildlife Center and the Carousel, or pop over to the Brooklyn Botanic Garden and the Brooklyn Museum—incredibly, these are all within a few minutes' walk of one another. Flushing Meadows is my destination of choice in **Queens,** where you can see both the New York Hall of Science and Queens Wildlife Center in one easy go. In the **Bronx,** the huge Bronx Zoo and the equally huge New York Botanical Garden are right across the road from each other. Getting to **Staten Island** is even more fun because you get to take a ferry ride, and the children's museum there is only a short bus ride from the ferry docks.

Many museums court families by designing weekend and holiday workshops for kids—these are detailed in chapter 9, where you'll also find everything you'll need to know about having fun outdoors in New York's great parks, playgrounds, and neighborhoods.

WHAT'S IN A name?

Here's a trivia quiz to test your kids' knowledge of New York City history:

1. Who was the Hudson River named after?
2. Who was the Verrazano Bridge named after?
3. Where does the downtown street name Wall Street come from?
4. Where does the name Harlem, for the uptown neighborhood, come from?
5. Why is the street leading down to South Street Seaport named Fulton Street?
6. What does the name of the New York Mets refer to? (*Hint:* Think of the opera and the big art museum.)
7. What other two area sports teams have names that rhyme with the Mets?
8. Why is Times Square called Times Square?
9. Carnegie Hall, the famous concert hall at 57th Street and Seventh Avenue, is named after whom? And how do you get there?
10. Who is buried in Grant's Tomb?

ANSWERS: 1. English explorer Henry Hudson, who sailed up the river in 1609. 2. Italian explorer Giovanni da Verrazano, the first European to enter the Narrows, in 1524. 3. In the original Dutch settlement, a wall was built at that point to keep out invaders. 4. Nieuw Haarlem was a separate Dutch settlement in the mid-1600s, named after the Dutch city of Haarlem. 5. Ferry service, operated by steamship inventor Robert Fulton, crossed the river at that point, linking Manhattan to Brooklyn (until the completion of the Brooklyn Bridge in 1883). 6. It's short for Metropolitans. 7. The New York Jets football team and the New Jersey Nets basketball team. 8. Because the headquarters of the *New York Times* newspaper is there (an earlier paper, the *New York Herald,* lent its name to Herald Square, a few blocks south at 34th St.). 9. It's named for the man who built it, industrialist/philanthropist Andrew Carnegie (his former mansion is now the Cooper-Hewitt Museum). How do you get there? Practice, practice, practice. 10. Why—it's Grant, of course (that's Ulysses S. Grant, Civil War commander and U.S. president), alongside his wife, Julia.

Sightseeing Suggestions

If you're trying to cram a lot of sightseeing into a short time, you may want to consider buying **The New York Pass** (☏ **877/714-1999;** www.newyorkpass.com), 1-, 2-, 3-, and 7-day passes that provide entry to 55 attractions (including the Empire State Building, Madame Tussauds, the Statue of Liberty, the Museum of Modern Art, Top of the Rock, Circle Line River Cruise), a 160-page guidebook, and line-skipping privileges. One-day passes cost $75 adult, $55 child 4 to 12; 2-day passes $120 adult, $100 child 4 to 12; 3-day passes $150 adult, $130 child 4 to 12; and 7-day passes $190 adult, $150 child 4 to 12 (look for online discounts). At issue, of course, is how many attractions you and your family can reasonably cram into the day to make the passes worth the price; and keep in mind that the card is valid for use only on consecutive days. You can order your passes in advance (and pay shipping fees) or pick them up at **Time Square Planet Hollywood** (45th St. and Broadway; open daily 8am–midnight) when you get to the city.

Another pass worth considering is the CityPASS, which gives you entry to six popular attractions: the American Museum of Natural History, the Metropolitan Museum of Art and The Cloisters, the Museum of Modern Art, the Empire State Building observation deck, the Guggenheim Museum or the Top of the Rock, and the Circle Line cruise around Manhattan or a cruise to Ellis Island or the Statue of Liberty. Good for a 9-day period, passes cost $79 for adults and $59 for youth 6 to 17. Buy them at the admission desk of any of these attractions or online at www.citypass.com/new-york. The sights—including the Guggenheim, whose nautilus shape enthralls kids—all have tremendous kid appeal, and you'd still save money on the adult pass if you did only five (it comes out about even on the kid pass, because the art museums don't charge admission for children).

Head to the website of the city's official tourism organization, **NYC & Company,** for the latest on what's happening (**www.nycgo.com**).

IF YOU HAVE ONLY 1 DAY

Talk to the animals at the **Central Park Zoo,** followed by a spin on the nearby **Carousel.** (If it's summer, take the little ones on the old-fashioned amusement-park rides at the **Victorian Gardens at Wollman Rink;** conversely, if it's cold, you might want to rent a pair of skates and hit the ice rink.) Grab a hot dog for lunch in the park; then head up Central Park West to the **American Museum of Natural History,** with its magnificent dinosaur bones and wildlife dioramas. If you've got enough stamina, wind up with an hour or so at the **Children's Museum of Manhattan,** a couple of blocks away on West 83rd Street.

IF YOU HAVE 2 DAYS

Spend day 1 as above. On day 2, start out at **Rockefeller Center** (if you're early enough you can join the crowds watching the *Today* show broadcast live), where you can hang over the railing at Rockefeller Plaza and delve into the downstairs concourse to see the underground city in action. Go up to the **Top of the Rock** for a view of Manhattan's glittering cityscape, then cross Fifth Avenue to slip into **St. Patrick's Cathedral.** Swing over to 54th Street to the **Museum of Modern Art (MoMA),** where younger kids can play in the interactive art room and older kids can quickly move from floor to floor on the escalators, admiring cool stuff like a real helicopter hanging from the ceiling, tables made out of paper, and a superb collection of eye-pleasing art.

After a spell at the museum, head west to the neon razzmatazz of **Times Square.** If you have young kids in tow, take a spin on the Ferris wheel at **Toys "R" Us.** (Interested in the theater? Check out what's being offered at the **TKTS** half-price ticket booth for tonight's shows.) If you've still got the energy, end your day with a visit to the pricey-but-memorable **Madame Tussauds New York** on 42nd Street, capped by dinner at **Carmine's, Virgil's Barbecue,** or another of Times Square's many restaurants (see chapter 6).

IF YOU HAVE 3 DAYS

Spend days 1 and 2 as above. On day 3, get up early to be first in line for the Circle Line ferry to the **Statue of Liberty** and **Ellis Island.** Viewing her close up is awesome. Proceed via the ferry to Ellis Island, where you can browse around the fascinating immigration displays. Catch the ferry back to Manhattan, where you've got three options: Zip over to the **National Museum of the American Indian,** do a lobby-hopping tour around the Wall Street area (see chapter 8), or take a cab over to **South Street Seaport** and the **South Street Seaport Museum** for a peek into Manhattan's 19th-century maritime past.

IF YOU HAVE 4 DAYS

Spend days 1 to 3 as above. With older kids, start out day 4 by taking the hour-long tour of the **United Nations,** have an early lunch in the Delegates' Dining Room (make reservations in advance), and then cab it uptown for an afternoon at the **Metropolitan Museum of Art.** If you have younger kids, start out at the Metropolitan first thing in the morning (when the crowds are lighter and the guards a trifle more patient), have lunch inside the museum or at an East Side coffee shop, and then go to **Central Park playgrounds** so your youngsters can let off some steam (see chapter 9 for playground details). Work your way up Fifth Avenue to 103rd Street, where you can pop in to check out the toy gallery (including vintage dollhouses) at the **Museum of the City of New York,** and end your day with a stroll through the **Conservatory Garden.**

IF THE WEATHER'S COLD

To cram the most into 1 day with a minimum of exposure to the elements, start out at the **American Museum of Natural History;** then scoot across Central Park on the 79th Street crosstown bus (just as quick as a taxi) and dive into the **Metropolitan Museum of Art.** Or do it the other way around, depending on which you think your child will want more time for. Both have good on-site cafes, so you won't have to venture outside to eat.

IF THE WEATHER'S HOT

East River breezes make **South Street Seaport** a refreshing spot in summer, and you can always duck inside the air-conditioned shops and museums when the sun beats down too strongly. As the sun moves westward, so should you: Cab it across town to **Battery Park City,** where you can take in an afternoon movie at the Regal Battery Park Stadium 11 multiplex, emerging in time to stroll down the breezy Esplanade along the Hudson and watch the sun set behind Lady Liberty—or even walk down to South Ferry and take a spin on the **Staten Island Ferry.** Another good warm-weather refuge is the **Cloisters,** the Metropolitan's medieval art annex located up in Fort Tryon Park, where

you can chill out amid the dim light and cool stone of transplanted European chapels.

Tip: Do not be tempted to do the Statue of Liberty and Ellis Island on a really hot day—though the ferry ride may be refreshing, the wait in line for the boat will be unbearable.

IF YOU HAVE A SITTER

The clock is ticking, right? If you have an afternoon off, visit one of the art museums kids aren't as happy in—like the **Frick,** the **Whitney Museum of American Art,** or the **Asia Society Galleries,** all on the Upper East Side. Or prowl around the Wall Street area: Visit the **New York Stock Exchange,** venerable **Trinity Church,** and the surprisingly small but ornate **City Hall.** You probably won't have time to do both a **leisurely dinner** at an elegant restaurant and a **Broadway show** or a concert at **Carnegie Hall** or **Lincoln Center.** So have your long, leisurely dinner and pop into a **jazz club** for a nightcap and a quick set. Or take an evening stroll on the **High Line,** the beautifully converted elevated freight line in the Meatpacking District. For complete details on all such grown-up activities, pick up a copy of *Frommer's New York City.*

KIDS' TOP 10 ATTRACTIONS

American Museum of Natural History ★★★   All ages. This is the city's one real don't-miss if you're with kids. The excitement begins even in the subway station below (B and C trains to W. 81st St.), where the walls feature wonderful ceramic bas-reliefs of dinosaurs, insects, birds, and mammals. When you enter the rotunda at the top of the Central Park West steps, a huge rearing skeleton of a mommy dinosaur protecting her baby from a small, fierce predator clues you in that the dazzling fourth-floor **dinosaur halls** are the perennial star attraction; they feature interactive consoles, glass-floored walkways that bring you up to the dino's eye level, and please-touch displays illustrating key points of evolution. But our favorite sights are the superb dioramas in the **North American Mammals** section (first floor)—the grizzly bear raking open a freshly caught salmon, majestic elks lifting their massive antlers, wolves loping through eerie nighttime snow—or, on the floor above, the bi-level **African Mammals Hall,** where you can circle around a lumbering herd of perfectly preserved elephants or check out the giraffes browsing by their water hole.

A circuit of the first floor alone could take a whole day. The PC-but-never-preachy **Hall of Biodiversity** features an immense multimedia re-creation of an African rainforest and a display of Earth's entire family tree, with more than 1,500 specimens

NATURAL HISTORY MUSEUM treasure hunt

The American Museum of Natural History is so vast, kids can easily tire if you trudge willy-nilly from hall to hall without a set plan. Make your visit a more interactive one with this treasure hunt, designed by my sons, Hugh and Tom, to keep kids busy exploring. Younger children may get through only one floor in an afternoon, but persist—I swear, it's all here.

First Floor

1. **North American Mammals**—Where is the rabbit hiding from the lynx?
2. **Ocean Life**—Who's talking back to the orca? (Hint: Orca is another name for a killer whale.)
3. **New York State Environment**—How many baby chipmunks are sleeping in the spring burrow?
4. **Human Biology and Evolution**—Find the cave of mammoth bones.
5. **Minerals and Gems**—Where are the rocks that glow in the dark?

Second Floor

6. **African Peoples**—Find the xylophone.
7. **Birds of the World**—How many stuffed penguins are there?
8. **Asian Peoples**—Who's getting married?
9. **Rose Center**—How soon after the Big Bang did our solar system start to form?

Third Floor

10. **African Mammals**—Who's watching the ostriches fight the wart hogs?
11. **Reptiles and Amphibians**—Which is the crocodile, and which is the alligator?

Fourth Floor

12. **Saurischian Dinosaurs**—Find the fossil dinosaur teeth.
13. **Ornithischian Dinosaurs**—Touch the triceratops horn.

ANSWERS: 1. Behind the bush. 2. The leopard seal. 3. Four. 4. Toward the end of the exhibit, in the Earliest Architecture display. 5. In the first gem room, the southeast corner. 6. Midway through the hall, on the west wall, across from the guys in straw skirts who look like Cousin Itt from The Addams Family. 7. Twenty in all—16 adults, 4 babies. 8. In the Chinese section, a bride in her ornate ceremonial sedan chair. 9. Eight billion years. 10. The mouselike elephant shrew, behind a dead log. 11. Facing each other by the entrance at the north end of the hall—the gator (on your right) has the snub snout; the croc (on your left) has the pointy snout. 12. On the south wall. 13. On the east wall.

—Holly Hughes

and models spread out along a 100-foot wall. We love the dimly lit **Millstein Hall of Ocean Life,** where a gargantuan model of a blue whale soars overhead and water-dappled lights play against the walls; it has informally become known as the place where toddlers can stretch their legs, racing and twirling around the vast open space. Around the corner, the less-well-visited **North American Forest dioramas** are a peaceful part of the museum, where you can hunt for blue jays in oak trees and rattle-snakes behind the cactus. Most people hurry through here to get to the interactive **Human Biology and Evolution** exhibits, which seem always full of busy grade-schoolers. Past that lies the **Mineral and Gem room,** where little kids can thrust their hands into a huge geode while older kids gape in awe at the jewels on display.

The museum is not all animals, by any means (remember that Margaret Mead was only one of many brilliant anthropologists whose research was supported by this museum over the years). Studying Native Americans? On the first floor, by the 77th

Uptown Attractions

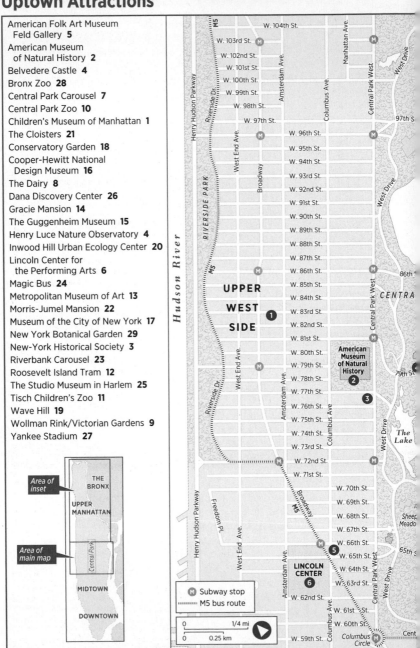

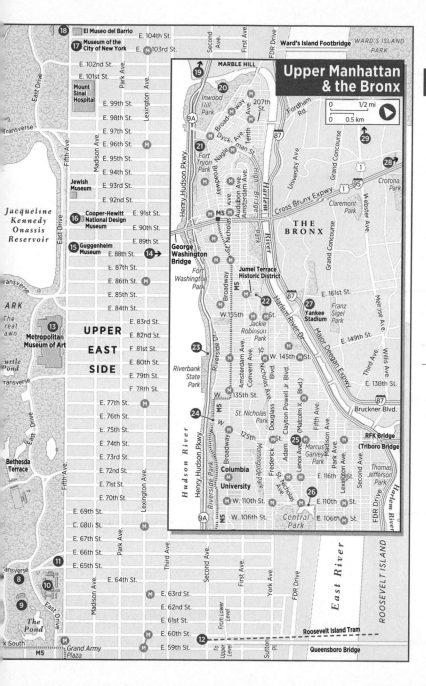

Midtown Attractions

7

Kids' Top 10 Attractions

EXPLORING NEW YORK CITY WITH YOUR KIDS

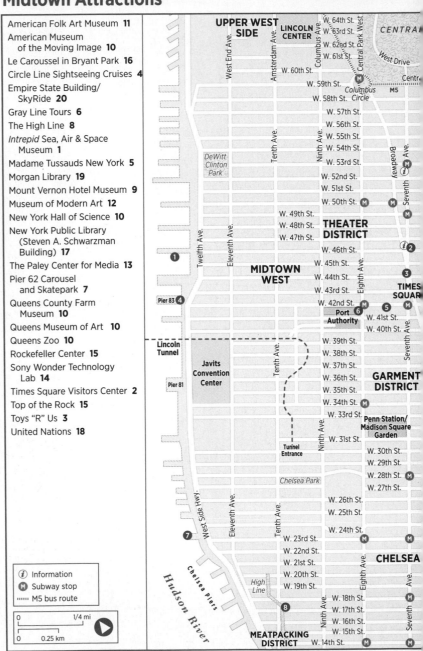

Street entrance, is the astounding collection of **Northwest Coast Indian** totem poles immortalized by J. D. Salinger in *Catcher in the Rye*. The haunting soundtracks in the **African and Asian peoples** sections (on the second floor) lull you into studying the precisely detailed displays there too. The stunning **Rose Center for Earth and Space** is a seven-story glass cube that holds the Hayden Planetarium, where you can take a thrilling virtual ride through the Milky Way to the edge of the universe, step on a scale that shows your weight on Saturn, see an eerie phosphorescent model of the expanding universe, and touch cosmic debris. At night the sphere floating inside the Rose Center is lit in an ethereal blue hue.

The **Discovery Room,** on the first floor by the 77th Street entrance (near the immense outrigger canoe), is a special spot where kids 5 through 12 can touch and feel and fiddle with items related to the displays; it's open Monday to Thursday from 1:30 to 5:10pm, Saturday and Sunday 10:30am to 1:30pm and 2:15 to 5:10pm (summer daily 10:30am–1:30pm and 2:15–5:10pm). Kids over 7 years will appreciate "Meet the Scientist" events, held in the Discovery Room on the first Saturday afternoons of February, April, June, August, October, and December. For preschoolers, the Discovery Room hosts "Gateway Storytime," where 2½- to 5-year-olds explore natural science through story, song, and a visit to a related museum hall; it's held on Monday mornings during the school year at 10:15am with a second program at 11am.

Here comes my only quibble with the museum: On top of the already significant admission price, there are substantial extra fees, even for members, for special exhibits, and even for regular features such as the space show *Cosmic Collisions* at the **Hayden Planetarium** and the various films shown in the **IMAX theater** (see below for prices). These can add up awfully fast to make a visit here quite expensive. Believe me, there's enough to do here that you don't need to go for the extras (I personally find the space shows a letdown). Shops at every turn lure you to spend more money, though there are always at least a few inexpensive items.

Where to Eat: The excellent **Museum Food Court** (open 11am–4:45pm) offers a wide range of sophisticated sandwiches, salads, fruit, and snacks, as well as hot food, including hamburgers and french fries. There's also **Café on One** for gourmet finger food, salads, and sandwiches. On weekends, you can also grab a light meal at the **Café on 4** (on the fourth floor by the 77th St. elevators) and **Cafe 77** (by the 77th St. entrance on the first floor).

Central Park West (at 79th St.). 📞 **212/769-5100** for reserved tickets to Space Show and other special exhibits. 📞 **212/769-5200.** www.amnh.org. Suggested admission for nonmembers (includes admission to museum and the Rose Center): $16 adults, $12 students and seniors, $9 children 2–12; nonmember admission Plus One ticket (includes admission to museum and the Rose Center plus one special exhibition, IMAX film, or Hayden Planetarium space show) $24 adults, $17 students and seniors, $13 children 2–12; Super Saver Packages (includes admission to museum and the Rose Center plus all special exhibitions, IMAX films, and Hayden Planetarium space shows) $32 adult nonmembers, $16 members, $20 nonmember children (2–12), $12 member children, free for children 1 and under. Daily 10am–5:45pm. Closed Thanksgiving and Dec 25. Limited parking available on-site (enter on W. 81st St. btw. Central Park West and Columbus Ave.). Subway: B, C to 81st St./Museum of Natural History; 1 to 79th St.

Bronx Zoo ★★ **All ages.** The big kahuna of New York City's wildlife parks, the Wildlife Conservation Society's Bronx Zoo covers 265 acres and boasts more than 4,000 animals, from Siberian tigers and snow leopards to condors and vultures to naked mole-rats and meerkats. Though there's a scattered number of indoor exhibits—the **World of Reptiles;** the **Monkey House;** the **World of Birds;** the **Giraffe House; Madagascar!;** and **Jungle World**—most of the animals live outdoors in

Downtown Attractions

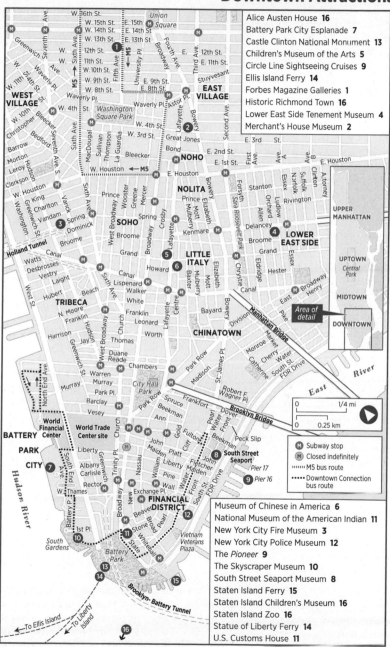

Alice Austen House **16**
Battery Park City Esplanade **7**
Castle Clinton National Monument **13**
Children's Museum of the Arts **5**
Circle Line Sightseeing Cruises **9**
Ellis Island Ferry **14**
Forbes Magazine Galleries **1**
Historic Richmond Town **16**
Lower East Side Tenement Museum **4**
Merchant's House Museum **2**

0 ____ 1/4 mi
0 ____ 0.25 km

Ⓜ Subway stop
Ⓜ Closed indefinitely
······· M5 bus route
····· Downtown Connection bus route

Museum of Chinese in America **6**
National Museum of the American Indian **11**
New York City Fire Museum **3**
New York City Police Museum **12**
The *Pioneer* **9**
The Skyscraper Museum **10**
South Street Seaport Museum **8**
Staten Island Ferry **15**
Staten Island Children's Museum **16**
Staten Island Zoo **16**
Statue of Liberty Ferry **14**
U.S. Customs House **11**

A (Real) Night at the Museum

The nationwide trend of children spending an adventure-filled night in a major museum has arrived in New York City with a bang, at the American Natural History Museum's summer **Sleepovers** ★★ (ages 7–13). What could be cooler? (Well, I've always wanted to spend a night at Bergdorf's, but that's another story.) You arrive at the museum with sleeping bag and pillow in tow, and with your trusty flashlight guiding the way, you explore the halls in search of T-Rex, a herd of thundering buffalo, and erupting volcanoes. You sleep under the big blue whale in the Millstein Hall of Ocean Life, next to a lifelike brown bear in the Hall of North American Mammals, or in the Hall of Planet Earth. Just know that you won't be alone: The museum can handle some 465 people for a night's sleepover. Families are welcome; one adult is required to chaperone every one to three children. Preregistration is required (✆ 212/769-5200; www.amnh.org/kids/sleepovers; $129 per person, $119 members, including evening snack and light breakfast, cots, IMAX film, and take-home activities).

large enclosures constructed to replicate the species' native environment as closely as possible. The **Himalayan Highland** is an atmospheric thicket of bamboo and paperback maples inhabited by red pandas, white-naped cranes, and a beautiful snow leopard named Leo. The handsome lions on the **African Plains** look almost airbrushed; the big cats pose regally as they sit atop the grassy savanna. The **Sea Lion Pool** is a delight; when we visited, a young pup thrilled the crowd with exuberant leaps and teases. New zoo residents include **brother-and-sister hyenas** who stalk their enclosure with as much menace as anyone with comical ears and furry spots can project. **Peacocks** are everywhere. Know that certain creatures are viewable only at a distance (you'll see plenty, don't worry)—and know that kids 4 and under may be overwhelmed if you try to do too much. This doesn't mean they won't love the zoo—it just means you've got to organize your visit sensibly.

You can run into several added charges once you get inside the gates, so I recommend opting for the **Total Experience ticket plan**—it saves you not only money, but also time, because you can bypass individual ticket booths inside (look for Web-only discounts). (Or consider buying a 1-year family membership [$124–$154], which also gives you access to the city's four Wildlife Conservation parks anytime during the next year; you'll be supporting valuable conservation efforts as well.) The Total Experience ticket includes every special exhibit except the seasonal camel rides ($6); among them, the open-sided tram known as the **Zoo Shuttle** ($3) rattles in a big loop around the main part of the zoo, making express stops only. Maneuvering the zoo with children is certainly doable on foot (strollers are essential), but the shuttle becomes a smart option when kids get pooped. The other special exhibits include the narrated **Wild Asia monorail ride** ($4, May–Oct), which offers fleeting glimpses of rhinos, exotic deer, and birds in outdoor habitats, but riding that slender skein of metal over the Bronx River is admittedly a thrill. This is where the remaining **two elephants** have been moved (citing a growing body of research that deems elephants unsuited for captivity, the Bronx Zoo in 2006 announced that it would close the exhibit once these elephants pass). On the **Zucker Bug Carousel** ($3) the riding steeds are colorful grasshoppers, praying mantis, and dung beetles. The **Children's Zoo** ($4), open April to October, is surprisingly fun even for 8- or 9-year-olds, with

Brooklyn Attractions

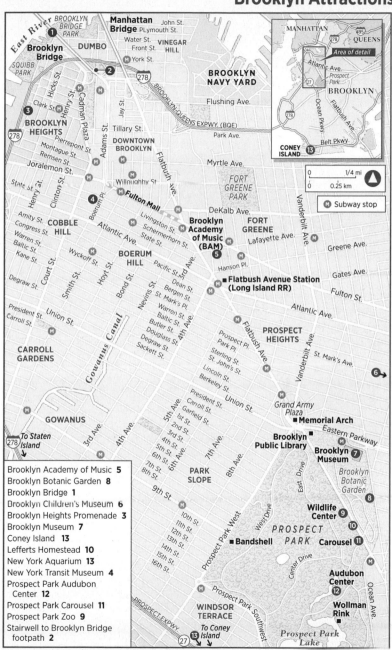

Brooklyn Academy of Music **5**
Brooklyn Botanic Garden **8**
Brooklyn Bridge **1**
Brooklyn Children's Museum **6**
Brooklyn Heights Promenade **3**
Brooklyn Museum **7**
Coney Island **13**
Lefferts Homestead **10**
New York Aquarium **13**
New York Transit Museum **4**
Prospect Park Audubon
    Center **12**
Prospect Park Carousel **11**
Prospect Park Zoo **9**
Stairwell to Brooklyn Bridge
    footpath **2**

lots of interactive exhibits (like a spider-web rope climb and a prairie dog burrow that kids can climb through) and a petting zoo. The zoo also tacks on $5 and $3, respectively, for two of its star exhibits, the **Congo Gorilla Forest** ★ and the **Butterfly Garden** ★ (open Apr–Oct only). Both are wonderful and fascinating—on a good day you can practically go snout-to-snout with our huge simian cousins through a wide glass window or have immense tropical butterflies land on your outstretched hand. But the newer **Tiger Mountain** ★ gives you the same close-up access to its big striped cats for no extra charge. This exhibit is a doozy, with a handful of astonishingly beautiful Siberian tigers lazing under trees or splashing around in a "swimming hole" cross-sectioned in the glass windows, with fish skirting beneath the big cat's paws.

New in summer 2010 is **Dora & Diego's 4-D Adventure** ($5; included in the Total Experience ticket), a digital 3-D film with added sensory effects like water mist, snow, bubbles, scents, even vibrating seats.

During winter, when many of the outdoor animals aren't on view, the park lures visitors with fanciful animal sculptures spangled with lights, as well as the indoor exhibits (still enough species on view to fill a smaller zoo); there's a certain pleasure in visiting during this uncrowded season.

The zoo has several entrances: The Southern Boulevard/Crotona entrance brings you in near the Children's Zoo; the Asia entrance (pedestrians only, closest to the subway station) brings you in near Wild Asia. In any case, study the zoo map as soon as you enter, and plot which animals you want to visit and the simplest route to pass them. Operate on the assumption that you can't see everything in 1 day, even if your kids are good walkers. Relax, take your time, and enjoy yourselves.

Getting There: By **subway,** take the no. 2 or 5 to East Tremont Avenue/West Farms Square; walk straight ahead on Boston Road, and you're 1 block from the zoo's Asia gate entrance. By **train,** take Metro-North from Grand Central Terminal to Fordham Road, change to the Bx9 bus, and ride to the zoo's Southern Boulevard entrance. By **bus,** BxM11 express buses (call ℂ **718/330-1234**) run about every 15 to 30 minutes, making stops along Madison Avenue in Manhattan between 26th and 99th streets, and then travels directly to the zoo's Bronx River gate. A **taxi** might cost $20 to $35 one-way, depending on your Manhattan starting point or destination. By **car,** take exit 6 off the Bronx River Parkway.

Where to Eat: The zoo's **Dancing Crane Cafe** is open year-round, and five open-air cafes operate seasonally. Expect fast-food-ish menus, with slightly high (but not outrageous) prices. Stop by the **Grizzly Goodies Corner** near the grizzly bears or pick up a snack at **Asia Plaza** near Jungle World. Pack a picnic lunch if you can— there are plenty of places to sit and eat outdoors. But why come all the way up and miss Arthur Avenue, the Little Italy of the Bronx? Unlike Manhattan's Little Italy, this neighborhood has some of the best Italian restaurants in the city—and all are extremely family-friendly. It's also walkable from the Bronx Zoo (inquire at the ticket office; it's closer to the Fordham Rd. gate), but you can also call a cab. You can't go wrong at **Dominick's** (2335 Arthur Ave.; ℂ **718/733-2807**), **Mario's** (2342 Arthur Ave.; ℂ **718/584-1188**), or **Pasquale's Rigoletto** (2311 Arthur Ave.; ℂ **718/365-6644**).

In Bronx Park, Bronx River Pkwy. and Fordham Rd. ℂ **718/367-1010.** www.wcs.org or www.bronxzoo.com. Admission $16 adults, $14 seniors, $12 children 2–12, free for children 1 and under; Total Experience tickets (include 7 special exhibits and/or rides) $27 adults, $21 students and children, and $23 seniors; admission fees optional Wed, but charges still apply to ticketed exhibits and rides. Stroller rental $10 single, $12 double stroller with $20 deposit (inquire at park entrances). Apr–Oct Mon–Fri 10am–5pm, Sat–Sun and holidays 10am–5:30pm; Nov–Mar daily 10am–4:30pm. Parking $13.

Central Park Zoo and Tisch Children's Zoo ★★   All ages. Beautifully organized, this pair of tiny zoos is perfect for young animal lovers—there's nothing bigger than a polar bear here, you can get pretty close to every species on display, and you don't have to walk very far to see everything. The centerpiece of the main zoo is the oval **Sea Lion Pool,** which has glass sides so everyone can watch the sea lions swimming underwater. A few steps to the west is **Monkey Island,** where a troop of snow monkeys scramble over the rocks and swans glide on the water. To the north lies the **Polar Circle,** with a big flock of penguins indoors (including new Emperor penguins) and polar bears outside, cavorting in and out of their rock-edged pool. Up on the hill behind Monkey Island is the **Temperate Territory,** which stars an otter, some ducks, and a pair of shy red pandas; at the south end you can stand on the bridge over a mucky turtle pond and look for frogs sunning themselves. The greatest number of species in the zoo are inside the **Tropical Zone,** a two-story enclosed aviary, featuring exciting creatures like piranhas and bats and snakes—not to mention golden lion tamarins, whose wizened faces remind us of the flying monkeys from *The Wizard of Oz.* Be sure to climb to the upper levels and stand out on the stairways, looking for the bright plumage of tropical birds flitting from tree to tree. Always warm and humid, the Tropical Zone is a great refuge on a chilly day. The newest inhabitant in the zoo is the magnificent **snow leopard,** a solitary female with a Garbo complex (she wants to be alone); see if you can spot her spotted coat as she oversees her rugged habitat.

Check signs near the entrance to see when the sea lion and penguin feedings are scheduled; there's often a crowd for these, but it's fun to see the animals scamper over to their keepers for their fish. (No, they don't do tricks.)

The **Tisch Children's Zoo** is a short stroll north, on the other side of the Delacorte Arch. Wooden bridges cross over a tidy central pond, cedar-chip paths circle around, and at the back is a giant spider web kids can clamber over. Children can get right up close to most of the animals here, so who cares if most are domestic species? To many a city kid, pigs, goats, sheep, and baby llamas are pure exotica (and here you can feed them by hand!).

Where to Eat: The **Leaping Frog Café,** within the Park's Wildlife Center, has indoor and outdoor seating and decent "self-serve" standards such as burgers, hot dogs, pizzas, and sandwiches. There's usually also a cart selling drinks and ice cream in the central courtyard. Note that drinks are served without straws, since a straw tossed into an animal's enclosure could be harmful.

In Central Park, near the park entrance at Fifth Ave. and 64th St. ☏ **212/439-6500.** www.centralpark zoo.com. Admission (includes both zoos) $12 adults, $9 seniors, $7 children 3-12, free for children 2 and under. Mon–Fri 10am–5pm; Sat–Sun 10am–5:30pm (closes 4:30pm Nov–Mar). Subway: N, R, W to Fifth Ave./59th St.; 6 to 68th St.

Ellis Island Immigration Museum ★★★   Ages 4 & up. From the mountain of ragtag luggage stacked right inside the front doors, to the cramped dormitories and medical examination rooms upstairs (cough the wrong way, and you could be sent right back to Europe), to the family heirlooms immigrants brought with them in the **Treasures from Home** collection—this place really brings history to life. We can't help but linger over the first-floor **Peopling of America** exhibit, with a life-size "family tree" and huge three-dimensional bar graph tracking immigration patterns over the years. The second-floor **Registry Hall** is awesome, with its soaring vaulted ceiling faced with white tile; this is where new arrivals waited in endless lines to be interviewed by immigration officials. On a **Wall of Honor** outside, some 700,000 immigrants' names are inscribed in steel. Free ranger-guided tours are held on a regular basis. There's a self-guided audio tour ($8 adults and $7.25 seniors and children 11 and under), or you can pick up handsets at various displays to hear narration; the stirring documentary *Island of Hope, Island of Tears* runs frequently throughout the day (free, but you need a ticket). You can easily spend 2 hours here.

Getting There: The **Statue Cruises ferryboats** make frequent trips, running a loop from Battery Park to Liberty Island to Ellis Island and back to Battery Park (from New Jersey, you can board ferries in Liberty State Park). In Battery Park, you can buy tickets at Castle Clinton, where there are some interesting exhibits to help pass the time before your ferry. The wait in line can take a while, and security procedures include metal detectors, bag searches (bags larger than a milk crate aren't allowed on the ferry), and waiting in several different holding pens—perhaps an appropriate introduction to the immigrant experience. Once on the ferry (best views are from the top deck on the right-hand side), you can disembark at either island and board a later boat to continue your trip. Schedules vary, but the service generally runs daily starting at 9am (the last trip starts around 3:50pm); allow at least half an hour beforehand to clear security. Boats depart every 30 minutes (every 20 min. on busy weekends); sailing time is about 15 minutes to Liberty Island, another 10 minutes to Ellis Island, and 10 minutes back to Manhattan. The Reserve Ticket allows priority entry to security check-in and provides access to Liberty Island and the Ellis Island Immigration Museum; tickets adults $12, seniors $10, children (ages 4–12) $5. With audio tour add $7–$8 per ticket. For the same price there's the Flex Ticket for one-time use within a 3-day period. A specific start date is required for access to Liberty Island and Ellis Island, including the grounds of Liberty Island and the Ellis Island Immigration Museum. For information and current schedules, call ✆ **877/523-9849** or go to **www.statuecruises.com**. For advance tickets, call ✆ **800/600-1600.**

Where to Eat: There's a big food court on the site, as well as a snack bar on the ferry. Bring a picnic lunch if you can—there are plenty of places to sit out and eat.

On Ellis Island in New York Harbor. ✆ **212/363-3200.** www.ellisisland.org and www.nps.gov/elis/index. htm. Free admission. Daily 9:30am–5pm (extended hours in summer). Closed Dec 25. Subway: 4, 5 to Bowling Green; 1 to South Ferry; R to Whitehall Station. Walk through Battery Park to Castle Clinton to purchase tickets.

The High Line ★★ All ages. It's been open less than a year and it's not even close to completion, yet the High Line has become one of the city's top attractions, embraced by locals and visitors alike. A 1930s-era elevated freight-train track, abandoned and weed-strewn, has been utterly reinvented as a 1½-mile-long public park—an "integrative landscape" with concrete or planked pathways winding through a range of innovative outdoor habitats, including big-sky grasslands, dense thickets of wildflowers, and a canopy of sumac trees known as the "Woodland Flyover." There's even a place to wade barefoot in a scrim of cool water. This is no whitewash of an old rusted landscape; the old rail tracks lie hither and thither, and some of the newly planted growth look like the sorts of native flotsam that pops up in abandoned city lots—by design, much of the plantings are indigenous New York species.

For urban kids, strolling the High Line is a real kick. Each turn in the track brings another delightful outdoor habitat. More than anything, the High Line is a meditative *passeggiata* above the urban din, a communal stroll amid artfully designed outdoor rooms pillowed in wildflowers and biblical grasses and uncluttered river and sky views. It's as if someone superimposed a bucolic country lane onto a gritty city tableau.

Section 1 (Gansevoort St. to 20th St.) of the High Line project was completed in 2009; **Section 2** (20th St. to 30th St.) was projected to open in 2011. Currently, the High Line has five access points (all with stairs): Gansevoort Street, 14th Street (elevator access), 16th Street (elevator access), 18th Street, and 20th Street. Prohibited are bikes, skates, dogs, and booze.

Manhattan's West Side, Gansevoort St. to 34th St. (btw. Tenth and Eleventh aves.). ✆ **212/500-6035.** www.thehighline.org. Free admission. Daily 7am–10pm. Subway: A, C, E, L to 14th St./Eighth Ave; C, E to 23rd St./Eighth Ave.

Metropolitan Museum of Art ★★★   All ages. You can have a great time at the Metropolitan, even with toddlers, as long as you remember two rules: Go at their pace, not yours (forget about standing transfixed for 10 min. in front of that wonderfully serene Vermeer), and don't let the gruff museum guards intimidate you. They're the city's most fervent believers that children should be seen and not heard—they'll level stern, disapproving glares if your child so much as skips for joy or exclaims above a whisper. Naturally, don't let youngsters touch the precious works of art or press their fingers against glass cases, but otherwise, let your own common sense prevail.

Granted, the $20 admission price can be off-putting, but remember that children 11 and under get in free. And it's only a suggested donation—if you think your kids' attention spans are too short for a lengthy visit, don't be shy about paying less. A better strategy to get your money's worth, however, is to inquire at the information desk about what children's programs may be available that day—these are free with admission, and they're a brilliant way to get the kids immersed in the collection. Among the museum's numerous family programs are regular **drop-in drawing sessions** (all ages), **global "art trcks"** (ages 5–12), and **story time** in Nolen Library (ages 3–7), among others. Also be sure to pick up (or download from the website) the museum's **family map** or one of the many **family guides** for kids.

The echoing marble-clad Great Hall is a monumental entrance—point out the ginormous sprays of flowers on either side. Kids love to climb the awesome central stairway up to the European painting galleries, the museum's prize jewel, but you may want to skip those galleries—they go on forever.

Here are the galleries kids are more likely to enjoy: the **arms and armor** (first floor), the extensive **Egyptian rooms** (also on the first floor—make a beeline for the glorious mummies), **musical instruments** (second floor, off the American Wing's courtyard), the **Costume Institute** (ground floor—rotating installations will be of varying interest to kids), and the **European** and **American period rooms** (all over the place). Much of the newly renovated **American Wing** has been reopened, including the sun-splashed **Charles Engelhard Court** with plantings, benches, and statues kids can actually relate to (a mountain lion and her cubs, a pensive Indian brave) and **20 period rooms** (dating from 1680 to 1914) that captivate older kids. It also has a nice new place to get a bite to eat, the **American Wing Café.** Bring lots of small change for them to throw into the pool here and in the pool in front of the Egyptian Wing's momentous **Temple of Dendur** (but *not* in the Chinese scholars' court goldfish pool in the second-floor Asian art galleries!). Wander around this immense museum, keep your eyes open, and concentrate on those sections that seem of most interest your children. Young ballerinas may love the **Degas ballet paintings** in the Modern Art gallery on the second floor. Older kids who are beginning to appreciate art may go for the **Impressionist gallery** (second floor) or the **Robert Lehman Wing,** set up to evoke the feel of the wealthy benefactor's own town house—it's art in small enough doses that it doesn't overwhelm. Everyone will love the **roof garden,** where you feel as if you're floating above the treetops, and iconic skyscrapers pepper the horizon.

The huge **museum gift shop** has a lot of wonderful stuff for kids (see "A World of Museum Shops," on p. 254).

Where to Eat: The museum's main restaurant, the **Cafeteria,** has moved; it's still on the first floor but now behind the Medieval Hall and offers self-serve dining from a menu of hot entrees, sandwiches, salads, and snacks as well as booster seats and highchairs. The Taxi CabKids Meals (pasta, PBJ sandwiches, chicken fingers) come packaged in cute yellow cardboard taxis. Two other sun-filled cafes have opened: The **American Wing Café** serves sandwiches, salads, snacks, and cocktails from 11am on; and the **Petrie Court Café and Wine Bar** is a European-style a la carte restaurant where you can get breakfast, lunch, dinner (Fri–Sat), and Sunday brunch. (The **Roof Garden Café** also serves cocktails and light snacks.) Or, since your museum badge allows reentry, go outside and sit on the splendid Fifth Avenue steps (one of the city's best impromptu grandstands) to eat a hot dog bought at a nearby pushcart.

1000 Fifth Ave. (at 82nd St.). ℂ **212/535-7710.** For daily tours and programs call ℂ **212/570-3930.** www.metmuseum.org. Suggested donation (includes same-day admission to the Cloisters) $20 adults, $15 seniors, $10 students, free for children 11 and under with adult. Tues–Thurs and Sun 9:30am–5:30pm; Fri–Sat 9:30am–9pm. Closed Jan 1, Thanksgiving, and Dec 25; open some school-holiday Mon (check website). Baby carriers are available at the coat checks, and strollers are allowed in all galleries, unless otherwise noted. Subway: 4, 5, 6 to 86th St.

Museum of Modern Art (MoMA) ★★★ **All ages.** My 4-year-old races through these galleries, pulling me along to see one "amazing" thing after another. For a young kid, what's not to like? It's a visceral banquet of color, shape, and texture, and instant gratification around every corner. It's also a wonderful lesson in the infinite possibilities of creative expression. Why is a chair made out of accordioned paper? *Why not?* Floor-to-ceiling windows offer neatly framed cityscapes. The greatly expanded galleries offer more space for some of the best in 20th-century art, from Picasso to Pollock, but the museum expands vertically (you don't have far to walk to get from one gallery to another; escalators zip you from floor to floor) and exhibition spaces aren't overwhelmingly big, making visiting and viewing breezy for kids. A favorite spot is the splendid central sculpture garden. The museum has a terrific interactive **children's "lab"** ★ that changes every 7 months or so, where kids can play and design with shapes or colors or swing from geometrics to organic to 3D. The children's lab is based on real graphic-design prompts, and there's always a facilitator on hand to offer suggestions and connections to images in the museum collection. It's located in the Lewis B. and Dorothy Cullman Education and Research Building at 4 W. 54th St. Kids 15 and under get in to the museum free with one adult admission, so a visit here may end up costing no more than an afternoon at the American Museum of Natural History. Even better: The winter/spring **Family Programs**—including the hour-long Tours for Fours, Tours for Tweens, and Family Art Workshops—are absolutely free and include a free five-member Family Pass to the museum! Sign up for news about upcoming family events by going to **www.moma.org/enews** or calling ℂ **212/708-9805.** All family programs begin in the Lewis B. and Dorothy Cullman Education and Research Building; tickets are distributed on a first-come, first-served basis beginning at 10am, and these programs fill up; it's recommended that participants get here a little before 10am to snag a ticket. Of course, with a family membership ($150), you get free admission for two adults and two children 18 and under for a

VISITING MOMA: advice from the pros

For the optimum family experience, the staff at MoMA recommends the following:

1. **Visit early in the morning** or on **Friday evenings** (open to 8pm). On Thursday evenings in July and August, the museum is open until 8:30pm and Brazilian music is played in the outdoor sculpture garden.

2. **Skip the special exhibitions;** the crowds can be unsettling.

3. **Hit the museum highlights:** Kids love the mind-blowing designs in the Architecture and Design gallery (third floor); the big, splashy paintings and 3-D sculptures in the Painting and Sculpture galleries (fourth and fifth floors); and the glass ceiling on the top floor. There's much to see even riding the escalators: An actual helicopter hangs from the ceiling, and the perspective changes as you go up and down.

4. **Let kids lead a little bit.** Don't spend too much time looking on your own; you're on your kids' time.

5. **Download the children's audiotape** (free at the museum), which directs children to prime kids' stops to the accompaniment of music, poetry, and cool sound effects.

whole year. Before you leave home, check out MoMA's interactive children's website **Destination Modern Art** (www.moma.org/interactives/destination).

11 W. 53rd St. (btw. Fifth and Sixth aves.). © **212/708-9400.** www.moma.org. Admission $20 adults, $16 seniors, $12 students, free for children 15 and under when accompanied by an adult; pay what you wish Fri 4–8pm. Wed–Mon 10:30am–5:30pm (until 8pm Fri). Subway: E, V to Fifth Ave.

South Street Seaport and the Seaport Museum ★★ **All ages.** New York City was built around its mighty harbor and the brawny sailing ships that brought the world to its door. At the South Street Seaport, a charming jumble of restored warehouses and maritime shops on the cobblestone East River waterfront, you'll timetravel back to New York Harbor's clipper-ship heyday. Here are some of New York's oldest structures, relics from the city's brash beginnings. Like its counterparts in Boston and Baltimore, the waterfront section of the South Street Seaport was in the 1980s converted into a "festival marketplace"—let's face it, it's a mall—containing an inordinate number of chain stores and general junk for sale; the unexciting food court upstairs is mostly fast food, but the views above the East River are terrific. Walk along narrow **Front** or **Water Street** from Fulton Street to Dover Street to get a fuller sense of the history here. This small but burgeoning neighborhood is converting 18th-century warehouses into charming restaurants, condos, and boutiques. Plus, architect David Rockwell's innovative **Imagination Playground** on Burling Slip was recently completed and is now open to the public (see chapter 9).

But most important, fork over admission to the **South Street Seaport Museum** (see details below), and you'll get to the heart of this historic spot. The South Street Seaport Museum encompasses the restored historic buildings of the Seaport, including a working **19th-century printing shop** (at 211 Water St.); a **gallery** with permanent and rotating historic exhibits; a **marine conservation lab; an archaeology center;** and the jewel of the collection: the largest privately owned **fleet of historic ships** in the country. You and your kids can actually climb aboard and tour these old ships—a fleet that includes wooden schooners, four-masted barks, tugboats, and

THE while-waiting-in-line-at-lady-liberty QUIZ

1. The Statue of Liberty weighs
   a. 225 tons.
   b. 25 tons.
   c. 225 pounds (when she's been to her step-aerobics class).

2. The statue's full official name is
   a. The Gatekeeper of Liberty.
   b. Liberty Enlightening the World.
   c. Liberty Looking for a Lost Contact Lens.

3. Sculptor Frédéric-Auguste Bartholdi is said to have modeled the statue after
   a. the Mona Lisa.
   b. Napoleon Bonaparte's girlfriend.
   c. his mommy.

4. Emma Lazarus's poem The New Colossus ("Give me your tired, your poor . . . ") is engraved
   a. on the tablet Liberty cradles in her arm.
   b. on a plaque inside the base of the statue.
   c. on a tattoo on every park ranger's left biceps.

5. The engineer who designed the statue's tricky steel skeleton is also known for
   a. the Eiffel Tower in Paris.
   b. the Brooklyn Bridge.
   c. the Spaceship Earth sphere at Epcot.

6. The French intellectual who first proposed the idea for the statue was
   a. the Marquis de Lafayette.
   b. Edouard René Lefebvre de Laboulaye.
   c. Pepe Le Pew.

7. Once completed and shipped in sections to the United States, the statue almost wasn't erected because
   a. Americans lost the instructions on how to put it together.
   b. Americans hadn't raised enough money to build a pedestal for it.
   c. everybody thought it was so ugly.

8. Lady Liberty looks green because
   a. the statue's hammered-copper sheathing has oxidized as expected.
   b. pollution from New York Harbor has corroded it.
   c. she gets seasick from watching the ferries chug past all day.

9. The statue's nose is
   a. 4½ feet long.
   b. 10 feet long.
   c. 100 feet long (she could use some plastic surgery).

10. The Statue of Liberty was given to the people of the United States by the people of France
    a. because there was no room for it in Paris.
    b. in repayment of old war debts.
    c. to symbolize a special friendship between the two countries.

ANSWERS: 1. a 2. b 3. c 4. b 5. a 6. b 7. b 8. a 9. a 10. c.

full-rigged iron maidens. Inside the museum are beautifully detailed ship models and artifacts including vintage ocean liner memorabilia, scrimshaw, and the last message sent by the captain of the Lusitania before it sank.

Harbor cruises on the *Zephyr* or the historic *Pioneer,* an 1885 schooner, also leave from here (see "Boat Tours," later in this chapter). Special children's workshops and storytelling hours are organized all over the place—pick up a schedule at the visitor center or call ✆ **212/748-8758.** The Land & Sea Pass provides admission to the galleries and entry onto the historic ships. You can also buy a ticket to see the ships alone ($10 per person). What with the ocean air whipping in off the river, you'll feel like old salts before the day is through.

Seaport: Pier 17, Fulton and South sts. 📞 **212/SEA-PORT** (732-7678). www.southstreetseaport.com. Free admission. Mon–Sat 10am–9pm; Sun 11am–8pm. **Museum:** 12 Fulton St. 📞 **212/748-8786.** www. seany.org. Admission (Land & Sea Pass) $15 adults; $12 seniors, youth, and students; free for children 1 and under. Children 16 and under must be supervised by an adult at all times. Tues–Sun 10am–6pm. Subway: 2, 3, 4, 5 to Fulton St.; A, C to Broadway/Nassau St.

Statue of Liberty ★★ Ages 3 & up. The symbol of New York is impressive enough from across the harbor, but close up—man, this chick is *big.* Ranger-led tours explore the promenade (right inside the entrance is displayed her original torch, replaced at the statue's centennial in 1986), and once again you can also climb up into her crown (closed to the public 2001–09) with a special ticket. Or simply head to the 10th-floor observatory to look at fascinating exhibits and peer up through a glass ceiling into her copper-clad steel skeleton. Timed-pass tickets for these tours must be reserved in advance, although a certain number are available on a walk-in basis at the ferry ticket office at Castle Clinton. Even if you don't have a tour reservation, it's fun to stroll around Liberty Island to gaze out over the harbor. For some kids, the ferry ride over is more fun than the statue itself. *Note:* The Statue of Liberty is scheduled to close for security upgrades in late 2011; you will still be able to visit Liberty Island, but the crown, base, and pedestal will be closed for approximately 1 year.

Getting There: The **Statue Cruises ferryboats** make frequent trips, running a loop from Battery Park to Liberty Island to Ellis Island and back to Battery Park (from New Jersey, you can board ferries in Liberty State Park). In Battery Park you can buy tickets at Castle Clinton, where there are some interesting exhibits to help pass the time before your ferry. The wait in line can take a while, and security procedures include metal detectors, bag searches, and waiting in several different holding pens— you'll come to appreciate the statue's poem about huddled masses yearning to be free. (Keep in mind that if you're carrying belongings that can't fit into a milk crate, you won't be allowed onto the ferry to Liberty or Ellis islands.) Once on the ferry (best views are from the top deck on the right-hand side), you can disembark at either island and board a later boat to continue your trip. Schedules vary, but the service generally runs daily starting at 9am (the last trip starts around 3:50pm); allow at least half an hour beforehand to clear security. Boats depart every 30 minutes, every 20 minutes on busy weekends; sailing time is about 15 minutes to Liberty Island, another 10 minutes to Ellis Island, and 10 minutes back to Manhattan.

Where to Eat: There's a **snack bar** on the ferry and a food concession on Liberty Island. If you bring a picnic lunch, watch out for marauding sea gulls.

On Liberty Island in New York Harbor. Buy tickets online or in Castle Clinton National Monument. 📞 **212/363-3200** (general info). www.nps.gov/stli. Free admission; ferry ticket to Statue of Liberty and Ellis Island: $12 adults, $10 seniors, $5 children (ages 4–12). With audio tour add $7–$8 per ticket (📞 877/523-9849; www.statuecruises.com). Daily 9am–4pm (last ferry departs around 3pm); extended hours in summer. Scheduled for closure for renovations in 2011. Please call ahead. Subway: 4, 5 to Bowling Green; 1 to South Ferry.

United Nations ★★ Ages 8 & up. Technically it's not even part of New York City, but an international zone all its own—step onto U.N. property and you can say you visited each of its 192 member nations in a day. This stunning East River site, its serene lawns and gardens cantilevered cleverly over the FDR Drive, makes a grand setting for that memorable postmodern design: the low dome of the General Assembly building tucked in at the base of the sheer glass plinth of the Secretariat Building. You'll mingle with an international cast of characters, African and Asian and

Scandinavian and Middle Eastern and Latin American bureaucrats chattering in a Babel of different tongues: It really brings home how big the world is and what an amazing feat it is to get all these people to agree on *anything.*

Walk past the long line of flagpoles (one for every member nation) to reach the visitors' entrance at 46th Street and First Avenue; go through security and proceed through the lobby to get on a **guided tour** in English. These run from 9:45am to 4:45pm and last nearly an hour (call ✆ **212/963-TOUR** [963-8687] to find out about tours in other languages); keep in mind that children 4 and under are not admitted on tours. These information-loaded talks fill you in on the organization's history while you cruise around to the complex's major highlights—the General Assembly Hall, the Security Council chamber, and other major meeting halls. The modernist interiors, mostly furnished in sleek Scandinavian style, look a little worn and frayed since their 1950s inception, but many details will impress older kids—the earpieces for simultaneous translations, the glassed-in booths for TV cameras, the horseshoe-shaped Security Council table, and massive pieces of internationally commissioned art and sculpture. A sobering exhibit of relics from the 1945 bombing of Nagasaki and Hiroshima reminds us of why the U.N. was formed in the first place; an exhibit on the horrors of land mines reminds us why it still is necessary.

The various U.N. agencies operate year-round, so there's always plenty of activity on the grounds. But things heat up when the General Assembly is in session, from the third Tuesday in September to sometime near the end of December. The **Gift Center** downstairs is great for finding unusual international handcrafts, including a delightful collection of dolls of all nations.

Where to Eat: There is a **coffee shop** near the gift shops, but for a more special experience, try the **Delegates Dining Room** ★ (reservations required—call ✆ **212/963-7625,** and be sure to bring a photo I.D.; jackets are required for men, and no sneakers or shorts are allowed), open to the public Monday through Friday from 11:30am to 2:30pm. Even if it's not exactly packed with high-level diplomats, the river views are great. Each week features a different culinary theme.

On the East River from 42nd to 48th sts. (entrance at First Ave. and 46th St.). ✆ **212/963-TOUR** (963-8687). www.un.org. Admission $16 adults, $11 seniors and students, $9 ages 5–12. Mon–Fri 9:30am–4:45pm. No tours Jan 1, Thanksgiving, Dec 25; limited schedule Sept–Oct. Subway: S, 4, 5, 6, 7 to 42nd St./Grand Central. Bus: M15, M27, M42, M104.

BEST VIEWS

Battery Park City Esplanade ★ **All ages.** The Statue of Liberty, Ellis Island, the Verrazano Bridge, and the Jersey City skyline punctuate the harbor views from this landscaped riverside walkway in a stunning residential/office development at the lower edge of Manhattan. People loll on the benches reading the *Times,* coffee mugs in hand; dog owners walk frisky pets on leashes; in-line skaters and cyclists weave patiently around pedestrians; and children hang on the inward-curved railings watching yachts cruise past on their way to the boat basin at the north end. No panhandlers, no T-shirt vendors, no ice-cream carts—it's a wonderfully civil scene.

On the Hudson River, btw. Chambers St. and Battery Place. Subway: A, C to Chambers St.

Brooklyn Heights Promenade ★ **All ages.** The calm here is so palpable, you'd never know that the Brooklyn-Queens Expressway is rumbling beneath your feet. On one side are the back gardens of lovely Brooklyn Heights town houses; on the other, the East River and a drop-dead view of Lower Manhattan and the harbor. It faces

24-hour PARTY CITY

Children's parties are big business in Manhattan, where the competitive stakes are high and the possible venues truly fantastic. But hey: Simply celebrating a birthday in the fizzy, heady atmosphere of the Big Apple can be a thrill in itself. If you want to do it yourself, in a restaurant, say, or a prime picnic spot in Central Park with the Manhattan skyline for cinematic backdrop, here are a few places to get the supplies you need. For decorations, balloons, party dishware, and party favors, **Party City** (38 W. 14th St., btw. Fifth and Sixth aves.; ☎ **212/271-7310**) is the spot. You can get colorful balloon bouquets created by "Certified Balloon Artists" and fun party favors at the **Balloon Saloon** (133 W. Broadway; ☎ **800/540-0749;** www.balloonsaloon.com), in TriBeCa. You can get the cake topper of your child's dreams and candles to match at **N.Y. Cake & Baking Dist.** ★ (56 W. 22nd St.; ☎ **212/675-CAKE** [675-2253]; www.nycake.com).

Following are just a few of the nifty places you can hold a child's birthday party in the city.

- **Carnival, Bowlmor Lanes.** Let kids loose in an indoor Coney Island, where they play carny games, eat cotton candy, and watch strolling performers do magic tricks or feats of amazement (110 University Place; ☎ **212/255-8188;** www.carnivalnyc.com; $700–$1,200 for 15 children and full buffet; 2hr.).
- **The USS** *Intrepid.* Birthday parties include museum admission, party hosts, food and cake, and a choice of themes, such as "pilot for a day" or "junior astronaut" (Pier 86, W. 46th St.; ☎ **212/957-3701;** www.intrepid museum.org; birthday packages $900–$1,800 for 30 guests [15 children/15 adults]; additional guests $40–$70).
- **The NBA Store.** Hoops-crazed celebrants (ages 6–12) will have exclusive use of the store's Center Court, pizza lunch and drink, a basketball cake, personalized team jersey, and video and All-Star Photocard favors (666 Fifth Ave.; ☎ **877/NBA-EVENT** [622-3836]; www.nba.com; $4,500 for up to 24 children, additional children $25 each; 2 hr.).
- **New York Fire Museum.** Birthday celebrations for the 4- to 6-year-old crowd at this downtown museum are surrounded by vintage fire engines. Kids get fire-truck-decorated cake, juice, balloons, and One Alarm loot bags with a fire chief hat, medals, and other fire-themed goodies (☎ **212/691-1303,** ext 15; www.nycfiremuseum.org; $700 for 16 children; 2 hr.; Sat–Sun only).
- **Swedish Cottage Marionette Theatre.** Private puppet show followed by party in child-size seats in room adjoining 1876 puppet theater; you'll need to cart in your own food and party favors (☎ **212/988-9093;** www.cityparksfoundation.org; $650 for birthday child and 15 guests; 2½ hr.).

west, which means that the view is especially terrific near sunset. Best of all, if you're with little kids, there's a superb neighborhood playground at the south end, near Pierrepont Street. Combine this with a walk across the Brooklyn Bridge or a visit to the New York Transit Museum (p. 172), and you've got a great day trip.

West of Columbia Heights (btw. Montague and Cranberry sts.), Brooklyn Heights, Brooklyn. Subway: 2, 3 to Clark St.; then follow Clark St. west to reach the Promenade.

Empire State Building ★   Ages 6 & up. The Empire State Building is the classic skyscraper observation deck—after all, this is where Cary Grant and Deborah Kerr missed their rendezvous in *An Affair to Remember* and Tom Hanks and Meg Ryan made theirs in *Sleepless in Seattle*. And, of course, this is where Fay Wray and King Kong had their own kind of rendezvous. The Art Deco lobby is still a looker, and the location puts you squarely in the middle of Manhattan, with close-up views to all sides. Tickets for the observation deck are sold up on the second-floor concourse, where you can also waste some money on the **New York Skyride** attraction (see later in this chapter). Lines zip along, but there are a fair number of them, and it may take an hour simply to get to the observation deck. An elevator whizzes you up to the 80th floor, where you change elevators to zoom up to the small enclosed observation deck on the 86th floor. It has narrow outdoor promenades on all sides, though the parapets are too high in many places for youngsters to see over. If you invested the extra dough downstairs, you can go even farther up to get porthole-type window viewing from the 102nd floor (1,250 ft. up). An excellent audio tour, available for $8, tells you exactly what you're looking out at—not a bad investment if you're an out-of-towner. Gift shops in the main lobby and on the 86th floor sell all kinds of New York City, Empire State Building, and (of course) King Kong knickknacks.

350 Fifth Ave. (at 34th St.). ☏ **212/736-3100.** www.esbnyc.com. Admission $20 adults, $18 seniors and students 12–17, $14 children 6–11, free for children 4 and under. ESB Express Passes $45 in advance. Observatories daily 8am–2am; last elevator goes up at 1:15am. Subway: B, D, F, N, R, V to 34th St./ Herald Square.

Top of the Rock ★   Ages 6 & up. Though the Empire State Building deck is higher, I'd recommend the Deco-detailed observation terraces atop Rockefeller Center's GE Building, especially for folks who get uneasy with heights—they're cleaner, roomier, and more securely enclosed with big glass panes that don't hinder the view. And don't worry: You'll see plenty. The 67th-floor deck is mostly indoors, a boon if the weather's rainy or cold; an escalator takes you on up to floor 69, where wide terraces ring the building (this is the only level where you can take in views to the west), and stairs lead up to the narrower 70th-floor outdoor deck. The elevator ride up is fun—the elevator car has a glass ceiling that allows you to look right up the shaft as you zoom upward; another fun feature is the Target Breezeway on floor 69, where colored lights behind opaque white panels switch on and off in response to people's movements around the room.

30 Rockefeller Center (entrance 50th St. btw. 5th and 6th aves.). ☏ **212/698-2000.** www. topoftherocknyc.com. Admission $21 adults, $14 children 6–12, $19 seniors. Daily 8am–midnight. Subway: B, D, F, V to 47th–50th sts./Rockefeller Center.

MORE MANHATTAN MUSEUMS

American Folk Art Museum   All ages. For whatever reason, even young kids get the point of folk art—in fact, young kids often enjoy this stuff more than older kids who think they know what "good" art is. The shows here change continually, but the collection is a charming mishmash of paintings and sculptures and collages—all by untutored artists, past and present—quilts, weather vanes, bottle-cap sculptures, an immense canvas covered with obsessively tiny handwriting, whatever. **"Families and Folk Art,"** interactive tours and artwork activities for kids 4 to 12, is held on the first

Saturday of every month (1–2:30pm; free with museum admission; ☎ **212/265-1040,** ext. 148). If your kids are good for only about 20 minutes of museum-going, pop into the small **Lincoln Square** branch on the Upper West Side (2 Lincoln Sq., on Columbus Ave. btw. 65th and 66th sts.; 1 train to 66th St./Lincoln Center; open Tues–Sun noon–7:30pm), where admission is free. The gift shop features a fabulous selection of toys you won't see everywhere else (see "A World of Museum Shops," on p. 254).

45 W. 53rd St. (btw. Fifth and Sixth aves.). ☎ **212/265-1040.** www.folkartmuseum.org Admission $9 adults, $7 students and seniors, free for children 11 and under, free to all Fri 5:30-7:30pm. Tues–Sun 10:30am-5:30pm (Fri until 7:30pm). Closed Mon and legal holidays. Subway: B, D, F to 47th-50th sts./ Rockefeller Center; V to Fifth Ave./53 St.

Children's Museum of Manhattan ★ Ages 1 to 10.
Best for the under-8 crew (and perfect for preschoolers), it's full of things they can touch, and has space for them to run and jump, make-believe environments, and opportunities to experiment. The museum's four floors also include a playroom especially for 4-and unders; a carpeted reading room with a puppet theater where kids can do their own impromptu shows; a few computers for older kids to mess around on; an interactive "TV station" where they can project themselves into a broadcast; and an activity-packed basement area that's periodically remodeled with a new literary theme. Young readers may appreciate the fun upstairs corridor that pays homage to various children's-book authors. There are always daily activities (check schedules when you enter) like face painting, storytelling, and shows in the auditorium. On rainy days and during school vacations, the joint gets pretty crowded, and the high-ceilinged spaces reverberate with noise; but it's still worth checking out.

212 W. 83rd St. (btw. Broadway and Amsterdam Ave.). ☎ **212/721-1223.** www.cmom.org. Admission $10 adults and children, $7 seniors, free for children under 1. Free admission 5-8pm on the first Fri of every month. Tues–Sun 10am-5pm; open school holidays. Subway: 1 to 79th or 86th St.; B, C to 81st St./ Museum of Natural History.

Children's Museum of the Arts ★★ Ages 1 to 10.
This interactive art-themed museum is a funky, charming gem—and it's much, much more of a creative-arts play space than a stodgy old museum (although it does have a collection of more than 2,000 artworks by children from around the globe, including vintage pieces made by kids under a WPA children's arts workshop in the 1930s). The museum is bi-level and paint-splashed messy (with the feel of a real artist's lair), the ideal habitat for pent-up urban kids and a great place for budding artists to express their creative selves. It's a highly interactive experience, and most kids dive right in, whether participating in the supervised art workshops or making a Jackson Pollock on their own. The CMA is highly active on Governors Island in the summer, with free family arts workshops on the weekends (ages 7–14; Nolan Park, Governors Island; Fri–Sun 11am–3pm June 5–Oct 3). **Note:** The museum was scheduled to move to a new space in the Saatchi & Saatchi Worldwide Headquarters at 375 Hudson St.; call before you visit.

182 Lafayette St. (btw. Broome and Grand sts.). ☎ **212/274-0986.** www.cmany.org. Admission $10, free for children under 1; pay what you wish Thurs 4-6pm. Wed-Sun noon-5pm (Thurs until 6pm); open school holidays. Subway: 6 to Spring St.; N, R, W to Prince St.

The Cloisters ★★ All ages.
Of course your kids aren't into medieval art—that's not the point. For families, the point of the Cloisters, the Metropolitan's beautiful medieval art annex, is the sheer otherness of it—a conglomeration of chapels and

rainy days & MONDAYS

Given that Monday is New York City's standard museum closing day, many a visitor on a tight schedule has been disappointed to find sights shuttered up on Monday. A number of family-friendly attractions are open on Monday, however, including the following:

o American Museum of Natural History
o Cooper-Hewitt National Design Museum
o Ellis Island and the Statue of Liberty
o Empire State Building/New York Skyride
o Guggenheim Museum of Art
o Madame Tussauds New York
o Merchant's House Museum
o Museum of Modern Art in Queens
o National Museum of the American Indian
o New York Public Library

o New York Transit Museum's satellite gallery in Grand Central Station
o New York Unearthed
o Queens County Farm Museum
o South Street Seaport Museum
o Top of the Rock
o The Toys "R" Us Ferris Wheel
o United Nations
o Yankee Stadium

All five of the city's zoos are open 7 days a week as well. The New York Botanical Garden and Brooklyn Botanic Garden, while usually closed on Monday, are open on Monday during 3-day holiday weekends. And to accommodate the schoolchildren who are their core audience, three outer-borough attractions—the Brooklyn Children's Museum, the New York Hall of Science, and Historic Richmond Town—stay open on Mondays during the summer school-vacation period.

courtyards and refectories lifted from European convents and monasteries, brought in packing crates to America, and reconstructed here on a bluff-top site in Fort Tryon Park. Wander from room to room, soaking up the time-stands-still atmosphere; go out on the terrace for splendid views of the Hudson River and the New Jersey Palisades; and poke around the monks' herb garden. Talk with your kids about unicorns before you go—there's one fascinating gallery devoted to a series of tapestries depicting a unicorn hunt (a medieval version of an adventure comic strip?).

It's a long trek up here, but your children might actually enjoy the bus or subway ride, which won't take forever if you're coming from the Upper West Side (combine the Cloisters with visits to St. John the Divine and Riverside Church for a full day of Gothic-ness). If you're doing this in the same day as the Metropolitan (which makes sense, since your pricey admission covers both sites), compare what you see up here to the Met's first-floor medieval galleries.

In Fort Tryon Park, at 193rd St. and Fort Washington Ave. ℂ 212/923-3700. www.metmuseum.org. Suggested donation (includes same-day admission to Metropolitan Museum of Art) $20 adults, $15 seniors, $10 students, free for children 12 and under. Tues–Sun 9:30am–5:15pm (closes at 4:45pm Nov–Feb). Closed Jan 1, Thanksgiving, and Dec 25. Free parking. Subway: A to 190th St. Bus: M4 to the end of line.

Cooper-Hewitt National Design Museum Ages 5 & up. Check to see what exhibit is currently running at this Smithsonian branch devoted to design and decorative arts: A surprising number of them appeal to kids (clothing, furniture, advertising posters), and the accompanying material is usually so lucid that even a young kid can

WHAT GOES AROUND COMES AROUND:
new york's carousels

Most kids are suckers for old-fashioned merry-go-rounds, no matter how corny the music, and New York is well supplied with them. The best known is probably the vintage hand-carved 1908 **Central Park Carousel** (midpark near 64th St.; $2 ride; Apr–Oct Mon–Fri 10am–5 or 6pm, Sat–Sun 10am–7pm), with its elaborately carved wooden horses spinning around for 4 minutes to creaky tunes like "Rainy Days and Mondays" and Beatles medleys; it's not far from either the zoo or the Wollman Rink, another plus. Our other antique choice is also near a good zoo: the **Prospect Park Carousel** (Flatbush Ave. entrance, Prospect Park; $1.50 ride; Apr–June and Sept–Oct Thurs–Sun noon–5pm; July to Labor Day Thurs–Sun noon–6pm), which has giraffes and zebras and other exotics in addition to horses, all painted in fanciful pastels.

These being postmodern times, however, a new generation of retro carousels has sprung up recently, just as meticulously handcrafted but often with a clever twist. The newest, the **Pier 62 Carousel,** a 36-passenger beauty on the waterfront in the Hudson River Park, next door to Chelsea Piers, has 33 hard-caved wooden figures based on indigenous Hudson River Valley fauna and one lone chariot ($2 ride; Mon–Thurs 11am–7:30pm, Fri–Sat 11am–9:30pm, Sun 11am–8:30pm). In Bryant Park, **Le Carrousel** (btw. 40th and 42nd sts. along Sixth Ave.; $2 ride; Sun–Thurs 11:30am–9pm, Fri–Sat 11:30am–10pm) is small but enchanting, with a riot of pastel floral decorations and a deer, a frog, and a bunny alongside the traditional horses. Though its ornate style is French-inspired, it was manufactured in good old Brooklyn, by the same firm that made the distinctive **Totally Kid Carousel** ★ (Riverbank State Park, 145th St. and Riverside Dr.; $1 ride; open Fri–Sun in summer); this one is most memorable, with its wonderfully whacked-out steeds designed by young neighborhood kids themselves. The lucky schoolchildren whose drawings were chosen to be reproduced—fanciful creatures like winged frogs replacing the traditional horses—were awarded free rides for life. Now there's a lottery worth winning. ***Note:*** Look for the aquatic-themed **SeaGlass Carousel** to open in Battery Park in 2011.

grasp what's interesting about the displays. What's more, it gives you a chance to get inside industrial tycoon Andrew Carnegie's surprisingly homey neo-Georgian mansion—don't forget to check out the beautiful plaster ceilings and the elegant leaded-glass conservatory, and point out to the kids how low some of the doorways are (Carnegie, a short man, wanted the house built to *his* scale). There's a nice garden out back and a super gift shop with a number of clever toys and kids' books (see "A World of Museum Shops," on p. 254); it's set in Carnegie's library—look at the inlaid designs in the wood paneling.

2 E. 91st St. (at Fifth Ave.). © **212/849-8400.** www.cooperhewitt.org. Admission $15 adults, $10 students and seniors, free for children 12 and under. Mon–Fri 10am–5pm; Sat 10am–6pm; Sun 11am–6pm. Closed major holidays. Subway: 4, 5, 6 to 86th St.

Forbes Magazine Galleries ✦ **All ages.** An obsessive collector, publishing magnate Malcolm Forbes had enough money to turn his obsessions into a strange and wonderful little museum. Basically, he collected five things: toy boats, toy soldiers,

Monopoly games, medals and trophies, and lavishly bejeweled Fabergé eggs. The eggs were sold, alas, for a princely sum, but that leaves plenty that kids do love. This labyrinth of small galleries won't tax youngsters' attention spans, though they should be warned ahead that this is a sedate don't-touch kind of place. (No strollers permitted inside, either.) The display windows aren't always low enough for small children, so expect to do a lot of lifting. Your kids may not want to linger as long as you do over the minutiae of the collection—remember, Forbes was a grown-up when he collected this stuff, with an adult's idea of what made something valuable. But there's still plenty here to make kids press their noses against the glass for a good half-hour or so, more if they're older. Be sure to book a free tour in advance.

60 Fifth Ave. (at 12th St.). ℂ **212/206-5548.** www.forbesgalleries.com. Free admission, but children 15 and under must be accompanied by an adult. Tues–Wed and Fri–Sat 10am–4pm. Closed major holidays. Subway: N, R, 4, 5, 6 to 14th St.; L to Union Square.

Guggenheim Museum Ages 6 & up. The Guggenheim's rotating exhibits of 20th-century art may or may not appeal to your kids—Norman Rockwell maybe yes, Mark Rothko maybe no. No matter. The main reason for including this museum in your NYC itinerary is the museum building itself: Frank Lloyd Wright's glorious, streamlined, totally wacky inverted spiral, which displays the art along one long ramp coiling down around a huge central atrium. I mean, can you imagine doing the Guggenheim on a *skateboard*? Since kids 11 and younger get in free, it may be worthwhile to pay the adult admission just so you can enjoy this visionary interior for half an hour. In any case, the side galleries display some artworks kids might enjoy, by such masters as Degas, Cézanne, and Picasso.

1071 Fifth Ave. (at 89th St.). ℂ **212/423-3500.** www.guggenheim.org. Admission $18 adults, $15 students and seniors, free for children 11 and under. Sun–Wed and Fri 10am–5:45pm; Sat 10am–7:45pm. Subway: 4, 5, 6 to 86th St.

Intrepid Sea, Air & Space Museum ★★ Ages 4 & up. The aircraft carrier known as the "Fighting I" served the U.S. Navy for 31 years, suffering bomb attacks, kamikaze strikes, and a torpedo shot. In 1982 it opened as a sea, air, and space museum on the New York waterfront. It's easily one of the city's top attractions for kids. Inside the **Exploreum** (on the hangar deck), you can crawl inside a wooden sub from the American Revolution; inspect a nuclear missile submarine; or enter the cockpit of an A-6 Intruder and manipulate the controls. How cool is that? You can even climb into the captain's bridge, where kids can fiddle with the controls and former Intrepid crew members are on hand to answer questions—but be warned that strollers aren't allowed and there are no elevators; you'll have to carry toddlers up (and back down) several sets of steep, narrow stairs. Summers are crowded; get here early or buy tickets online. Some 30 vintage aircraft are displayed on and around the flight deck.

Pier 86, 12th Ave. and 46th St. ℂ **212/245-0072.** www.intrepidmuseum.org. Admission $22 adults, $8 students and seniors, $17 children 3–17, free for children 2 and under. Apr 1–Sept 30 Mon–Fri 10am–5pm, Sat–Sun 10am–6pm; Oct 1–Mar 31 Tues–Sun 10am–5pm. Bus: M42 to 12th St. and Hudson Ave. Subway: A, C, E, S, 1, 2, 3, 7, 9 to 42nd St./Times Square.

Lower East Side Tenement Museum ★★ Ages 5 & up. A collection of 19th-century tenement buildings has been converted into this brilliant small museum that picks up the immigrant story where Ellis Island leaves off—in the poor neighborhoods where the new arrivals landed. Once you've seen these bare, cramped living quarters, all too authentically furnished, your kids may never fight again over sharing a bedroom. (It's the perfect antidote to all those ornate period rooms at the Metropolitan Museum.) The restored tenement apartments can be seen only via hour-long guided tours; book ahead to make sure you get onto the right tour. Furnishings and other artifacts tell the stories of immigrants from different homelands and eras of immigration; the best one for kids (ages 5 and up) would be the 60-minute living-history **Confino Family Tour.** The Confinos were Greek Sephardic immigrants who lived in the Lower East Side tenement around 1916. Featuring costumed interpreters, the tours are held only on weekend afternoons and are limited to 15 people; so reserve in advance, especially for Sunday. Weekend walking tours widen the scope to include the whole neighborhood—they're wonderful if your kids are old enough to keep up with the pace.

108 Orchard St. (below Delancey St.). 🅒 **866/606-7232.** www.tenement.org. Tours $20 adults, $15 students and seniors. Tours daily 10:30am–5pm. Subway: J, M, Z to Essex St.; B or D to Grand St.; F to Delancey St.

Madame Tussauds New York ★ **Ages 7 & up.** Transplanted from London, this wax museum to the stars has adapted its slightly creepy signature attraction to the Big Apple by featuring wax replicas of quintessential New Yorkers such as former mayor Rudolph Giuliani, Woody Allen, Joe DiMaggio, Yoko Ono, Jacqueline Kennedy Onassis, Donald Trump, and Andy Warhol. Newer models include Sean ("Diddy") Combs. (Never fear, you can still see Tussauds favorites like Princess Di and the Beatles.) The admission fees are outrageous, granted, but you can have a whopping good time here, prowling through room after room of these meticulously crafted effigies. Evening hours mean that you can fit this into your schedule after most of the regular museums have closed for the day. Young children may get freaked out by the all-too-lifelike statues; it's better for kids old enough to recognize the celebrities and the great figures from the past. Be sure to bring a camera so that you can pose next the statue of your choice and show off your new best friend to the folks back home. *Note:* The ghoulish section re-creating the French Revolution is rife with blood and dismemberment (another Tussauds trademark).

234 W. 42nd St. (btw. Seventh and Eighth aves.). 🅒 **800/246-8872.** www.madametussauds.com/ NewYork. Admission $36 adults, $33 seniors, $29 children 4–12, free for children 3 and under. Look for discounted online specials. Daily 10am–10pm. Subway: A, C, E to 42nd St./Port Authority; B, D, F, V to 6th Ave./42nd St.; N, R, S, 1, 2, 3, 7 to 42nd St./Times Square.

The Morgan Library ★ **Ages 8 & up.** The Morgan Library's refined gallery space exhibits prints and drawings, which may or may not be of interest to your kids—past shows about A. A. Milne or Saint-Exupéry's *The Little Prince* were totally delightful for youngsters, but that isn't always the case. What kids will appreciate is the McKim-designed wing J. P. Morgan actually used as a library, especially his sumptuous wood-paneled study with its ceiling-high shelves of rare books, gorgeously bound in leather. By the time you read this, the newly refurbished library will have reopened, buffed and polished to a golden patina and outfitted with state-of-the-art lighting, newly designed display cases, and the original pendant chandelier (in mothballs for 70 years) in place at the library entrance.

225 Madison Ave. (at E. 36th St.). 🅒 **212/685-0008.** www.themorgan.org. Admission $12 adults; $8 students, seniors, and children 16 and under; free for children 12 and under. Tues–Thurs 10:30am–5pm; Fri 10:30am–9pm; Sat 10am–6pm; Sun 11am–6pm. Closed holidays. Subway: 6 to 33rd St.

Museum of Chinese in America **Ages 5 & up.** Now ensconced in a larger space, this museum mounts fascinating rotating exhibits, mostly drawn from its huge collection of photographs and artifacts—tiny shoes for a Chinese woman's bound feet, tin tea canisters, brocaded Chinese opera costumes, the heavy irons used in a laundry. The gallery is a stunning surprise, with angled translucent walls creating the illusion of being inside a giant Chinese lantern. Saturday afternoons are a great time to visit, to take advantage of free hands-on workshops for kids (teaching about paper folding, shadow puppets, and so on) or in-depth themed walking tours of Chinatown.

211–215 Center St. ✆ 212/619-4785. www.mocanyc.org. Suggested admission $7 adults, $4 students and seniors, free for children 11 and under. Mon and Fri 11am–5pm; Thurs 11am–9pm; Sat-Sun 10am–5pm. Subway: N, R, 6 to Canal St.

The Paley Center for Media   **Ages 5 & up.** Formerly known as the Museum of Television & Radio, this sleek Midtown museum (with a sister branch in L.A.) is where junior couch potatoes can gorge on all kinds of broadcast media, from vintage commercials to 1960s sitcoms to TV coverage of the first moonwalk. Get here early in the day and make a reservation to use the library, where you can search the database on a Mac and then call up a program on an individual console with headphones. If you can't get a reservation, at least stop by the fifth-floor radio-listening room to sample sound bites from timely preselected programs or attend any of the screenings running frequently in a number of cushy small theaters. Weekends are the best time for kids, when there are hands-on workshops in the morning and uncrowded screenings of top international children's TV shows in the afternoon; the staff is genuinely friendly to youngsters. If your child's hooked on TV Land, plan for hours of browsing.

25 W. 52nd St. (btw. Fifth and Sixth aves.). ✆ 212/621-6600 or 621-6800. www.mtr.org. Admission $10 adults, $8 students, $5 children 13 and under. Wed-Sun noon-6pm (until 8pm Thurs). Closed major holidays. Subway: E or M to Fifth Ave./53rd St.; N or R to 49th St./7th Ave.; 1 to 50th St.; B, D, F, or M to 47th-50th St./Rockefeller Center.

Museum of the City of New York ★ 👜   **Ages 3 & up.** If you're on Museum Mile already, your kids may enjoy this more than the art museums farther south (be sure to skip across the street afterward to Central Park's lovely Conservatory Garden—see p. 180). The biggest draw for kids is the spectacular exhibit of dolls and dollhouses in the Toys Gallery, though some kids I know like to come here just to parade up and down the gorgeous staircase in the entrance hall. Perhaps the most famous dollhouse in the collection is the **Stettheimer Dollhouse** ★★, the exquisite creation of Carrie Walter Stettheimer, a theater set designer in the 1920s. The dollhouse has period wallpaper, delicate paper lampshades, and walls hung with 15 original miniature works of art by such famous avant-garde artists as Marcel Duchamp (15 other miniature masterpieces made for the dollhouse are now on exhibit nearby). Prowling through re-created bedchambers and parlors and gazing at displays of famous New Yorkers' fashionable outfits is a great way for kids to peek back in history. Theater lovers won't want to miss the Broadway exhibit, displaying posters and mementos from the Great White Way (including a costume Barbra Streisand wore in *Funny Girl*). Peter Pan fans will be blown away upon seeing the black net "shadow" that Wendy sewed back onto Peter Pan's toes in the old Mary Martin musical—that's the kind of awesome stuff this museum has hidden away.

1220 Fifth Ave. (at 103rd St.). ✆ 212/534-1672. www.mcny.org. Suggested admission $10 adults, $6 students and seniors, free for children 12 and under, $20 families. Tues-Sun 10am–5pm. Subway: 6 to 103rd St.; 2 or 3 to Central Park North (110th St.). Bus: M1, M2, M3, M4.

National Museum of the American Indian 🏛   **Ages 5 & up.** A branch of the Smithsonian, this museum enjoys a fabulous setting in the ornate 1907 U.S. Customs House, a Beaux Arts gem that your kids may recognize from the movie *Ghostbusters II*.

To enter the exhibition galleries, you pass through the awesome Great Rotunda—don't miss looking up at the painted dome. The museum has vast holdings, only a small portion of which are on display here (especially now that the Smithsonian has opened its main NMAI museum on the Mall down in Washington, D.C.). It isn't big on interactivity, but wend your way through the series of rooms and you should be able to find something of interest, particularly if your kids have studied Native American culture in school—a hanging bison hide they can stroke, a glass case filled with hundreds of moccasins, mysterious Mesoamerican clay figures, or some eye-opening art by contemporary Native American artists.

1 Bowling Green, beside Battery Park. ℰ **212/514-3700.** www.nmai.si.edu. Free admission. Daily 10am–5pm (until 8pm Thurs). Closed Dec 25. Subway: 4, 5 to Bowling Green; R to Whitehall St./South Ferry.

New York City Fire Museum Ages 3 & up. Though small, this two-story museum in a converted firehouse is worth the money if your kids are into fire trucks. There's an awesome collection of antique fire engines, including several horse-drawn ones (the horses aren't on display, unfortunately, but there's a stuffed fire dog that used to be the mascot of one Brooklyn firehouse). A lot of the museum is most interesting to adults patient enough to pore over the mementos of 19th-century firefighting, but there are enough bells, alarms, pickaxes, and nozzles to hold the youngsters' interest for 45 minutes or so. Best of all, there are usually retired firefighters on hand eager to explain each apparatus to admiring youngsters.

278 Spring St. (btw. Varick and Hudson sts.). ℰ **212/691-1303.** www.nycfiremuseum.org. Suggested admission $7 adults; $5 seniors, students, and children. Tues–Sat 10am–5pm; Sun 10am–4pm. Subway: 1 to Houston St.; C, E to Spring St.

New York City Police Museum 🗡 Ages 6 & up. With everything from vintage uniforms to a mock-up of a crime scene and a computer simulation of what it would be like to be confronted with a gun-wielding criminal, this collection of police memorabilia should mesmerize any child who's into cops and robbers. Confiscated weapons (including Al Capone's machine gun), counterfeit money, old patrol cars and motorcycles, badges and radios and alarms and nightsticks . . . the mind boggles. It's in a beautiful neo–Italian Renaissance Hunt & Hunt building that was built as the First Precinct police station house in 1911 and is staffed by NYPD officers.

100 Old Slip (at South St.). ℰ **212/480-3100.** www.nycpolicemuseum.org. Suggested admission $7 adults; $5 students, seniors, and children 3–18; free for children 2 and under. Mon–Sat 10am–5pm. Subway: 2, 3 to Wall St.; R to Whitehall St.; J, M, Z to Broad St.; 4, 5 to Bowling Green.

New-York Historical Society ★ Ages 4 & up. Rotating exhibits here have been noteworthy in recent years—the blockbuster Alexander Hamilton exhibit, for example, exhibits of presidential campaign memorabilia, or the occasional opportunity to gaze upon John James Audubon's stunning original art for his classic *Birds of America.* Older children may be ready to browse through the fourth-floor exhibit space, crammed with treasures from the society's vast holdings—George Washington's camp bed from Valley Forge, the desk where Clement Clarke Moore wrote *A Visit from St. Nicholas,* a glorious collection of Tiffany lamps, and a portrait of an early governor of New York dressed as a woman. Note that work is being done on the museum's Central Park West facade and new galleries, but the museum will remain open during the work.

170 Central Park West (btw. 76th and 77th sts.). ℰ **212/873-3400.** www.nyhistory.org. Admission $12 adults, $9 educators and seniors, $7 students, free for children 11 and under. Tues–Sat 10am–6pm (until 8pm Fri); Sun 11am–5:45pm. Subway: B, C to 81st St./Museum of Natural History.

New York Public Library (Stephen A. Schwarzman Building) ★ **Ages 8 & up.** Though most little kids fall in love with the noble pair of lions—*Patience* and *Fortitude*—poised beside the front steps, the exhibits mounted inside the main branch of the New York Public Library are usually of interest to older kids only. The library branch, which now bears the name of one of Wall Street's private-equity-firm kings, has an extraordinary collection of first editions, manuscripts, letters, prints, maps, and other treasures on paper and often puts together fascinating shows, but whether or not your youngster will be intrigued all depends on the theme. Otherwise, pop in for a few minutes just to gape at the Beaux Arts architecture, from the dignified marble lobby to the extraordinary third-floor Main Reading Room, where anyone can join the scholars and writers at endless ranks of tables poring over research materials from the NYPL's famous stacks. Note that behind the library is **Bryant Park,** which is filled with cafes, free chairs and tables for alfresco dining, and its own spiffy little **carousel** ($2).

One good reason to pop in to the library these days is to see the original **Winnie-the-Pooh animals** ★ displayed in their new home here in the city's main library.

Note that the beautiful marble steps can be slippery in rain and snow.

Fifth Ave. at 41st St. ⓒ **212/275-6975.** www.nypl.org. Free admission. Mon and Thurs–Sat 10am–6pm; Tues–Wed 10am–9pm. Subway: B, D, F, V to 42nd St.; 7 to Fifth Ave.

The Skyscraper Museum ★ **All ages.** How far is it, really, from stacking building blocks to building skyscrapers? This museum is located, appropriately enough, at the south end of Manhattan, at the foot of Wall Street's shoulder-to-shoulder jumble of skyscrapers. The muscular icons of the Manhattan skyline, skyscrapers were born out of the needs of a hubristic and rapidly expanding metropolis—tall buildings carved real estate out of the sky. This museum pays homage to the city's amazing vertical architecture, much of which went up in the skyscraper boom of the early 20th century. A must-see for young and old: the Lilliputian wooden panoramas of New York, hand-carved by an amateur Arizona model maker, so exquisitely small that 10 city blocks can fit into the palm of your hand. The museum is very family-friendly and offers regular Saturday workshops where kids get to, yes, stack blocks and build their own skyscrapers.

Ritz-Carlton Hotel (ground floor), 39 Battery Place, Battery Park City. ⓒ **212/968-1961.** www.skyscraper.org. Admission $5 adults, $2.50 seniors and students, free for children 11 and under. Wed–Sun noon–6pm. Subway: 4, 5 to Bowling Green; R, W to Whitehall St.; 1 to South Ferry; J, M, Z to Broad St.

Sony Wonder Technology Lab ★ 🐾 **Ages 6 & up.** Though no doubt it helps sell Sony products, this wonderful interactive exploratorium isn't annoyingly self-serving. Sony Wonder actually lets people experiment with all types of high-tech equipment, from TV cameras to industrial robots to ultrasound scanners; you can play at being a game designer, a movie director, or an electronic musician or just mess around in a multisensory interactive environment. When you first enter the lab, you get your own **personal card,** which becomes magnetically encoded with your name and photo (and even voice); as you continue through four floors of activities, every time you slide the card through the scanner on a new terminal, your name and photo are inserted into whatever program is up. On your way out, you can print out a personalized certificate recording all the activities you tried. To prevent overcrowding, the Sony Wonder folks have set up a timed-ticket system; call 1 week to 3 months ahead to reserve your time slot, especially if you're planning to come before 2pm on a weekday September through June (this place is *very* popular with school groups). If you haven't reserved a slot, you'll be admitted on a first-come, first-served basis, which may mean you'll have to wait in line in the lobby (a comic robot, b.b. wonder-bot, helps you pass the time with goofy interactive chat).

550 Madison Ave. (entrance on 56th St.). ⓒ **212/833-8100;** for reservations call 212/833-5414 Mon–Fri 8am–2pm. www.sonywondertechlab.com. Free admission. Tues–Sat 10am–5pm; Sun noon–5pm. Subway: N, R, 4, 5, 6 to 59th St.; E, M to Fifth Ave.

The Studio Museum in Harlem **Ages 6 & up.** It all depends on what the current exhibition is, but this savvy uptown museum mounts some very interesting art in its cool, high-ceilinged white galleries and often has good Saturday-morning family workshops. It's a reasonably sized place for a dose of art viewing, and a good start to a Harlem neighborhood exploration. Sundays are free!

144 W. 125th St. (btw. Lenox Ave. and Adam Clayton Powell Blvd.). ⓒ **212/864-4500.** www.studiomuseum.org. Suggested donation $7 adults, $3 students and seniors, free for children 12 and under. Thurs–Fri noon–9pm; Sat 10am–6pm; Sun noon–6pm. Subway: A, B, C, D, 2, 3, 4, 5, 6 to 125th St.

MUSEUMS IN THE OUTER BOROUGHS

In Brooklyn

Brooklyn Children's Museum ★★ **All ages.** Technically the oldest children's museum in the country, founded in 1899, the Brooklyn Children's Museum is also one of the best in the country, and the big yellow building reopened in 2008 with an array of hands-on exhibits that will interest kids up to age 14. The emphasis on technology, TV, and video will appeal to older children (witness the pair of hip New York boys, ages 10 and 12, who wandered into a *Sesame Street* exhibit, saw themselves on a monitor, and wound up happily clowning around alongside various *Sesame Street* characters they thought they'd outgrown). In the new **World Brooklyn** exhibit, kids can experience multiple cultures in a charming kid-scale cityscape. There's also an emphasis on nature, with exhibits exploring animals' eating habits and plants' growing habits in a hands-on greenhouse. In the **Neighborhood Nature,** staff members bring out the museum's permanent animal inhabitants, including a beautiful and enormous albino python named Fantasia, to demonstrate their traits. There's also a kitchen-sink exhibit called **Collections Central,** a rotating display of the 30,000 objects in the museum's collection, including toys, rocks, fossils, amulets—the sorts of odd and fascinating things that kids like to squirrel away in shoe boxes. Children 5 and under can explore the bright tactile learning environment of **Totally Tots.** Look for ongoing story times on the calendar of events.

The museum's daffodil-yellow expansion features a lobby, a theater, a kids' cafe, and much more gallery space. It's also expected to be the city's first official "green" museum, awarded LEED certification for its sustainable structural features.

Getting There: By **subway,** take the no. 3 to the Kingston Avenue station, walk 6 blocks (with traffic flow) on Kingston Avenue to St. Mark's Avenue, and turn left for 1 block. Or take the no. A to the Nostrand Avenue station, walk 6 blocks on Kingston Avenue (against traffic) to St. Mark's Avenue, turn right, and go 2 blocks. By **car,** take Atlantic Avenue east to Brooklyn Avenue, turn right, and drive 4 blocks south; or follow Eastern Parkway east from Grand Army Plaza to New York Avenue, turn left, and go 6 blocks north to St. Mark's Avenue, where you turn right and go 1 block east. Unmetered on-street parking is nearby.

Brower Park, 145 Brooklyn Ave. (at St. Mark's Ave.), Crown Heights. ⓒ **718/735-4400.** www.brooklynkids.org. Suggested admission $7.50 per person, free for children under 1. Tues–Sun 10am–5pm.

Brooklyn Museum ★   Ages 6 & up. The superb Egyptian collection, full of over-the-top mummy cases, is the best reason to visit this big, underappreciated museum in Brooklyn, near neighbor to the Brooklyn Botanic Garden and Prospect Park; even if you're going to spend only an hour or so in the museum, there are enough other things to do nearby to justify the excursion. If your kids like history, they can wander past 27 detailed American period rooms from 1675 to 1928, including an eye-popping Moorish-style smoking room from John D. Rockefeller's own town house. If they're old enough to appreciate great art, the American and European galleries are strong, with lots of Impressionism and a load of Rodin bronzes. There's also a special gift shop just for kids, as well as lots of weekend drop-in programs for children.

200 Eastern Pkwy., at Prospect Park, Brooklyn. © 718/638-5000. www.brooklynart.org. Admission $10 adults, $6 students and seniors, free for children 11 and under. Wed–Fri 10am–5pm; Sat–Sun 11am–6pm (1st Sat of the month 11am–11pm). Parking $3 for 1st hour, $2 per hour after that. Subway: 2, 3 to Eastern Pkwy.

Jewish Children's Museum   All ages. Multimedia and hands-on are the watchwords for this museum out in Crown Heights, dedicated to explicating Judaism to youngsters of all faiths. Push buttons to trigger a multimedia "re-creation" of Creation; clamber around a large-than-life replica of a Shabbat table setting and shop in a Kosher supermarket; play Mini-Golf's Six Holes of Life; be a newscaster reporting on the miracle of the oil from the war with the Maccabees; feel the rush of the Red Sea parting on either side of you and stand atop Mount Sinai to receive the Ten Commandments alongside Moses—yep, it's all simulated here. Developed under the guidance of Rabbi Menachem M. Schneerson, otherwise known as the Lubavitcher Rebbe, this handsome facility offers a pretty persuasive reason to head out to Brooklyn.

792 Eastern Pkwy. (at Kingston Ave.), Brooklyn. © 718/467-0600. www.jcmonline.org. Admission $10, free for children 1 and under. Mon–Thurs 10am–4pm; Sun 10am–6pm. Closed Jan 1 and all Jewish holidays. Subway: 3 to Kingston Ave.

Lefferts Homestead Children's Historic House Museum   All ages. This Dutch colonial farmhouse has been filled with exhibits for kids—old-fashioned toys, puppets, storybook corners, art activities—and absolutely everything in it is touchable. It's a little shabby, but who cares when your kids are allowed to run up and down the stairs and jump off the porch and just enjoy themselves? On summer Sundays, come for the afternoon songs and story hours under the big tree outside, and go on to visit the nearby Prospect Park Zoo (p. 179) and take a spin on the stunning carved animals of the vintage Prospect Park Carousel.

Flatbush Ave., Brooklyn. © 718/789-2822. Free admission. Apr–Nov Thurs–Sun noon–5pm (until 6pm July to Labor Day). Subway: B, Q, S to Prospect Park.

New York Transit Museum ★   Ages 3 & up. This museum is set in an old subway station, with exhibits sprawling down the tunnels—talk about awesome! Small kids love the pair of bus cabs they can climb into and pretend to drive and the set of vintage subway cars they can lope through, hanging on straps and swinging around poles. Beyond that, the collection dwells on antique turnstiles and fare boxes, switching apparatus, and subway-station mosaics. The sheer amount of stuff makes this place good for an hour, more if your kid is transportation-obsessed.

At the corner of Boerum Place and Schermerhorn St., Brooklyn. © 718/694-1600. www.mta.nyc.ny.us/mta/museum. Admission $5 adults, $3 seniors and children 17 and under. Tues–Fri 10am–4pm; Sat–Sun noon–5pm. Subway 2, 3, 4, 5 to Borough Hall; A, C, G to Hoyt/Schermerhorn sts.; A, C, F to Jay St./Borough Hall; M, R to Court St.

In Queens

American Museum of the Moving Image ★★ **Ages 8 & up.** *Note:* At press time, this Astoria museum was closed for a major $67-million expansion but was scheduled to reopen in January 2011; check the website for the latest updates. This superb resource for cinephiles is housed in the Kaufman Astoria Studio, where talkies were made long ago and *Sesame Street* is filmed today (unfortunately, you cannot tour the set). At interactive workstations, you can fiddle with sound effects, dub in new dialogue, call up different soundtracks, create your own digital animation, and even star in your own personal flipbook. Many of the historic artifacts on display (a 1910 wooden Pathé camera, a 1959 Philco TV set, Charlton Heston's chariot from *Ben-Hur*) may mean nothing to youngsters, but the extensive costume gallery should grab them (items like Robin Williams's padded housedress from *Mrs. Doubtfire*), as will the ghoulish masks in the makeup exhibition and the special effects artifacts—you'll see a character model of Yoda from 1980's *The Empire Strikes Back,* before computer animation rendered such puppetry obsolete. The new expansion will include a three-story addition, a 264-seat film theater, a 68-seat screening room, a cafe, and a big new outdoor space, the Courtyard Garden.

35th Ave. and 36th St., Astoria, Queens. ℂ **718/784-0077.** www.ammi.org. Admission (includes film and video programs) $10 adults, $7.50 students and seniors, $5 children 5–18, free for children 4 and under. Wed–Thurs 11am–5pm; Fri 11am–8pm (free admission after 4pm); Sat–Sun 11am–6:30pm. Subway: N, W to Broadway; G, R, V to Steinway St.

New York Hall of Science ★★ **Ages 3 & up.** Like the wonderful Imaginarium in San Francisco, this is a completely hands-on museum that makes learning really fun—you can pedal furiously on a bicycle to turn a huge propeller; you can watch a bank of rotating electric fans create wind; you can hunt for microbes and fungi with microscopes; you can use colored Plexiglas tiles to make your own rainbow; you can watch your brother get really huge and then really tiny as he walks across an optically distorted room. Put your ear to glass pipes, and you can hear different pitches; stand in front of a special light scope, and you can cast three different-colored shadows at once.

Best of all, no activity takes more than a minute to execute, which means that kids sprint from one to another instead of hogging a demo station—you rarely have to wait your turn to try anything. And the **Science Playground** (additional $4; appropriate for kids 6 and older; closed Jan–Feb) is an awesome 60,000-square-foot space with loads of interactive activities indoors and out, including a gigantic teeter-totter, a light-activated kinetic sculpture, windmills, and a water-play area. The colorful **Rocket Park Mini Golf** exhibition (additional $6 adults, $4 children), which opened in 2009, is both a 9-hole minigolf course and an interactive lesson in rocket science. Opt for the Combination Ticket (see below) if you want to hit all the museum highlights.

The cafe is limited; you'd be better off packing a lunch—there aren't many options in the neighborhood. Definitely combine the science museum with a stop at the nearby Queens Zoo and/or Queens Museum of Art (both later in this chapter).

47-01 111th St., Flushing Meadows-Corona Park, Corona, Queens. ℂ **718/699-0005.** www.nysci.org. Admission $11 adults, $8 children 2–17 and seniors; Science Playground fee $4; Rocket Park Mini Golf $6 adults, $4 children and seniors. Combination Ticket (museum, Science Playground, Rocket Park Mini Golf): $19 adults; $15 seniors, students, and children 2–17. Free to all Fri 2–5pm and Sun 10–11am Sept–June. Sept–June 27 Tues–Thurs 9:30am–2pm, Fri 9:30am–5pm, Sat–Sun 10am–6pm; June 28–Aug 31 Mon–Fri 9:30am–5pm, Sat–Sun 10am–6pm. Closed major holidays. Parking $14. Subway: 7 to 111th St.

Queens County Farm Museum ★ **All ages.** Still a working farm, this 18th-century homestead is a bucolic spot of fields and orchards and barns full of animals, with ongoing demonstrations of agricultural arts—plowing, planting, apple picking, reaping, milking cows, birthing foals, incubating chicks, and so on. Come on a weekend, when you can go inside the simple three-room frame farmhouse, built in 1772, and take a hayride ($2 per person). From mid-September to November, weekend visitors can try to find their way through the **Amazing Maize Maze,** a giant corn maze ($8 adults, $5 children 4–11, free for kids 3 and under).

73–50 Little Neck Pkwy., Floral Park, Queens. ℂ **718/347-3276.** www.queensfarm.org. Free admission (except for special events). Mon-Fri 10am–5pm (grounds only); Sat-Sun 10am–5pm (house and grounds). Subway: E, F to Kew Gardens/Union Tpk., then Q46 bus to Little Neck Pkwy.

Queens Museum of Art **Ages 8 & up.** Besides the fact that it's parked next to the Unisphere, that famous stainless steel globe from the 1964 World's Fair, the chief reason for children to visit this museum of 20th-century art is the **Panorama** ★, an awesomely huge three-dimensional re-creation of the New York skyline. Originally built in 1964, it's been faithfully updated; laser-light shafts stand in place of the World Trade Center, replicating the "Tribute in Light" that marked the towers' place for a few months after the 9/11 tragedy. The lights are timed to show the progress of a day every 9 minutes. Kids will love picking out familiar landmarks; anyone who enjoys dollhouses, Polly Pockets, and Micro Machines can marvel over the incredibly detailed small-scale rendering of a city that's often all too large-scale. The museum's **Family Drop-in Art Workshops** (ages 5–12; free) are some of the best in the city.

NYC Building (next to the Unisphere), Flushing Meadows-Corona Park, Queens. ℂ **718/592-9700.** www.queensmuseum.org. Admission $5 adults, $2.50 students and seniors, free for children 4 and under. Wed–Sun noon–6pm; Fri in July–Aug until 8pm. Subway: 7 to Willett's Point/Shea Stadium, then walk south over ramp into park and head for the Unisphere.

On Staten Island

Historic Richmond Town ★ **Ages 5 & up.** Somewhat off the beaten track, this 100-acre re-creation includes 27 buildings spanning the 17th to the early 20th century—which may create a disjointed effect for historical purists, but kids generally don't care. Three little streets are set up like a small village, and kids can run in and out of the house, shops, inns, and schoolhouses (there are even a couple of outhouses!) and basically just have a ball. Many buildings were moved here from other sites on Staten Island; they range from a neoclassical courthouse to a little schoolhouse dating from 1695, the oldest elementary school building in the country. Costumed interpreters are in action July and August, demonstrating crafts like basket weaving, spinning, weaving, tinsmithing, and printing. A good full day's expedition.

441 Clarke Ave., Staten Island. ℂ **718/351-1611.** www.historicrichmondtown.org. Admission $5 adults, $4 seniors, $3.50 children 5-17, free for children 4 and under. Sept–June Wed–Sun 1-5pm; July–Aug Wed–Sun 11am–5pm. From the Staten Island Ferry, take bus no. S74 to Richmond Rd./St. Patrick's Place.

Staten Island Children's Museum ★ **Ages 10 & under.** Of all the area's children's museums, this one has the loveliest setting—on the lawns and gardens of the Snug Harbor Cultural Center, formerly a home for retired seamen. There's already plenty to do on-site, with weekend workshops and a host of interactive exhibits that help children explore the wonders of water, insects, computers, and animals (there's more of an emphasis on natural sciences here than at its more urban counterparts).

A bonus: You get here via the Staten Island Ferry, with only a short added bus ride from the terminus.

Snug Harbor Cultural Center, 1000 Richmond Terrace, Staten Island. © **718/273-2060.** www.staten islandkids.org. Admission $6, free for children under 1 (grandparents free on Wed). Tues–Sun noon–5pm when public schools are open and 10am–5pm when public schools are closed (until 8pm Wed July–Aug). From the Staten Island Ferry, take the S40 bus (Richmond Terrace) to the Snug Harbor center, with its black wrought-iron gate. The museum is in Building M.

In New Jersey

The Liberty Science Center ★★ **All ages.** This science center just across the river in Jersey City, New Jersey, reopened in 2007 after a 2-year, $110-million expansion that doubled its size. The museum has not so much been refurbished but literally *reinvented,* shifting its mission from, in its own words: "encouraging science literacy to inspiring science activism." It has six large interactive exhibition spaces, the country's largest IMAX Dome theater, and the Joseph D. Williams 3D Science Theater. Among the permanent exhibitions: **I Explore,** where kids age 1 through 5 can play a xylophone made up of hanging rock slabs or explore beneath the street; **Eat and Be Eaten,** where you explore the food chain in imaginative ways; and **Skyscraper!,** where you can walk amid a scaled-down cityscape. There's much to do here—it's a blast. You can take public transportation to get here (see below) or ride in a Liberty Landing Ferry **water taxi** from the World Financial Center to Liberty State Park—but you'll have a 20-minute walk from the ferry landing to the museum; see the website for the latest schedule (© **201/604-5799;** www.libertylandingferry.com; round-trip $14 adults, $12 seniors, $10 children 7–12, and free for kids 6 and under).

Liberty State Park, 222 Jersey City Blvd. (btw. Philip and Wilson sts.). © **201/200-1000.** www.lsc.org. Admission $16 adults, $12 seniors and children 7–12, free for kids 6 and under. Combination tickets available. Daily 9am–5pm. Take the PATH train to Exchange Place or Pavonia/Newport, transfer to the Hudson-Bergen Light Rail to Liberty State Park. Ferries to points nearby also available. Check website for details.

BEST RIDES

Coney Island ★ **All ages.** Open during the summer months, this cluster of small private amusement parks is on the rebound, with the spruced-up boardwalk, the Brooklyn Cyclones ballpark, and the New York Aquarium within easy walking distance. At 10th Street, the vintage **Cyclone** roller coaster (www.coneyislandcyclone. com; $8), built in 1927 and now a city landmark, offers riders over 54 inches tall the thrill of an eight-story drop at one point. The Cyclone is pretty much all that remains of the 1960s-era amusement park **Astroland,** which closed its doors in 2008. **Deno's Amusement & Kiddie Park** (www.wonderwheel.com) next door at 12th Street features the landmark **Wonder Wheel** ($6), an ingenious double Ferris wheel built in 1920 that circles high over the boardwalk, as well as lots of old-school kiddie rides: a carousel, flying elephants, Red Baron airplanes, even a sea serpent roller coaster ride (kiddie rides $3–$6; $40 for 20 rides). Paying homage to the 1903 amusement park of the same name, **Luna Park** flipped the switch on its considerable neon wattage in summer 2010. Luna Park features 19 spiffy new rides, a number of which are family- and kid-friendly (www.lunaparknyc.com; unlimited-ride wristbands $26–$34). The area also has minigolf, go-carts, a museum, and even a freak show, not to mention the original Nathan's hot dog stand.

Coney Island USA, 1208 Surf Ave., Brooklyn. ℭ **718/372-5159.** www.coneyislandfunguide.com. Admission to parks free. Deno's **Amusement & Kiddie Park:** Open daily 11am–midnight Memorial Day to Labor Day; weekends and school holidays only noon–8pm (weather permitting) Apr–May and Sept–Oct;. **The Cyclone:** Open daily noon–closing May 22 to Labor Day; weekends only noon–closing Apr 5–May 22. **Luna Park:** Open May 29–Sept 6 Mon–Fri noon–midnight; Sat–Sun and holidays 11am–midnight; weekends only Sept–Oct. Subway: D, N to Coney Island/Stillwell Ave.; F, Q to W. 8th St.

New York Skyride 👣 **Ages 5 & up.** "Passengers" are seated on a large platform that begins to tilt and jolt and careen wildly while a big screen shows you "crashing" your way around New York landmarks, with lots of ear-splitting recorded sound effects. There's zero sightseeing information—it's just a crazed 8-minute simulation of speeding through the cityscape. Count on a long line, up to 30 minutes at times. Not worth the tourist-soaking price.

In the Empire State Building (2nd floor), Fifth Ave. at 34th St. ℭ **888/SKYRIDE** (759-7433) or 212/279-9777. www.skyride.com. Admission $30 adults, $23 children 12–17 and seniors, and $16 children 5–11; combination tickets with Empire State Building $40 adults, $25 seniors, $32 children 12–17, $19 children 5–11. Daily 10am–10pm. Subway: B, D, F, N, Q, R, V, W to 34th St.

Roosevelt Island Tram 🚡 **All ages. Note:** At press time, the tramway was scheduled to reopen in fall 2010 after an extensive modernization and upgrades. A pair of big red cable cars swing over the East River alongside the 59th Street/Queensboro Bridge to Roosevelt Island. Though most of the trip is actually over an unglamorous wedge of East Side real estate, it does go over the river, and you're high up enough to get good views of Manhattan up and down (and it has been the star of several movies—including *Spider-Man* in 2002). There are few seats—only a narrow hard bench at either end of a car that holds 30 or so—so get onboard quickly to grab a seat by the front windows. Once you're on Roosevelt Island, site of a former smallpox hospital, you can turn right around and ride back—or you can take a ride on the red shuttle bus to loop around this island housing development, a sprawl of modern apartment blocks with lots of riverside green space and little playgrounds tucked away everywhere. The village's main street looks like something out of the 1960s British TV series *The Prisoner*—a curved main street cutting between bland shop fronts (one of everything: post office, library, church, deli, Chinese restaurant, bank, school). Getting there on the cable car is more than half the fun.

Manhattan terminus: Second Ave. and 60th St. ℭ **212/832-4540.** www.rioc.com. Fare $4.50 round-trip including children 5 and older, $2 seniors with MetroCard, free for children 4 and under. Subway: 4, 5, 6 to 59th St.

Staten Island Ferry ★ 🚢 **All ages.** Walk right on at the South Ferry Terminal, and you can chug across New York Harbor, past the Statue of Liberty, to Staten Island, where you walk around the barriers and get on again for the return ride. The whole round-trip should take about an hour. Most of the ferry decks are now glassed in, alas, but the views are still great. A friend of mine tells me that his mother used to herd her kids onto the ferry on hot summer nights to sleep when their un-air-conditioned apartment got too hot; that's the kind of wonderful institution the Staten Island Ferry is in the hearts of New Yorkers.

Departing from South Ferry in Battery Park. ℭ **718/727-2508.** Free tickets. Subway: R, W to Whitehall St.; to South Ferry.

Toys "R" Us Ferris Wheel **All ages.** Inside the three-story atrium of this immense Times Square toy-o-rama, there's an honest-to-goodness 60-foot-tall Ferris wheel with fun, funky cars resembling licensed characters and toy icons like Uncle

Moneybags from Monopoly. For the money, it seems a fairly short ride, but kids seem to love it.

1514 Broadway (at 44th St.). © **646/366-8800.** Tickets $4, free for children 1 and under. Children under 40 in. must be accompanied by an adult. Mon–Thurs and Sun 10am–10pm; Fri 10am–11pm; Sat 9am–11pm. Subway: N, R, S, 1, 2, 3, 7 to 42nd St./Times Square.

Victorian Gardens at the Wollman Rink ★   Ages 2 to 12. In summer months Central Park's skating rink is overtaken by this delightful kiddie amusement park, featuring a dozen rides and games kept in immaculate, ultraclean shape. It's geared to small children: There's a sweet little roller coaster, a fabulous airplane ride, a goofily fun Rocking Tug, and some semi-scary rides for older kids. It's a wonderful Manhattan option for a summer afternoon, but it's a little pricey: It costs $6.50 ($7.50 weekends) just to get into the park, and the unlimited-ride wristband ($12) is the best option if you want to ride more than six rides—which adds up to around $20 a person. Keep in mind that the park can be overrun with camp groups and there's very little shade—so it can be simmering on a hot day.

Wollman Rink, Central Park (enter E. 62nd St.). © **212/982-2229.** www.victoriangardensnyc.com. Admission Mon–Fri $6.50, Sat–Sun $7.50; children under 36 in. free with paid adult. Rides $2 each (climbing wall $10). Unlimited-ride wristband $12 Mon–Fri, $14 Sat–Sun. Mid-May to mid-Sept Mon–Thurs 11am–7pm; Fri 11am–8pm; Sat 10am–9pm; Sun 10am–8pm. Subway: A, B, C, D, 1 to 59th St./Columbus Circle; F to 57th St.; N, R to Fifth Ave./59th St.

HISTORIC HOUSES

Alice Austen House ★   Ages 6 & up. Many things about pioneer photographer Austen's house make it a great bet for kids. First, it's really just a cozy cottage, a lowslung gingerbread-trimmed bungalow with rolling lawns that offer dynamite views of New York Harbor. Second, Austen herself is such an appealing character, a spunky turn-of-the-20th-century woman who started taking pictures when she was 10 and just never stopped. Lots of her work is on display, and the garden has been replanted according to her photos of the original grounds. Third, you get to ride the Staten Island Ferry over. What more could you ask for?

2 Hylan Blvd., Staten Island. © **718/816-4506.** www.aliceausten.org. Suggested admission $2 adults, free for children 12 and under. Thurs–Sun noon–5pm. From the Staten Island Ferry terminal, take the S51 bus 2 miles to Bay St./Hylan Blvd. Walk 1 block toward water; museum is on right.

Gracie Mansion   Ages 8 & up. Dating back to the early 19th century, this yellow frame house—formerly a wealthy family's country house—has since 1942 been the official residence of the mayor of New York. The current mayor, Michael Bloomberg, chooses to live in his much tonier Upper East Side town house, so visitors can tour the residential areas for the first time in years, as well as the public rooms on the main floor. The tours last 45 minutes, and it's not much of a window into the past—many restorations have wiped away original features and furnishings—but it's a lovely home, nonetheless.

Carl Schurz Park, East End Ave. at 88th St. © **311** (within NYC) or **212/570-4751** for tour reservations. Admission $7 adults, $4 seniors, free for children. Reservations required. Wed 10am, 11am, 1pm, and 2pm. Subway: 4, 5, 6 to E. 86th St.

Merchant's House Museum ★   Ages 8 & up. The most interesting thing about the Tredwell family—who lived in this house continuously from 1835 to 1933—is that they weren't famous or unusual at all, just a stable, prosperous, upper middleclass family whose house and furniture happened to survive intact, wallpaper and all, until it became a house museum in the mid–20th century. The house itself is a fairly notable example of Greek Revival, but your kids will probably be more struck by the old-fashioned furnishings and clothing (poignant details like a piece of needlework tossed onto a table, never to be finished). A nice trip back in time on a quiet side street not far from NYU and the East Village's funky St. Mark's Place.

29 E. 4th St. (btw. Bowery and Lafayette St.). ℰ **212/777-1089.** www.merchantshouse.org. Admission $10 adults, $5 students and seniors, free for children 11 and under accompanied by an adult. Thurs–Mon noon–5pm. Subway: N or R to 8th St.; 6 to Astor Place or Bleecker St.

Morris-Jumel Mansion ★ Ages 10 & up. Dating back to 1765, this imposing mansion with its Georgian front columns had a major brush with history when Gen. George Washington used it as his headquarters in 1776. As they tour the house, however, your kids may become more interested in Eliza Jumel, the wealthy, brazen 19th-century woman who lived here for many years, during her marriage to, and after her divorce from, Aaron Burr. It's too bad this big, elegant mansion is so far off the beaten path for tourists.

65 Jumel Terrace (at 160th St.). ℰ **212/923-8008.** www.morrisjumel.org. Admission $5 adults, $4 students and seniors, free for children 12 and under. Wed–Sun 10am–4pm. Mon and Tues by appt. only. Subway: C to 163rd St.

Mount Vernon Hotel Museum and Garden ★ 👜 Ages 6 & up. Back in the 1820s and 1830s, when this part of the Upper East Side was considered a country retreat, the Mount Vernon Hotel was a fashionable day resort for genteel travelers. What's surprising is how much this site still feels like a retreat, surrounded by city as it is: The surrounding gardens, planted in 18th-century style, offer a welcome whiff of horticulture, and eight period rooms inside this former carriage house—restored by the Colonial Dames of America—re-create what life in the old inn might've been like. Considering its convenient location, it's curious that this museum isn't better known. Guided tours, which leave from the gift shop, can be geared toward younger visitors.

421 E. 61st St. (btw. First and York aves.). ℰ **212/838-6878.** www.mvhm.org. Admission $8 adults, $7 students and seniors, free for children 12 and under. Tues–Sun 11am–4pm (June–July Tues until 9pm). Closed major holidays and Aug. Subway: F, N, R to Lexington Ave./59th St.; 4, 5, 6 to 59th St.

ZOOS & AQUARIUMS

Aside from the following, check out the **Bronx Zoo** (p. 148) and the **Central Park Zoo** (p. 153).

New York Aquarium All ages. After an hour-long subway ride from Manhattan—an adventure in itself—you hit the ocean at Coney Island beach, skirting the amusement parks, and walk to the left down the boardwalk to the aquarium. In summer, you may need to plan a full day so you can also enjoy the beach or the rides, or even get a ticket for a Brooklyn Cyclones game (see chapter 11). If you go in spring, know that many of the exhibits are outdoors, and it may still be too chilly to linger while watching the otters, penguins, and walruses on their rocky sea-cliff habitats— but out of season has its own charm, with the beach deserted and the ocean misty, cold, and gray. The interactive **Explore the Shore** exhibit with its re-created salt marsh is a blast. Time your schedule so you can catch the sea lion demonstrations. The **Planet Earth 4D Theater** experience costs extra for a multisensory visit to the ocean floor.

Surf Ave. and W. 8th St., Coney Island, Brooklyn. ℂ **718/265-3400** or 265-FISH (3474). www.ny aquarium.com or www.wcs.org. Admission $13 adults, $10 seniors, $9 children 2-12. Deep Sea 3D $6. Total Experience Ticket (includes museum admission plus Planet Earth 4D Theater) $17 adults, $14 seniors, $13 children. Mon-Fri 10am-5pm; Sat-Sun and holidays 10am-5:30pm (hours are extended in summer). Parking $13. Subway: F or Q to W. 8th St./NY Aquarium.

Prospect Park Zoo ★ All ages. Like the Central Park Zoo, this is right at the level of preschoolers and young grade schoolers. The fanciful abstract sculptures arching over the walkway from the side entrance tell you right away you're in kid territory, and on it goes, to the Animals in Our Lives exhibit and the outdoor Discovery Trail, where kids can hop like a wallaby, squat on their own lily pads, or huddle inside a giant turtle shell. There's a mini-amphitheater built in front of the glass-enclosed environment where a troop of hamadryas baboons scamper around—somebody here knows which animals kids most like to watch. It's small, clean, safe, and tons of fun. Once you're out here, make it a full day by visiting nearby Lefferts Homestead (p. 172), New York's only historic house set up just for kids, and by taking a ride on the gorgeous antique Prospect Park Carousel (p. 165), only steps from the zoo entrance. The subway ride from Manhattan isn't all that long, leaving you off only a block or so from the zoo.

450 Flatbush Ave., Prospect Park, Brooklyn. ℂ **718/399-7339.** www.prospectparkzoo.com or www. wcs.org. Admission $8 adults, $6 seniors, $5 children 3-12, free for children 2 and under. Mon-Fri 10am-5pm; Sat-Sun 10am-5:30pm. Subway: B, Q, or S (Franklin Ave. Shuttle) to Prospect Park.

Queens Zoo All ages. Though it may not merit a trip out to Queens from Manhattan on its own account, this smart little zoo is a natural add-on to a New York Hall of Science excursion (p. 173) and a good excuse for a tramp through the old World's Fair grounds. The zoo's focus is on North American species (don't expect exotics here, though my sons considered the American bison plenty exciting) arranged along a handsomely landscaped walking trail. You feel surrounded by wilderness, yet the pathway is actually pretty short—it won't tax young legs—and the loop shouldn't take more than 15 or 20 minutes. Across the park road is a minifarm with domestic animals that'll satisfy the yen for feeding and stroking warm, furry creatures.

53-51 111th St. (at 54th Ave.), in Flushing Meadows Park, Queens. ℂ **718/271-1500.** www.wcs.org. Admission $8 adults, $6 seniors, $5 children 3-12, free for children 2 and under. Mon-Fri 10am-5pm; Sat-Sun 10am-5:30pm. Subway: 7 to 111th St. (Queens).

Staten Island Zoo All ages. The little Staten Island Zoo isn't under the umbrella of the Wildlife Conservation Society, as are the other zoos around here, and it's definitely a poor cousin. But you may want to combine this with a visit to the Staten Island Children's Museum (p. 174), especially if you're into snakes—the reptile collection is a standout. The 8 acres are also home to a small aquarium and a fair number of birds. You won't see a lot of large animals, but several small mammal species that kids love to gaze at—the red panda, bush babies, otters, meerkats, and the colorful snout of a mandrill. Feeding times are frequent attractions, and there's a small children's zoo, for younger kids who like their nature hands-on.

614 Broadway, Barrett Park, Staten Island. ℂ **718/442-3101.** www.statenislandzoo.org. Admission $8 adults, $6 seniors, $5 children 3-14, free for children 2 and under; admission by donation Wed after 2pm. Daily 10am-4:45pm. Closed Thanksgiving, Dec 25, and Jan 1. Free parking except for special events. From the Staten Island Ferry, catch the S48 bus, get off at Broadway and Forest Ave., turn left, and go 2½ blocks up Broadway.

GARDENS

Brooklyn Botanic Garden ★★ **All ages.** Every month, something new is blooming at this 52-acre garden beside the Brooklyn Museum and across from Prospect Park. Starting in spring, Daffodil Hill dazzles the eye with a field of stunning yellow; then delicate pink cherry blossoms fringe the Japanese Pond (local Japanese families flock in for blossom viewing). A riot of roses fills the Cranford Rose Garden as summer sets in, and thickets of rhododendron bloom near the Eastern Parkway entrance. There's also a fragrance garden for those who are blind, coupled with a sweet little Shakespeare Garden featuring all sorts of plants mentioned in Shakespeare's plays. Year-round, you can stroll through the **Steinhardt Conservatory,** with its outstanding bonsai collection, orchids, waterlilies, and the Trail of Evolution, a pathway lined with increasingly sophisticated plant forms. You'll also find a terrace cafe, a lovely gardening gift shop, and frequent **weekend workshops** for children and families. Kids may get a kick out of the Celebrity Path, inlaid with the names of famous Brooklynites from Mae West to Woody Allen.

1000 Washington Ave. (at Eastern Pkwy.), Brooklyn. ✆ **718/623-7200.** www.bbg.org. Admission $8 adults, $4 students and seniors, free for children 15 and under; free Tues and Sat until noon. Tues–Fri 8am–6pm; Sat–Sun and holidays 10am–6pm (Nov 6–Mar 13 closes 4:30pm). Open Mon holidays; closed Thanksgiving, Dec 25, and Jan 1. Subway: 2, 3 to Eastern Pkwy.; B, Q, or S to Prospect Park; 4 to Franklin Ave. (the B train does not run to Prospect Park on weekends).

Conservatory Garden 🏛 **All ages.** Central Park's only patch of formal garden is a delightful 6-acre surprise in Manhattan that's rarely crowded. Walk through glorious wrought-iron gates (which once fronted the Fifth Ave. mansion of Cornelius Vanderbilt II), and turn left to find the Children's Garden, with beds of flowers blooming around a wishing well with a statue of the children from Frances Hodgson Burnett's *The Secret Garden.* The central section of the garden is a long lush lawn flanked by a pair of walkways lined with flowering trees; the northern end has a circular design, with the *Three Dancing Maidens* fountain surrounded by flower beds—a blaze of tulips in spring and chrysanthemums in fall. On spring and summer weekends, there's nearly always a wedding party here getting photographed. With restrooms and a fair-weather outdoor cafe, it's a welcome refuge, a perfect place to let your kids stretch their legs after a Museum Mile trek.

Central Park at 105th St. ✆ **212/360-2766.** www.centralparknyc.org. Free admission. Daily 8am–dusk. Subway: 6 to 96th St., then walk up Fifth Ave.

New York Botanical Garden ★★ **All ages.** This lushly planted 250-acre park—five times bigger than the Brooklyn Botanic Garden (see above)—is a real magnet for families. The stunning 8-acre **Everett Children's Adventure Garden** (separate admission $3 adults, $2 seniors and students, $1 children 2–12) tempts youngsters with cunning minitrails and mazes and topiaries and fanciful sculptures, not to mention hands-on stations where they can learn about pollination, chlorophyll, root systems, and all that good stuff. Other highlights are the **Ruth Rea Howell Family Garden,** where young city dwellers can plant, weed, water, and compost tidy little garden plots; the 19th-century **Snuff Mill,** perched on its riverside terrace; the magnificent **Peggy Rockefeller Rose Garden;** a steep rhododendron valley; and the immense Victorian-era greenhouse complex of the **Enid A. Haupt Conservatory** (admission $5 adults; $4 students and seniors; and $3 children 2–12), which alone makes the garden a delightful destination year-round. A new summer and fall

Holiday Train Show at the New York Botanical Garden

Few places celebrate the Christmas holidays with as much sheer theatricality as New York. Still, it's hard to outbedazzle the New York Botanical Garden's wonderful **Holiday Train Show** ★★★, where model trains and trolleys zip around a glittering holiday landscape composed of architectural reproductions of well-known New York landmarks and historic buildings—replicas made *entirely out of plant materials.* It's an astonishing feat of artistry, with dollhouse-size versions of icons such as Yankee Stadium, Grand Central Station, and the Empire State Building crafted from twigs, pine cones, acorn caps, palm and magnolia leaves, dried moss—even walnut shells and orange slices. Kids of all ages are entranced. Each year brings a new creation; in 2010 the show featured the Trans World Airlines Flight Center (✆ 718/817-8700; www.nybg.org; $20 adults, $7 children 2–12, free for children 1 and under). Take the 20-minute Metro-North Railroad from Grand Central to the Botanical Gardens stop. The train show runs from November to early January.

exhibition, the **Edible Garden,** features four kitchen gardens, cooking demonstrations, and a family harvest weekend in October.

A narrated **tram** ($2 adults, $2 children 2–12) swings around the grounds to help you cover the territory. Spring is intoxicating here, what with the huge stands of azaleas, magnolias, dogwood, and lilacs, but it's a blast even in winter, when the **Holiday Train Show** ★★★ is set up in the Conservatory—where vintage trains wend their way through fanciful landscapes and past amazingly crafted miniature replicas of New York landmarks (see below). Although the botanical garden is right next to the Bronx Zoo (p. 148), you'd have to be very ambitious (and very good walkers) to do justice to both in 1 day, since their sites are so spread out—but if you're game, it can be done.

Note that the grounds-only admission does not include admission to the Enid A. Haupt Conservatory, the Everett Children's Adventure Garden, the Rock and Native Plant Gardens, the Tram Tour, or any special exhibitions. If you want to do and see it all (and you absolutely should), it makes sense to buy the All-Garden Admission ticket.

Getting There: Metro-North trains from Grand Central Terminal make the 20-minute trip to the Botanical Garden Station; cross Southern Boulevard, and you're right at the entrance. One-way adult fare is $5 off-peak or $7 peak ($2.75–$3.50 child). By **car,** take the Henry Hudson Parkway to the Mosholu Parkway; at the end of the Mosholu, turn right onto Kazimiroff Boulevard, and follow the garden perimeter to the entrance. By **subway,** take the B, D, or 4 train to Bedford Park Boulevard. Walk east 8 blocks or take the Bx26 bus to Garden.

200th St. and Kazimiroff (Southern) Blvd., the Bronx. ✆ **718/817-8700.** www.nybg.org. Admission to grounds only, $6 adults ($5 Bronx residents), $3 seniors and students, $1 children 2–12, free for children 1 and under. All-Garden Admission ticket (covers all extra charges) $10–$20 adults, $9–$18 students and seniors, $4–$7 children 2–12. Tues–Sun and Mon holidays 10am–6pm (Nov–Mar until 5pm). Parking $12.

Wave Hill ★★ **All ages.** A very suburban enclave in the Bronx, Riverdale has some fine houses on its Hudson River shore, notably this 28-acre estate with two mansions and extensive gardens. Over the years many famous people lived here, as tenants or as guests (writers Mark Twain and William Makepeace Thackeray, conductor Arturo Toscanini, Theodore Roosevelt); at one time the Tudor-style house was also the official residence of Great Britain's ambassador to the U.N. But there's not much to see inside the houses—just let your kids play on the grounds, which offer one of the few unobstructed views across the Hudson to the magnificent New Jersey Palisades.

Nobody minds if youngsters run on the grass, and the formal gardens are world famous. Favorite spots include the **Aquatic & Monocot Garden,** with a pair of pergolas enclosing a formal pool; the nook-filled **Wild Garden;** and a terraced series of small walled gardens showing off cactuses and alpine flowers. Below the mansions' smooth lawns sprawls a 10-acre woodland with walking trails that give kids a nice bit of a hike. Excellent children's workshops and "Stories in the Gardens" are held on weekends; call or check the website for a current schedule.

Getting There: Wave Hill provides **free van service** to and from the **Metro-North train station** at Riverdale and to and from the terminus of the **no. 1 subway train** at West 242nd Street. The one-way adult fare on the **Metro-North train** (℃ **212/532-4900;** www.mta.info) to the Riverdale stop is $7 peak and $5.25 off-peak ($2.75–$3.50 children). The **MTA** (℃ **718/330-1234**) bus no. BxM1 (from the East Side) or BxM2 (from the West Side) goes to 252nd Street; then walk west across the parkway bridge and follow the signs to the main gate. The fare is $5 one-way; a child under 45 inches may sit on a parent's lap free. By **car,** take the Henry Hudson Parkway to the 246th Street exit and drive straight north to 252nd Street; turn left to cross the parkway overpass, turn left at the light, and drive south to 249th Street, where you turn right and follow it to the Wave Hill gate.

675 W. 252nd St., Riverdale, the Bronx (entrance at 249th St. and Independence Ave.). ℃ **718/549-3200.** www.wavehill.org. Admission $8 adults, $4 students and seniors, $2 children 6 and over, free for children 5 and under; free to all Tues, Sat before noon, and daily Nov–Apr and July–Aug. Tues–Sun 9am–5:30pm (mid-Oct to mid-May closes 4:30pm, June–Aug Wed until 9pm). Parking $8.

NATURE CENTERS

Note that Central Park is covered in-depth on p. 208 in chapter 9.

The Dairy   All ages. This charming 19th-century structure, with patterned roof tiles and gaily painted gingerbread trim, actually started life as a dairy, back in the days when people grazed cows on Central Park's meadows (children could stop here to buy a cool cup of milk fresh from the udder). There aren't too many Guernseys left in Manhattan, so nowadays the Dairy is the park's chief visitor information center, with a roomful of displays about the park's landscape. There are always a few hands-on activities for youngsters, and it's a pleasant short stroll from the carousel, the zoo, or Wollman Rink.

In Central Park, midpark at 65th St. ℃ **212/794-6564.** Free admission. Tues–Sun 10am–5pm. Subway: 6 to 68th St.; A, B, C, D, 1 to 59th St./Columbus Circle.

Dana Discovery Center ★   All ages. After Harlem Meer was dredged out in the early 1990s and its banks beautifully relandscaped, this pretty structure on its north shore opened as a nature-study center, bringing visitors uptown for the first time in years. If your kids are keen to catch a fish, they can head to the Meer in warm months to try their hands at catch-and-release fishing (Apr–Oct Tues–Sun 10am–4pm). Weekend family workshops run year-round (usually at 1pm, but call for schedules), and a room overlooking the Meer's serene waters is set up with hands-on nature exhibits. Stroll around the Meer to the neighboring Conservatory Garden (p. 180).

In Central Park at 110th St., near Fifth Ave. ✆ **212/860-1370.** www.centralpark.com. Free admission. Tues–Sun 10am–5pm (closes 4pm in winter). Subway: 2, 3 to 110th St. Bus: M2, M3, or M4 to 110th St./ Fifth Ave.

Henry Luce Nature Observatory at Belvedere Castle ★ All ages. Inside this tiny folly of a castle, built in 1872 as an optical illusion to make the lake to the south look bigger (the woods of the Ramble have since grown so high they now obscure the lake view), children enjoy interactive exhibits on Central Park's natural habitats and even bird-watching kits. But the real thrill is outside, where visitors can stand on the rocky terrace hanging high over Turtle Pond and the outdoor **Delacorte Theater,** or walk onto the castle's upper-level terraces for some super views of the Upper West Side, including the American Museum of Natural History. This castle even has a U.S. Weather Service station on top—note the twirling weather vanes on the tower. Stroll down the hillside west of the castle, a neatly planted **Shakespeare Garden** (appropriate, since the neighboring Delacorte is home to the Public Theater's free Shakespeare in the Park series), or scamper down the long slope to the east, where turtles and ducks populate the adjacent pond.

In Central Park, midpark at 79th St. ✆ **212/772-0210.** Free admission. Tues–Sun 10am–5pm. Subway: B, C to 79th St.

Inwood Hill Urban Ecology Center All ages. This Art Deco canoe house, tiled in aqua and white, holds weekend walking tours of the surrounding park, with its marsh, meadow, and steep rock cliffs. A telescope inside the center lets kids zoom in on details of the neighboring marsh and meadow; other exhibits include hands-on geology displays, an aquarium, and a flipbook of pictures of the native plants and animals. Few Manhattanites venture up to this northern tip of the island, but it's a stunning site.

Inwood Hill Park, 218th St. and Indian Rd. ✆ **212/304-2365.** Free admission. Daily 11am–4pm. Subway: 1 to 215th St., then walk several blocks to Indian Rd.

Prospect Park Audubon Center ★ All ages. Set inside a magnificently restored century-old Beaux Arts boathouse on the shore of a 60-acre man-made lake, the Audubon Society's Brooklyn outpost offers two stories of child-friendly exhibits on the local bird population—songbirds, waders, raptors, woodpeckers, and the rest of the avian crew. Kids can pore over books, videos, feathered models, and computer simulations—even climb inside a human-size bird nest—all against a background of piped-in birdcalls. Nature walks and boat tours of the lake start from the boathouse as well.

Inside Lincoln Rd./Ocean Ave. park entrance, The Lake, Prospect Park, Brooklyn. ✆ **718/287-3400.** www.prospectpark.org/audubon. Free admission. Thurs–Sun and holidays noon–5pm (weekends only Jan–Mar). Subway: B, Q, S to Prospect Park.

KID-FRIENDLY TOURS
Bus Tours

Hop-on/hop-off bus tours are ubiquitous in New York, with colorful double-decker sightseeing buses clogging the thoroughfares year-round, whether sun, rain, or snow. Among the companies offering hop on/hop off bus service are **Gray Line** (see below), **CitySights NY** (✆ 212/812-2700; www.citysightsny.com), and **Big Taxi Tours** (✆ 212/685-TOUR [685-8687]; www.bigtaxitours.com).

Gray Line Tours Double-Decker Bus Tours   All ages. Though lengthy narrated bus tours can make some younger children squirm like crazy, they're convenient for seeing a lot of sights without running your kids ragged. Hop-on/hop-off tours provide a happy medium—you get driven around and spoon-fed information, and when your kids get restless, you just jump off at the next stop, expecting to get back on again later.

Operating both red double-decker buses and bright red trolley buses, Gray Line offers so many options, it could make your head spin. Besides the 2-day **All-Loops Tour,** which would take 5 hours if you didn't hop on and off, there's a **Lower Manhattan loop,** an **Upper Manhattan loop,** the **Grand Tour plus Statue of Liberty 2-day option,** and the **Lower Manhattan plus Statue of Liberty 1-day option.** More traditional escorted sightseeing tours—the kind where you have to stick with the same groups of bus pals throughout—include both half-day and full-day Manhattan routes that involve a buffet lunch, as well as escorted Harlem tours (the Sun version includes a gospel church service).

Main stop at Port Authority Bus Terminal (42nd St. and Eighth Ave.). ℂ **800/669-0051** or 212/397-2600. www.graylinenewyork.com. Full city tour $50 adults, $40 children 11 and under; Upper or Lower Manhattan loop $40 adults, $30 children 11 and under, free for children 4 and under if sitting in adult's lap. Daily 8am–6pm.

Magic Bus (M5 city bus) 🎈 **All ages.** It's an ordinary city bus route, but it happens to rumble past a host of sights you'd like to see in its 90-minute loop, and you may even get some narration over the PA. You can board anywhere along the route, which is marked with a dotted line on the three city maps in this chapter. I recommend catching the bus at 125th Street and Riverside Drive, where you'll first wheel past **Grant's Tomb** (122nd St.) and gleaming neo-Gothic **Riverside Church** with its carillon bell tower (120th St.). You'll proceed down handsome residential **Riverside Drive** (Riverside Park and the Hudson lie out the right-side window) to 72nd Street, where the route jogs east to Broadway and then south past **Lincoln Center.** At Columbus Circle it turns east and goes across 59th Street—also called Central Park South because it borders the south side of the park (look to your left)—where it turns right at the ornate **Plaza Hotel** at 58th Street. Down Fifth Avenue you'll go, past **Tiffany & Company** (on your left on the south side of 57th St.); **St. Patrick's Cathedral** (on your left at 51st St.); **Rockefeller Center** (on your right from 51st to 48th sts.); the main research library of the **New York Public Library** with its famous stone lions (on the right from 42nd to 40th sts.); the **Empire State Building** (on the right at 34th St.); the narrow wedge-shaped **Flatiron Building** (on the left at 23rd St.); to the white arch of **Washington Square** (facing the foot of Fifth Ave.). After turning east on 8th Street to Broadway, you'll head south along lower Broadway, through SoHo and past Chinatown and City Hall. You'll zip down past the canyons of Wall Street and past Battery Place, and after circling Peter Minuit Plaza, you'll go back north up Church Street (what will become Sixth Ave.), passing the World Trade Center site. From 16th to 23rd streets you zip past **Ladies' Mile,** the late-19th-century department store district (many of the old stores have been restored for megastore tenants like Barnes & Noble and Bed Bath & Beyond); the Herald Square shopping intersection where **Macy's** department store presides at 34th Street; **Bryant Park** (on your right from 40th to 42nd sts.), which was the site of a World's Fair in 1853; more of Rockefeller Center, including **Radio City Music Hall** (on your right at 50th St.); and back to 59th Street to retrace the route north, as far as West 178th Street.

Recommended starting point: 125th St. and Riverside Dr. Fare $2.25, exact change or MetroCard.

Boat Tours

Circle Line Sightseeing Cruises ★ **Ages 3 & up.** Circle Line dominates the market on from-the-water sightseeing cruises, operating out of two locations: Pier 83, midtown at the Hudson River end of 42nd Street, and downtown at South Street Seaport's Pier 16. The experience of being out on the water with the wind in your hair is wonderful by itself, but getting a minicourse in New York history and architecture is a definite bonus. Go early in your trip to get a firm sense of Manhattan as a whole.

Starting from 42nd Street, the classic New York City experience is the **3-hour tour** ($35 adults, $30 seniors, $22 children 12 and under) that chugs around the entire Manhattan island in a low-slung steamer. Sit on the left-hand side of the boat for the best views. On the first leg, you deconstruct the Midtown skyline, get a good look at the Chelsea Piers, pass Battery Park City, and swoop past Ellis Island and the Statue of Liberty. Then the boats cut across New York Harbor and go up the east side of the island, past Wall Street and South Street Seaport, and under the East River bridges, getting a view of the other end of Midtown, with the United Nations looming over the river at 42nd Street. You'll continue north past the Upper East Side, seeing the mayor's official residence, Gracie Mansion. You get to go through Hell Gate (where the East River merges with the Harlem River), glimpse Yankee Stadium on the Bronx bluffs to your right, and slide through Spuyten Duyvil, where the Harlem River empties into the Hudson. There's not much to see on the northern end of the island, but the guides gamely fill in with lots of trivia. (It really is the guide that makes the trip—it's great to have a narrator who is full of wonderful obscure trivia.) When you pass under the George Washington Bridge, look for the little red lighthouse

---

Seeing NYC from the Deck of a Historic Fireboat

The fireboat *John J. Harvey* served New York City from 1931 to 1994. Saved from the scrap yard by a group of boat lovers who purchased her in 1999, the *Harvey* is being lovingly and painstakingly preserved and restored, mostly by volunteer labor, and is now on the National Register of Historic Places. Currently docked at Pier 66 on the West Side of Manhattan (btw. 26th and 27th sts), the boat offers occasional free tours around the harbor and up the Hudson River from May through autumn, periodically unleashing the "deck pipes" (water guns) to spray all around (at 18,000 gallons a minute). Expect to get soaked! Check the calendar at **www.fireboat.org** to see if you're lucky enough to be in town when one of these tours is offered, to learn more about the historic and heroic boat and her crew, or make a donation to help fund her restoration. Even after starting its second life, the fireboat answered the call for New York City once more: on September 11, 2001, the *John J. Harvey* left its slip to head down to Ground Zero, and the crew rigged its pumps to draw water from the Hudson when downtown's fire hydrants weren't working after the attack on the World Trade Center. The boat and its crew pumped water for 80 hours. For more about the *John J. Harvey* and how New York Harbor and the Hudson River have shaped New York City and the United States from the Colonial era through today, pick up a copy of Jessica DuLong's *My River Chronicles: Rediscovering the Work That Built America* (Free Press, 2009), a personal memoir and history of the river and its times by the *Harvey*'s acting chief engineer.

◉ The Little Red Lighthouse

Also known as Jeffrey's Hook Lighthouse, this little red lighthouse located under the George Washington Bridge in Fort Washington Park on the Hudson River was the inspiration for the 1942-children's book classic, *The Little Red Lighthouse and The Great Gray Bridge,* by Hildegarde Swift and Lynd Ward. Built in New Jersey in 1880 and reconstructed and moved to its current spot in 1921, it was operational until 1947. The lighthouse was to be removed in 1951, but because of its popularity there was a public outcry and it was saved. It's now a New York City landmark and on the list of National Register of Historic Places. It's a fun place for the kids to explore and scenic picnic spot in nice weather. It's open to the public, with guided tours by the **New York City Urban Park Rangers** (📞 **212/304-2365**) from spring through fall.

featured in Hildegarde H. Swift's classic children's book *The Little Red Lighthouse and the Great Grey Bridge.*

Also **departing from 42nd Street** are 2-hour **semicircle cruises** ($31 adults, $27 seniors, $20 children 12 and under), which go as far as the U.N. and then loop back; and 75-minute **Liberty Cruises** ($26 adults, $23 seniors, $18 children 12 and under), which steam past Liberty and Ellis islands. But if your kids are like the ones I know, they'll want to do the 3-hour circuit instead because it's cool to go *all the way around.* That's the *point,* Mom. Of course, you can always save time *and* score coolness points by taking the high-speed boat *The Beast* (daily May–Sept; $23 adults and seniors, $17 children 12 and under; must be over 40 in.), its hull painted with huge chomping shark teeth to look like it's eating the waves before it. Cruising at speeds up to 45 mph, the Beast buzzes past the New York skyline, pausing briefly at the Statue of Liberty, and then zips back to port, all within an adrenaline-pumping 30 minutes.

From the Seaport, 30-minute thrill rides are offered on a similar high-speed boat called *The Shark* (daily June to mid-Sept and weekends in May; $23 adults, $20 seniors, $16 children 4–12). The hour-long, narrated *Zephyr* Seaport Liberty Cruise (daily Apr–Dec; $27 adults, $23 seniors, $16 children 4–12) crosses the harbor to swing past Ellis Island and the Statue of Liberty and then back to the Seaport. Restrooms and a snack bar are onboard.

(1) Pier 83, at the foot of W. 42nd St. at the Hudson River. 📞 **212/563-3200.** www.circleline42.com. Parking $20. Bus: Westbound M42 to the Hudson River. (2) Pier 16 at South Street Seaport. 📞 **212/809-0808.** www.circlelinedowntown.com. Subway: 2, 3, 4, 5 to Fulton St.; A, C to Broadway/Nassau St.

The Pioneer **All ages.** Two-hour harbor cruises aboard a historic schooner depart (schedules vary) from South Street Seaport in July and August. The time warp experience of setting sail from the old seaport is somewhat diluted by the views of modern downtown skyscrapers and the chug of barges, tugboats, and tour boats on the water around you, but it's still a memorable throwback to an earlier era. New York viewed from the water is quite a sight in any circumstance.

Departing from Pier 16 at South Street Seaport. 📞 **212/748-8786.** www.seany.org. Family sail package: $100 for 2 adults, 2 children; $20 extra child.

Private Group Tours

Small Journeys, Inc. ★ **All ages.** These custom-designed group tours may be a tad expensive for individual families, but if you can hook up with another two or three broods, it's actually a good deal. It's worth it because Steven Kavee and his guides really gear their tours to kids' interests. In one 4-hour block of time, families can see the whole city with a knowledgeable, entertaining guide. The company also designs behind-the-scenes field trips for school groups, going on-site to meet professionals in fashion, art, theater, music, interior design, whatever. You're charged a flat fee for the standard 4-hour tour no matter how many in your group (within reason). Transportation costs—Small Journeys uses a 24-passenger minicoach—are additional, depending on the sights involved. You can save money by doing the tour on foot, for which older children will be better suited. Arrange well in advance.

114 W. 86th St., New York, NY 10024. ☎ **212/874-7300** or 914/762-4700. www.smalljourneys.com. $311 4-hr. standard tour, $65 each additional hour.

Studio Tours

Little Airplane Productions **All ages.** The popular commercial-free network for preschoolers, Nick Jr. (formerly Noggin), has produced a number of hit kids' animated shows, among them *The Wonder Pets* (initially produced for Nick Jr.) and *Jungle Junction*. The studio that creates and produces these two shows (and others) is actually located in the South Street Seaport. Little Airplane offers studio tours on Tuesday and Thursday (and one Sat a month), in which visitors can see where the shows' animation, voice-overs, and music are made. The small Little Airplane shop has a sprinkling of toys, Wonder Pets paraphernalia, and original artwork. Tours are limited to 10 people.

207 Front St. ☎ **212/965-8999.** www.littleairplane.com. Tickets $10 per person. Tues and Thurs 11am and 4pm (call about Sat times). Reservations required.

Walking Tours

For detailed strolls around the city and even Brooklyn, you may want to check out *Frommer's Memorable Walks in New York.* Take into account, however, that some of the walks (such as the Greenwich Village literary tours) may not be of much interest to kids.

Several organizations run a number of tours; check the schedules in *Big Apple Parent, New York Family,* or *New York ParentGuide,* available free at children's bookstores and clothing stores all over town.

Big Onion Walking Tours (☎ 212/439-1090; www.bigonion.com) are designed primarily for adults, but kids 8 and up will respond to many of their lively topics, which often touch on the multiethnic dimensions of New York's mosaic. Tours can last as long as 2½ hours; they cost $15 for adults, $12 for students and seniors. The **Grand Central Partnership** (☎ 212/883-2420) sponsors a free 90-minute walking "Grand Tour" ★ along East 42nd Street—an area that includes such Midtown classics as the Chrysler Building, the Daily News Building, and the old Bowery Savings Bank. With its historical/architectural emphasis, this award-winning tour led by historian Justin Ferate may be a bit scholarly for younger kids, but the length (and the price) makes it worth trying out. Tours depart Friday at 12:30pm from the Sculpture Court at the Whitney Museum at Altria, 120 Park Ave., at 42nd Street. The **Municipal Arts Society** (☎ 212/935-3960 for reservations and details,

212/439-1049 to get a schedule by mail; www.mas.org) tours explore the city's architecture and neighborhoods from an urban-design perspective; they may run as long as 7 hours and cost between $10 and $15, but the knowledgeable, enthusiastic guides make it worthwhile. For some of the popular weekend tours, you may need to reserve a couple of weeks in advance; call for times.

ARTime (✆ **718/797-1573**), as its name implies, runs walking tours oriented toward the fine arts, usually focusing on museums and galleries. Because they don't cover as much physical ground as some of the neighborhood and architectural tours (no more than 2 or 3 blocks between art galleries), they're quite suitable for younger kids—as long as the kids are into art. Tour guides gear their talks to children ages 5 to 10. Tours last about 1½ hours and cost $25 for one adult plus a child and $5 for each additional child (an extra adult tagging along is free). You can usually book a tour in advance—they run from October to June, the first Saturday of every month at 11am.

NEIGHBORHOOD STROLLS

M anhattan is one of the great walking cities of the world. On this densely packed island, it seems there's something new to see every half a block—an intriguing shop, a museum, a beautiful piece of architecture, or an eccentric fellow pedestrian. Even children who normally drag their feet when forced to walk from the far end of a parking lot may cover several blocks without noticing, absorbed by the continual stream of sights. Almost every place you want to go can be reached on foot, often more quickly, and for sure more cheaply, than via taxi, subway, or bus. And along the way you'll get a great window on the way New Yorkers live.

If you're already planning to go to one of the neighborhoods described in this chapter to visit an attraction, restaurant, or shop, allow extra time to explore the immediate area. Most of these sections of the city are worth a visit simply so you can drink in the kaleidoscope of street life that is New York.

MIDTOWN
Lobby Hopping

Start at the biggie: the **Empire State Building** (p. 162), 34th Street and Fifth Avenue, whose streamlined 1931 interior includes murals of the Seven Wonders of the World. Then head up Fifth Avenue to the **New York Public Library** at 41st Street, where you can walk up the steps between the famous lions (Patience and Fortitude) and peek into the ornate lobby, eternally cool in white marble. Turn east onto 42nd Street to pop into **Grand Central Terminal** on the north side of 42nd Street at Park Avenue, which, though technically not a lobby, has a gloriously restored main room that'll knock your socks off. Gaze up at the constellations painted or electronically twinkling on the soaring azure ceiling; check out the elegant waiting room; and then descend into the marbled catacombs to find a shopping concourse and a food court, populated with commuters scurrying for their trains. Try out the whispering gallery in the large tiled vault outside the Oyster Bar—if two people face the walls in diagonal corners, they can hear each other's softest speaking voices. One block farther east on 42nd Street, on the northeast corner of 42nd and Lex, you can duck into the **Chrysler Building,** whose steel-tipped Deco spire is so notable on the skyline. The small lobby is surprisingly warm and rich looking (think luxury-car glove compartment), with black marble and inlaid wood. Continue east to the end of 42nd Street to visit the **United Nations** (p. 159); even if you don't plan to do a U.N. tour, walk around the U.N. complex's beautiful Rose Garden, with broad paved walkways overlooking the East River.

Rockefeller Center Area

The heart of Midtown is Rockefeller Center, a huge streamlined office/retail complex of pale limestone built in the 1930s by the famously wealthy Rockefeller family. Start on Fifth Avenue between 49th and 50th streets at the **Channel Gardens,** which lie between the British building on the north and the French building on the south (like the English Channel lies between Britain and France—get it?). The Channel Gardens slope down to **Rockefeller Plaza,** the center's heart. Beneath the colossal gilded statue of the Greek god Prometheus, there's a jewel of an ice-skating rink (in winter) or an open-air restaurant, the Rock Center Café (in summer). Behind Prometheus, where the giant Christmas tree stands every December, rises **30 Rockefeller Plaza** (aka **30 Rock**), home of the NBC TV network; if you're here between 7 and 10am, stop outside the glass pagoda on the north side of 49th Street to watch the *Today* show being broadcast live. Hosts Meredith Viera and Matt Lauer often take to the streets outside to film various segments.

Head across 50th Street toward Sixth Avenue (excuse me, the Avenue of the Americas) to find the entrance for the **Top of the Rock** observation deck (p. 162) atop 30 Rockefeller Center; from here you'll get a dynamite view of the entire city. Once you've come back down to earth, roam inside 30 Rock's lobby, studying the monumental murals by José Maria Sert. Take the escalators down from the lobby and you can prowl the maze of concourses and tunnels connecting the Rockefeller Center buildings in an underground world of shops and restaurants (good to know about on rainy days). Leaving 30 Rock through the Sixth Avenue entrance, turn around to see the glittering mosaics decorating the portico. On 50th Street are massive stone bas-relief figures framing the doors, jauntily dressed in nothing but attitude and a little city soot. Across 50th Street is **Radio City Music Hall.** Go west to Sixth Avenue for the best views of Radio City's neon-jazzed streamlined facade. This landmark Art Deco theater still hosts live stage shows as well as a continual lineup of pop concerts; see chapter 11 for details.

Return to Fifth Avenue along 50th Street and turn left to pass the **International Building,** with its famous bronze statue of Atlas carrying the world. Across the street is Rockefeller Center's famous neighbor, **St. Patrick's Cathedral,** seat of the Archdiocese of New York. Step inside for a look at this graceful circa-1879 neo-Gothic church—if you're lucky, there'll be a wedding to watch.

Times Square

There was a time, not so long ago, when New York families strenuously avoided the Times Square area when out on the town with their kids. Those days are gone: The old Forty Deuce of two-bit porn shops and poor-man's peep shows has given way to the über-G-rated 42nd Street, a family-friendly theme park with neon razzle-dazzle to spare. It's a sight, alright, with giant animated billboards and illuminated jumbotrons.

The neighborhood's revival has been a boon to the glorious old Broadway theaters pocketed along the side streets of Times Square. (**Note:** Try to avoid this stroll before or after theater times; the crowds can be dense and the going slow as molasses.) If you start at the intersection of 42nd Street and Seventh Avenue and head west on 42nd Street, you'll pass two gloriously restored theaters—Disney's ornate **New**

Amsterdam Theater on the south side of the street and the **New Victory Theater** on the north—both of which specialize in family entertainment; farther west on the south side, you'll find a bustling theater-themed 24-hour McDonald's and the New York branch of **Madame Tussauds** (p. 167). Toward the end of the block, two megamultiplex cinemas face off across 42nd Street closer to Eighth Avenue—the 13-screen **Loews** (with an homage-to-Broadway lobby and a great retro neon sign flashing on the facade) and the 25-screen **AMC Empire,** which boasts the gilded moldings and frescoed dome of an old Broadway theater as its lobby. Flanking them are two new chain hotels: a Hilton on the south side and a Westin across the street. Take a moment at the Hilton's street entrance to admire the adorable little bronze figures by Tom Otterness scampering about the doorway.

If you head north up Broadway from 42nd Street, your kids may not allow you to cruise past the **Toys "R" Us** flagship store at the northeast corner of Broadway and 47th Street without stopping in. Early mornings, ABC's *Good Morning America* gang holds court on the southeast corner of 44th and Broadway, and later in the afternoon *Late Night with David Letterman* may be filming segments on the street outside the **Ed Sullivan Theater,** up at 53rd and Broadway. Tourists flock into the bright and busy restored **Embassy Movie Theatre** lobby that now features the **Times Square Visitors Center** on Seventh Avenue between 46th and 47th streets, and hopeful theatergoers line up for half-price tickets at the **TKTS** booth on the mid-Broadway island.

You don't need to pay any entrance fee just to marvel at the intersection's immense high-definition advertising signs, designed to be as bright and as gimmicky as possible. Despite the changes in display technology, one advertiser has remained constant: For decades there's been a **Coca-Cola** sign facing south at 47th Street. Just plant yourselves on one of the mid-Broadway islands and crane your neck. Don't be ashamed to gawk; we all do.

DOWNTOWN
Wall Street Lobby Hopping

The narrow urban canyons of this skyscraper-crammed neighborhood are another iconic Manhattan sight, familiar even to youngsters—they're the prototype of many a futuristic movie and video game landscape.

Begin at the corner of Broad and Pearl streets, where the modern **85 Broad St.** building pays tribute to the archaeological past: The curved lobby shows where old Stone Street used to run, and the Pearl Street sidewalks outside contain glassed-over pits revealing foundations of the old **Stadt Huys,** the town hall of 17th-century Nieuw Amsterdam. Follow Pearl Street down to State Street, and turn left. Even if you're not visiting the **National Museum of the American Indian** (p. 168), go inside the **Alexander Hamilton Customs House** on Bowling Green, Broadway, and State Street, across from Battery Park. Just past the museum's front desk (admission is free) is the glorious Grand Rotunda, with a huge circular ceiling mural celebrating New York history. Outside, Bowling Green may be a simple patch of concrete today, but in the Revolutionary era there was a famous riot here, in which outraged colonists toppled a statue of the English king; you can still see the broken spikes on the iron fence, which originally were topped by little crowns.

Heading up Broadway, you'll pass the venerable Gothic-style **Trinity Church,** tucked among the skyscrapers at the head of Wall Street (Alexander Hamilton and Robert Fulton are among the famous New Yorkers buried in its graveyard). Wall

The Big, Big Apple

From 1913 to 1974, New York City could boast of the tallest building in the world. The **Woolworth Building** was the tallest from 1913 to 1930, when it was supplanted by the **Chrysler Building** on 42nd Street. The Chrysler Building didn't hold its title very long—it was taken over a few months later, in 1931, by the **Empire State Building,** which ruled until the **World Trade Towers** arrived in 1972. New York lost the crown soon, however, when the Twin Towers were edged out by Chicago's Sears Tower in 1974. (The tallest building today? That would be the 2,717-foot Burj Khalifa, in Dubai.)

Street marks the limits of the original Dutch settlement, where a wooden wall was built in 1653 to protect the settlers. Turn right down Wall Street to see, on the north side, the Greek Revival **Federal Hall,** with its statue of George Washington marking the spot where our first President took his oath of office in 1789; turn right down Broad Street to see the **New York Stock Exchange** (8 Broad St.), with mythological figures crowding its triangular pediment.

Return to Broadway and turn right (north); between Dey and Fulton streets, **195 Broadway**—built from 1915 to 1922 as AT&T headquarters—looks like a wedding cake stacked with several levels of classical columns (in fact, it has more exterior columns than any other building in the world). Go in the lobby to see even more columns. Then proceed uptown to the **Woolworth Building** at Park Place and Broadway, the world's tallest building from 1913 to 1930. The Woolworth Building is a splendid example of neo-Gothic skyscraper design, and the lobby's sculptured ceiling is worth several minutes' study. Ask your kids to look for the self-portrait of the architect hugging his building in his arms and a Scrooge-like caricature of Mr. Woolworth hoarding his wealth.

Greenwich Village

Start in the heart of the Village, **Washington Square,** with its white triumphal arch at the foot of Fifth Avenue. The handsome red-brick houses on the north side of the square date from a time when Greenwich Village really was a separate country village. Much of the rest of Washington Square is now surrounded by the modern buildings of **New York University,** but the park's crowd is an eclectic swirl of all sorts of New Yorkers, not just college students. Weekends usually attract street performers, and on many afternoons there are informal speed-chess competitions going on beneath the shade trees at the southwest corner of the park. A top-to-bottom renovation was expected to be completed by early 2011.

For a taste of the bohemian Village, go south from the park (down Thompson, Sullivan, or MacDougal) to **Bleecker Street,** lined with inexpensive restaurants, cafes, and long-established music clubs. Turn right to go west on Bleecker Street. A couple of vintage coffeehouses remain just off Bleecker on MacDougal: **Cafe Dante** (83 MacDougal St.) and **Caffe Reggio** (119 MacDougal St.), holdouts from the Village's beatnik days (Dante has been here since 1915; Reggio since 1927). At Sixth Avenue, Bleecker takes an unpredictable angle north, like many West Village streets, and changes into a foodie neighborhood, with some great food shops selling bread, pastries, sausage, pizza, and seafood. You can get some great homemade Parmesan cheese sticks and cheese puffs at **Murray's Cheese Shop,** at 254 Bleecker St.

Return to Sixth Avenue, and go north to West 9th Street; the castle-like red-brick building on your left is **Jefferson Market,** originally a courthouse and now a branch of the public library. Its lovely outdoor garden is sometimes open to the public in the afternoon. Turn right (east) onto West 11th Street. The brick wall on your right surrounds a tiny cemetery, one of several belonging to **Shearith Israel,** the oldest Jewish congregation in the country. Continue down the block, lined with classic brick town houses, until you see one that's startlingly modern: **18 W. 11th St.** Inside the large picture window, the owner's stuffed Paddington bear is usually dressed in a timely fashion, with a yellow slicker on if it's raining or a Yankees or Mets cap in baseball season, depending on which team is winning. The modern structure replaced the original Greek Revival home, which was accidentally destroyed in 1970 by members of the radical Weathermen group, who were making bombs in the basement.

Follow 11th Street to Fifth Avenue—turn right to get back to Washington Square or left to make a stop at the **Forbes Magazine Galleries** (p. 165), with its collections of toy soldiers and toy boats.

The East Village

The funky East Village is a magnet for preteens and teenagers determined to score high on the hipness scale. Start on **Astor Place,** the busy intersection of Fourth Avenue, Lafayette Street, and East 8th Street, where sidewalk peddlers usually hawk everything from hammered silver jewelry to vinyl LPs to well-thumbed paperbacks to secondhand lamps and furniture. The hulking brownstone building to the south is **Cooper Union,** a progressive school of architecture, art, and engineering founded in 1859. Head east on what should be 8th Street, here called **St. Mark's Place;** busy day and night, the block of St. Mark's between Third and Second avenues is lined with vintage-clothing stores, food shops and cheap restaurants, and bars. Beatniks hung out here in the 1950s, hippies in the 1960s, and punks in the 1970s. Interestingly, this neighborhood also has long-established enclaves of Ukrainian immigrants, centered on 7th Street, and Russian immigrants, on 9th and 10th streets, as you can see if you stroll around farther. The city's "Little Tokyo"—a conglomeration of Japanese restaurants, noodle shops, sake bars, and grocery and snack shops—is centered on 9th Street between Second and Third avenues.

At Second Avenue, you may want to turn left and go 2 blocks north to the field-stone **St. Mark's-in-the-Bowery Church,** the city's oldest continually used church building—Peter Stuyvesant, the famous governor of the Dutch colony of Nieuw Amsterdam, used to worship here. In fact, this area used to be his farm, and **Stuyvesant Street,** which angles south back to Astor Place, is named for him. Stroll past the early-19th-century town houses on Stuyvesant Street and try to imagine what the Village looked like back then—before the beatniks, hippies, and punks took over.

If you're looking for club-kid coolness, follow St. Mark's Place until it ends at Avenue A. (Manhattan widens here, requiring a set of lettered avenues to be added east of the numbered ones—hence the neighborhood's nickname, Alphabet City.) You'll be at **Tompkins Square** (bounded by Ave. A, E. 7th St., Ave. B, and E. 10th St.), much spruced up (and with a spiffy children's park) since the late 1980s, when it held a resident camp of homeless people. Nowadays much of this neighborhood, long the low-rent-or-no-rent domain of squatters, struggling artists, and anarchists, has been gentrified, and Avenue A is lined with restaurants, shops, and cafes.

Chinatown

Begin on **Canal Street,** the major thoroughfare cutting across Manhattan at this point; Canal Street used to be the northern boundary of Chinatown before its population spilled over into Little Italy and the Lower East Side. Walk east from Centre Street to the Bowery on the south side of Canal Street, where produce and fish stores pile their wares on the sidewalks. Point out to your kids the Chinese lettering on every sign and the pagoda-shaped pay phone stations. Turn right (south) at the Bowery. On the Bowery's east side, a gargantuan statue of the Chinese philosopher Confucius dominates the little plaza in front of **Confucius Plaza,** a modern red-brick residential development.

Continue south on the Bowery 2 blocks to the frantic intersection called **Chatham Square,** with its big Chinese arch in the middle. Then backtrack on the Bowery a few steps to narrow sloping Pell Street, where you turn left. A Hong Kong–like jumble of restaurants and neon signs, Pell leads you west 1 block to busy Mott Street, filled with Chinese restaurants and shops selling souvenirs, colorful Chinese slippers and hats, and lots of fun, dirt-cheap tchotchkes (Chinese dragons, back scratchers, little Buddhas, plastic swimming frogs) that little kids find irresistible. Barbecued ducks hang in glass storefronts, and dim sum shops draw big lunchtime crowds. Turn right on Mott and go 1 block to Bayard Street, where you should turn left and go a block to Mulberry. **Columbus Park** is on your left, where Chinatown residents old and young congregate.

Little Italy

There's not much left of this classic tenement neighborhood, what with Chinatown encroaching on the south and SoHo on the west; you and your kids can easily do the whole bit in half an hour, even if you stop along the way to eat lunch. On weekends Mulberry Street becomes a pedestrian mall, which makes it even easier to traverse with young ones. From Canal Street, walk up **Mulberry Street** to Houston Street, past several Italian restaurants that thrive on the tourist trade; what used to be **Umberto's Clam House** (which moved 2 blocks away, to 86 Broome St.), at 129 Mulberry St., was the site of a famous 1972 Mafia hit when a wiseguy named Joey Gallo was rubbed out while reportedly dining on scungilli with clam sauce.

Along Mulberry and the streets branching off it, look for stores selling religious medals and figures and others selling glorious foodstuffs—fresh pastas and raviolis, imported olive oil, and vinegars. At the intersection of Mulberry and Broome streets, **Caffé Roma,** 385 Broome St., is a great old-fashioned tin-ceiling pastry shop where you can stop for cannoli and espresso. Look above the shop signs to see the tracery of iron fire escapes hanging out over the street, a distinguishing feature of these turn-of-the-20th-century tenement buildings, which slumlords designed to cram in as many small rooms as possible onto the narrow lots.

Lower East Side

Once a teeming slum for waves of new immigrants, the Lower East Side has been transformed of late into a hipster hangout. The main shopping drag, **Orchard Street,** though still full of discount-clothing and dry goods stores (many of them still Jewish-owned and shut up tight on Sat), now also has renovated storefronts and trendy boutiques. While you'll admire the changing retail mix and classic tenement architecture, lure your kids to walk with the promise of a good nosh. Start out at

Kossar's (367 Grand St., btw. Essex and Norfolk sts.), a glorious time warp of a bagel factory where customers can watch the bakers slide trays full of ring-shaped dough into a vintage oven. The bialys are incredibly dense and flavorful, especially when you get them warm. Return to Orchard Street, turn right, and head north to Broome Street for the fascinating **Lower East Side Tenement Museum** (p. 166), which explores the district's immigrant past. (Sadly, **Guss' Pickles,** last located across the street at 85 Orchard St., has up and moved to Brooklyn.) Window-shop your way north 4 more blocks to East Houston Street, where you can take care of whatever appetite you may have: **Katz's Delicatessen** (E. Houston St. at Ludlow St., 1 block east of Orchard) has sit-down service for such deli favorites as pastrami (best in town), corned beef, and luscious brisket sandwiches; the long-established family deli **Russ and Daughters** (179 E. Houston St., btw. Orchard and Allen sts.) specializes in lox, whitefish, and herring; and **Yonah Schimmel Knishes** (137 E. Houston St., at Forsyth St.) offers an amazing selection of Yiddish knishes—pockets of thin dough stuffed with everything from kasha to blueberries to sweet potatoes.

UPTOWN
Morningside Heights

The upper end of the Upper West Side, this neighborhood is Manhattan's college town. The place to start, however, is at 112th Street and Amsterdam Avenue, on the front steps of the Episcopal **Cathedral of St. John the Divine.** This will be the largest cathedral in the world if they ever finish building it; they've been at it for over a century, since 1892, but if your kids have studied medieval history at all, they'll know that most of the great European cathedrals took a couple of centuries to complete, too. St. John the Divine is so huge that the Statue of Liberty could fit under the central dome, and the tiny-looking figure of Christ you see in the rose window over the front doors is actually life-size. Notice how only two of the arches over the front doors have statues in them; empty niches in the other arches await future stone carvers' work. Go inside and stroll around, stopping on the north aisle at Poet's Corner, where paving stones honor selected American poets. Go out to the garden just south of the cathedral to see the Children's Fountain, a fanciful huge sculpture surrounded by peewee sculptures created by local schoolchildren. On the lawns of the surrounding cathedral close, you can sometimes spot a pair of peacocks strutting and preening.

Go north on Amsterdam Avenue to 117th Street, where you can pass through wrought-iron gates into **Columbia University,** New York's Ivy League college. As you cross the campus, notice the broad steps of Low Memorial Library on your right; kids will recognize it as the place Peter Parker visited for a fateful high-school field trip in *Spider-Man.* Exit the campus through the matching set of gates onto Broadway and cross the street to enter the gates of **Barnard College,** Columbia's all-women sister college. Or head north on Broadway to 120th Street: Columbia's **Teachers College** is the big, dark, red-brick building on the northeast corner (read the roll call of history's greatest teachers inscribed around the roofline). The **Union Theological Seminary** is the medieval-looking gray stone complex on the northwest corner of 120th Street, complemented by the red-brick **Jewish Theological Seminary** on the northeast corner of Broadway and 122nd Street. Turn left on 120th Street and go west to Riverside Drive, where **Riverside Church** stands on the right. If its pale limestone reminds you of a Gothic version of Rockefeller Center, it's no coincidence,

NEW YORK TOP 10 movie & tv sites

If New York didn't exist, Hollywood would've had to invent it to get the perfect movie set. Film companies shoot on location here so often, my kids learned from an early age what it means when we run into a phalanx of trailers, lighting equipment, and headset-wearing production assistants: *They're making a movie!* Here are 10 of the most famous sites around town, with an emphasis on those flicks and television shows that kids have seen:

1. **Columbia University Low Library steps** (Upper West Side, 117th St. btw. Broadway and Amsterdam Ave.)—where *Spider-Man* recovers after his fateful spider bite, where Mary-Kate Olsen tries to save Ashley's scholarship in *New York Minute,* and where three fired Columbia professors decide to go into business as *Ghostbusters.*

2. **Tom's Diner** (Upper West Side, 112th St. and Broadway)—where Jerry and his pals from Seinfeld hold their endless discussions, while Jerry eats cornflakes, Elaine devours big salads, and George tries to avoid the bill.

3. **Grove and Bedford streets** (Greenwich Village)—where TV's *Friends* live, in the apartment building on the southeast corner. Go a little farther west to where Grove crooks north and peer through a gate to see the fountain where they splash around in the credits.

4. **14 Moore St.** (TriBeCa)—where the *Ghostbusters* set up office in an old firehouse (it's still a working firehouse).

5. **The Plaza Hotel** (Midtown, 59th St. and Fifth Ave.)—where Eloise scampers in the many Eloise TV movies, and Macaulay Culkin rings up a whale of a room service bill in *Home Alone 2.*

6. **The Empire State Building** (Midtown, 34th St. and Fifth Ave.)—where Tom Hanks and Meg Ryan meet in *Sleepless in Seattle,* just like the reuniting lovers did in the many versions of *An Affair to Remember.* And who could forget what *King Kong* did to this place?

7. **55 Central Park West** (Upper West Side)—where the ancient spirit Gozar must be driven out of Sigourney Weaver in *Ghostbusters* (the top of this varicolored Art Deco building looks significantly different in the movie, though—an elaborate rooftop was matted in). Later in the movie, the nerdy accountant played by Rick Moranis roams glassy-eyed outside Tavern on the Green, the festively lit restaurant across the street in Central Park.

8. **The American Museum of Natural History** (Upper West Side, Central Park West at 79th St.)—where the mermaid in *Splash* escapes, where Cary Grant works on his dinosaur in *Bringing Up Baby,* and where the Macy's parade begins in *Miracle on 34th Street.* And don't forget that *Friends'* Ross Geller works here as a paleontologist.

9. **The front steps of the New York Public Library** (Midtown, Fifth Ave. at 41st St.)—where Holly Golightly researches eligible millionaires in *Breakfast at Tiffany's,* an apparition flips open card catalogs in the opening of *Ghostbusters,* and Peter Parker sees his beloved uncle slain in *Spider-Man.*

10. **The central fountain in Lincoln Center Plaza** (Upper West Side, 64th St. and Broadway)—where Bialystock and Bloom dance in *The Producers.*

since John J. Rockefeller was one of its founders in 1930. Across Riverside Drive and several yards north sits the columned neoclassical **Grant National Memorial Monument,** where President Ulysses S. Grant and his wife, Julia, are buried. (Ask your kids the corny old joke: "Who's buried in Grant's Tomb?") Admission is free—step inside and peer down into the sunken chamber where the couple's dark marble tombs are laid. The high-ceilinged memorial offers excellent exhibits about Grant's life and the Civil War he won for the Union, but most kids' favorite part is outside, in the plaza around the tomb, with its whimsical mosaic benches designed by local public school students.

BROOKLYN

Crossing the Brooklyn Bridge

As thrilling a sight as this beautiful brown-hued East River bridge is from afar, with its Gothic-style towers and lacy mesh of cables, the view from the bridge is even more thrilling. A boardwalk-like pedestrian walkway goes all the way across, raised slightly above the car traffic. One mile long, it should take about half an hour to traverse—except you'll be tempted to stop more than once to ooh and ahh at the vision of Manhattan's skyscrapers thrusting upward, with the great harbor and Verrazano Bridge beyond.

Why has the Brooklyn Bridge captured the popular imagination so much more than its neighbors to the north, the Manhattan and Williamsburg bridges? Well, for one thing, it was the very first steel-wire suspension bridge in the world when it opened in 1883. Until then, the only way to get from Manhattan to Brooklyn, at that time separate cities, had been via ferry (crossing from Manhattan's Fulton St. to Brooklyn's Fulton St., both named after steamship inventor Robert Fulton, who operated the ferry company).

Since then, however, the Brooklyn Bridge has become a byword in New York lore. The standard old joke defines a con artist as a guy trying to sell rubes the deed to the Brooklyn Bridge ("Brother, have I got a bridge to sell you . . . "). Cocky teenage hoodlums have proved their bravado by shinnying up its cables, and suicides with a flair for the dramatic have plummeted to their deaths from those same cables into the tidal currents below. The bridge has appeared in countless movies and TV shows, its outline practically synonymous with New York City.

The Manhattan entrance ramps to the bridge begin by the plaza in front of the city's **Municipal Building,** along Centre Street just south of Chambers Street;

The Curse of the Brooklyn Bridge

The Brooklyn Bridge took 16 years to build, from 1867 to 1883, and it seemed to have a bit of a curse on it—the original designer, John A. Roebling, died from tetanus contracted when his foot was crushed while surveying the site, and his son, Washington, who took over the job, fell ill with the bends after diving in the river to supervise the workmen laying the pilings. A virtual invalid afterward, Washington Roebling watched the bridge going up through a telescope from his house in nearby Brooklyn Heights, while his wife actually supervised much of the completion of the project.

pedestrian ramps on the other side empty out into Brooklyn's downtown, which is a bit of a wasteland on weekends, but it isn't a far walk from here to **Brooklyn Heights,** one of the loveliest brownstone neighborhoods you'll ever see. Go armed with a map. If your kids aren't hardy urban trekkers, walk halfway to get the view and then double back to Manhattan. Be aware that it can get awfully windy once you're over the water!

FOR THE
ACTIVE FAMILY

D on't make the mistake of assuming that New Yorkers are soft, flabby city folk—on the contrary, we end up walking much more than car-dependent suburbanites do, and the city's huge complement of parks and recreational pathways makes it easy to ride a bike, play tennis, jog or stroll, toss a Frisbee, fly a kite, skate, or skateboard. And what do you do when you have a dog in New York City? Well, you don't just open a door and put him out in the back yard. You walk the animal, sometimes several times a day.

But the gritty streets of New York have never been an easy place to carve out space to play, perfectly encapsulated in Helen Levitt's classic 1930s photographs of urban kids at play in a treeless concrete tableau.

Kids still play ball in the streets and dance in the spray of fire hydrants on sweltering days. But since Levitt's day (and especially in the 20 years we've lived here), the city has become, well, downright outdoorsy, with cleaner air and seas, more than 600 miles of bike lanes, and long stretches of alfresco breathing room where sea and sky are the focal points. We've thrilled to the rescue and refashioning of derelict piers and long-neglected waterfront sites into beautiful, thriving recreational areas like the 550-acre **Hudson River Park.** The latest public incentive is **NYHarborWay** (www.nyharborway.com); its goal is to connect by bike and water the city's revitalized waterfront sites in a mutually sustainable live-work-play ecosystem. Urban blight has been cannily repurposed in the "integrative landscape" of the **High Line** (see chapter 7), now a favorite spot for a restorative stroll—the leisurely Italian *passeggiata* on display in the go-go Meatpacking District. Rooftop gardens are thriving. Public playgrounds have never been in better shape, and the city's beloved big green spaces are healthier than they have been in years. Dive in and play to your heart's content.

GREEN NEW YORK: THE TOP PARKS

Though New York is studded with squares where you can find a patch of grass and some benches, it has only a handful of parks large enough for a real exploration. Some of these are somewhat off the beaten track: **Flushing Meadows–Corona Park** in Queens (take the no. 7 train to 111th St. or Willets Point/Shea Stadium) and **Van Cortlandt Park** in the Bronx

Central Park Attractions

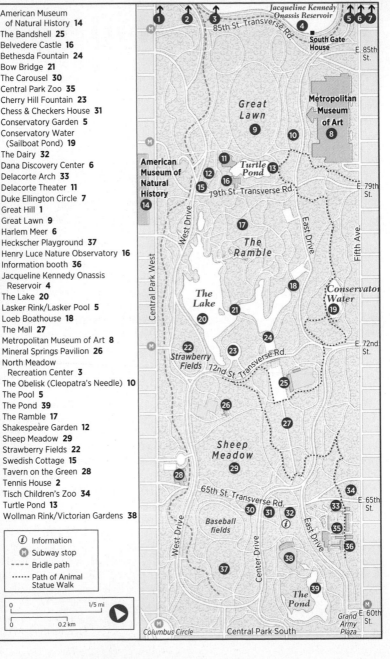

American Museum
  of Natural History **14**
The Bandshell **25**
Belvedere Castle **16**
Bethesda Fountain **24**
Bow Bridge **21**
The Carousel **30**
Central Park Zoo **35**
Cherry Hill Fountain **23**
Chess & Checkers House **31**
Conservatory Garden **5**
Conservatory Water
  (Sailboat Pond) **19**
The Dairy **32**
Dana Discovery Center **6**
Delacorte Arch **33**
Delacorte Theater **11**
Duke Ellington Circle **7**
Great Hill **1**
Great Lawn **9**
Harlem Meer **6**
Heckscher Playground **37**
Henry Luce Nature Observatory **16**
Information booth **36**
Jacqueline Kennedy Onassis
  Reservoir **4**
The Lake **20**
Lasker Rink/Lasker Pool **5**
Loeb Boathouse **18**
The Mall **27**
Metropolitan Museum of Art **8**
Mineral Springs Pavilion **26**
North Meadow
  Recreation Center **3**
The Obelisk (Cleopatra's Needle) **10**
The Pool **5**
The Pond **39**
The Ramble **17**
Shakespeare Garden **12**
Sheep Meadow **29**
Strawberry Fields **22**
Swedish Cottage **15**
Tavern on the Green **28**
Tennis House **2**
Tisch Children's Zoo **34**
Turtle Pond **13**
Wollman Rink/Victorian Gardens **38**

(i) Information
Ⓜ Subway stop
---- Bridle path
••••• Path of Animal
     Statue Walk

0 ——————— 1/5 mi
0 ——————— 0.2 km

(take the no. 1 train to 242nd St.) are both loaded with recreational facilities, but they're so big and spread out, you can't just ramble around aimlessly. **Fort Tryon Park,** at the northern end of Manhattan (take the A train to 190th St.), a wooded strip of park on high ground overlooking the Hudson River, is lovely but off the beaten path—it's not worth a special trip unless you're already coming to visit **The Cloisters** (which you definitely should do—p. 163). Then there's compact **Riverbank State Park,** perched over the Hudson River at the western end of 145th Street, which offers a slew of top-notch recreational facilities (see "Sports & Games," later in this chapter) but hardly any untrammeled grass. For other green pleasures in the city, see "Gardens" and "Nature Centers" in chapter 7.

New Yorkers, however, more than make do with the **five great parks** listed below. The larger three—Central Park, Riverside Park, and Prospect Park—were laid out in the 19th century by the team of Frederick Law Olmsted and Calvert Vaux, a pair of inspired amateurs who virtually invented the art of urban landscape design. These guys really knew how to maximize space, with twisting paths and artful hills and dales that make you feel as though you've left the city as soon as you're 10 paces inside the park. Later, park commissioners slapped on recreational amenities like tennis courts and playgrounds that may not strictly have been what Olmsted and Vaux envisioned, but nothing has seriously marred the beauty of these detailed landscapes.

Central Park ★★★   At 840 acres, this park—one of the world's greatest—is a vital resource for the city. Set right in the middle of things, with frequent entrances cut into its low brownstone wall, it separates the Upper West Side from the Upper East Side, lying between Midtown at the south end and Harlem at the north end. It's big enough to give you a real sense of escape, and when you're walking around the park, the only roads you have to deal with are the circular park drive and one crosscut at 72nd Street; both are closed to car traffic weekdays 10am to 3pm and 7 to 10pm, as well as 7pm Friday to 6am Monday (holidays are traffic free, too). Four other east-west streets cross the park—66th, 79th, 86th, and 96th—but because they're cunningly hidden beneath overpasses, you'll never notice them.

The section of the park below 72nd Street is somewhat formal. Starting at 59th Street and Fifth Avenue—where **horse-drawn carriages** line up to give tourists a ridiculously overpriced (about $50 plus tip for the first 20 min.!) ride through the park—you'll find the **Pond,** a picturesque small body of water reflecting Midtown skyscrapers. Just northwest of this you'll find the **Wollman Rink** (p. 224), where you can ice-skate in winter and visit an amusement park in summer, and **the Dairy** visitor center (p. 182). From the Dairy, follow a path west under an arch to the **Central Park Carousel** (p. 165). The **ball fields** west and south of here are fun even for spectators on summer weekday evenings, when some very competitive after-work leagues (including Broadway actors) slug it out. As you walk up the West Drive past the former **Tavern on the Green** restaurant, your kids may be interested to know that it was originally built as a sheepfold in 1870 when the **Sheep Meadow,** the broad fenced-in green lawn on your right, was still used for grazing sheep. The **Mineral Springs Pavilion,** just north of the Sheep Meadow, has a snack bar and restrooms.

Go north across 72nd Street to **Strawberry Fields,** a gem of a bit of landscape laid out in memory of Beatle John Lennon, who lived across Central Park West

stalking the animal statues IN CENTRAL PARK

In the course of half an hour's walk, you and your kids can bag a couple dozen animals in the wilds of Central Park—statue animals, that is.

Start on the northwest corner of East 79th Street and Fifth Avenue. A few steps into the park, on your right are **three bronze bears,** a copy of a Paul Manship statue that's in the Metropolitan Museum directly north. Continue on the path into the park, going through a vaulted tunnel under the East Drive and veering to your left (south) to reach the east end of Turtle Pond. There you'll find King Jagiello of Poland astride a **magnificent horse.** Stroll uphill to your left to the drive and walk downtown (south) on the road, keeping to the right-hand jogging path if there's car traffic in the park. About halfway down the hill, atop a massive rock outcropping on your right, crouches a **bronze panther,** peering out of the foliage ready to pounce on unsuspecting joggers.

Cross the East Drive at the pedestrian crossing near the Loeb Boathouse and walk down a short, steep, grassy slope to a path leading south to the Conservatory Water. The *Alice in Wonderland* statue at the pond's north end has not only the **White Rabbit** but also the **Cheshire Cat,** the **Dormouse,** Alice's **kitten Dinah,** and the **Mad Hatter,** along with the usual number of children climbing all over the giant mushrooms. Swing around to the west side of the pond to find the **Ugly Duckling** waddling past the statue of Danish storyteller Hans Christian Andersen.

Take either path leading south from the Conservatory Water up the hill to the 72nd Street Transverse; cross 72nd Street, turn right to cross the circular drive, and then veer left to follow the drive southward. On your right, the ground rises to the Rumsey Playground (less a playground these days than a plaza for special events). Set amid the steps rising to Rumsey's entrance gate is a big **stone goose,** with who else but Mother Goose riding on its back. (Walk around to identify carved scenes from various nursery rhymes.) Go west, away from the drive, past Rumsey downhill to

from here in the Dakota apartment building. It seems there are always flowers laid in tribute to Lennon on the black-and-white mosaic medallion that reads IMAGINE. Across the drive to the northeast lies the **Lake,** a body of water larger than the Pond—large enough, in fact, for boating. To rent rowboats, cross the park along the 72nd Street Transverse. Along the way, though, stop off at two postcard views that your kids may recognize from scores of movies and TV shows: Turn left at **Cherry Hill Fountain** and walk over lovely **Bow Bridge,** or take either the lakeside path or 72nd Street to **Bethesda Terrace,** a grand lakeshore plaza featuring the **Bethesda Fountain.** The lakeside path continues, winding north to the **Loeb Boathouse ★** (*(C)* **212/517-2233;** www.thecentralparkboathouse.com), where you can rent boats and also get something to eat (in clement weather) with smashing views of the lake and Bethesda Terrace. The fast-food **Express Café** specializes in burgers, soups, salads, and snacks and serves breakfast, lunch, and dinner (daily 8am–8pm). The casual **Boathouse Bar & Grill** (Apr–Nov 11am–11pm) is a sit-down alfresco cafe where you can dine on grilled chicken, crab cakes, and shrimp cocktail; it's a bit of a singles hang at happy hour—lunch may be the ideal time to come. The more upscale **Lakeside Restaurant** here serves lunch and dinner Monday through Friday, brunch and dinner on weekends (Mon–Fri the plaza in front of the Bandshell (watch for roller skaters on weekends!). At the western edge of the plaza, you'll find a **pair of eagles** devouring a hapless **mountain goat.** Bear right to return to the 72nd Street transverse, where a left turn will take you west. On your left, just before 72nd Street meets the West Drive, look up on another big outcropping to find the **falcon** lighting on the glove of the falconer.

Retrace your steps a short distance east on 72nd Street to the Dead Road, a broad asphalt lane bordering the Sheep Meadow, where skaters and volleyball games proliferate on warm-weather weekends. Turn right and follow the Dead Road south to find the Indian hunter with his faithful **dog.** Turn left, following the circular drive past the foot of the Mall; cross under the drive via a brick-vaulted tunnel (try out the echoes). The path swings uphill on the east side of the drive to reach one of the most famous animal statues in the park, **Balto the sled dog,** hero of the

1995 animated film and a real-life hero in the Alaska wilds in 1925.

From here the path leads south through another underpass past the gates of the Children's Zoo; look for a **pair of goats** prancing atop the zoo's wrought-iron entrance arch. On through a second underpass, you'll come up to the red-brick Delacorte Arch. In a niche to the right of the arch is a bronze **dancing bear,** and the glockenspiel on top of the arch features a **hippo,** a **goat,** a **penguin,** a **kangaroo,** an **elephant,** and a **penguin**—plus a **pair of monkeys** squatting on top, hammering the bells. The musical clock plays nursery rhymes on the hour and half-hour; it's worth sticking around to see the animals dance. Then proceed south on the walkway past the Central Park Zoo; at the southern end of the zoo's red-brick structures, turn to your right to see another niche with a **dancing goat** inside.

Which leaves you right near the gates of the zoo, ready to see the real deal.

noon–4pm and 5:30–9:30pm; Sat–Sun 9:30am–4pm and 6–9:30pm; dinner only Apr–Nov). The boathouse is open March through October daily from 10am to dusk, depending on the weather; rowboat rental is $12 per hour (cash only, $30 cash deposit required; maximum five people per boat).

Across East Drive and just above 72nd Street, the **Conservatory Water** (also known as the Sailboat Pond) is a fun area even for the littlest ones, with its large, serene formal pool. The *Alice in Wonderland* statue at the north end features a giant mushroom that just begs to be clambered on. From April to October you can rent one-quarter-scale radio-controlled model sailboats ($11 per half-hour) at the **Kerbs Memorial Boathouse** (𝄢 **917/522-0054**); check out www.sailthepark. com. There's also a cafe and restrooms.

Stroll back south through a shady green strip with winding paths, passing a couple of good playgrounds (see "The Playground Lowdown," later in this chapter). As you head downhill toward a rugged stone arch, expect to see a gaggle of sidewalk performers on weekends, some of whom are delightful to watch—allow for a little dawdling time. Passing through the arch brings you to the **Tisch Children's Zoo,** then south to the Delacorte Arch, with its delightful glockenspiel chiming every hour, and finally to the **Central Park Zoo** (p. 153).

North of the Lake, the **Ramble** is a compact wilderness that's easier than you'd think to get lost in; navigate with care, and stick to daylight hours when there are plenty of other folks around. Situated on a major North American flyway, this is, against all odds, a bird-watcher's paradise right in the middle of the big city; the **Henry Luce Nature Observatory** (p. 183) at the nearby Belvedere Castle can provide you with equipment to find and identify several species. Look overhead for nests and along the lake's marshy northern shore for frogs.

Above 79th Street, two museums dominate the park: the **Metropolitan Museum of Art** (p. 155), inside the park at East 82nd Street, and the **American Museum of Natural History** (p. 142), facing the park at West 79th Street and Central Park West. Midpark, between them, lies the **Great Lawn,** a huge stretch of grass and ball fields where crowds happily congregate in summer for gatherings ranging from Metropolitan Opera concerts to special events like Disney premieres and major rock concerts. At the south end of the Great Lawn, **Turtle Pond** (and its island, **Turtle Island**) protects a habitat for turtles and migrating birds. To the west of it lie the **Delacorte Theater,** home of summer's free Shakespeare in the Park (and another essential set of restrooms); the picturesque wooden **Swedish Cottage Marionette Theatre** (p. 276), where daily marionette shows are held; and, up on the hill, the **Shakespeare Garden** and **Belvedere Castle** with its nature center.

Between 86th and 96th streets, the major feature of the park is the **Jacqueline Kennedy Onassis Reservoir,** named in 1995 in honor of the former First Lady who lived for years nearby at 1040 Fifth Ave. (at 85th St.). She was often seen running along the cinder track, which makes a 1½-mile loop around the reservoir, much of it lined with cherry trees that are breathtaking in spring; you may prefer to walk along the bridle path circling the reservoir, where not so long ago experienced riders brought their mounts from the old **Claremont Stables,** which closed its doors in 2007. You'll still see horseback riders trotting down the bridle path, but don't worry: It's spacious enough for you and the horses. North of the reservoir is the tan stucco **Tennis Center** (see "Tennis" under "Sports & Games," later in this chapter), which also has restrooms.

Above 96th Street, the east side of the park has two big attractions: the **Conservatory Garden** (p. 180), at 105th Street and Fifth Avenue, which has restrooms, and **Harlem Meer,** the graceful pond at the northeast corner of the park, where the **Dana Discovery Center** (p. 182) runs nature workshops and hands out fishing poles so even youngsters can try their hand at angling in the meer. Midpark, right off of the 97th Street Transverse, on the recently renovated North Meadow, the **North Meadow Recreation Center,** undiscovered by many Manhattanites, has lots of sports facilities, including well-groomed ball fields, handball courts, basketball courts, and climbing walls. See "Sports & Games," later in this chapter, for more details; the staff here will even lend you bats, balls, Frisbees, and hula hoops free (call *C* **212/348-4867** to reserve equipment; all you need is a valid photo ID).

On the west side of the park, a stroll above 96th Street will take you to a picturesque and little-known area at West 100th Street: the **Pool,** a willow-fringed pond with a lively waterfall at the east end; you can hang over the railing on the bridge and watch the cascading waters beneath. North of here, the **Great Hill** has a high, broad lawn perfectly suited to picnics. At the top of the park, at 110th Street, is the

Lasker Rink, which converts in summer into the **Lasker Pool.** Note that the neighborhoods can be a little dicier up this way, and the social scene at the pool can be rough in summer.

From 59th to 110th sts., btw. Central Park West (Eighth Ave.) and Fifth Ave. ✆ **212/310-6600;** visitor center 212/794-6564; event hot line 888/NY-PARKS (697-2757) or 212/360-3456. www.centralparknyc. org. Subway: 1 to 59th St./Columbus Circle; N, Q, R, W to 57th St./Seventh Ave.; N, R, W to Fifth Ave./59th St.; B, C to any stop from 59th St./Columbus Circle to 110th St.; 4, 5, 6 to any stop from 59th St. to 103rd St.

Riverside Park ★★ Long, narrow Riverside Park really shows off designer Frederick Law Olmsted's ingenuity: Beneath it lie miles of underground railroad tracks, while the Henry Hudson Parkway, a major thoroughfare out of the city, bisects it lengthwise (you can't always get to the river shore as a result). But between West 83rd and West 96th streets, Riverside Park features a broad paved **promenade** with stone railings where you can lean over and gaze west over the Hudson; the pavement here makes it super for leisurely biking and skating, though you'll have to weave through strolling crowds on summer Sundays. The **dog run** near 86th Street always manages to entertain children even if they don't have a pooch to exercise, and the **community garden** along the median strip at 91st Street is simply glorious.

The southern end of Riverside Park, from 72nd to 83rd streets, is flatter and more open than the rest of the park, and it is unbelievably beautiful in spring, when all the flowering trees unfurl. If you want to fly a kite, this can be a good place for it, with breezes blowing in from the river. Above 96th Street, the park gets more rustic and less crowded, with some very steep paths plummeting down the slope from Riverside Drive.

At 72nd Street, 79th Street, and 86th Street, paths dip under the West Side Highway to the park's lower section, which hugs the banks of the Hudson River. At the southern end, the **72nd Street recreational pier** offers a wonderful view up and down the Hudson; a wide riverside path leads north from there to the **79th Street Boat Basin**—a marina full of bobbing houseboats, not all necessarily seaworthy. The grassy shade behind the esplanade makes a good place for a picnic, or you can stop for a good, casual meal at the **Boat Basin Café** (p. 105), with splendid river views. Follow the bike path on north, past a platoon of ball fields and tennis courts and a sister cafe at 105th Street; the bike path meanders along the river more or less all the way to the George Washington Bridge.

Btw. the Hudson River and Riverside Dr., from 72nd to 153rd sts. ✆ **212/496-2103.** Subway: 2, 3 to 72nd St. or 96th St.; 1 to any stop from 72nd St. to 125th St.

Prospect Park ★★★ Designers Frederick Law Olmsted and Calvert Vaux considered this Brooklyn park their crowning achievement. The main draws for kids are the super trio of attractions on the park's east side, along Flatbush Avenue: the **Prospect Park Audubon Center** (p. 183), the **Lefferts Homestead Children's Historic House Museum** (p. 172), and the **Prospect Park Carousel** (p. 165). Across Flatbush Avenue, you'll find the **Brooklyn Museum** (p. 172) and the **Brooklyn Botanic Garden** (p. 180), which aren't part of the park proper but were always considered part of the overall scheme.

The focus for nature lovers in Prospect Park is in the park's southern end at the **Boathouse,** a glorious Italianate tiled structure dating from 1905, where the

Audubon Center & Cafe (✆ 718/287-3400; admission free; Apr 5–Nov 23 Thurs–Sun and holidays noon–5pm; Nov 29–Mar 29 weekends and school holidays noon–4pm) offers two floors of exhibits, nature workshops for kids, and nature walks, both ranger-led and self-guided, along the Lullwater and through the wooded Ravine. **Electric-boat tours** leave from the landing in front of the boathouse for $6 per ride for ages 13 and up, $3 for children 3 to 12. Prospect Park's own **Wollman Rink** sits on the northern shore of the 60-acre lake.

If outdoor play is on your agenda, head for the **Long Meadow,** 90 acres of rolling greensward just inside the park's ornate entrance on Grand Army Plaza. Warm-weather weekends always see plenty of picnic action on the meadow, with lots of families tossing Frisbees and working on little sluggers' pitching arms; it's not so great for kite flying, since the meadow is set down in one huge gentle hollow. Brooklyn's sizable Middle Eastern and Caribbean populations give cookout hours here a special spicy aroma. In winter the slopes along the edges of the meadow are just the ticket for trying out that new sled or pair of cross-country skis. The park's circular drive follows a 3.5-mile loop that's great for biking or in-line skating.

Bounded by Prospect Park W. (Ninth Ave.), Eastern Pkwy., Flatbush Ave., Parkside Ave., and Prospect Park S., Brooklyn. ✆ **718/965-8951;** events hot line 718/965-8999. www.prospectpark.org. Subway: 2, 3 to Grand Army Plaza or Eastern Pkwy.; Q to Prospect Park or Parkside Ave.; F to 15th St./Prospect Park.

Carl Schurz Park ★ Though not as extensive as its West Side counterpart, Riverside Park, Carl Schurz Park—named after a prominent 19th-century German immigrant who was a newspaper editor, senator, and cabinet member—offers some very good East River views, and behind them, a few delicious green landscaped dells to wander through. Along the river, **John Finley Walk** (which actually continues south for several blocks past the park) is a paved promenade with wide-open views of the Triborough Bridge to the northeast, the railroad bridge spanning the rough waters of Hell Gate, and, across the river, the small lighthouse on the northern tip of Roosevelt Island; otherwise, it's just warehouses and boxy modern apartment complexes across the water.

No bikes or skating are allowed, but there's an enclosed **dog run** just inside the park about halfway up; come right before dinnertime, and watch the dogs romp. Walk to the north end of the promenade, where it loops around **Gracie Mansion,** the mayor's yellow clapboard residence (built as a country house in 1799, when this still was country); stand by the railing and face south to see how this tranquil park is built over four lanes of car traffic, on the busy FDR Drive—another good example of New York City maximizing its real estate.

Along the East River from E. 84th to E. 90th sts. Subway: 4, 5, 6 to 86th St.

Hudson River Park ★★ The long-term plan is to create a nearly continuous strip of park along the 5 miles of Manhattan's Hudson waterfront from Battery Park to West 59th Street. It's a narrow strip of landfill, but it's a beaut, with landscaped gardens, recreational piers, and lots of places to sit and moon over the water. It's Manhattan's best-developed strip of riverside, and its determined reopening after the 9/11 tragedy sent a strong signal to New York (and the world) that downtown Manhattan would prevail.

The oldest section, city-run **Battery Park,** is southernmost, occupying the tip of Manhattan Island. An expanse of grass with some fine old trees, it's crisscrossed by paved paths and dotted with statues; round brownstone **Castle Clinton National Monument** stands here, where you can purchase ferry tickets to the Statue of Liberty and Ellis Island—the ferries embark from Battery Park's waterfront pilings. Hot dog carts, T-shirt vendors, and street musicians are abundant in Battery Park—and it can get plenty crowded with visitors and ferry riders in the summer.

Embraced by the mouth of the mighty New York Harbor, the beautiful **Robert F. Wagner, Jr. Park** and **Esplanade** is a curved greensward that feels like the prow of a ship; it has a sit-down restaurant and lots of shady trees to picnic under. At the northern end, the **Museum of Jewish Heritage** presides over a terrace with great harbor views; the wooded area around **South Cove** is fun for kids, where they can scamper over a small bridge and up into a postmodern gazebo echoing the Statue of Liberty's crown.

Battery Park City comes next, a large residential/retail development built in the early 1980s, with a wonderful tree-shaded **Esplanade** serving as its spine. The heart of the complex—the World Financial Center's retail mall, the **Winter Garden Atrium**—features massive palm trees and a cascade of marble steps leading down to a huge glass window and outdoor plaza. The atrium faces the **North Cove yacht basin,** where gleaming white yachts are moored.

North of Battery Park City, the park traces the Hudson shore. Opening in fall 2010 is **Pier 25,** between Chambers and N. Moore streets, a multi-use recreational pier with a beautiful new playground and facilities for beach volleyball, skating, basketball, and miniature golf; to the south will be mooring facilities for small boats and water taxis. A wonderful toddlers' playground is the **Pier 51 Water Park** at Jane Street.

Newly opened in 2010 is **Pier 62** in Chelsea at 23rd Street. It's a haven of trees and gardens, with a beautiful **carousel** and a state-of-the-art **skatepark. Kayak** lessons and launchings are available at **piers 40, 66, and 96.**

GOVERNORS ISLAND: country in the city ★★

The city is transforming this former military base into a big seasonal playground (open Fri–Sun June 5–Oct 10), with car-free bike paths, art projects, a waterfront promenade with views of Wall Street and shimmering New York Harbor, and lots of wide-open greenswards. Mile-long **Governors Island,** which is within shouting distance (800 yds.) of lower Manhattan, is easy to reach: A free ferry runs from the Battery Maritime Building (next door to the Staten Island Ferry) at 10 South St. on the hour on Friday and every 30 minutes on Saturday and Sunday. You can bring bikes on the ferry or rent them when you arrive ($10–$15/2 hr.; $20–$25/full day; quad-cycles and tandem bikes also available). The island has lots of food vendors and even a beach (Water Taxi Beach) to dip your toes in the sand. Plans are afoot for the repurposing of old asphalt parking lots into green recreational spaces, a revitalized promenade, and even landscaped hills. For details, go to **www. govisland.com.**

The bike path continues north to 59th Street, with recreational piers and loads of athletic facilities tucked between busy West Street and the river, with strips of fiercely green lawn and flower-filled planters wherever possible. These riverside swaths of green are a perfect spot to get away from it all—and on a sunny afternoon, when the wide sky arches overhead and the broad Hudson sparkles a stone's throw away, it's an exhilarating place to be.

West of West St., from W. 59th St. to the bottom tip of Manhattan. ℂ **212/627-2020.** www.hudsonriver park.org. Subway: 1, 2, 3 to Chambers St. and stations north; E to Chambers St./World Trade Center; 4, 5 to Bowling Green.

THE PLAYGROUND LOWDOWN

The first municipally built public playground, **Seward Park,** opened on New York's Lower East Side in 1903; by 1915, the number had grown to 70 public playgrounds. Today the city maintains more than 1,000 playgrounds in all five boroughs. These days, the buzzword is designer playgrounds, with architects cherry-picking innovations from around the world and big-name designers muscling into the play fray. Among them are David Rockwell, whose Imagination playground of "loose parts" opened in the South Street Seaport in summer 2010, and Frank Gehry, who is fashioning a $10-million playground in Battery Park City—plans include a birdhouse for kids.

For the latest news on the playgrounds of metropolitan New York City, go to the **New York City Department of Parks & Recreation** website at **www.nyc govparks.org**.

Central Park

Central Park's "adventure playgrounds," most built in the 1980s, feature imaginative designs incorporating lots of places to climb, jump, slide, and hide out, as well as lots of sand to dig in or safely land on. In the 1990s, a new generation of playground arrived, with retrofitted rubber-mat ground surfaces (as opposed to asphalt) and large, complex structures of metal bars coated with tough plastic, usually in primary colors. The city's public playgrounds are surrounded by iron palings so kids don't wander away unsupervised; they all have drinking fountains, operational from Memorial Day to Labor Day, though none has restrooms; and many have sprinklers to make summertime play a whole lot cooler (which makes up somewhat for the city's appalling lack of decent public pools).

The playgrounds listed below have bucket swings for toddlers and babies and either tire swings or flat swings for older kids.

THE WEST SIDE   The largest playground in Central Park, **Heckscher Playground ★**, midpark at 62nd Street, sprawls over 1.8 acres of swings, slides, and climbers. Its most appealing feature is the wide-open center space, covered in patches of artificial turf and soft springy asphalt—perfect for tag. Though very little of the playground is shaded by trees, there are cooling jets of spray in summer.

Just north of the former Tavern on the Green, the **West 67th Street Playground** has **Adventure Playground,** with a stone sand fortress, a treehouse, and a very cool climbing pyramid. The sprinkler is set on a large compass.

The well-shaded **Diana Ross Playground ★** at West 81st Street—so named because the singer donated money to the park after violent incidents marred her Central Park concert in the early 1980s—was one of the first adventure playgrounds.

The weathered wood structures, set in sand pits, are complex enough to inspire some really fun games, with webs of chains to climb on, suspension bridges to bounce on, and fireman's poles to slide down. But the design isn't geared to younger kids, who may have some trouble climbing where they want to go (which means you'll have to climb up after them to give them a boost). There are two hulking climbing structures set right in the middle; the sightlines can be a problem. Two giant pluses: There are public restrooms nearby (next to the Delacorte Theater—usually dirty but infinitely preferable to soiled undies), and you're only a block north of the American Museum of Natural History.

The **Abraham and Joseph Spector Playground** at West 86th Street sits on a rise of land with lots of picnickable grass around it. Its two best features are the nice fenced-off toddler area (baby swings, sandbox, sprinklers) and an irresistible rambling wooden treehouse with a giant rope to swing on, Tarzan-style. Many of the playground's structures are set in sand, however, and a long wooden bridge arches over the middle of the immense sand pit, which makes sightlines problematic if you're in the toddler area and trying to keep an eye on older kids down by the treehouse. The paved sprinkler area gets very active in summer. Across the drive are some bucket swings midpark in the shady cool of the **Arthur Ross Pinetum Playground,** an open collection of pine trees with swings and picnic tables.

The delightful **Safari Playground ★** at West 91st Street is an imaginative playscape where children scramble over a herd of hippo sculptures and hop in and out of a green rowboat embedded in the pavement. It has no swings or slides and only two rudimentary climbing structures, but kids hardly notice—they're so busy with jump-ropes and hopscotch and sidewalk chalk and running in and out of the sprinklers. With picnic tables and lots of shade, it attracts swarms of preschoolers. At West 93rd Street, the **Wild West Playground** is extremely popular with uptown families, especially in summer, when sprinklers send water rushing down the long central gully into a circular wading pool at the far end. Four square fort-like wood towers at the center make this a great spot for playing all sorts of war games; three of the towers anchor big sand pits surrounded by low wooden palisades, with tire swings, slides, a bouncy suspension bridge, and weathered wood climbing structures (the fourth has a rubber-mat surface that's good for playing ball). The towers in the center make the sightlines a bit of a problem, and the combination of water gully and sand pit means lots of wet, gravelly muck in your kids' shoes when you get home.

At West 96th Street, the **Rudin Family Playground** is set on an island between two busy transverse roads, meaning a bit more noise and exhaust than at other playgrounds; the gate leads straight out to Central Park West, which can also be a problem. But in other respects it's a pleasant place, with a central paved sprinkler area, a vine-hung pergola shading a set of benches, and a trio of brightly colored pipe-rail climbing gyms that modulate from low toddler-friendly structures to a fairly demanding set of parallel bars and swinging rings. There's only one small concrete-edged sandbox, but there are lots of well-shaded bucket swings for babies. The newly reconstructed Tarr Family Playground, at West 100th Street, has a treehouse, swings, and a cone-shaped climber.

The **West 110th Street Playground** has a spongy rubber surface (poured in place), with one section devoted to school-age kids and the other, with a sandbox and climbing sets, to toddlers. There are good lawns nearby for picnicking, and right across the drive are the North Meadow playing fields.

Manhattan Playgrounds

Map of Manhattan Playgrounds showing numbered locations across Harlem & Morningside Heights, East Harlem (El Barrio), Upper West Side, Yorkville, Upper East Side, Central Park, Riverside Park, and surrounding areas including Hudson River, East River, Roosevelt Island, and Queensboro Bridge.

CENTRAL PARK PLAYGROUNDS

West Side

Abraham and Joseph Spector
   Playground 17
Diana Ross Playground 21
Heckscher Playground 31
Arthur Ross Pinetum Playground 18
Rudin Family Playground 6
Safari Playground 14
West 67th Street Playground 28
Tarr Family Playground 7
Wild West Playground 12

East Side

Ancient Playground 19
Bernard Family Playground 4
Billy Johnson Playground
   (aka Rustic Playground) 29
East 72nd Street Playground 27
East 96th Street Playground 10
Robert Bendheim Playground 8
James Michael Levin Playground 25
Lenox Avenue Playground 3
Pat Hoffman Friedman Playground 22

**RIVERSIDE PARK
PLAYGROUNDS**

Claremont Playground 1
Dinosaur Playground 5
Neufeld Playground
   (Elephant Park) 23
Hippo Playground 13
River Run Playground 16
West 110th Street
   Playground 2

**OTHER MANHATTAN
PLAYGROUNDS**

The Upper West Side

Sol Bloom Playground 11
Tecumseh Playground 24

The Upper East Side

Carl Schurz Park
   Playground 20
Hunter School Playground 9
John Jay Park 26
Ruppert Park 15
St. Catherine's Playground 30

Midtown

DeWitt Clinton Park 32
Sutton Place Park 33
Tudor City Playground 34

Chelsea & the Flatiron District

Augustus Saint-Gaudens Park 37
Chelsea Waterside Park 35
Clement Clarke Moore Park 36
Union Square Playgrounds 38

*Greenwich Village
& the East Village*

Downing Street Playground 43
Bleecker Street Playground 40
Pier 51 Water Park 39
Tompkins Square Park 41
Washington Square Park
   Playgrounds 42

SoHo, Little Italy & Chinatown

Columbus Park 47
De Salvio Playground 45
First Street Playground 44
Vesuvio Playground 46

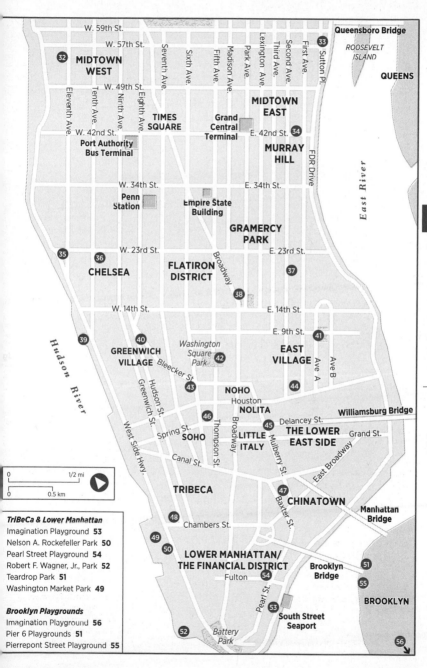

TriBeCa & Lower Manhattan
Imagination Playground **53**
Nelson A. Rockefeller Park **50**
Pearl Street Playground **54**
Robert F. Wagner, Jr., Park **52**
Teardrop Park **51**
Washington Market Park **49**

Brooklyn Playgrounds
Imagination Playground **56**
Pier 6 Playgrounds **51**
Pierrepont Street Playground **55**

THE EAST SIDE At East 67th Street, the **Billy Johnson Playground** ★ (also known as the **Rustic Playground**) is one of the park's most imaginative play spaces. You enter through a leafy wooden arbor; straight ahead is an arched stone bridge that looks very much like the famous Bow Bridge over the Lake to the north, connecting a pair of lushly planted islands. On your left is a midsize sand pit with a slide; on your right, a terrace with picnic tables. Best of all, behind the stone bridge, steps lead up a steep rock outcropping to the top of a 45-foot-long curved metal slide actually set into the face of the rock; daredevil kids in the know bring a square of corrugated cardboard to sit on to make the slide superfast, sort of like a waterless log-flume ride. The big problem with the Rustic Playground is that you can't see past the bridges and islands in the center; if one of your children is doing repeat trips down that slide—it can be addictive—you can't monitor the rest of the playground if your other children are elsewhere. Still, it's a wonderful place for a pre- or post-zoo frolic.

The **East 72nd Street Playground** is another dinosaur from the era of brown timber, brick pyramids, metal slides, and concrete. These hulking shapes make the sightlines pretty bad, and the ground surface, mostly sand, looks a bit dirty. It's quite shady, though, and the entrance is set safely inside the park. Kids in this neighborhood prefer to go to the newly renovated **James Michael Levin Playground,** set well inside the park near East 76th Street, with a small iron entrance gate everyone conscientiously keeps latched. The centerpiece of this graceful wide-open playground is a fountain featuring scenes from *Alice in Wonderland;* kids swarm between the climbing structure near the gate and a decent-size concrete sandbox at the other end, with plenty of open pavement in between for skating, hopscotch, and the like. Sightlines are super, and the people here are pretty well behaved; but the place gets crowded after school. On the north side of East 79th Street, the **Pat Hoffman Friedman Playground** is a well sheltered small area behind a replica of the Metropolitan Museum's American Wing's statue *Three Bears,* by Paul Manship; geared more to the 6-and-under set, it's got a nice curly slide that deposits kids in a sandbox, bucket swings, and a few climbing bars. It's a handy place for a quick stop right after a visit to the Metropolitan.

The handsomely reconstructed **Ancient Playground** ★ at East 84th Street, just north of the Metropolitan Museum of Art, pays homage to the museum's Egyptian Temple of Dendur, visible through the glass wall right across the road. It's got pyramid-shaped climbers and an obelisk in the sandbox as well as two cool water-spray features. Be sure to admire the beautifully restored Osborn Gates at the playground entrance; these bronze gates were created in 1953.

The popular **East 96th Street Playground** sits at the top of a short, steep rise from Fifth Avenue. A good-size toddler area is set off by iron palings in the center; other separately defined areas include a rubber-matted zone with tire swings and wooden pilings to climb on; a large modern metal-bar structure with all sorts of bridges, ladders, towers, and plastic slides; a cool little treehouse platform in a shady back corner; and a paved expanse surrounding a big water sprinkler. Sightlines are very good.

The well-shaded **Lenox Avenue Playground,** at 110th Street and adjacent to the Harlem Meer and the Charles A. Dana Discovery Center, has great views of the lake. It's next to an extensive lawn that sees lots of ball playing and picnic action on weekends. The **Robert Bendheim Playground,** at East 100th Street, has a coil of red steel that becomes a run-through tunnel of spraying water in summer and an imaginative climbing structure with lots of inspiring nooks for all sorts of make-believe. Best of all, this playground is wheelchair accessible. On the east shore of Harlem Meer, at 108th Street, the **Bernard Family Playground** features large steel-bar climbing equipment, painted maroon and forest green, mounted on black rubber matting. It also has a small, clean sandbox; a paved sprinkler section; and a few bucket swings. Only a few yards away, there's a marvelous tiny sand beach where small children can happily dig, sift, and mold sand beside the lapping meer water.

Riverside Park

The **Neufeld Playground** at West 76th Street is commonly known as the **Elephant Park,** after a set of five plump little stone pachyderms set around an open expanse of asphalt. This pleasant playground also has two modern climbing structures, a fenced swing area, a small fenced sandbox with very clean sand, and restrooms (hallelujah!) actually kept decently clean. There's an active set of basketball courts next to it. The only drawback is that traffic roars on the West Side Highway right past the bushes on the other side of the back fence. At the **River Run Playground** at West 83rd Street, a sprinkler feeds into a sculpted replica of the Hudson River; this, in turn, flows into a whimsical 35-foot sandbox, with sculptural forms of castles, classical gods, and woodland animals frolicking around it. Parents appreciate another form of running water here—the working restrooms.

The **Hippo Playground** (down a steep hill from Riverside Dr., at W. 91st St.) derives its nickname from the wonderful hippopotamus sculptures in the middle, which children can climb on. It has swings for both tots and big kids, smallish sandboxes, and sprinklers in summer. An energetic group of neighborhood parents has organized drop-in arts-and-crafts classes in summer, as well as regular attendants to keep the restrooms clean and safe.

A few blocks north at 97th Street and Riverside Drive, the **Dinosaur Playground** also has sculptures (dinosaurs, naturally) and a huge sprinkler area, great for cooling off in summer, though it gets crowded after school. There are restrooms here as well. Set alongside the Riverside Drive promenade on the park's upper level, the **West 110th Street Playground** has small climbing structures, bucket swings, and little sandboxes that make it best for toddlers. The farthest north, the shady **Claremont Playground,** at West 124th Street (right behind Grant's Tomb), has spouting porpoise sprinklers, a sandbox shaped like a huge rowboat, and—ta-da!—more restrooms.

The Upper West Side

Sandwiched between Riverside and Central parks, the West Side has plenty of access to playgrounds, though few between the parks. If you're at the American Museum of Natural History, it may be handy to stop on Amsterdam Avenue at 77th Street (northeast corner) at the **Tecumseh Playground,** which features a rootin' tootin' Western theme, with climbing structures shaped like Conestoga wagons and longhorn cattle. On West 92nd Street between Central Park West and Columbus Avenue, the **Sol Bloom Playground** not only has two great climbing structures (one toddler-scaled) on a soft red-and-black checkerboard surface, but also is the focus of lots of neighborhood athletics, with basketball hoops, a paved softball diamond, and a handball court.

9

FOR THE ACTIVE FAMILY — The Playground Lowdown

The Upper East Side

The **Carl Schurz Park Playground ★**, at 84th Street and East End Avenue, is my top choice on the East Side. This large, well-shaded playground was recently renovated and has several multilevel climbing structures of red-and-green plastic-coated steel and weathered wood—ladders, slides, bridges, steering wheels, climbing chains, and sliding poles provide plenty of playtime interest. It also has a separate sprinkler area and lots of open pavement in the middle that just cries out for a rousing game of Red Rover or Prisoners All. You'll see lots of little girls in uniforms in the afternoons, after nearby Chapin and Brearley schools let out. Adjacent **Carl Schurz Park** (p. 206) has a superb riverside promenade.

St. Catherine's Playground, on the west side of First Avenue between 67th and 68th streets, is undeniably urban—iron palings, asphalt paving, traffic churning past on three sides—but it's definitely a welcome spot in this near-Midtown neighborhood, roomy and fairly shady with a couple of terraced levels. The park is designed after the floor pattern of the Santa Maria sopra Minerva church in Rome—and the play areas represent the church pews. There's a set of happening basketball and handball courts on the other side of a chain-link fence. **John Jay Park,** on 76th Street east of York Avenue, has some nice up-to-date climbing structures for toddlers in the shady outer area and some for older kids inside the chain-link fence. There are also wide-open asphalt surfaces to run (and fall) on, a small East River lookout, and an outdoor pool open in summer (see "Swimming" under "Sports & Games," later in this chapter).

Ruppert Park (89th to 90th sts., along Second Ave.) has limited playground equipment, but smaller children have fun frolicking on the landscaped series of terraces, with lots of curved paths, flower beds, and benches for play-date tête-à-têtes. The **Hunter School Playground,** on Madison Avenue between 94th and 95th streets, is notable for its Madison Avenue entrance, which incorporates a red-brick castle-like facade, the remnant of a demolished turn-of-the-20th-century National Guard armory. (A similar armory, still intact, is down Park Ave. btw. 66th and 67th sts.) Though this playground is open to the public only after school hours, it may be worth a special detour to let your kids scamper up and down the steps between the stout brick towers, through a wide arch that just cries out for a moat and drawbridge.

Midtown

At the east end of 42nd Street, the **Tudor City** residential complex is set on a terrace above First Avenue; halfway up the stairs that rise on the south side of 42nd Street just past Second Avenue is a small fenced playground with a rubberized surface and primary-colored climbing structures. Overlooking the river, **Sutton Place Park** is set in a quiet cul-de-sac where East 57th Street dead-ends just past Sutton Place. This tiny brick-paved play area—a few steps down from street level, on a terrace above the FDR Drive, with lots of shade and some great views of the 59th Street Bridge arching over the East River—is best for infants and toddlers, since there's no playground equipment to speak of, just wooden benches, one absurdly small iron-fenced sandbox, and a large bronze wart hog (Pumbaa!) on a pedestal.

Over on the far West Side, in a grimy neighborhood once called Hell's Kitchen (nowadays more gentrified and relabeled Clinton), the **DeWitt Clinton Park** playground (btw. 52nd and 53rd sts. on Eleventh Ave.) is set behind a balding set of ball fields, with the West Side Highway rumbling beyond a fence. Still, the playground equipment is excellent, set in pleasant shade, with a nicely executed Erie Canal theme (DeWitt Clinton was the politician who got the Erie Canal built a couple centuries ago—but you already knew that, right?).

Chelsea, Union Square & Gramercy Park

Chelsea Waterside Park, right across 11th Avenue from the Chelsea Piers recreational complex at 23rd Street, has a cheery little playground nestled beside the turf athletic fields. The newly opened **Pier 62** has a brand-new **carousel** (p. 165) and a California-style skatepark. Named for the clergyman who wrote *A Visit from St. Nicholas* (better known as *The Night Before Christmas*), **Clement Clarke Moore Park** (southeast corner of Tenth Ave. and 22nd St.) is a pleasant, shady, paved corner lot with benches, concrete sculptures, and one rubberized-steel climbing structure.

The most centrally located is newly refurbished **Union Square playground ★**, also known as Evelyn's Playground, near Broadway and 16th Street. The 15,000-square-foot fenced-in playground opened in early 2010 after a major renovation; it's split into two distinct sections, side by side—all of it with a cushiony rubber checkerboard surface. The toddler section is colorful but cramped, with lovely meadowlike plantings and brand-new climbers. The German-made equipment in the larger section is utterly inventive (a slanted "teacup" to spin around in; a large, stainless-steel dome to clamber onto; people-size metal cattails; a swing carousel)—and so unlike anything else in the city that the playground is often overrun with kids. The **Union Square Greenmarket,** operating Monday, Wednesday, Friday, and Saturday, is only a few steps away, which makes playground picnics very handy—and colorful public-use tables and chairs are set up under the park's big shade trees. Somewhat off the beaten track in the Gramercy Park area is **Augustus Saint-Gaudens Park** (19th St. and Second Ave.), which has shade, good climbing structures, and lots of open pavement, some with basketball hoops.

Greenwich Village & the East Village

The focal point of the Village, **Washington Square Park,** at the foot of Fifth Avenue (btw. 4th and 6th sts., though the names are changed here for a couple of blocks), has undergone a major renovation and refurbishment; the old shade trees form a canopy for wide lawns rimmed with densely planted flower meadows. The larger children's playground is being thoroughly redesigned and should be open by the time you read this; a smaller, fenced playground to the west is perfect for smaller tots.

Farther west, at Sixth Avenue and Bleecker Street, the **Downing Street Playground** was being newly renovated at press time. It's buffered from the surrounding traffic by a red-brick wall. Follow Bleecker Street west to the point where it dead-ends at Hudson Street to find the always-hopping **Bleecker Street Playground,** fenced off with iron palings. It's got swings, a sandbox, picnic tables, sprinklers, and a stretch of asphalt just big enough for hopscotch or a round of double Dutch jump-roping.

Way over west on the banks of the Hudson, the wonderful **Pier 51 Water Park ★** in the Hudson River Park (west of West St. btw. Jane and Horatio sts.)

The Playground Lowdown

not only has a shallow lazy river for foot wading, water sprinklers, and cool things to climb, but is literally built on the pier, with sparkling riverside views. It's got a spongy surface and is remarkably clean—a perfect spot for the under-6 set.

Once-derelict **Tompkins Square Park** ★ has become a leafy haven in the increasingly gentrified East Village, and it has no fewer than three good-size fenced-off playgrounds with black rubberized ground surfaces and rubber-coated metal play structures in bold primary colors; it's even got a small 3-foot pool for a cool summertime soak. The biggest playground is along Avenue A at East 9th Street and has spectacular jungle gyms; the other two are along East 7th Street. After a vigorous play session, head down the avenue for pizza at **Two Boots** (p. 128).

SoHo, Lower East Side & Chinatown

The **Vesuvio Playground** (formerly known as the Thompson Street Playground) ★, on the east side of Thompson Street between Prince and Spring streets, is a welcome romping spot for young children in SoHo. A 2008 renovation has only made it better, with climbing structures on a forgiving surface, a sparkling 3-foot minipool, and flowering cherry trees. Good for stretching limbs in fair weather, it's about halfway between the New York Fire Museum and the Children's Museum for the Arts, both on Spring Street. At the corner of Mulberry and Spring streets in Little Italy, the **De Salvio Playground** has a couple of bright modern climbers set in a paved, fenced-in corner lot, with a few benches under the trees.

Tucked between First Street and Houston Street just west of First Avenue, the neatly enclosed **First Street Playground** is the pleasantest Lower East Side playground for younger kids, with shade trees and colorful coated-steel climbing structures. In the tree-shaded **Columbus Park,** at Worth Street between Baxter and Mulberry streets in Chinatown, hordes of Asian and Asian-American children scramble over the climbing structures and dangle on the swings, while elderly men play chess nearby. This is one of the city's oldest urban parks. A 2007 renovation added a state-of-the-art playing field, spiffy new landscaping, and a restored historic pavilion. It's hard to fathom that throughout much of the 19th century this park was the center of one of the city's most notorious and dangerous slums.

TriBeCa & Lower Manhattan

Washington Market Park ★, on Greenwich Street between Chambers and Duane streets, is one of the nicest small greenswards in the city, a shady 2½-acre lawn sprouting up where the city's rough-and-tumble wholesale food markets used to be. The gentle rises of the grassy area, punctuated with a delightful gazebo, are perfect for picnics and Frisbee games, and there's a fanciful maritime-themed wrought-iron fence at the south end, where PS 234 sits. A pleasant fenced **playground** is enclosed along the park's eastern wall, with lots of wooden climbing sets and shade. Nearby is the little **Teardrop Park** ★, tucked away in a cool, shady spot between Murray and Warren streets, which basically consists of a long (two-story) tubular slide built over rock boulders that delivers sliders into a big sand pit.

The **Nelson A. Rockefeller Park** ★, at the west end of Chambers and Warren streets, is a thriving swath of green along the river esplanade, a great place for toddlers to run with abandon. The super climbing structures, made of weathered wood and royal-blue steel, provide bridges and platforms where kids can scamper aboveground; on ground level are three good-size sand areas, one wheelchair

Imagination Playground: A Playscape of Loose Parts

In July 2010 one of the most unusual and exciting playgrounds in New York City was opened for heavy-duty play. The **Imagination Playground** at Burling Slip in the South Street Seaport forgoes typically static playground equipment—slides, swings, climbing sets—for an unstructured, constantly changing environment of sand, water, and "loose parts" where kids are invited to play in unique and creative ways. The playground is the brainchild of David Rockwell, the award-winning architect of Broadway stage sets, restaurant spaces, and theaters. Go to www.imagination playground.org for the latest details.

accessible. The northern section of the playground is set aside for toddlers, with a delicious bronze dodo bird set in a tiny splashing area; there's another sprinkler area for older kids, with a stone elephant and hippo. At the southern end is one of the coolest pieces of playground equipment in the city: a red steel whirligig seating eight, powered by pedals mounted beneath every other seat. Go up the esplanade to the fanciful sculpture park with its wade-in fountain, too.

Across the street from South Street Seaport, iron fences surround a triangular lot at Fulton and Pearl streets, where the **Pearl Street Playground** has a delightfully complicated climbing structure where kids can let off steam.

Brooklyn

In the new **Brooklyn Bridge Park, the Pier 6 Playground ★**, located along the Brooklyn waterfront below the Brooklyn Bridge, opened in summer 2010. It's billed as a "destination playground," and it's pretty spiffy, with a large "Water Lab" with cool boulders, a miniature marshland with misting machines, and three sculptural slides. At the south end of the Promenade in Brooklyn Heights, the excellent **Pierrepont Street Playground** has restrooms (not always clean, however), a separate yard for the very young, lots of shade trees, and loads of slides. Add to that plenty of neighborhood buzz and a peerless view across the East River to Manhattan. The **Imagination Playground ★** in Prospect Park (east side of the park, near the Lincoln Road entrance) is as fanciful as its name promises: a bronze dragon spouts water, a black-and-white-striped bridge twists like a helix, child-size masks are mounted for children to peek through, and a central sculpture features the little boy Peter and his dog Willie from Ezra Jack Keats's beloved children's books. (It is not, however, connected to David Rockwell's playground of the same name; see box above.)

SPORTS & GAMES

Baseball

Organized Little League games around the city in spring snap up most of the groomed baseball fields on spring weekends; after work, grown-up leagues fill the parks on weekday evenings. Central Park has some very nice fields: at the **Great Lawn** (midpark btw. 81st and 86th sts.), **Heckscher Ballfields** (midpark btw. 63rd and 66th sts.), and the **North Meadow** (midpark btw. 97th and 100th sts.).

Anyone can reserve a ball field for use; call the Parks & Recreation department at ☎ 212/408-0226 and find out what's available for the time you want. The cost is $10 per 2-hour session (after 5:30pm, $8 gets you a 1½-hr. session). If you don't want to get that formal, try the North Meadow facilities, which are sometimes free on a walk-in basis, provided no one has reserved them; a handful of other Manhattan parks, including **DeWitt Clinton Park** (btw. 52nd and 53rd sts. on Eleventh Ave.) and **Riverside Park** (west of Riverside Dr., in the section north of 103rd St.; take stairs down from the promenade level), have baseball diamonds with chain-link backstops that are usually free for pickup games.

If your slugger just wants to work on batting form, check out **batting cages** at **The Baseball Center NYC,** 202 W. 74th St., between Broadway and Amsterdam Avenue (☎ 212/362-0344; www.thebaseballcenter.com; $50 per half-hour, $80 per hour, for one to five players); at the **Chelsea Piers Field House,** 23rd Street and the West Side Highway, Pier 62 (☎ 212/336-6500; www.chelseapiers.com; $2 per 10 balls); in **Hudson River Park** on West Street, just north of Chambers Street (☎ 212/627-2020; www.hudsonriverpark.org; $2 per 15 balls); or at **Randall's Island Family Golf Center,** across the Triborough Bridge on Randall's Island (☎ 212/427-5689; $2 for 15 balls).

Basketball

Several city-run playgrounds have asphalt half courts where some pretty aggressive games of one-on-one take place. The famous courts at **Sixth Avenue and West 4th Street**—known as "The Cage"—are a breeding ground for serious hoop-dreamers; the action (not to mention the trash talk) is so fast and furious, kids are better off watching than playing. *Insider tip:* The McDonald's across 4th Street has an upstairs seating area with picture windows overlooking the courts, practically as good as a skybox. Intrepid kids may be able to get a pickup game at **St. Catherine's Playground** (First Ave. btw. 67th and 68th sts.); **Central Park**'s courts just northeast of the Great Lawn (midpark at 85th St.); **Riverside Park** courts at West 76th Street; the **Sol Bloom Playground** (W. 92nd St. btw. Central Park West and Columbus Ave.); or **Goat Park** (Amsterdam Ave. and 99th St.), named after Earl "the Goat" Manigault, a high-jumping, high-scoring street player who watched his peers win NBA offers while his own life unraveled in disappointment and drug addiction. Manigault redeemed himself by running athletic programs for kids in this very park, for which he will be forever remembered.

If you didn't bring your own ball, head to the paved outdoor courts at Central Park's **North Meadow Recreation Center** (midpark, just north of the 97th St. transverse road); at the recreation center's offices right next to the courts, you can borrow a basketball, along with a whole bag full of other sports equipment. If pickup games aren't your style, organize a group of kids and book a basketball court at the **Chelsea Piers Field House,** Pier 62 at Chelsea Piers, 23rd Street and the West Side Highway (☎ 212/336-6500; www.chelseapiers.com; $235 per hour to reserve a court, $10 an hour to walk in and play; call for availability).

Bicycling

The Bloomberg Administration has made a serious effort to make the city more bike-friendly, and at press time the metropolitan area had more than 620 miles of bike lanes, some 30 miles of which are on traffic-free greenways or along city waterfront where motorized vehicles are not allowed. Miles of bike lanes have been added to city streets, and most every bridge has a car-free bike path, including the beauteous Brooklyn Bridge. Most bike shops and rentals offer the latest free **NYC Cycling Map;** you can also download a version at **www.nyc.gov/html/greenyc**.

Manhattan's bicycle rental shops stock adults' and kids' bikes; most have a limited number of child carriers and tagalongs for rent (even child-pedal trailers and tandems). All offer helmets, locks, and maps. **Bike and Roll** (© 212/260-0400; www. bikeandroll.com/newyork) has four locations in the city: Central Park (at the Merchant's Gate entrance, just north of Columbus Circle), Riverside Park (Hudson River Greenway btw. 70th and 71st sts.), Governors Island, Pier 84 (the Greenway and W. 43rd St.), and Battery Park (Battery Place and West St.). **Pedal Pusher,** 1306 Second Ave., at 69th Street (© **212/288-5592;** www.pedalpusherbikeshop.com; Wed–Mon 10am–6pm), charges $6 per hour, $25 per day; baby seats are $13 per day. Downtown, check out **The Hub,** at Charles and Washington streets (© **212/965-9334;** www.hudsonurbanbicycles.com; daily 9am–8pm), charging $5 per hour weekdays and $7 weekends, $10 bike with toddler seat, $35 per day; it's just 2 blocks from the Hudson River.

Bike the Big Apple Tours (© **877/865-0078;** www.Bikethebigapple.com) offers an array of bike tours, and kids as young as 8 years old have participated (they have no toddler bike seats, however).

The marked **Hudson River bike path** runs all the way from the Battery Park at the southern tip of the island to the George Washington Bridge, which crosses the Hudson at 181st Street. One section, around 125th Street, is still hard to navigate; you may have to turn to city streets for a few blocks at this point (and keep in mind that at certain marked points along the road, traffic will cross the path). But otherwise, it's smooth, level, and clear sailing all the way, with amazing river views. The trail begins with the **Battery Park Promenade,** then runs north along West Street, past Greenwich Village and then Chelsea Piers. Things get pretty urban as you follow the bike lane beside the West Side Highway through Midtown (keep an eye out for turning traffic), but at 72nd Street you'll enter **Riverside Park.** The path cruises along through Riverside's lower section and continues north of 125th Street as a strip of green tucked between the river and the West Side Highway, neatly paved and landscaped.

The circular drive in **Central Park** is probably the city's most popular biking road, but it's not the best spot for amateur or beginning cyclists on weekends, when entering the bike slipstream can require some skill. The 6-mile-long circuit includes a couple of fairly grueling hills; younger kids may want to stick to the relatively flat lower loop, which shortcuts across at 72nd Street, or even the footpath looping around the Great Lawn, midpark from 81st to 86th streets; it's off-limits to bikes, but trikes are usually tolerated. The wide sidewalk bordering the park walls is also good for young riders, with few cross streets to negotiate; follow it up either Fifth Avenue or Central Park West. Park drives are closed to traffic weekdays 10am to 3pm and all weekend long, from 7pm Friday to 7am Monday. Bike traffic circles the park clockwise.

Riverside Park also offers a flat, wide promenade from 83rd to 96th streets, perhaps better for younger bikers. And like Central Park, Riverside is bordered by wide sidewalks, either of asphalt or of distinctive hexagonal paving stones, so you can cruise along the west side of Riverside Drive from 79th Street up to 125th Street with very few cross streets to worry about.

On weekends, there's little traffic in **Lower Manhattan,** and it's great fun circling the deserted skyscrapers along Wall Street. Just south of City Hall, broad entrance ramps lead onto the Brooklyn Bridge, with broad bike/pedestrian lanes leading you over the river (see "Crossing the Brooklyn Bridge," on p. 197).

The circular road in Brooklyn's **Prospect Park** is another great traffic-free place to ride on weekends; it's only 3½ miles long and has just one really tough hill.

Bowling

Bowlmor Lanes ★★ Down in the Village, 42-lane Bowlmor survives as a sort of hip throwback, with a long, sleek bar, a restaurant, a lounge, and lots of post-modern touches (for example, glow-in-the-dark pins). You wouldn't know by the modest entrance and the cramped, creaky elevator that takes you slo-o-owly up to the lanes that this 1938 relic is the highest-grossing bowling alley on the planet. Bowlmor is one well-oiled machine; they take excellent care of families here, and the food (good sliders, nachos, hummus, pizza) is more than decent. Prime family bowling times are midday and afternoon weekends; no one 17 or under is allowed after 7pm (Mon–Thurs) and it's 21 and over after 7pm on Friday and Saturday. There's automatic scoring, and gutter bumpers are available to keep kids' balls in the alley. Upstairs, in what used to be the bubble-topped Village Tennis courts, the popular **Carnival ★** (Thurs–Sun) presides with real Carnival games, strolling carny performers, and two bars; it's a kids' party space during the day and a lounge at night. *Trivia fans take note:* The first *Bowling for Dollars* TV game show was shot here, and Nixon bowled here regularly in the 1950s.

110 University Place (btw. 12th and 13th sts.). ✆ **212/255-8188.** www.bowlmor.com. Best family bowling times: Fri–Sun 11am–7pm. Mon–Thurs $12 per person per game; Fri–Sun $13. Shoe rental $6. Subway: N, Q, R, W, 4, 5, 6 to 14th St.; L to Union Square.

Bowlmor Times Square ★ Opened in fall 2010, this 90,000-square-foot mega-entertainment complex in Times Square has 50 bowling lanes in seven city-themed sections and a David Burke restaurant, the **Gray Lady,** the nickname given the *New York Times* and a nod to the newspaper formerly housed in the building. It's quite an enterprise.

Times Square Building, W. 44th St. (btw. Seventh and Eighth aves.). ✆ **212/680-0012.** www.bowlmor. com. Best family bowling times Fri–Sun 11am–7pm. Mon–Thurs $12 per person per game; Fri–Sun $13. Shoe rental $6. Subway: R, S, W, 1, 2, 3, 7 to 42nd St./Times Square.

Chelsea Piers AMF Bowling ★ This sparkling 40-lane facility at Chelsea Piers (it's in the next building south from the Field House) sees lots of family action on weekends. There's also a games arcade, and waiters from the on-site restaurant will bring food right to your lane. Gutter bumpers are much in demand here.

Pier 60 at Chelsea Piers, 23rd St. and the West Side Hwy. at the Hudson River. ✆ **212/835-2695.** www. chelseapiers.com. Bowling for children Mon–Wed and Sun 9am–11pm; Thurs–Sat 9am–9pm. Mon–Fri 9am–5pm $8 per person per game; Sat–Sun 9am–5pm $9; Sun–Thurs after 5pm $10; Fri–Sat after 5pm $11. Shoe rental $6. Subway: C, E, F, N, R, V, W, 1 to 23rd St. station. Bus: M23 across 23rd St.

Harlem Lanes Gospel Bowling on Monday nights? Let me guess: This must be Harlem. Just off the 125th Street strip, this sleek 24-lane facility occupies two floors of the same building as the Alhambra Ballroom; the third floor is best for families, while more of a lounge atmosphere prevails on the fourth floor. The Family Fun Pack special bowling package is available Sunday 11am to 8pm (1 hr. bowling $40 family of four). The cafe has some tempting food, from Jamaican meat patties and jerk chicken to Cajun BBQ shrimp.

2116 Adam Clayton Powell Blvd. at 126th St., 3rd and 4th floors. ✆ **212/678-2695.** www.harlemlanes. com. Sun–Thurs 11am–11pm; Fri–Sat 11am–2am (no children allowed after 6pm Fri–Sat); Sun 11am–9pm. $6 per person per game Sun–Thurs; $8 all day Fri–Sat. Shoe rental $5 adults, $3 children. Subway: A, B, C, D, 2, 3 to 125th St.

Leisure Time Bowl   Located in the unattractive Port Authority bus terminal, this modern and stylish 30-lane bowling facility is on the second floor of the terminal's South Wing.

625 Eighth Ave. ✆ **212/268-6909.** www.leisuretimebowl.com. Mon–Wed 10am–midnight; Thurs 10am–1am; Fri 10am–3am; Sat 11am–3am; Sun 11am–11pm. $7.50 per person per game Mon–Fri before 5pm; $9.50 after 5pm Mon–Sat. Shoe rental $5. Subway: A, C, E to 42nd St./Port Authority.

Chess

It's possible to play at the outdoor chessboards beside the **Central Park Chess and Checkers House,** midpark at 67th Street, just west of the Dairy; the boards are built into the stone tables and you can pick up chess pieces at the Dairy. The real scene for kids, however, is in Greenwich Village, where two chess stores sit a few doors away from each other on Thompson Street between 3rd and Bleecker streets: **Chess Forum,** 219 Thompson St. (✆ **212/475-2369**), and the **Chess Shop,** 230 Thompson St. (✆ **212/475-9580;** www.chess-shop.com). Loads of kids stream in to play, especially on Saturday, and the charges are minimal—children play free at the Chess Forum. The Chess Shop is also the site of the **Chess Academy** (✆ **212/475-8130**), where you can arrange private lessons with master-level instructors for $55 per hour.

Climbing

Open Youth Rock-Climbing Sessions ($30/50 min.) are available for kids 5–9 at the **Chelsea Piers Field House.** Chelsea Piers also offers **Rock-n-Roll** sessions: 45 minutes of rock climbing and 45 minutes on the trampoline (Pier 62, 23rd St. and the West Side Hwy. (✆ **212/336-6500;** www.chelseapiers.com; $30 for 1½-hr. session; Mon–Fri 4–5:45pm and Sat 12:30–2pm for children 5–16). You can also get private ($85) and semiprivate rock-climbing lessons ($115 for two kids).

Fishing

Believe it or not, you actually can fish in Manhattan. At the north end of Central Park, the **Harlem Meer** has been stocked with fish; April to October, take your kids before 3pm to the Dana Discovery Center on the north shore (near E. 110th St.; ✆ **212/860-1370**) and the staff will give them simple fishing poles and some bait. The Hudson River Park Trust sponsors **Big City Fishing,** catch-and-release fishing off piers 46 and 84 on summer weekends (www.hudsonriverpark.org; 10am–4:30pm); fishing poles, gear, bait, and even instructions are provided free.

Golf

Golf Club at Chelsea Piers   This is truly an amazing facility: a four-level driving range, where 52 golfers at a time can slam balls out into a huge open space bounded by high-tech mesh, all the while enjoying incredible Hudson River views. Stalls are heated for year-round play, and you don't have to lug around buckets of balls—a computerized system in the floor slides a new ball up on your tee as soon as you've hit the previous one. You pay for as many balls as you want and get a magnetized card to swipe in a slot at the tee; the computer subtracts how many you hit and you can come back whenever you want to hit the rest. There's also a 1,000-square-foot practice putting green, and pros are available for lessons at the attached Jim McLean Golf Academy.

Pier 59 at Chelsea Piers, 23rd St. and the West Side Hwy., at the Hudson River. © **212/336-6400.** www.chelseapiers.com. Minimum charge $25, which gets you 90 balls at peak times, 147 off-peak times. Apr–Sept daily 6:30am–midnight; Oct–Mar daily 6:30am–11pm. Subway: C, E, F, N, R, V, W, to 23rd St. station. Bus: M23 across 23rd St.

Randall's Island Golf Center   Randall's Island is one of the city's best-kept sports secrets; with lots of ball fields, it's a haven for amateur athletes and a quick drive across the Triborough Bridge from Manhattan. Along with a driving range, batting cages, a golf shop, and a snack bar, there's a nifty minigolf course at this golf complex on the island. If you don't have a car, you can take a shuttle bus ($10), leaving from the northeast corner of Third Avenue and 72nd, 77th, 86th, and 96th streets every hour on the hour (11am–11pm weekdays; 9am–11pm weekends, on the half-hour 11am–6pm).

1 Randall's Island. © **212/427-5689.** www.randallsislandgolfcenter.com. Driving range $13 for bucket of 160 balls (112 balls after 2pm), $9 for 85 balls (68 balls after 2pm). Minigolf $7 adults, $5 children 11 and under. Batting cages $2 for 15 pitches. Mar 1–Apr 4 daily 9am–9pm; Apr 5–Oct 31 7am–11pm. Free parking; shuttle available (see above).

Horseback Riding

Note: The 115-year-old **Claremont Stables,** the only riding stables close to Central Park, shuttered the doors of its charming 1892 stables in 2007.

Bronx Equestrian Center   Right off the Hutchinson Parkway on City Island, this small stable offers not only lessons and ring riding, but also trail rides in quiet woodlands. Pony rides are available for younger riders.

Shore Rd. S., City Island, the Bronx. © **718/885-0551.** www.bronxequestriancenter.com. Trail rides $35 per hour; private lesson $40 per half-hour, $65 per hour. Pony rides $5. Daily 9am–7pm.

Kensington Stables 🏇   To me, this is one of the best horseback deals in New York City, provided the schlep to Brooklyn doesn't daunt you. For $37 per hour, you can join a guided trail ride through leafy Prospect Park, riding either English or Western saddle; because there's a guide along, even inexperienced riders can join in. Lessons at the stable can be English or Western saddle. Call ahead if you want to book a lesson; drop-ins are welcome for the trail rides.

51 Caton Place, Brooklyn. © **718/972-4588.** www.kensingtonstables.com. $57 per hour private lesson, $34 per half-hour private lesson; $47 per hour group lesson for 3 or more. Daily 10am–sundown. Subway: F to Fort Hamilton Pkwy.

New York City Riding Academy 🏇   Yet another of the many sports options on Randall's Island is this 20-year-old riding stable in a quiet area on the East River shore, a good bet for beginners. The major riding programs are Western and English; ponies are available for smaller riders.

Wards Island Park (take E. 102nd St. footbridge from Manhattan; by car, go over Triborough Bridge, follow road past golf center and psychiatric hospital, continue past baseball fields and turn right). ℂ **212/860-2986.** www.newyorkcityridingacademy.org. Lesson $30 per half-hour. Daily 9am–6pm.

Riverdale Equestrian Centre Founded by former Olympians Rusty Holzer and Ashley Nicoll Holzer, this 21-acre stable in spacious Van Cortlandt Park offers quality instruction and well-cared-for mounts, with some spacious outdoor rings and jumping instruction. Ask about its Young Rider program. It also now offers guided trail rides for experienced riders in Central Park (through Nov). All saddles are English; riders must be over 6. Call a few days in advance to book lesson time.

In Van Cortlandt Park at W. 254th St. and Broadway, Riverdale, the Bronx. ℂ **718/548-4848.** www. riverdaleriding.com. $85 per hour private lesson, $45 per half-hour private lesson; $65 per hour semi-private lesson (for advanced riders only), $40 per half-hour semiprivate lesson. Mon–Fri 11am–7pm; Sat–Sun 11:30am–5pm. Subway: 1 to 242nd St. Bus: Liberty Lines BxM3.

Ice-Skating

Lasker Rink ♦ Cheaper and less crowded than its Central Park cousin the Woll-man Rink, uptown's Lasker is well populated by families on weekends. The ice here doesn't get as chewed up as Wollman's. Night skating is available on Tuesdays and Fridays.

In Central Park at 110th St. and Lenox Ave. ℂ **212/534-7639.** Admission $6.50 adults, $3.50 children. Skate rental $5.50. Nov–Mar daily; hours vary. Subway: 2, 3 to 110th St.

Riverbank State Park This roomy, open-air rink on Riverbank's topmost level is very much in demand with school hockey teams, but public skating sessions are lei-surely and pleasant—a boon for tentative young skaters. It's rarely crowded, though some fast and furious teenage skaters here don't always watch out for little ones. In summer it converts to a roller rink.

145th St. and Riverside Dr. ℂ **212/694-3642.** Admission $5 adults, $3 children 12 and under. Skate rental $6. Nov–Mar Fri 6–9pm, Sat–Sun 1–4pm and 5–8pm. Subway: 1 to 145th St. Bus: M11, Bx19.

Rockefeller Plaza Rink No doubt the most famous rink in town—and the easiest to find if you're a first-time visitor staying in a Midtown hotel—the Rock-efeller Plaza Rink does have undeniable charm, especially in December, when you get to skate under the gargantuan Christmas tree. The golden statue of Pro-metheus reclines at rinkside, and tourists crowd around the railings above, staring down as you pirouette around (though the ice is sunken far enough below street level that you're hardly aware of your audience). It's expensive (particularly around the holidays), you have to pay again if you want to skate for more than 45 minutes, and the rink is so small you can't get up much speed; there's usually a crowd, which means a wait in line to get in as well as a bit of jostling once you're on the ice. But do it once for the glamour of it.

Lower Plaza, Rockefeller Plaza (off Fifth Ave. btw. 49th and 50th sts.). ℂ **212/332-7654.** Admission Jan–Apr Mon–Thurs $10 adults, $7.50 seniors and children 11 and under; weekends and holidays $14 adults, $8.50 children 11 and under; skate rental $8. Admission in high season (Nov to New Year's) weekdays $13–$14 adults, $9–$10 children 11 and under; weekends and holidays $15–$17 adults, $12 children 11 and under; skate rental $8. Lunchtime skating Mon–Thurs (excluding holidays) 11:30am–1pm: $5. Skating sessions daily Oct–Apr; call for exact schedule. Subway: B, D, F, V to 47th–50th sts./ Rockefeller Center.

Sky Rink ★   Open 7 days a week year-round, this facility offers not one but two permanent ice rinks—the benefit of permanent ice being that the skating surface has more give than ice rinks laid down on top of other surfaces. (This is how Sky Rink justifies its relatively high prices.) The East Rink is booked up pretty solid with figure skating classes and hockey programs, but the West Rink is open for general skating sessions every afternoon, somewhere between noon and 6:30pm, and some evenings to 9pm (call for the current schedule). If you're a good enough skater to look around, you can gaze out the windows to a wide-open Hudson view. It's a special treat to skate here in summer, wearing a T-shirt and shorts.

Pier 61 at Chelsea Piers, 23rd St. at the Hudson River. ☎ **212/336-6100.** www.chelseapiers.com. Admission $13 adults, $11 children 12 and under. Skate rental $7.50; helmet rental $4; coin-operated lockers 75¢ (bring 3 quarters). Call for schedule of public skating sessions. Subway: C, E, F, N, R, V, W, 1 to 23rd St. Bus: M23 across 23rd St.

Wollman Rink   Central Park's chief skating rink, at the southern end of the park nearest to Midtown, makes a super place to spin around the ice outdoors, with a rock-music soundtrack piped in and a skyscraper skyline rising right beyond the trees. After school and on weekends, the ice can be thronged, but since skaters aren't limited to set session times, you can still get your money's worth if you hang out at the rink for a while, maybe refortifying yourself with food and hot chocolate from the snack bar while the Zamboni reslicks the ice surface.

In Central Park; enter at E. 62nd St. ☎ **212/439-6900.** www.wollmanskatingrink.com. Admission $10–$15 adults, $5.50–$5.75 children 11 and under. Skate rentals $6.25. Mon–Tues 10am–2:30pm; Wed–Thurs 10am–10pm; Fri–Sat 10am–11pm; Sun 10am–9pm. Subway: N, R to Fifth Ave. B, Q to 57th St.

In-Line Skating & Roller Skating

In **Central Park,** the top place for skating on weekends is the plaza by the Bandshell (just south of 72nd St., at the end of the Mall). The entire 6-mile loop of the circular drive is generally popular with skaters on weekends, though it includes some challenging hills that may be too much for young skaters; they should stick to the so-called Inner Loop, from 72nd Street down to 60th Street, which is mostly level. **New York Skate Out** (☎ **212/486-1919** or 917/257-7648; www.nyskate. com) organizes skating lessons and tours for kids 5–12 ($50 per session) weekend mornings and Tuesday through Thursday after school, meeting at the Fifth Avenue entrance at 72nd Street; it runs a free kids' skate Saturday from 3 to 4pm.

Other favorite skating pavements around the city are the promenade in Riverside Park, West 83rd to 96th streets; the Upper East Side's walkway on the bank of the East River from 60th Street on north; the riverside Promenade in Battery Park City; and the skate path of Hudson River Park from Chambers Street up to 59th Street.

Skate-rental outlets have proliferated in Manhattan, but not all rent skates in children's sizes. Try **Blades Board & Skate** at one of its Manhattan locations; the branch at 120 W. 72nd St., between Columbus Avenue and Broadway (☎ **212/787-3911**), is closest to Central Park. If you don't have your own wheels, you'll have to go to the following rinks, where skates are available for use at the rink only.

Riverbank State Park   Perched above the banks of the Hudson, this sizable roofed rink catches lots of cooling breezes in summer, though it's an uptown trek.

Sports & Games

FOR THE ACTIVE FAMILY

145th St. and Riverside Dr. 🕾 **212/694-3642.** Admission $1.50. Skate rental $6. May–Sept Mon–Thurs 3–6pm, Fri–Sun 2–5pm and 6–9pm. Subway: 1 to 145th St. Bus: M11.

Kayaking

During the summer months, the volunteer-run **Downtown Boathouse** (🕾 **646/ 613-0740;** www.downtownboathouse.org; no reservations; check website for updated schedules) organizes free walk-up kayaking Saturday and Sunday on the Hudson River at **Pier 40** (West St. near Houston St.) and **Pier 96** (at 56th St.); they also have a Hudson River location at 72nd Street. Children 15 and under must be accompanied by an adult in the same boat; young children must go in a double kayak with one or two adults. Life jackets, kayaks, and paddles are provided; you can take a kayak out onto the water for 20 minutes. Come wearing a bathing suit, or a T-shirt and shorts that you don't mind getting wet.

Play Spaces

Chelsea Piers Field House Children 6 months to 3 years old can occupy themselves happily in the **Little Athletes Exploration Center,** a separate playroom with soft climbing structures.

Pier 62 at Chelsea Piers, 23rd St. and the West Side Hwy., at the Hudson River. 🕾 **212/336-6500.** Admission $12 to Little Athletes Exploration Center. Call for schedule. Subway: C, E, F, N, R, V, W, to 23rd St. station. Bus: M23 across 23rd St.

Skateboarding

A brand-new primo site for skateboarders is the California-style 15,000-square-foot **Skatepark at Pier 62** (23rd St. and West Side Hwy.; free; daily 8am–dusk; closed in winter). Ramps have been set up for aggressive skateboarding in **Riverside Park,** at about 108th Street, west of the promenade (🕾 **212/408-0239;** May–Oct; admission $3); and at the **Hudson River Skate Park** (West St. just north of 30th St.; free). You can also try Midtown's **Penn Plaza** (next to Penn Station), the **Seagram Building** on Park Avenue and 52nd Street, and the **Grace Building** plaza at 43rd Street and Sixth Avenue, and, downtown, spots near City Hall, including the **Police Plaza** and the **Brooklyn Banks,** those swerving concrete ramps around the entrance to the Brooklyn Bridge. The top source for boards, either sale or rental, is **Blades Board & Skate;** of its several locations all over town, the handiest for these skateboarding sites is at 120 W. 72nd St., between Broadway and Columbus Avenue (🕾 **212/787-3911**).

Swimming

The city parks' public pools range from the big, noisy, and overrun to small oases in busy urban parks. Still, they have improved by leaps and bounds in the past few years in regard to cleanliness, upkeep, and orderliness—and a number are simply stunning. **Hamilton Fish,** on the Lower East Side (128 Pitt St., btw. Houston and Stanton sts.; 🕾 **212/387-7687**), is an Olympic-size pool with a smaller kids' pool. **Lasker Pool** (🕾 **212/534-7639**), in a beautiful north Central Park location overlooking the Harlem Meer, is an ice rink in winter and a swimming pool in summer. I also like the 3-foot-deep minipools at **Tompkins Square Park** in the East Village and **Vesuvio Park** (formerly the Thompson Street Park) in SoHo—both perfect for kids 7 and under (see "Playgrounds," earlier in this chapter). The city's outdoor pools are open July and August; go to **www.nycgovparks.org** for the details on all of the city's 54 public pools.

An option worth knowing about is the Upper East Side's **Asphalt Green,** York Avenue between 90th and 91st streets (© **212/369-8890;** www.asphaltgreen.org). You can take advantage of the **weekend family swim time** without a membership (Sat noon–3:30pm, Sun noon–3pm; $35 adults, $10 children 16 and under). Asphalt Green has two marvelous, clean pools: one 25-yard-long heated outdoor pool, and an Olympic-size 50m indoor pool, with a raised lower section ideal for young swimmers. The city's only other Olympic-size pool is at **Riverbank State Park,** 145th Street and Riverside Drive (© **212/694-3665**), which also offers a smaller outdoor pool in summer; use of the Riverbank pools is far cheaper than Asphalt Green, at $2 for adults and $1 for kids 15 and under, free for children 4 and under, and it's available daily from 9am to 6pm.

Tennis

Very few public tennis courts are available in Manhattan, where most serious tennis players belong to private clubs. **Riverside Park** offers two sets, one at 116th Street and Riverside Drive, the other a well-maintained set of 10 clay courts at 96th Street in the lower section of the park. Play is first-come, first-served, but there's not usually much of a wait. At the city's premier public facility, the **Central Park Tennis Center,** midpark at West 93rd Street, matters are somewhat more complicated. Players who have bought an annual tennis permit ($100 adults, $20 seniors, $10 juniors) can make advance reservations by phone for $7 by calling weekdays from 10am to 2pm or 4 to 7pm (© **212/316-0800** for information and reservations). Anyone else can get a single-play ticket for $7 at the Tennis Center on the day of play, entitling you to an hour of court time (2 hr. for doubles players). You can sign up for a specific court time—in person only—or put your name on the no-show list to take the next available court; players who don't show up 15 minutes before their booked court time get bumped, so plenty of folks from that standby list do get to play. When the hourly bell rings, there's a mass exodus from the courts—26 Har-Tru and 4 hard courts. If you don't have your own racket, you can rent one at the pro shop ($5 for 1 hr.), and they do have kid-size rackets. The Tennis Center is open daily from 6:30am to dusk, April to November. Staff pros also offer lessons; call for prices and availability.

It may be worth an excursion into Queens just to play on the site of the U.S. Open, the **U.S.T.A. Billie Jean King National Tennis Center** in Flushing Meadows–Corona Park (take the no. 7 subway to the Shea Stadium stop). Call the center at © **718/760-6200** to reserve a court, no more than 2 days in advance. Per-hour fees for outdoor courts are $18 to $56. The center is open Monday to Saturday 6am to midnight, Sunday 11pm.

Trapeze

Yes, that's right—in New York City your child can take a trapeze lesson, in a special trapeze arena on top of Pier 40 beside the West Side Highway in Hudson River Park, run by **Trapeze School New York** (Pier 40; West and Houston sts.; © **917/797-1872;** www.trapezeschool.com). Classes are offered even for total novices, as long as they are 6 years or older (accompanied by a parent or guardian, of course); don't worry, Mom, all sorts of reassuring nets and harnesses are provided. As you might expect, it'll cost you plenty—classes last 2 hours and cost $60 to $70, depending on the skill level and time of day, and that's on top of an initial $22 registration fee (indoor classes at 518 W. 30th St. are also offered). Still, it's an exhilarating experience, and those I know who've done it thought it was worth every penny. Take lots of videos.

CLASSES & WORKSHOPS
Art & Science Workshops

Dana Discovery Center   Summer weekends usually see free entertainment out on the plaza here, and arts-and-crafts workshops, science displays, puppet shows, and the like are regularly held inside this beautiful pondside facility, a short walk north of the Conservatory Garden.

In Central Park at the Harlem Meer, 110th St. at Lenox Ave. *C* **212/860-1370.** Tues–Sun 10am–5pm. Subway: 2, 3 to 110th St. Bus: M2, M3, M4 to 110th St./Fifth Ave.

Metropolitan Museum of Art   Indisputably one of the world's great museums, the Met scores big points with families for its frequent programs—they require no reservations and are free with museum admission, which means you can drop in on the spur of the moment and have a transforming experience. MuseumKids offers **Art Treks** (ages 5–12) and **Start With Art at the Met** (ages 3–7), and lots of other great family programs during the school year. Check the online calendar or at the information desk in the entrance hall to find out what's happening when.

Uris Center for Education, Metropolitan Museum of Art, 1000 Fifth Ave. (at 82nd St.). *C* **212/535-7710;** for program schedules, call *C* **212/570-3930.** www.metmuseum.org. Suggested museum admission $20 adults, $10 students and seniors, free for children 12 and under. Tues–Thurs and Sun 9:30am–5:30pm; Fri–Sat 9:30am–9pm. Subway: 4, 5, 6 to 86th St.

92nd Street Y   Affiliated with the YMHA (Young Men's Hebrew Association), this is one of the city's greatest cultural resources, with loads of evening programs in music and the arts, and a vast roster of sign-up classes for adults and children. Call to ask what is currently available on a drop-in basis.

1395 Lexington Ave. (at 92nd St.). *C* **212/996-1100.** www.92y.org. Subway: 4, 5, 6 to 86th St.

Drop-In Crafts

The Craft Studio   Plasterwork painting is a big draw here—superheroes, harlequin masks, rainbows, cars, picture frames, puppies, kittens, dinosaurs, you name it, you can paint it (with a little help from the friendly staff). You pay according to the price of the piece you choose. Terra-cotta pots are available for painting (think Mother's Day presents), as are other assorted ceramic items. The space is roomy and well lit, with a rainforest decor, and the shop carries a good number of excellent crafts and toys.

1657 Third Ave. (btw. 92nd and 93rd sts.). *C* **212/831-6626.** www.craftstudionyc.com. Mon–Sat 10am–6pm; Sun 11am–6pm. Subway: 4, 5, 6 to 86th St.; 6 to 96th St.

Little Shop of Crafts   Pick a piece of precast plaster from wall racks—there are more than 1,000 pieces to choose from—and you can paint it whatever colors you choose, daub on designs in finger wax, sprinkle glitter all over, and just generally make

NEW YORK KIDS' TOP FIVE cheap thrills

1. Ride in the front car of the subway train, standing at the front window to watch the train hurtle down the tunnel.
2. Stand on the street gratings above a subway line when the train comes thundering along underneath.
3. Run into the middle of a flock of pigeons, and make them all fly up at once.
4. In a skyscraper elevator, stand on tip-toe when the elevator starts to go up, and lower to a squat as you speed upward.
5. On the double-long accordion-style city buses, sit in the seats right in the hinge so you can swivel when the bus turns a corner.

it your own masterpiece. There's no charge except the price of the plaster pieces, which are $13 and up. The staff helps out as much as you need; teenagers labor intently for hours over incredibly detailed curlicues, while little kids are allowed to happily slap on paint as they please. They also carry a full line of functional pottery pieces to decorate; you can't take them home for about a week, but shipping is available for out-of-towners. Bead crafts and T-shirt painting are also on the menu, or you can stuff your own cuddly cloth animal to take home.

(1) 431 E. 73rd St. (btw. First and York aves.). ℂ **212/717-6636.** (2) 711 Amsterdam Ave. (corner of 96th St.). ℂ **212/531-2723.** www.littleshopny.com. Mon–Tues 11am–6:30pm; Wed–Fri 11am–10pm (after 6:30pm adults only); Sat 10am–8pm; Sun 10am–6:30pm. Subway: 6 to 77th St.

Make The ceramic items that customers paint here must be glazed and fired in a kiln, which means you pick them up a week after you've painted them—not as good on the instant-gratification score as the plaster-painting shops described above. On the other hand, you'll end up with a real piece of pottery, from a mug to a piggy bank to a pitcher to a platter, a keepsake that's also functional. Make now has a prime location in FAO Schwarz.

(1) FAO Schwarz. 767 Fifth Ave. (at 58th St.). ℂ **212/644-9400.** Subway N, R to Fifth Ave. (2) 1566 Second Ave. (btw. 81st and 82nd sts.). ℂ **212/570-6868.** Subway: 4, 5, 6 to 86th St. (3) 506 Amsterdam Ave. (btw. 84th and 85th sts.). ℂ **212/579-5575.** Subway: 1 to 86th St. www.makemeaning.com. Mon–Wed 10am–7pm; Thurs–Sat 10am–10pm; Sun 10am–6pm; after 5pm, adults only. Cost is base charge for item ($3–$60), plus $6 per half-hour work time.

Museum Weekend Workshops

On weekends, a number of major Manhattan museums seek to attract families by offering children's workshops, usually free with museum admission. Times vary, so be sure to call ahead.

The **Children's Museum of Manhattan,** 212 W. 83rd St., between Amsterdam Avenue and Broadway (ℂ 212/721-1223; www.cmom.org; admission $10, free for children under 1), always has a lineup of fun workshops, often themed to holidays. The **Children's Museum of the Arts,** 182 Lafayette St., between Broome and Grand streets (ℂ 212/274-0986; www.cmany.org; admission $10, free for children under 1), sets up hands-on art projects every day, providing materials for kids to create anything from papier-mâché masks to found-art collages to giant mobiles; weekend projects are even more ambitious. Midtown's **The Paley Center for Media,** 25 W.

52nd St., between Fifth and Sixth avenues (© **212/621-6600;** www.paleycenter. org; admission $10 adults, $8 students, $5 kids 13 and under), has fun Saturday workshops, including a series in which kids can re-create old radio scripts ($300 per group). The magnificent **Cathedral of St. John the Divine,** 1047 Amsterdam Ave., at 114th Street (© **212/662-2133;** www.stjohndivine.org), offers family stained-glass or medieval art workshops Saturday mornings at 10am for a $5 fee (cathedral admission is free).

At least once a month, the **Asia Society,** 725 Park Ave., at 70th Street (© **212/288-6400;** www.asiasociety.org; admission $10 adults, $5 students, free for kids 15 and under), comes up with really super Family Day workshops exploring various facets of different Asian cultures—Chinese storytellers, Indonesian puppets. And less frequently, the **China Institute,** 125 E. 65th St., between Park and Lexington avenues (© **212/744-8181;** www.chinainstitute.org; admission $7 for adults, $4 students, free for children 12 and under), offers similar workshops usually around the Chinese New Year or connected with current rotating shows in its galleries.

If art is your child's special interest, don't miss the excellent family programs offered by the **Museum of Modern Art,** 11 W. 53rd St., between Fifth and Sixth avenues (© **212/708-9400;** www.moma.org; admission $20 adults, $16 seniors, $12 students, free for children 15 and under), which organizes Saturday tours for 4-year-olds, drop-in tours for children ages 5 to 10, Tours for Tweens, hands-on classes for the entire family, and family-oriented programs of classic short films. The **Whitney Museum of American Art,** 945 Madison Ave., at 75th Street (© **212/570-3600;** www.whitney.org; admission $18 adults, $12 students, free for kids 11 and under); the **American Folk Art Museum,** 45 W. 53rd St., between Fifth and Sixth avenues (© **212/265-1040;** www.folkartmuseum.org; admission $12 adults, $8 students, free for kids 11 and under; $1 materials fee for workshops); and the **Studio Museum in Harlem,** 144 W. 125th St., between Lenox Avenue and Adam Clayton Powell Boulevard (© **212/864-4500;** www.studiomuseum.org; admission free for workshop participants), present interactive tours and frequent art workshops highlighting aspects of their collections or current exhibitions.

SHOPPING WITH YOUR KIDS

A s any serious grown-up shopper knows, the world capital of finance is also a world capital of conspicuous consumption. The children's market is no different. New York City offers a staggeringly wide range of ways for you to spend money on your kids—whether in boutiques selling state-of-the-art children's frocks, toy stores crammed with imported marvels, wondrous hobby shops stocked with rarities, or bookstores piled high with a mind-boggling selection of books. Some of these stores are destinations in themselves (think the Times Square Toys "R" Us store, with its giant animatronic dinosaur, or fabled FAO Schwarz, its doormen dressed splendiferously as toy soldiers); others are small, serendipitous gems you stumble upon as you round a corner. Still others showcase goods with price tags that may have you whistling a happy tune out the door. Luckily, you'll have little trouble getting your hands on fun, goofy souvenirs and cool New York–abilia that doesn't cost a pretty penny.

Without a doubt, some of the best children's stores in the city are museum stores, many with innovative offerings you won't find anywhere else. So that means you can get in some quality museum time *and* do some serious shopping, all in one fell swoop.

THE SHOPPING SCENE
Shopping Hours & Sales Tax

Neighborhood stores are generally open daily from 10am to 7pm; stores may not open until noon on Sunday. Street fairs and flea markets are generally weekends-only operations.

New York City has an **8.375% sales tax,** although on clothing and shoe purchases you don't have to pay sales tax at all. Takeout food, groceries, and services are exempt from sales tax.

Top Shopping Districts

CHELSEA   The best of the city's two baby megastores, **buybuy BABY,** is located here, on 7th Avenue and 25th Street. Don't miss **Books of Wonder,** one of Manhattan's best children's bookstores.

CHINATOWN　　This is cheap tchotchkes central, with oodles of irresistible MADE IN CHINA toys for sale on the sidewalks. You can also get colorful paper umbrellas, Chinese dragons and lanterns, kids' Chinese slippers and cheongsams, and other inexpensive exotica.

THE EAST VILLAGE　　The shops here have a funky edge, but you'll find lots of adorable clothes and unique toys. The toy-filled **Dinosaur Hill** is a good place to start; you can find chic-clothing with a downtown sensibility at the boutiques **Crembebè** and **Sons + Daughters.** Have any aspiring punksters head to St. Marks Place to **Trash & Vaudeville** (4 St. Marks Place; ✆ **212/982-3590**) or **Andy's Chee-Pees** (St. Marks Place; ✆ **212/253-8404;** www.andyscheepees.com) for rock-star duds, vintage leather jackets, and faded Levis.

GREENWICH VILLAGE　　This neighborhood has an increasing number of notable shops, including **Kid O,** with its brilliant selection of toys and books; **Doodle Doo's,** a toy store/haircutting salon; and **Ibiza Kidz,** with its racks of Splendid Little, Cotton Caboodle, and other incredibly soft, deliciously fashionable clothes. For older kids who are into comics, trading cards, vintage records, and sci-fi/fantasy stuff, there's **Forbidden Planet.** Greenwich Village is also chess central: On Thompson Street just south of Washington Square, the **Chess Shop** and the **Chess Forum** sell beautiful chess sets and let kids play for hours.

MIDTOWN　　This is where you'll find the big boys of retailing, as well as those stores designed as much for tourist gawping as for actual shopping. FAO Schwarz is a must-see attraction for kids of all ages. **American Girl Place** is without question an essential stop for girls between the ages of 6 and 12, with the flagship store of **Build-A-Bear Workshop** just down Fifth Avenue a huge draw for younger boys and girls as well. The truly impressive **Toys "R" Us** flagship store in the Times Square area is worlds away from the chain's usual strip-mall outlets. The cleverly designed **Niketown** and **NBA Store** are magnets for sports-loving older kids. A number of big department stores reign over Midtown, including **Saks Fifth Avenue, Bloomingdales,** and **Macy's**—all with choice children's departments. Don't miss the jewel box of a baby boutique inside the serene interiors of **Takashimaya,** the elegant Japanese department store on Fifth Avenue.

NOLITA/LITTLE ITALY　　Nolita, a small grid of streets east of Broadway and south of Houston (and once part of Little Italy), is packed with hip boutiques and cafes; the original St. Patrick's Cathedral occupies a central, shaded spot. It has few children's stores, however. If you're looking for **cheesy souvenirs**—catnip to kids, of course—Little Italy has a smattering of tourist-oriented souvenir emporiums.

SOHO　　Not so long ago, this fabled neighborhood, with its cobblestoned streets and landmark cast-iron architecture, was the domain of pioneering loft-dwelling artists and cutting-edge art galleries. It's now shopping central, with designer boutiques cozying up to retailers like J. Crew (and **Crewcuts**) and cosmetics stores— the art galleries have largely fled to funkier pastures. The charming, all-purpose **Giggle** opened its first New York store here, with übermodern, high-end furniture, clothes, and toys. For sophisticated French imports, head to **Julian and Sara** or **Les Petits Chapelais.** Older kids go for the aggressively ironic boutique **Kidrobot.** Back in the 1970s and 1980s, the large cast-iron buildings (formerly manufacturing businesses) along Broadway below Astor Place were where teens and preteens flocked for jeans and vintage clothes, army surplus, and Doc Martens. Alas, these funky businesses have been largely displaced by big retailers like **Old Navy, H&M, UNIQLO,** and even a downtown **Bloomingdales,** which replaced the much-lamented old Canal Jeans store. **Sneaker emporiums** are ubiquitous along lower Broadway, however, and the **Scholastic toy and bookstore** (at Broadway and Prince) is a perennial favorite for kids who love Scholastic faves like Harry Potter and Clifford the Big Red Dog.

SOUTH STREET SEAPORT/WALL STREET This historic neighborhood along the East River has seen a spurt of family gentrification since the departure of the Fulton Fish Market. The piers at **South Street Seaport** feature a characterless mix of lower- to midrange chain stores, but the area just north has developed into a small but appealing neighborhood of cobblestoned streets, renovated landmark buildings, boutiques, and restaurants. The **World Financial Center** has few shops kids will be interested in, but the Winter Garden Atrium is a stunning space with a long cascade of marble steps that kids seem to find irresistible. You can also stroll (or bike) along the Battery Park City waterfront ★ and watch boats skim the water and have a good view of the Statue of Liberty and Ellis Island.

TRIBECA This is the city's newest Gold Coast, with big media money filling huge loft apartments and a baby boom filling an army of Bugaboos. I also think it's the most kid-friendly neighborhood in town, with an almost small-town vibe: Its spacious, uncrowded sidewalks are great for strolling, with minimal traffic, kid-friendly restaurants, and a beautiful children's park. Oh, and a small but enviable concentration of kids' stores (among them **Shoofly, Boomerang,** and **Babesta**).

UNION SQUARE The city's other baby megastore, **Babies "R" Us,** is here, on the east side of the park. A large **Barnes & Noble,** with a very good children's department (and scheduled story times), is located in a beautiful landmark building on the north side of Union Square. The city's largest greenmarket is here 4 days a week.

THE UPPER EAST SIDE This neighborhood has the largest concentration of children's clothing stores in the city. And, as befitting its demographics, it also has some of the priciest (and preppy-est) kids' shops in town. If you're shopping without kids in tow, a serious Madison Avenue expedition could take all day—many designer kids' boutiques are located between 62nd and 96th streets (**Jacadi** and **Bonpoint** among them). Shops along Lexington and Third avenues are a little more reasonable, especially in the toy realm: **Mary Arnold Toys** and **Zitomer's Zittles** (and **Homboms** is worth the extra walk over to First Ave.). Older boys can augment their card collections at **Alex's MVP Cards & Comics.**

THE UPPER WEST SIDE This has long been a down-to-earth, family-centric neighborhood, with lots of toy and clothing shops (although UWS fixture Morris Brothers—clothing neighborhood children since 1940—shuttered its doors in 2007, a victim of rising rents) and family-friendly dining. Don't miss the outstanding shops in the **American Museum of Natural History** and the Children's Museum of Manhattan. A number of good toy stores are located on Amsterdam Avenue between 79th and 86th streets, including the generic but stocked-to-the-gills **West Side Kids.**

SHOPPING WITH YOUR KIDS | The Shopping Scene

Department Stores

Barneys New York ★   The kids' stuff is way up in the nosebleed section of the 9th floor—but oh, what a delicious bouquet of designer frocks! The clothes here make Manhattan's cutting-edge kids' boutiques seem ho-hum. How about Junior Gaultier? Little John Gallianos? Look for new or lesser-known brands (and solid end-of-season sales) and a small but choice selection of toys. On the same floor is the newly relocated **Fred's,** with park views; kid-friendly lunch items include pizza margherita and chicken soup. 660 Madison Ave. (at 61st St.). ✆ **212/826/8900.** www.barneys. com. Subway: N, R to Fifth Ave.

Bergdorf Goodman   Some people are intimidated by this fabled store's exclusive reputation and the intimate, gallery-like departments. Don't be: Once you get past the frosty first floor, you'll find a memorable, even welcoming shopping experience, with excellent sales. The children's department (on the seventh floor) is small but choice, with brands such as Splendid, Ella Moss, and Noodle and Boo and a good assortment of fine layette. 754 Fifth Ave. (at 57th St.). ✆ **800/558-1855.** www. bergdorfgoodman.com. Subway: N, R to Fifth Ave.

Bloomingdale's   Unlike the rest of the store, which can feel claustrophobic, the kids' clothing department is cavernous, with clothes grouped by age (and brand) on two levels split by a swirling staircase (there's no toy department to speak of). It's also been pretty quiet during the times I've stopped in. It's built around boutique-style brand-specific sections; look for Juicy Couture, Ralph Lauren, Uggs, and Diesel—that's about as cutting edge as it gets. It has a fairly sizable tween fancy-dress section. 1000 Third Ave. (at 59th St.). ✆ **212/705-2000.** www.bloomingdales.com. Subway: 4, 5, 6 to 59th St.

Lord & Taylor   This formerly frumpy Midtown matron has gotten a spiffy makeover, but it's still blessedly free of crowds most of the time. It stocks traditional layette items and children's clothes. Its **Christmas window displays** ★★ are among the best in town—with meticulously detailed historic scenes featuring tiny costumed moving figures. 424 Fifth Ave. (at 39th St.). ✆ **212/391-3344.** www.lordandtaylor.com. Subway: B, D, F, V to 42nd St.

Macy's Herald Square   Macy's flagship in Midtown is one of the world's biggest department stores, with a solidly middle-class orientation and a reputation for moving the merchandise with ongoing (often deeply discounted) sales. It's within crawling distance of a number of subway stations and usually packed to the gills with people chasing the markdowns. However, the children's departments are huge and carry a broad range of merchandise, including lots of sturdy basics and playwear for boys and girls. This is the only Manhattan department store with a significant toy department, though the selection is fairly run-of-the-mill. At Christmastime, Macy's still mounts a free Santaland on its eighth floor, a state-of-the-art extravaganza with long lines and Santa himself taking requests. 151 W. 34th St. (from Broadway to Seventh Ave.). ✆ **212/695-4400.** www.macys.com. Subway: B, D, F, N, Q, R, V, W to 34th St.

Saks Fifth Avenue   Sleek and chic, Saks does best for the very young, with a fairly good infant-wear department, but its departments for older kids often have special themed characters and fun events. It's worth including in your Rockefeller Center expeditions, especially since the store's restaurant, **Café SFA,** is such a winner. 611 Fifth Ave. (at 50th St.). ℂ **212/753-4000.** www.saksfifthavenue.com. Subway: B, D, F, V to 47th–50th sts./Rockefeller Center.

Baby Megastores

Babies "R" Us   This three-story Union Square baby emporium has all the basics you need to keep your little one well fed, bathed, rested, and properly clothed— and the competition from buybuy BABY (see below) has prodded them to offer better (and trendier) brands. Don't expect much help from the staff, though. It's the franchise's only location in Manhattan. 754 Fifth Ave. (at 57th St.). ℂ **800/558-1855.** www.bergdorfgoodman.com. Subway: N, R to Fifth Ave.

buybuy BABY ★   This is the best baby department store in the city when it comes to feeding and bathing items, linens, strollers, car seats, and furniture; the clothing line is fairly pedestrian but reasonably priced. It's a Bugaboo specialist, with all the latest models and accouterments. 1000 Third Ave. (at 59th St.). ℂ **212/705-2000.** www.buybuybaby.com. Subway: 4, 5, 6 to 59th St.

Greenmarkets/Street Fairs

The city's largest greenmarket, **Union Square Greenmarket,** 16th Street between Broadway and Park Avenue South, runs Monday, Wednesday, Friday, and Saturday and has some truly glorious produce from rural New York State, New Jersey, and Pennsylvania. There's a newly renovated playground directly south of the greenmarket, so pick up lunch (crisp apples, apple cider, fresh cheddar cheese, muffins, or hearty seven-grain bread in fall; fresh berries, heirloom cherry tomatoes, just-squeezed juices in summer) and eat on a bench while the kids clamber away.

From May to October various stretches of Manhattan streets are closed to traffic for **street fairs,** featuring booths selling everything from T-shirts to audiotapes to potted palms and hand-knit Peruvian sweaters. The food booths are even more fun—sizzling-hot stir-fries, heaping tacos, or foot-long hot dogs. Sometimes, there'll be a petting zoo or one of those inflated bouncing castles. You tend to see the same vendors weekend after weekend, and little that's for sale is really special. But the main things are the crowd, the sunshine, and the car-free strolling. To find out where street fairs will be held throughout the city, look under "Events" in the "Spare Times" section of the Friday *New York Times.*

SHOPPING A TO Z

The last couple of years have not been easy ones for the city's boutique and mom-and-pop stores, many of which did not survive the financial downturn. The economy was still in recovery mode at press time, so be sure to call before you go out of your way to visit a store.

Books

Note that many of these bookstores offer story hours and appearances by children's book authors—for details see "Story Hours," in Chapter 11.

Bank Street College Book Store This narrow, bright uptown store has a wonderful selection of more than 40,000 titles and an extremely knowledgeable staff. It's connected to an outstanding education college, so there's also a great section for parents and teachers. 610 W. 112th St. (at Broadway). ✆ **212/678-1654.** www.bankstreetbooks. com. Subway: 1 to 110th St.

Barnes & Noble Far from being bland mall outlets, the Manhattan branches of this megastore have great children's sections (especially the 86th St., 21st St., and Union Square locations), with informed salespeople, frequent story hours, and plenty of room for kids to frolic, where the salespeople never complain if your toddler pulls every board book off the shelf and leaves it on the floor. The store's cafes are a good option for a midday snack, too, and there are big, clean restrooms available. A giant new Barnes & Noble has just opened in TriBeCa next door to a Whole Foods supermarket (97 Warren St., at Greenwich St.; ✆ **212/587-5389**). (1) 240 E. 86th St. (btw. Second and Third aves.). ✆ **212/794-1962.** Subway: 4, 5, 6 to 86th St. (2) 2289 Broadway (at 82nd St.). ✆ **212/362-8835.** Subway: 1 to 79th St. (3) Citicorp Building (at Third Ave. and 54th St.). ✆ **212/750-8033.** Subway: E, V to Lexington Ave./53rd St. (4) Rockefeller Center, 600 Fifth Ave. (at 48th St.). ✆ **212/765-0590.** Subway: B, D, F, V to 47th–57th sts./Rockefeller Center. (5) Union Square, 33 E. 17th St. (btw. Broadway and Park Ave.). ✆ **212/253-0810.** Subway: N, Q, R, W, 4, 5, 6 to 14th St.; L to Union Square. (6) 396 Sixth Ave. (at 8th St.). ✆ **212/674-8780.** Subway: A, B, C, D, E, F, V to W. 4th St.

Bookberries A cozy little carpeted nook has been partitioned off for kids in this small East Side store. The selection is fairly good, though the picture books may be haphazardly alphabetized—probably because so many little hands have pulled them out—a good sign. 983 Lexington Ave. (at 71st St.). ✆ **212/794-9400.** Subway: 6 to 68th St.

Books of Wonder ★ One of the few specialty children's bookstores left in town, this great Flatiron shop has a lot of hard-to-find titles, as well as collectors' items (the Oz books, original Nancy Drews, illustrators' original art). The staff is friendly, helpful, and knowledgeable. Plus, it's got an outpost of the **Cupcake Cafe** (p. 109) right in the store, with gorgeously decorated cupcakes to eat on-site or cakes for celebrations later. 18 W. 18th St. (btw. Fifth and Sixth aves.). ✆ **212/989-3270.** www.booksofwonder.com. Subway: 1 to 18th St.

Borders This chain megastore has a large and welcoming children's section, with plenty for older kids as well as picture books for the younger set. The atmosphere is very conducive to browsing. www.borders.com. (1) 10 Columbus Circle (at Eighth Ave.). ✆ **212/823-9775.** Subway: A, B, C, D, 1 to 59th St./Columbus Circle. (2) 461 Park Ave. (at 57th St.). ✆ **212/980-6785.** Subway: 4, 5, 6 to 59th St. (3) 550 Second Ave. (at 31st St.) in Kips Bay Plaza. ✆ **212/685-3938.** Subway: 6 to 33rd St. (4) 2 Penn Plaza (7th Ave. and 31st St.). ✆ **212/244-1814.** Subway: 1, 2, 3 to 34th St. (5) 100 Broadway (at Pine St.). ✆ **212/964-1988.** Subway: 2, 3, 4, 5 to Wall St.

Scholastic Store ★ Big, bright, and glossy, this outlet of the big children's publisher has an obvious motive for selling Scholastic books, activities, and tie-in toys, but considering how many of the titles your kids love are published by Scholastic—from Clifford the Big Red Dog to Harry Potter—it's a worthwhile SoHo stop. 557 Broadway (btw. Prince and Spring). ✆ **212/343-6166.** www.scholasticstore.com. Subway: R, W to Prince St.

Shakespeare & Co. The uptown branch of this local chain offers a decent children's section, with pint-size chairs and a carpet for in-store reading. The selection is intelligent, if skewed toward "worthy" picture books and classics. 939 Lexington Ave. (btw. 68th and 69th sts.). ℭ **212/570-0201.** www.shakeandco.com. Subway: 6 to 68th St.

The Strand The venerated used-bookseller touting "18 Miles of Books" actually has a great children's section, where you can get new bestsellers and classics at substantial discounts. 828 Broadway (at 12th St.). ℭ **212/472-1452.** www.strandbooks.com. Subway: N, R, 4, 5, 6 to 14th St.

Westsider Books This excellent little used-book store—narrow and dusky, with books to the ceiling—has a small children's section with some real finds. 2246 Broadway (btw. 80th and 81st sts.). ℭ **212/362-0706.** Subway: 1 to 79th St.

Candy, Chocolate & Sweets

Chocolate Bar Cashing in on the designer chocolate vogue, this boutique in the West Village will intrigue older kids who've outgrown stuffing their faces with Hershey's Kisses. You can sit down and sip a cocoa or latte while you're browsing. 19 8th Ave. (btw. W. 12th and Jane sts.). ℭ **212/366-1541.** www.chocolatebarnyc.com. Subway: A, C, E to 8th Ave./14th St.

Dylan's Candy Bar The creation of Ralph Lauren's daughter, Dylan's is a candy-colored, sweet-shoppe-themed bi-level boutique full of specialty candy, from imported sweets to store-brand designer chocolates. There's some hard-to-find stuff here, though prices can be, as I overheard one dad growl, "obscene." Its glossy shopping bags are a status symbol among the younger set. 1011 Third Ave. (at 60th St.). ℭ **646/735-0078.** www.dylanscandybar.com. Subway: 4, 5, 6 to 59th St.

Hershey's Times Square Store Gigantic Hershey bars, buckets of Kisses, and other lavish souvenir packages of Hershey-brand confectionery are piled ceiling-high in this bright and busy Times Square boutique, along with T-shirts, stuffed animals, and all manner of candy tie-ins. 1593 Broadway (at 48th St.). ℭ **212/581-9100.** www.hersheygifts.com. Subway: 1 to 50th St.; N, R, W to 49th St.

Li-Lac Chocolates A Greenwich village institution founded in 1923, this charming shop sells handmade chocolates molded into a delightful variety of shapes. www.lilacchocolates.com. (1) 40 Eighth Ave. (at Jane St.). ℭ **212/924-2280.** Subway: A, C, E to 14th St. (2) Park Ave. and 42nd St., The Food Market at Grand Central Terminal. ℭ **212/370-4866.** Subway: S, 4, 5, 6, 7 to 42nd St./Grand Central.

Mondel Chocolates 🎁 This old-fashioned little shop in the Columbia University area has beautiful handmade chocolates and other gift items for the sweet tooth in your family. Closed Sundays July through August. 2913 Broadway (near 114th St.). ℭ **212/864-2111.** www.mondelchocolates.com. Subway: 1 to 116th St.

Clothing
THE BIG CHAINS

You can find these stores all over the city—as well as in malls and shopping centers all over the United States, even the world. So why on earth would you stop in one while you're here? Well, for a number of very good reasons. Some of these stores are

NYC IS chocolate city

The Big Apple has become a city consumed by a near-feverish craving for chocolate. Many sweets shops around the city now are turning out homemade chocolates in every variety that are so good, the stores, like four-star restaurants, are bona fide destinations. If your brood is in search of that perfect chocolate taste, here are a few more places to keep in mind.

The best can be found just over the Brooklyn Bridge in DUMBO at **Jacques Torres Chocolate ★★**, 66 Water St., Brooklyn (✆ **718/875-9772;** www. mrchocolate.com). Torres, the former celebrated pastry chef at Le Cirque, ventured out on his own a few years ago and opened this mecca to chocolate, where your mouth will water as you watch chocolate being made—and don't neglect his nearby **Ice Cream Store** at No. 62. The variations here are staggering and include chocolate peanut brittle, chocolate-covered corn flakes, and champagne truffles. Take home a tin of the "wicked" hot chocolate, which features allspice, cinnamon, sweet ancho chile peppers, and hot chipotle peppers. Torres also has an uptown shop at 285 Amsterdam Ave. (at 73rd St.) and opens his chocolate-manufacturing facility to the public daily at 350 Hudson St., at King Street, in the Hudson Square neighborhood (✆ **212/414-2462**).

Just east of the Metropolitan Museum of Art is the Madison Avenue incarnation of the Paris import **La Maison du Chocolat,** 1018 Madison Ave., at 78th Street (✆ **212/ 744-7117;** www.lamaisonduchocolat.com). This boutique takes its chocolate very seriously. Here you will find possibly the best pure chocolate you've ever tasted. They abhor any bitterness in their chocolate and make it a point to claim that

they use nothing stronger than 65% cocoa. It is serious chocolate. If you're downtown, stop by their new shop at 63 Wall St. (✆ **212/952-1123**), or duck into the midtown 30 Rockefeller Center shop (✆ **212/265-9404**).

Lily O'Brien's Chocolate Cafe, across from Bryant Park at 36 W. 40th St., (✆ **212-575-0631;** www.lilyscafenyc. com), is the place to try superb 100% Belgian chocolate in many forms, served alongside some of the city's best pastries—a great follow-up to winter ice skating in the park.

Head to the Bowery for more diverse temptations, like the strawberry balsamic dark chocolate, vegan hazelnut chocolate, or the signature chocolate-covered pretzel at **Bespoke Chocolates,** 6 Extra Place, off 1st Street between Second Avenue and Bowery (✆ **212-260-7103;** www.bespoke chocolates.com).

More unconventional chocolate is found at **Kee's Chocolates,** 80 Thompson St., near Spring Street (✆ **212/ 334-3284;** www.keeschocolates.com), where owner Kee Ling Tong makes her own unique creations 7 days a week, like mango green tea and Thai chili. Further south in the Financial District, you can enjoy a delectable handmade Heavenly Hash—and other sumptuous variations on regular old candy bars—at **Evelyn's Chocolates,** 4 John St. (✆ **212/267-5170**).

If none of these sources are decadent enough for you, head to the Lower East Side's **Essex Street Market** (at Delancey St.) for some homemade truffles, caramels, or "pig candy"—that is, chocolate-covered bacon, if you can wrap your head around that—at **Roni Sue's Chocolates** (✆ **212/260-0421**).

Manhattan Clothes Shopping

Baby Mega Stores
Babies "R" Us **33**
buybuy BABY **30**

**CLOTHES SHOPPING
BY NEIGHBORHOOD**
Chelsea
Baby Depot at Burlington
Coat Factory **31**

East Village
Crembebé **46**
Jane's Exchange **41**

Flatiron
Space Kiddets **32**

Greenwich Village
Clementine **38**
Ibiza Kidz **35**
Lucky Wang **34**
Yoya **36**

NoLiTa
Soho Baby **45**

SoHo
Glory Chen **41**
Julian & Sara **43**
Kisan Concept Store **40**
Les Petits Chapelais **48**
Lilliput **44**
Patagonia SoHo **42**
Trico Fields **39**

TriBeCa
Babesta **51**
Koh's Kids **50**
Torlys's Kids **49**

Upper West Side
Berkley Girl **3, 23**
Bonne Nuit **5**
Greenstones **2, 19**
Z'Baby Company **4, 26**

Upper East Side
All Dressed Up **13**
Monnalisa **10**
Baby CZ **26**
Bonpoint **7, 27, 37**
Catimini **9**
Flora and Henri **20**
Flowers by Zoe **11**
Jacadi **6, 7, 25**
Lemonade **15**
Lester's **16**
Lily Pulitzer **17**
Magic Windows/Magic
  Windows for Teens **8**
Petit Bateau **10**
Prince & Princess **18**
Roberta Roller Rabbit **22**
Small Change **14**
Spring Flowers Children's
  Boutique **21, 28, 29**
Tutti Bambini **24**
Zittles
  (Zitomer Department Store) **19**

the chains' flagships; some are in spaces that really deserve a look—bigger and better (and more fabulously designed) than those in your hometown. Maybe you, like me, come from such an infinitesimal speck on the map that you don't have chain stores, much less *store* stores. In all likelihood, however, you already know what these chains have to offer, and that may be exactly what you need. And hey—you may just love the stuff and want to stock up. Here are the recommended big chains with solid children's selections.

CHILDREN'S PLACE   This chain store sells its own label of bright, simply cut casual wear in sizes newborn to 12 (up to size 8 in some stores). It's like a slightly cheaper version of the Gap, in all respects, but to fill out a wardrobe, a $10 polo shirt or plain $14 sundress isn't a bad idea. I don't find the clothes as well made as those at the Gap, however. Go to **www.childrensplace.com** for the latest Manhattan locations.

FOREVER 21   Twenty-one may actually be over the hill for this store; every time we visit, we see swarms of tweens and teens rummaging through racks bursting with clothes that threaten to go out of style before you even reach the cash register. Forever 21 has stores in prime locations in Union Square, lower Broadway, and near Macy's. For addresses, go to **www.forever21.com**.

GAPKIDS/BABYGAP   I love the kids' clothes at Gap—they're stylish, solidly constructed, made of good cotton, and priced to move. Wait for sales, and you can clean up. For the latest Manhattan locations, go to **www.gap.com**.

J. CREW CREWCUTS   J. Crew's smart and chic line of clothing, Crewcuts ★, is found only at a handful of J. Crew locations in Manhattan. For Manhattan locations, go to **www.jcrew.com**.

H&M   Not every NYC branch of this value-conscious Swedish clothing company carries children's lines, but you can find them at both 34th Street locations and the Harlem branch. Sizes up to 13 years, for both boys and girls, are designed to be durable, easy to move in, and seriously fashion-conscious. For the latest Manhattan locations, go to **www.hm.com**.

OLD NAVY   Featuring fun, casual clothing (the works: cotton knits, outerwear, sleepwear, beachwear) in the Gap mold (its parent company), this clothing chain is a favorite with New Yorkers, who love the surprisingly stylish clothing and rock-bottom prices—even Madonna has been known to shop for her brood here. Go to **www.oldnavy.com** for the latest Manhattan locations.

UNIQLO   This Japanese export specializes in quality, well-made casual wear. Teens and tweens love the soft cotton tees of all shapes and colors, cargo pants, and simple knit dresses—building blocks for a stylin' wardrobe at very reasonable prices. Go to **www.uniqlo.com/us** for the latest locations in Manhattan.

CONSIGNMENT STORES

Consignment stores selling gently used clothing and shoes can be highly rewarding shopping experiences, especially is an uncertain economy; just think of them as beloved hand-me-downs from older siblings.

Clementine ★   This Village basement shop is as adorable as the clothes it sells—and the excellent stock of upscale brands in baby and toddler sizes (up to size 6) is refreshed on a regular basis. 39½ Washington Sq. S. (at MacDougal St.). ℭ **212/228-9333.** www. clementineconsignment.com. Subway: A, B, C, D, E, F to W. 4th St.

Jane's Exchange   Crammed to the gills with kids' clothing, strollers, toys, games, you name it—Jane's Exchange is not as meticulously curated as Clementine, but the hunt for goodies can be more adventurous. Prices are very, very reasonable. 191 E. 3rd St. (btw. Ave. A and Ave. B). ℭ **646/677-0380.** www.janesexchangenyc.com. Subway: F to Second Ave.

CLOTHING BY NEIGHBORHOOD

A number of the following clothing stores also stock shoes, but for a complete listing of shoes-only stores, go to "Shoes," later in this chapter.

Keep in mind that a number of the following stores have more than one location, often in other neighborhoods altogether. That's why we've included listing information for all the stores' locations in Manhattan.

Chelsea

Baby Depot at Burlington Coat Factory   Clothing up to size 16, boys' and girls', can be found on the third floor of this big discount store in the megastore shopping district wedged between Chelsea and the Flatiron District. The brands are quite respectable—Carter's, Buster Brown, Guess—but not very appealingly displayed, jammed onto racks under fluorescent lighting. 707 Seventh Ave. (btw. 22nd and 23rd sts.). ℭ **212/229-1300.** www.coat.com. Subway: F, V to 23rd St.

East Village

Crembebè   This little shop has a real sense of style; it carries sophisticated European brands, popular American labels (Splendid), and cool downtown clothing from local designers in sizes newborn to 12 years. 68 Second Ave. (btw. 3rd and 4th sts.). ℭ **212/ 979-6848.** www.crembebe.com. Subway: 6 to Astor Place, F to Second Ave.

Flatiron District

Space Kiddets ★   I love this store for its splendid selection of adorable, trendy clothing for wee ones (up to teens)—it can be pricey, but the sales are terrific and the staff is always helpful. Look for brands like Kenzo as well as hipster and little-known brands you won't find anywhere else—my daughter loves her green furry spotted coat made by the Japanese company Boohomes. The stock from Space Kiddets' former toy-store offshoot on 21st Street (now closed) has been consolidated here. Look for classic toys and a good selection of puzzles and games from the French line Vilac. Closed Sunday. 26 E. 22nd St. (btw. Broadway and Park Ave. S.). ℭ **212/420-9878.** www.space kiddets.com. Subway: N, R, W, 6 to 23rd St.

Greenwich Village

Ibiza Kidz ★   In its new location on Broadway, this Village shop sells children's clothes with a bohemian sensibility (Splendid, Cotton Caboodle). The look is stylish and colorful, with a sense of whimsy. 830 Broadway (btw. 12th and 13th sts.). ℭ **212/228-7990** or 212/375-9984. www.ibizakidz.com. Subway: N, R to 8th St.

Lucky Wang ★   Adorable children's kimonos, colorful kimono tops, and flower-print wrap dresses: This store sells hip, charming ensembles you won't find anywhere else. 799 Broadway (at 10th St.). ℭ **212/353-2850.** www.luckywang.com. Subway: N, R, W to 14th St.

Yoya Gosh, the stuff in this baby and toddler boutique is beautiful, from the dresses (Judith Lacroix, Marie Chantal, Tocca, Tzawa) to the furniture (Netto, Bloom) to the sleek silver and gold rattles. And gosh, it's pricey (good sales, though). It's got an up-to-the-minute selection of Jellycat stuffed toys—priced reasonably and the perfect baby gift. 636 Hudson St. (at Horatio St.). ✆ **646/336-6844.** www.yoyashop.com. Subway: A, E to 14th St.

Nolita

Soho Baby This pleasant shop has a small but nicely curated selection of stylish clothing for sizes newborn to 6 years. It also has bedding, stuffed animals, and toys. 251 Elizabeth St. (btw. Prince and Houston sts.). ✆ **212/625-8538.** Subway: R, W to Prince St.; B, D, F, V to Broadway/Lafayette St.

SoHo

Glory Chen ★ The San Francisco shoe designer Glory Chen now has a small but utterly captivating collection of kids' shoes. The shoes are originally styled and beautifully made with Italian leather, but at press time only come in sizes 5 to 10½ (European sizes 21 to 27). 121 Greene St. (btw. Prince and Houston sts.). ✆ **212/677-2938.** www.glorychen.com. Subway: R, W to Prince St.

Julian & Sara For 15 years, this tiny SoHo shop has been selling lovely, upscale things in sizes for newborns to 16 years, for girls and boys. 103 Mercer St. (btw. Prince and Spring sts.). ✆ **212/226-1989.** www.julianandsara.com. Subway: R, W to Prince St.

Kisan Concept Store ★★ Arriving from Paris by way of Iceland, this 2-year-old shop sells "high-street" women's wear, menswear, art books, shoes, and a breathtaking selection of fine kids' clothes. Brands—largely European and fairly obscure in NYC—include Cotton & Milk, Megan Park, Quincy, Annette Pois, Littl by Lilit, Antipast, and Y-3. 125 Greene St. (btw. Prince and Houston sts.). ✆ **212/475-2470.** www.kisanstore.com. Subway: R, W to Prince St.

Les Petits Chapelais ★ The Brittany-inspired fashions by French designer Nathalie Simonneaux in this darling SoHo boutique are refreshingly child-appropriate, sturdy, and beautifully made. Sizes 0 to 10. 86 Thompson St. (at Spring St.). ✆ **212/625-1023.** www.lespetitschapelais.com. Subway: C, E to Spring St.

Lilliput ★ A fashion-conscious, European boho sensibility rules in these crammed-full shops (in two locations on the same street) carrying play and dressy clothes in sizes up to 18; expect such quality international labels as Petit Bateau, Repetto, and Lili Gaufrette. A battery of windup toys and a good-size selection of tulle skirts for dress-up fun give you a clue to the spirit of the place. (1) 265 Lafayette St. (btw. Prince and Spring sts.). ✆ **212/965-9567.** (2) 240 Lafayette St. (btw. Prince and Spring sts.). ✆ **212/965-9201.** www.lilliputsoho.com. Subway: 6 to Spring St.; B, D, F, V to Broadway/Lafayette St.

Patagonia SoHo This outdoor specialist has a small but excellent selection of solid kids' clothes—specializing, as you might guess, in winter fleece and down outerwear from toddler sizes on up. It's a big, handsome store, with wood floors and a warm, friendly staff. 101 Wooster St. (btw. Prince and Spring sts.). ✆ **212/343-1176.** www.patagonia.com. Subway: 6 to Spring St.; R, W to Prince St.

Trico Field ★ These highly original, highly wearable Japanese brands (Fith, Denim Dungaree, Go to Hollywood) have a countrified/bohemian sensibility, with lots of adult-pleasing plaid shirts, distressed denim, nubby textures, and sundresses in farmstead floral prints. Sizes run largely from 2 years to 7 years. Its only other American store is in Beverly Hills. 65 W. Houston St. (at Wooster St.). © **212/358-8484.** www.tricofield.net. Subway: R, W to Prince St.

TriBeCa

Babesta   If it's "plain vanilla" you're after, head elsewhere. This small clothing store makes no bones about its fun, contemporary rock-'n'-roll sensibility. That doesn't mean the cool kids' clothes aren't supremely wearable and good quality, because they are. Yes, you can get your Ramones T-shirts and psychedelic rompers here, but you can also get perfectly darling Kit+Lilli sundresses. **Babesta Cribs** (56 Warren St.) is just across the street, selling modern furniture, strollers, highchairs, and home decor. 66 W. Broadway (btw. Murray and Warren sts.). © **212/608-4522.** www.babesta.com. Subway: A, C, E, 1, 2, 3 to Chambers St.

Koh's Kids ★   This TriBeCa shop is crammed to the rafters with a terrific assortment of quality casual clothes and shoes for the newborn to size 14 set, as well as plenty of nifty toys and gifts. Good sales are ongoing. 311 Greenwich St. (btw. Chambers and Reade sts.). © **212/791-6915.** Subway: A, C, E, 1, 2, 3 to Chambers St.

Torly Kids NYC   Formerly Babylicious, this TriBeCa boutique stocks stylish children's clothes for newborns to age 7, as well as Jellycats stuffed toys and books. 51 Hudson St. (btw. Duane and Jay sts.). © **212/406-7440.** www.babyliciousnyc.com. Subway: A, C, E, 1, 2, 3 to Chambers St.

Upper East Side

Baby CZ ★   Designer Caroline Zapf fashions gorgeous, timeless frocks for babies and kids 2 to 12 in silks, cotton poplin and cotton voile, velvet, and cashmere. 820 Madison Ave. (btw. 68th and 69th sts.). © **212/288-8030.** Subway: 6 to 68th St.

Bonpoint ★   This boutique has some of the most expensive children's clothes in town (up to size 16 girls and 12 boys)—and the selection is beautiful. Everything sold is the store's private label, and the fabrics are gorgeous, no question about it; the styles are classic, understated, and perfectly cut. Bonpoint has two Upper East Side locations and a downtown store on newly fashionable Bleecker Street. www.bonpoint.com. (1) 1269 Madison Ave. (at 91st St.). © **212/722-7720.** Subway: 4, 5, 6 to 86th St. (2) 810 Madison Ave. (at 68th St.). © **212/879-0900.** Subway: 6 to 68th St. (3) 392 Bleecker St. (btw. W. 11th and Perry sts.). © **212/647-1700.** Subway: 1, 9 to Christopher St.

Catimini ★   These colorful French kids' clothes (mostly size 8 and under) show an ineffable sense of style, with sassy prints and deep-colored solids cut into simple, roomy clothes with real flair. The store has friendly staff. The clothes aren't cheap, but they're casual and sturdy enough that you'll get lots of wear out of them. It's right next door to a Cozy Cuts. Closed Sunday July to August. 1125 Madison Ave. (at 84th St.). © **212/987-0688.** www.catimini.com. Subway: 6 to 96th St.

Flora and Henri ★   This charming, timeless shop showcases a delightful designer line of drapey European knits, French sailor shirts, shoes, and bathing suits in sizes newborn to 12. 1023 Lexington Ave. (btw. 73rd and 74th sts.). © **212/249-1695.** www.florahenri.com. Subway: 6 to 77th St.

Flowers by Zoe   This shop is the only store of the stylish brand sold in so many other UES boutiques. Flowers by Zoe was started in 1993 by three New York–based owners, all of whom have a hand in designing the colorful, boho clothing (girls' sizes 12 months to 14 years old) you see in the store. The clothes are fun and fizzy, the store less so—and the overall effect of racks crammed with clothes is garish. 1070 Madison Ave. (btw. 80th and 81st sts.). ✆ **212/535-3777.** Subway: 6 to 77th St.

Jacadi   A French chain, Jacadi sells pricey, stylish clothes, cut for comfort, for boys and girls from babies up to age 12. Each season's line is color-coordinated, handy for mixing and matching. Jacadi has two locations on the Upper East Side and one store near Columbus Circle on the west side. www.jacadiusa.com. (1) 1242 Madison Ave. (at 89th St.). ✆ **212/369-1616.** Subway: 4, 5, 6 to 86th St. (2) 1841 Broadway (at 60th St.). ✆ **212/246-2753.** Subway: 1 to 59th St./Columbus Circle. (3) 1260 Third Ave. (at 72nd St.). ✆ **212/717/9292.** Subway: 6 to 68th St.

Lemonade ★   Opened in August 2009, this charming boutique offers a carefully edited selection of of-the-minute designer clothing for kids ages newborn to 7 years. Brands include Pink Chicken, Appaman, Chase 'n' Sky, and Hagel. 1534 Second Ave. (at 80th St.). ✆ **212/734-9292.** www.lemonadenyc.com. Subway: 6 to 77th St.

Lester's ★   This roomy shop is an East Side staple for clothing and shoes, ages newborn to 12—most of the stock is imported, and designer styles abound, but the prices aren't too out of whack. The girls' clothes are stocked with typical Upper East Side brands: Lili Gaufrette, Flowers by Zoe, Splendid. This is the place for boys to buy a real suit, with knowledgeable fitters and tailors available and a wide range of styles to choose from (more casual clothes are stocked, too). The layette department features imported and designer styles at fairly reasonable prices. 1534 Second Ave. (at 80th St.). ✆ **212/734-9292.** www.lestersnyc.com. Subway: 6 to 77th St.

Lilly Pulitzer ★   Think pink! It's preppie heaven at the brand's sherbet-hued flagship store, appropriately ensconced in a brightly upholstered town house on a tony Madison Avenue block. The candy colors and "unchained melody of prints" (the *New York Times*) are utterly irresistible in a city where black is perpetually the new black—and the cheerful staff makes you believe *everybody* dresses this way. In addition to adult wear, the store has girls' clothes in sizes 3 months to 14. 1020 Madison Ave. (at 79th St.). ✆ **212/744-4620.** www.lillypulitzer.com. Subway: 6 to 77th St.

Magic Windows/Magic Windows for Teens   Here you'll find East Side–conservative, traditional clothes, including baby clothes (sizes up to 6X), all in pastel blues and pinks, as well as tween and preteen clothing (up to 16). Look for a solid collection of special-occasion wear and such respectable high-end brands as Burberry, Lilly Pulitzer, and Ralph Lauren. When you graduate from Magic Windows, you get to buy party dresses from **Magic Windows for Teens** next door (with its own entrance). www.magicwindowskids.com. 1186 Madison Ave. (at 87th St.). ✆ **212/289-0028.** Subway: 4, 5, 6 to 86th St.

Monnalisa   The former location of Bambini, this boutique sells the upscale Italian children's brand Monnalisa, very stylish and beautifully made. 1088 Madison Ave. (btw. 81st and 82nd sts.). ✆ **212/249-9040.** Subway: 6 to 77th St.; 4, 5, 6 to 86th St.

Petit Bateau ★   As the flagship store for this upscale clothing label, this is a good source for classic, understated French style (meaning country-club-ish clothes of which *Maman* would approve). The baby clothes are meltingly soft and lovely, but keep in mind when sizing that the Petit Bateau baby is long and lean. Carries clothing for boys and girls up to size 18. 1094 Madison Ave. (at 82nd St.). ℂ **212/988-8884.** www.petit-bateau.us. Subway: 4, 5, 6 to 86th St.; 6 to 77th St.

Prince & Princess ★   If a coronation is on your calendar, this is the store to outfit your little ones. The small, spare, not particularly plush shop, just off Madison, sells gorgeous (taffeta, silk, velvet) special-occasion wear for boys and girls. The owner stocks the store with supreme-quality Italian-made clothing. "I buy only the best," she says. "I never ask prices." Closed Sunday. 41 E. 78th (btw. Park and Madison aves.). ℂ **212/879-8989.** www.princeandprincess.com. Subway: 6 to 77th St.

Roberta Roller Rabbit ★   Amid the hand-block-printed linens and colorful home furnishings is a small but choice selection of kids' clothing (girls sizes 6 months to 8 years) in pleasing East Indian–flavored prints and florals: largely kurtas and tunics, dresses, and pajamas. It's a sunny store, and the clothes are lovely. 1019 Lexington Ave. (at 73rd St.). ℂ **212/772-7200.** www.robertarollerrabbit.net. Subway: 6 to 77th St.

Small Change   As expensive children's clothing shops go, this isn't a bad choice, but it has a generic feel, with racks and racks of stock, much of it duplicates. Closed Sunday in summer. 1196 Lexington Ave. (at 83rd St.). ℂ **212/772-6455.** Subway: 6 to 79th St.

Spring Flowers Children's Boutique ★   The clothes here are beautiful and correspondingly pricey. But oh—those Italian bronze slip-ons with the grosgrain bow! The Audrey Dress in blue silk taffeta! You *can* buy big-skirt party gowns for only $100—but you can also pay $450 for that irresistible Audrey Dress. Don't come here for rock-star trendy: This stuff is conservatively styled, with creamy linen shorts and vests for little boys and tea dresses and classic cardigans for little girls. Spring Flowers has casual wear and shoes, but it's the classic dress-up stuff that catches the eye, round racks bulging with petticoats and crisp pinafores. Closed Sunday. www.springflowerschildren.com. (1) 1050 Third Ave. (at 62nd St.). ℂ **212/758-2669.** Subway: 4, 5, 6 to 59th St. (2) 907 Madison Ave. (at 72nd St.). ℂ **212/717-8182.** Subway: 6 to 68th St. (3) 538 Madison Ave. (at 55th St.). ℂ **212/207-4606.** Subway: 6 to 51st St.

Tutti Bambini ★   Carrying a wide range of labels—imported, made in the U.S.A., whatever—this busy little East Side shop knows its look: funky and fun. It carries sizes up to 10, with brand names like Lili Gaufrette, Marcel et Leon, JKKS, and Charlie Rockets, and tends toward designs adults wouldn't mind wearing. Most of the other shoppers I saw had kids in tow, which means they were picking out clothes the kids themselves like to wear—always a good sign. 1480 First Ave. (btw. 77th and 78th sts.). ℂ **212/472-4238.** Subway: 6 to 77th St.

Zittles (Zitomer Department Store)   Bursting at the seams, this landmark pharmacy has a second-floor children's clothing department (the toy store, Zittles, is on the third floor), stocked with upscale imported clothes (dresses in the $50–$500 range) that manage to look cheesy in the fluorescent light, jammed together on chrome racks as they are. But don't be put off; it's worth a stop if you're on a quest for something special—and regular sales bring the prices down to earth. 969 Madison Ave. (btw. 75th and 76th sts.). ℂ 212/737-5560. www.zitomer.com. Subway: 6 to 77th St.

Upper West Side

Berkley Girl ★ Fashion-conscious West Side girls from toddlers to size 16 can outfit themselves in the latest styles in this busy boutique across from the Natural History Museum. They'll know the labels, from Missoni to Juicy Couture. It now has a second location on the Upper East Side. www.berkleygirl.com. (1) 410 Columbus (btw. 79th and 80th sts.). ℂ 212/877-4770. Subway: B, C to 81st St. (2) 1418 Second Ave. (at 74th St.). ℂ 212/744-9507. Subway: 6 to 77th St.

Bonne Nuit Does your daughter dream of a pink taffeta party frock? Here's where you can find just the right one. This lingerie shop carries elegant clothes for both girls and boys, adult and children's loungewear, and some beautiful layette items. 30 Lincoln Plaza (at 63rd St.). ℂ 212/489-9730. Subway: 1 to 66th St./Lincoln Center.

Greenstones Upscale imported kids' clothes, in cuts and fabrics that kids can actually play in. Sizes run from newborn to 12 years (the East Side shops carry up to size 8 only). Greenstones also has two locations on the Upper East Side. (1) 442 Columbus Ave. (at 81st St.). ℂ 212/580-4322. Subway: B, C to 79th St. (2) 1184 Madison Ave. (btw. 86th and 87th sts.). ℂ 212/427-1665. Subway: 4, 5, 6 to 86th St. (3) 1410 Second Ave. (at 73rd St.). ℂ 212/794-0530. Subway: 6 to 68th St./Hunter College.

Z'Baby Company ★ Handily located both uptown and down, Z'Baby features hip and casual French and Italian clothes (boys' sizes newborn to 10, girls up to 14) with upscale labels. The dresses have an airy boho flair. (1) 100 W. 72nd St. (at Columbus Ave.). ℂ 212/579-BABY (579-2229). Subway: B, C, 1, 2, 3 to 72nd St. (2) 996 Lexington Ave. (at 72nd St.). ℂ 212/472-2229. Subway: 6 to 68th St.

Comic Books, Trading Cards & Collectible Figures

All these stores have a wide stock of cards and/or comics, but whether they've got that rare item you're looking for is always a question. If you're really on a quest for something special, call the whole lot until you strike gold. Otherwise, drop in for a browse at whichever shop you're nearest.

Alex's MVP Cards This friendly neighborhood store specializes in comics and sports cards and wax packs, as well as a decent supply of nonsports toys and supplies. 256 E. 89th St. (at Second Ave.). ℂ 212/831-2273. Subway: 4, 5, 6 to 86th St.

Chameleon Comics & Cards Here you'll find Marvel and DC comics, a wide range of sports cards, and action-figure toys and statues. Closed Sunday. 3 Maiden Lane (btw. Nassau St. and Broadway). ℂ 212/587-1603. www.chameleoncomics.com. Subway: A, C to Broadway/Nassau St.; 2, 3, 4, 5 to Fulton St.

Cosmic Comics This is a good source for comics, in addition to action figures, nonsports trading cards, T-shirts, models, trade paperbacks, and videos. 10 E. 23rd St. ℂ 212/460-5322. www.cosmiccomics.com. Subway: 6 to 23rd St.

Forbidden Planet This store is a valuable source for comics and assorted sci-fi and fantasy paraphernalia. 840 Broadway (at 13th St.). ℂ 212/473-1576. www.fpnyc.com. Subway: N, Q, R, W, 4, 5, 6 to 14th St.; L to Union Square.

Gotham City Comics & Toys A wide-ranging stock of comics, sports cards, action figures, and T-shirts, with some rarities—it's one of those places where collectors could browse happily for a long time. 796 Lexington Ave. (at 62nd St.), 2nd Floor. © 212/980-0009. Subway: 4, 5, 6 to 59th St.

Gotta Have It The trove of sports collectibles in the gallery here includes a good stock of sports cards, including plenty of rarities. It also has rock-'n'-roll and other entertainment memorabilia. Closed Sunday except during Thanksgiving and Christmas holidays. 153 E. 57th St. (btw. Lexington and Third aves.). © 212/750-7900. www.gottahaveit. com. Subway: 6 to 59th St.

Jim Hanley's Universe In the shadow of the Empire State Building, this classic comic-book store has been selling comics old and new, plus fantasy-role-playing games, for more than 25 years. 4 W. 33rd St. (btw. Fifth Ave. and Broadway). © 212/268-7088. www.jhuniverse.blogspot.com. Subway: B, D, F, N, Q, R, V, W to 34th St./Herald Square.

Kidrobot Purveying what the store itself describes as "urban vinyl action figures," this tiny SoHo shop is often packed with kids and slacker hipsters. You'll know your kid will dig this place if he or she recognizes these product lines: Homies, Kubriks, Dunnys, and Stifkas. 126 Prince St. (btw. Greene and Wooster sts.). © 212/966-6688. www.kid robot.com. Subway: R, W to Prince St.

St. Mark's Comics Anything comic-related can be bought here, including books, magazines, action figures, and toys; the shop has its own subculture buzz. www.stmarkscomics.com. (1) 11 St. Mark's Place (btw. Second and Third aves.). © 212/598-9439. Subway: 6 to Astor Place (2) 148 Montague St., Brooklyn. © 718/935-0911. Subway: M, R, 2, 3, 4, 5 to Court St./Borough Hall.

Toy Tokyo Showroom NYC 🎁 Pokemon! Godzilla! Super Mario! *Texas Chainsaw Massacre* and *Halloween 2* Living Dead Dolls! This fascinating little store carries all the latest domestic toys and dolls as well as rare and vintage collectibles

---

Beads, Beads, Beads!

Making jewelry, crafts, and art with beads is a passion that starts early; for many kids (and especially girls), it's an irresistible pastime. You can find beads all over the city, but the area just above Macy's (on and around Sixth Ave. and 36th and 37th sts.) has the city's largest concentration of bead stores. They run the gamut from Japanese-based **Toho Shoji** (999 Sixth Ave.; © 212/868-7465; www.tohoshoji-ny.com) to no-frills old-timer **Gampel Supply** (11 W. 37th St.; © 212/575-0767). Uptown, **Bruce Frank** (215 W. 83rd St.; © 212/595-3746; www.brucefrankbeads.com) is a snug little shop selling Indonesian art and antiques and an absolutely amazing selection of beads, from vintage glass European and Japanese beads to bone wood and ethnic beads. Downtown, it's hard to beat **Beads of Paradise** (16 E. 17th St.; © 212/620-0642; www.beadsofparadise nyc.com), a glittering, atmospheric shop packed with a colorful assortment of global and ethnic goods, including beads— from vintage 18th-century European glass beads to wooden prayer beads from Nepal to semiprecious stone beads.

and Japanese imports of vinyl figures, sought by connoisseurs (of which your own progeny may be one). 91 Second Ave. (btw. 5th and 6th sts.). ☎ **212/673-5424.** www.toytokyo. com. Subway: 6 to Astor Place.

Crafts, Models & Trains

The Craft Studio   The rainforest-themed site for parties has an excellent front section with lots of crafts kits, art materials, puzzles, and other toys. Walk in and paint on plaster, wood, or terra-cotta pots. Its private parties (for kids ages 3 and up) have 16 different craft themes, from doll making to chocolate to PJs and puppets. Closed Sunday July to August. 1657 Third Ave. (btw. 92nd and 93rd sts.). ☎ **212/831-6626.** www.craft studionyc.com. Subway: 6 to 96th St.

Games Workshop   Manhattan has three branches of this U.K.-based chain of stores, selling its own line of character models and hosting elaborate fantasy-game tournaments. For certain boys, it's a sort of clubhouse. www.gamesworkshop.com. (1) 1457 Third Ave. (at 83rd St.). ☎ **212/744-1390.** Subway: 4, 5, 6 to 86th St. (2) 269 72nd St. (at Amsterdam Ave.). ☎ **212/362-0726.** Subway: 1, 2, 3 to 72nd St. (3) 54 E. 8th St. (at University Place). ☎ **212/982-6314.** Subway: A, B, C, D, E, F, V to W. 4th St.

Jan's Hobby Shop   This stocked-to-the-rafters shop is a wondrous source for wooden boat models—in everything from balsa wood to mahogany—as well as plastic model kits (loads of Revell planes and race cars) and die-cast metal items for collectors. The display cases of military models are awesome. 1435 Lexington Ave. (btw. 93rd and 94th sts.). ☎ **212/861-5075.** Subway: 4, 5, 6 to 96th St.

N.Y. Cake & Baking Dist. ★   Cooking kids and adults alike love this old-time supply store (Martha Stewart shops here), packed with all sorts of baking pans, cake stands, ice-cream scoopers—as well as supremely cool stuff like edible sugar diamonds (to sprinkle on cupcakes), edible images, and an exhaustive selection of kids' cake toppers and candles—we're talking action figures, cartoon faves, carousels, you name it. 56 W. 22nd St. (btw. Fifth and Sixth aves.). ☎ **212/675-CAKE** (675-2253). www.nycake.com. Subway: N, R to 23rd St.

Red Caboose ★   New York's most intense model-railroad shop, the Red Caboose has been selling all gauges and scales of trains since 1942, as well as equipment and supplies desired by modelers. The stock of train and automobile kits is growing all the time, too. Closed Sunday (except during the holiday season). 23 W. 45th St. (btw. Fifth and Sixth aves.); enter the lobby and go downstairs at the back. ☎ **212/575-0155.** www.theredcaboose.com. Subway: B, D, F, V to 47th–50th sts./Rockefeller Center.

Trainland ★   True electric-train fanatics may want to venture out to this huge store for train sets. Note to *Sopranos* fans: As the website says, Bobby Bacala "bought it" at Trainland; this is where model-train aficionado Bacala is whacked. Closed Sunday. 751 McDonald Ave., Brooklyn. ☎ **718/436-7072.** www.trainworld.com. Subway: F to Ditmas Ave.

Dolls & Dollhouses

American Girl Place ★★   Just a store? Try telling that to the legions of little girls, dolls lovingly clasped in their arms, who converge on this Midtown site as if they were pilgrims heading to Mecca. If you've been on Mars for the past few years—or if you only have sons (which is the same thing)—you may not know about these pricey, beautifully made 18-inch dolls, each with her own carefully researched back story presented in a series of middle-grade-level books.

American Girl Place—one of only eight stores (the others are in Atlanta, Boston, Chicago, Dallas, Denver, Los Angeles, and Minneapolis) where you can buy these dolls in person, rather than by catalog or online—is like a shrine for young doll owners, and many bring their dolls with them to worship here. Technically, it is possible to visit without spending a penny, although if you can swing that, you deserve a medal. Besides the historical dolls, other doll lines such as Bitty Babies, Hopscotch School, Angelina Ballerina, and American Girls of Today are displayed, along with books, accessories, and a fair number of clothes for the doll owners themselves. There is a small **art gallery** displaying original illustration art for the books. On the second floor, detailed and delightful **historical dioramas** present each of the American Girl dolls in her time period. Often, craft activities and special celebrations are on tap, and if your daughter has brought her own Felicity or Kayla or Samantha or whomever, she can have the doll's hair restyled in the **doll salon.** The store also boasts a usually booked-up **cafe** (p. 110). 609 Fifth Ave. (at 49th St.). © **877/AG-PLACE** (247-5223). www.americangirl.com. Subway: E, V to Fifth Ave./53rd St.; B, D, F, V to 47th–50th sts./Rockefeller Center.

Manhattan Doll House Shop ★ Located as a dollhouse boutique in FAO Schwarz, this wonderful shop not only has a truly awesome selection of kits and finished dollhouses, but also carries all the furnishings, right down to electrical fixtures. Full-size dolls are also repaired and sold. FAO Schwarz, 767 Fifth Ave. (btw. E. 58th and 59th sts.). © **212/644-9400.** www.manhattandollhouse.com. Subway: 6 to 23rd St.

Mary Arnold Toys ★ This top-notch East Side toyshop includes an outstanding doll section—Madame Alexander, Corolle, Götz, and the like. Closed Sunday. 1010 Lexington Ave. (btw. 72nd and 73rd sts.). © **212/744-8510.** Subway: 6 to 77th St.

Tiny Doll House ★ In this small, well-organized shop, rows of perfectly put-together miniature rooms flank the side walls, while a few empty doll mansions preside regally over the center of the room. Wallpaper, carpeting, lamps, cutlery—a tasteful selection of all the tiny furnishings you'll ever need. Before you go inside, warn little would-be customers not to touch; the staff is somewhat gun-shy about kids breaking the delicate miniatures. Closed Sunday. 314 E. 78th St. (btw. First and Second aves.). © **212/744-3719.** Subway: 6 to 77th St.

Furniture, Cribs & Strollers

ABC Carpet & Home ★ You may not know that this fabulous home-furnishings store has a children's department, but it does, and it's a doozy. Just don't expect to go poking around in a bargain bin, because you won't find one here (although it does have occasional sales). Yes, like much of the rest of ABC's inventory, the kids' stuff is pricey, but choice. The shop sells hand-painted furniture as well as beautifully crafted wooden and iron cribs, bed canopies fashioned of vintage saris, sumptuous organic bedding, whimsical lamps. And toys. 888 Broadway (at 19th St.). © **212/473-5000.** www.abchome.com. Subway: N, R, 4, 5, 6 to 14th St.

Albee Baby Carriage Co. This store may be crowded and a little disorganized, but what these folks don't know about nursery equipment ain't worth knowing.

There's always an unwieldy mother-to-be collapsed in a glider rocker, looking glassy-eyed as she (and her mother and/or husband) orders a couple thousand dollars' worth of baby stuff—I wonder how many labors have started here over the years. Closed Sunday. 715 Amsterdam Ave. (at 95th St.). ☏ **212/662-7337.** www.albeebaby. com. Subway: 1, 2, 3 to 96th St.

Baby Depot at Burlington Coat Factory 🔖 Toil up to the third floor of this discount emporium to find a Toys "R" Us–ish collection of layettes, cribs, strollers, car seats, and clothing. The prices are fairly low—just don't expect top-of-the-line furnishings for your nursery. 707 Sixth Ave. (btw. 22nd and 23rd sts.). ☏ **212/229-1300.** www. burlingtoncoatfactory.com. Subway: F, V to 23rd St.

Bellini If you want to start your infant off with upscale tastes, this pricey baby-furniture boutique is where to do it. The service can be offhand (unless, of course, you're spending a bundle), but the look is pretty with an edge of fun, nothing way-out. 1305 Second Ave. (btw. 68th and 69th sts.). ☏ **212/517-9233.** www.bellini.com. Subway: 6 to 68th St.

Giggle ★ This complete baby and toddler lifestyle store in SoHo has become an essential all-purpose stop for hip and happening New York parents ever since it opened its flagship store in SoHo, with the latest hip and happening brands on display in colorful designer stores (complete with a stroller parking lot). The stores are so stylish and smartly laid out, it's a pleasure to shop here. Look for high-end furniture brands like Oeuf, Stokke, Peg Perego, Cabine—as well as organic cotton clothing and eco-friendly wares. It now has an Upper East Side location as well. www.giggle.com. (1) 120 Wooster St. (btw. Prince and Spring sts.). ☏ **212/334-5817.** Subway: R to Prince St. (2) 1033 Lexington Ave. (at 74th St.). ☏ **212/24904249.** Subway: 6 to 77th St. (3) 352 Amsterdam Ave. (btw. 76th and 77th sts. ☏ **212/362-8680.** Subway: 1 to Broadway/79th St.

Kids Supply Co. This boutique sells some intriguing children's furniture, featuring warm woods and bold colors and a sophisticated sense of style. Quality stuff, built to withstand children. Closed Sunday July through August. 1343 Madison Ave. (at 94th St.). ☏ **212/426-1200.** www.kidssupply.com. Subway: 6 to 96th St.

Little Folks Shop For more than 35 years, Little Folks has been selling a solid range of nursery outfittings and strollers plus layettes and clothes up to size 7. Look for top brands like Bugaboo, BOB Strollers, Mutsy, and Quinny. Closed Saturday. 123 E. 23rd St. (btw. Park and Lexington aves.). ☏ **212/982-9669.** www.littlefolksnyc.com. Subway: 6 to 23rd St.

Planet Kids ★ Big, bright, and bustling, this Upper East Side source has a wide range of furnishing and paraphernalia for babies and toddlers. It has an Upper East Side location (see contact info below) and a store near Lincoln Center. www.planetkids ny.com. (1) 247 E. 86th St. (btw. Third and Second aves.). ☏ **212/426-2040.** Subway: 4, 5, 6 to 86th St. (2) 191–193 Amsterdam Ave. (btw. 68th and 69th sts.). ☏ **212/362-3931.** Subway: 1 to 67th St.

Schneider's ★ This downtown source offers not only nursery essentials but also furniture for kids' and even teenagers' bedrooms, as well as strollers, car seats, and layette must-haves—all at competitive prices. Closed Sunday. 41 W. 25th St. (btw. Sixth Ave. and Broadway). ☏ **212/228-3540.** www.schneidersbaby.com. Subway: F, N, R, V, W to 23rd St.

Games

Chess Forum ★   Competing head-to-head with the Village Chess Shop right up the street, the Chess Forum is big on chess lessons for kids, along with selling a large variety of exquisite sets for chess, backgammon, cribbage, and dominoes. Celebrity customers include David Lee Roth, Sean Lennon, Yoko Ono, and Harvey Keitel. 219 Thompson St. (btw. 3rd and Bleecker sts.). ℂ **212/475-2369.** www.chessforum.com. Subway: A, B, C, D, E, F, V to W. 4th St.

Compleat Strategist ★   This specialist shop stocks a fairly mind-boggling array of games, from chess and backgammon to military simulations and role-playing games, but doesn't neglect board games for the younger set, including some noncompetitive games for nonreaders. Fun for browsing. Closed Sunday. 11 E. 33rd St. (btw. Fifth and Madison aves.). ℂ **212/685-3880.** www.thecompleatstrategist.com. Subway: 6 to 33rd St.

Village Chess Shop ★   Come to this 36-year-old shop to play or stock up on exotic chess sets, esoteric chess manuals, and a slew of related computer software, as well as clocks for speed chess. In the summer it has chess events in Bryant Park. 230 Thompson St. (btw. 3rd and Bleecker sts.). ℂ **212/475-9580.** www.chess-shop.com. Subway: A, B, C, D, E, F, V to W. 4th St.

Haircuts

Apple Seeds   This sprawling indoor family play space in the Flatiron District also features a celebrated kids' hair-cutting salon. 10 W. 25th St. (at Broadway). ℂ **212/792-7590.** www.appleseedsnyc.com. Subway: N, R, 4, 5, 6 to 23rd St.

Cozy's Cuts for Kids   Spanking clean and bright, Cozy's plays videos to keep kids happy in the chair—which may be a regular barber chair or a yellow Jeep. Après-cut, the little ones are rewarded with lollipops, balloons, and favors—all the usual bribes. Cozy's has enough quality toys to double as a toy store, which unfortunately means you've got to ward off toy requests when you come in only for a haircut, but what the hey, at least you have no trouble getting the kids in the door. Closed Sunday in summer. www.cozyscutsforkids.com. (1) 1125 Madison Ave. (at 84th St.). ℂ **212/744-1716.** Subway: 4, 5, 6 to 86th St. (2) 1416 Second Ave. (at 74th St.). ℂ **212/585-2699.** Subway: 6 to 77th St. (3) 448 Amsterdam Ave. (btw. 81st and 82nd sts.). ℂ **212/579-2600.** Subway: 1 to 79th St.

Doodle Doo's   Now in a much bigger location on Christopher Street, this pleasant downtown store is both a full-service kids' haircutting salon and a fully stocked toy store. The little ones can sit in a race car or a boat (or a regular barber's chair) and watch their favorite videos while the expert cutters work fast. 11 Christopher St. (near Greenwich Ave.). ℂ **212/627-3667.** www.doodledoos.com. Subway: 1 to Christopher St.

Kids Cuts   In its location inside Homefront Kids, this salon still cuts hair well at reasonable prices. Closed Monday. 202 E. 29th St. (at Third Ave.). ℂ **212/684-5252.** www. kidscutsny.com. Subway: 6 to 33rd St.

Kidville   There's a multitude of classes and activities for little kids at this Upper West Side hangout, but even if you haven't registered in a class, you can still drop by for a haircut. Kidville also has a salon at its Upper East Side location (163 E. 84th St. btw. Third and Lex aves.; (C) **212/772-8435**). 466 Columbus Ave. (btw. 82nd and 83rd sts.). (C) **212/362-7792.** www.kidville.com. Subway: 1 to 79th St.

Jewelry & Accessories

Claire's Costume jewelry, hair doodads, and a grab bag of slumber-party-worthy gift items make these bouncy chain shops a hit with tweens. www.claires.com. (1) 2267 Broadway (btw. 81st and 82nd sts.). (C) **212/877-2655.** Subway: 1 to 79th St. (2) 1385 Broadway (btw. 37th and 38th sts.). (C) **212/302-6616.** Subway: B, D, F, N, Q, R, V, W to 34th St. (3) 89 South Street Seaport (2nd Floor). (C) **212/566-0193.** Subway: 2, 3, 4, 5 to Fulton St.; A, C to Broadway/Nassau St.

Ricky's 🔖 For hair ornaments, youthful makeup, and great Halloween costumes, Ricky's has a definite cool quotient, especially with teens and tweens. Ricky's has 20 locations in Manhattan; the following are just a sampling. Check the website to see if there's one near you. www.rickysnyc.com. (1) 144 E. 8th St. (btw. Mercer and Greene sts.). (C) **212/254-5247.** Subway: N, R to 8th St. (2) 375 Broadway (btw. Franklin and White sts.). (C) **212/925-5490.** Subway: 1 to Franklin St. (3) 590 Broadway (btw. Houston and Prince sts.). (C) **212/226-5552.** Subway: R to Prince St.; 6 to Spring St. (4) 466 Sixth Ave. (btw. 11th and 12th sts.). (C) **212/924-3401.** Subway: 1,2 3 to 14th St. (5) 383 Fifth Ave. (btw. 35th and 36th sts.). (C) **212/481-6701.** Subway: B, D, F, N, Q, R, V, W to 34th St. (6) 1189 First Ave. (at 64th St.). (C) **212/879-8361.** Subway: 6 to 68th St. (7) 112 W. 72nd St. (btw. Broadway and Columbus Ave.). (C) **212/769-3678.** Subway: 1, 2, 3 to 72nd St. (8) 1380 Third Ave. (btw. 78th and 79th sts.). (C) **212/737-7724.** Subway: 6 to 77th St. (9) 472 Columbus Ave. (at 83rd St.). (C) **212/724-4590.** Subway: 1 to 86th St.

Magic & Gags

Abracadabra Harry Potter fans can indulge some serious fantasies at this ever-growing magic superstore, so large it even has a stage and a cafe on-site. Its several thousand feet of space are stocked with every magic trick, costume, and gag under the sun. Warning to parents of skittish youngsters: Some of the masks on display are extremely lifelike and as gruesome as all get-out. Closed Monday. 19 W. 21st St. (btw. Fifth and Sixth aves.). (C) **212/627-5194.** www.abracadabrasuperstore.com. Subway: F, V to 23rd St.

Tannen's Magic ★ Amateur or professional, magicians shop here, and the array of equipment is impressive. In the interests of developing future magicians, Tannen's also hosts ongoing lectures and classes in New York and runs a Magic Camp (for ages 12–20) in Pennsylvania (David Blaine is a former grad). Magic is serious business here. Closed Sunday. 45 W. 34th St., Suite 608 (btw. Fifth and Sixth aves.). (C) **212/929-4500.** www.tannens.com. Subway: B, D, F, N, Q, R, V, W to 34th St.

Music

Bleecker Bob's Golden Oldies ★ 🎒 Like a scene out of the movie *High Fidelity,* this Village hangout has bins full of vinyl, with some very obscure albums, and staff who really know their arcane music trivia. Older kids who are into esoterica and nostalgia might dig it. 118 W. 3rd St. (btw. Sixth Ave. and MacDougal St.). (C) **212/475-9677.** Subway: A, B, C, D, E, F, V to W. 4th St.

Colony Music Center ★ 🎒 Nobody ever sells sheet music anymore—well, nobody except for Colony, which has a mind-blowing assortment of song sheets and scores for your budding musician, including jazz, rock, and every Broadway show tune ever written. Even better, you'll be rubbing shoulders with real professional musicians as you browse the narrow aisles. The huge selection of easy piano books is great for beginners, and—who knew?—it's also the world's largest karaoke dealer. 1619 Broadway (at 49th St.). ✆ **212/265-2050.** www.colonymusic.com. Subway: 1 to 50th St.

Guitar Center Manhattan's only location of this national music chain is a two-story emporium selling guitars, drums, organs, the works. It's very user-friendly and a very cool place to be when a serious musician stops in to sample the wares. 25 W. 14th St. (btw. Fifth and Sixth aves.). ✆ **212/463-7500.** www.guitarcenter.com. Subway: F, V to W. 14th St.

House of Oldies 🏠 Like Bleecker Bob's (see above), the House of Oldies prides itself on hard-to-find vintage recordings, especially 45s and LPs. If your kids don't know what a "record" is, bring them here for a history lesson. Closed Sunday and Monday. 35 Carmine St. (btw. Bleecker and Bedford sts.). ✆ **212/243-0500.** www.houseofoldies.com. Subway: A, B, C, D, E, F, V to W. 4th St.

Manny's Music ★ In business since 1935 and located on Midtown's Music Row, Manny's is one store that welcomes kids to fiddle around on the instruments for sale. 156 W. 48th St. (btw. Sixth and Seventh aves.). ✆ **212/819-0576.** www.mannysmusic.com. Subway: B, D, F, V to 47th–50th sts./Rockefeller Center.

Matt Umanov Guitars ★ Unlike what it calls the "supermarket-style music stores," this intimate shop has been selling guitars—and only guitars (oh, and a few mandolins, banjos, and ukuleles)—in the Village since 1965. Check out its selection of gorgeous vintage guitars. 273 Bleecker St. (btw. Sixth and Seventh aves.). ✆ **212/675-2157.** www.umanovguitars.com. Subway: A, B, C, D, E, F, V to W. 4th St.

Shoes

East Side Kids Free popcorn is dispensed to shoe-shopping kids, which means the place looks like a pigsty by the end of the day. But the range of shoes is wide, from chic to totally playground-friendly. Closed Sunday. 1298 Madison Ave. (btw. 92nd and 93rd sts.). ✆ **212/360-5000.** Subway: 6 to 96th St.

Flight Club New York ★ As your sneaker-loving progeny may well know, some shoes are infinitely cooler than others. And some, for better or worse, have achieved legend status. This consignment store stocks authentic vintage Air Jordans, Nike dunks, and richly hued skateboarding sneaks in a wide range of prices and conditions (a slammin' pair of Nike Dunk High Pro SB "De La Soul" can be yours for $500). 812 Broadway (btw. 11th and 12th sts.). ✆ No phone. www.flightclub.com. Subway: R to 8th St.

Harry's Shoes for Kids ★ The bustling West Side shoe store finally spun off its children's shoe operation into a separate store up the street. It's a sweet place, with a great selection of quality shoes. Broadway (btw. 83rd and 84th sts.). ✆ **212/874-2034.** www.harrys-shoes.com. Subway: 1 to 86th St.

Ibiza Kidz ★ In its new location on lower Broadway, this Village kids' boutique sells a terrific collection of shoes from newborn through women's sizes, as well as books and stuffed animals. The stock shows real flair, with brands like Primigi, Naturino, Geox, Umi, and Saucony. 830 Broadway (btw. 12th and 13th sts.). ✆ **212/228-7990** or 212/375-9984. www.ibizakidz.com. Subway: N, R to 8th St.

A WORLD OF museum shops

New York City museums have really excellent gift shops, often selling items for children that you can't find anywhere else. Some are so good, we shop there without visiting the museum at all (and you don't have to pay admission to hit the shops). So when you're out and about in New York City, don't forget the following wonderful museum boutiques (see chapter 7 for more details about these and other NYC museums). Note that most make sure to stock lots of inexpensive impulse-buy items, knowing full well how the gift-shop bribe works for families.

The renowned gift shop at the **Metropolitan Museum of Art** (1000 Fifth Ave. at 82nd St.; ☎ **212/535-7710;** closed Mon) is filled with great gifts, books, toys, and games. The large children's department on the upper level includes beautiful books, craft kits, coloring books, art materials, dolls, puzzles, and games. Echoing the Met's great arms-and-armor galleries, there are loads of toy knights here, as well as toy Roman legionnaires and charioteers (in tribute to the vast classical art galleries) and Egyptian trinkets (tying into the mummies on display).

Farther north along the Upper East Side's Museum Mile, three other excellent choices are the **Cooper-Hewitt National Design Museum** (2 E. 91st St. at Fifth Ave.; ☎ **212/849-8300;** closed Mon), which offers some very clever toys and books in a gorgeous stately home setting; the **Jewish Museum** (1109 Fifth Ave. at 92nd St.; ☎ **212/423-3200;** closed Sat), a super source for children's books about Judaism as well as toys, games, and puzzles (plus the best dreidel selection in town); and **The Museum of the City of New York** (1220 Fifth Ave. at 103rd St.; ☎ **212/534-1672;** www.mcny. org; closed Mon), which has a pleasant selection of toys and books, in line with its excellent toy galleries inside.

On the Upper West Side, the intelligent toys and books sold at the **Children's Museum of Manhattan** (212 W. 83rd St. btw. Broadway and Amsterdam Ave.; ☎ **212/721-1234;** www.cmom.org; closed Mon in summer, Mon–Tues during the school year) never fail to delight. Some of the stock features tie-ins to special exhibits, but there's always a wide range of wholesome, educational-yet-fun items for kids 10 and under. At the nearby **American Museum of Natural History** (Central Park West at 79th St.; ☎ **212/769-5100;** www.amnh.org; open daily), you'll have to pay admission to visit most of the gift shops, with the exception of the

Lester's ★   This all-purpose children's clothing store provides one-stop shopping with a full-service shoe department in the back. 1534 Second Ave. (at 80th St.). ☎ **212/734-9292.** www.lestersnyc.com. Subway: 6 to 77th St.

Little Eric Shoes   This store may not look it, but high style is the watchword here—get your 4-year-old shod here if you want to wow the admissions officer at your kindergarten interview. Yes, they've got plain patent leather Mary Janes and classic penny loafers in peewee sizes, but also cowboy boots, beautiful Italian brands, and other trendy styles. 1118 Madison Ave. (at 83rd St.). ☎ **212/717-1513.** Subway: 4, 5, 6 to 86th St.

Naturino   This spare boutique is the prime source for imported children's shoes by Naturino, Moschino, and Oilily. Closed Sunday July to August. 1184 Madison Ave. (btw. 86th and 87th sts.). ☎ **212/427-0679.** Subway: 4, 5, 6 to 86th St.

Planetarium Shop near the West 81st Street entrance. If you're inside the museum anyway, though, you'll find an impressive array of educational toys, games, stuffed animals, and nature books in the main shop near the Central Park West entrance; smaller boutiques tucked around the museum may be geared to special exhibitions or particular interests.

If you're in Midtown, a trio of museums along West 53rd Street between Fifth and Sixth avenues offer a fun shopping diversion for kids: the **Museum of Modern Art** (11 W. 53rd St.; 𝒞 **212/708-9400;** www.moma.org; closed Tues) and the **American Folk Art Museum** (45 W. 53rd St.; 𝒞 **212/265-1040;** www.folkartmuseum.org; open daily). The MoMA shop is famous for its art books, cool games and puzzles, and visually appealing *objets,* and the narrow little gallery at the folk-art museum has a small but brilliant selection of things that will strike kids' fancy. The **Museum of Arts and Design** (2 Columbus Circle; 𝒞 **212/956-3535;** www.madmuseum.org; open daily) will be ensconced in its new Columbus Circle location by the time you read this, but should continue to sell such nifty gifts as handmade baseballs imprinted with

NYC street maps or the *New York Times* crossword puzzle.

Downtown, head to the **Rubin Museum of Art** (150 W. 17th St.; 𝒞 **212/620-5000;** www.rmanyc.org; closed Tues), which has a wonderful gift shop specializing in items from the Himalayas, from a fantastic Nepalese wool tiger rug ($750)—every kid's room needs one—to unique toys, books, and games.

Up in the Bronx, the **New York Botanical Garden** (Bronx River Pkwy., at Fordham Rd.; 𝒞 **718/817-8700;** www.nybg.org) has a fabulous store with a worthy kids' section, where you can find a good assortment of Thomas the Tank Engine toys, kids' gardening sets, Indonesian crocheted hats, games, books, and musical instruments.

Finally, some of the city's best places for stuffed animals are the gift shops at the various zoos. While you might not go to the Bronx or Prospect Park just to visit the zoos' boutiques, the one at the **Central Park Zoo** (in Central Park, near the park entrance at Fifth Ave. and 64th St.; 𝒞 **212/439-6500;** open daily) is incredibly handy, displaying even more plush species than the zoo's live ones. Again, it's outside the admission barriers, so anyone can walk in.

Shoofly ★   A whimsical collection of designer hats for kids hangs from tree branches poking out of one wall; low shelves, bins, and steamer trunks overflow with an assortment of shoes, sandals, socks, mittens, hair bows, belts, and ties, running the gamut from goofy to glam. It's always fun shopping here, even if you don't buy. The prices aren't outlandish, but the sense of style is—just what little New Yorkers need to look really cool. 42 Hudson St. (btw. Duane and Thomas sts.). 𝒞 **212/406-3270.** www.shooflynyc.com. Subway: 1, 2, 3 to Chambers St.

Tip Top Kids ★ 𝄢   Bright, cheerful, and relaxed, this children's annex to Tip Top Shoes has a vibe similar to Harry's Shoes (see above). Here the staff handles children with good humor, and the selection offers quality shoes at fair prices. Brands like Elefanten, Aster, Timberland, Sperry, and Bass, as well as Stride Rite and Adidas, are popular here. 149 W. 72nd St. (btw. Broadway and Columbus Ave.). © **212/874-1004.** www.tiptop shoes.com. Subway: 1, 2, 3 to 72nd St.

Village Kids Foot Wear   An offshoot of neighborhood shoe stalwart Foot Gear Plus, this new shop is nicely stocked with solid children's brands. 116 First Ave. (btw. 7th and 8th sts.). © **212/254-2172.** Subway: 6 to Astor Place.

Shower & Baby Gifts

Tiffany & Co. ★   Wanna score points? A silver spoon, rattle, teething ring, or baby cup from Tiffany's is still the classy way to celebrate a new arrival, and no new parent minds duplicates of these classics. Get the spoon or cup engraved for an extra touch; you can do it all by phone or online, though visiting this fabled store is a pleasure. 727 Fifth Ave. (at 56th St.). © **212/755-8000.** www.tiffany.com. Subway: N, R, W to Fifth Ave./59th St.

Software & Electronic Games

Electronics Boutique/Game Stop   Racks full of computer software and accessories, as well as those Game Boy, PlayStation 2, and Xbox games kids think they can't live without. The staff make it their business to know about the latest hot games, even if it means steering you away from a rip-off. Our family makes a supply stop here at least once a month. www.ebgames.com. (1) 30 Rockefeller Center, concourse level. © **212/765-3857.** Subway: B, D, F, V to 47th–50th sts./Rockefeller Center. (2) 901 Sixth Ave. (at 33rd St.). © **212/564-4156.** Subway: B, D, F, N, R, V to 33rd St. (3) 1282 Broadway (at 33rd St.). © **212/967-9070.** Subway: B, D, F, N, Q, R, V, W to 34th St. (4) 1470 Third Ave. (at 83rd St.). © **212/288-5370.** Subway: 4, 5, 6 to 86th St. (5) 128 E. 86th St. (btw. Park and Lexington aves.). © **212/423-1844.** Subway: 4, 5, 6 to 86th St. (6) 2330 Broadway (btw. 84th and 85th sts.). © **917/441-4160.** Subway: 1, 2, 3 to 86th St. (7) 2764 Broadway (at 106th St.). © **212/864-4292.** Subway: 1 to 103rd St. (8) 251 W. 125th St. (btw. Seventh and Eighth aves.). © **212/749-7434.** Subway: 1 to 125th St. (9) 324 First Ave. (at 19th St.). © **212/995-0085.** Subway: L, N, Q, R, 4, 5, 6 to 14th St./Union Square. (10) 107 E. 14th St. © **646/602-1483.** Subway: N, Q, R, 4, 5, 6 to 14th St.; L to Union Square. (11) 743 Broadway (btw. 7th and 8th sts.). © **212/979-7678.** Subway: 6 to Astor Place; N, R, W to 8th St. (12) 687 Broadway (btw. W. 3rd and W. 4th sts.). © **212/473-6571.** Subway: N, R, W to 8th St. (13) Pier 17 at South Street Seaport, 2nd Floor. © **212/227-1945.** Subway: 2, 3, 4, 5 to Fulton St.; A, C to Broadway/Nassau St.

Sports Stuff

Blades Board & Skate   In-line skaters and skateboarders gear up at this chain of specialty stores, where you can have your own board custom-built for $500 or so. Get your helmets and kneepads here as well. Rentals are available. See chapter 9 for skateboarding info. www.blades.com. (1) 120 W. 72nd St. (btw. Broadway and Columbus Ave.). © **212/787-3911.** Subway: B, C, 1, 2, 3 to 72nd St. (2) 659 Broadway (at Bleecker St.). © **212/477-7350.** Subway: B, D, F, V to Broadway/Lafayette St.

Eastern Mountain Sports   This place is big on camping gear and outdoor wear, along with equipment for climbing walls—the ideal place to buy a sleeping bag that doesn't have Mickey Mouse or Batman all over the lining. 530 Broadway (at Spring St.). © **212/966-8730.** www.ems.com. Subway: B, D, F, V to Broadway/Lafayette St.

Mets Official Clubhouse Shop   Mets fans stock up on blue-and-orange team paraphernalia and memorabilia here. You can buy game tickets too. Let's go, Mets! 11 W. 42nd St. (btw. Fifth and Sixth aves.). © **212/768-9534.** Subway: B, D to 42nd St.

NBA Store This three-story player in the Fifth Avenue Parade of Theme Stores celebrates hoop dreams in a big way, with lots of gleaming blond hardwood floors, high ceilings, and fun b-ball–themed merchandise. The jerseys in stock show a decided preference for New York–area teams (Knicks, Nets, Liberty), but there's plenty for fans of all stripes. The on-site cafe is reasonably priced and offers burgers, chicken fingers, and shakes—your usual arena food. 666 Fifth Ave. (btw. 52nd and 53rd sts.). **212/515-6221.** www.nba.com/nycstore. Subway: E, V to Fifth Ave./53rd St.

Niketown This glitzy temple to sports and sneakers is more of a museum/attraction than a place to buy shoes, with several interactive stations where kids can measure their feet, test their reach and reflexes, and generally try to be like Mike. 6 E. 57th St. (btw. Fifth and Madison aves.). **212/891-6453.** Subway: N, R to Fifth Ave./59th St.

Paragon Sports Paragon is crammed with sports clothing and total gear, including workout wear, swimsuits, tennis gear, ski stuff, and a golf department with a tiny putting green. It has a good shoe selection on the bottom floor. 867 Broadway (at 18th St.). **212/255-8036.** www.paragonsports.com. Subway: N, Q, R, 4, 5, 6 to 14th St.; L to Union Square.

Yankees Official Clubhouse Shop Bronx Bomber fans can indulge their merchandise-buying addictions here. Also a good source for tickets. (1) 393 Fifth Ave. (btw. 36th and 37th sts.). **212/685-4693.** Subway: 6 to 33rd St. (2) 110 E. 59th St. (btw. Park and Lexington aves.). **212/758-7844.** Subway: 4, 5, 6 to 59th St. (3) 745 Seventh Ave. (at 49th St.). **212/391-0360.** Subway: T to 50th St. (4) 294 W. 42nd St. (Times Square). **212/768-9555.** Subway: N, Q, R, S, 1, 2, 3, 7, 9 to 42nd St./Times Square; A, C, E to 42nd St./Port Authority. (5) 8 Fulton St., South Street Seaport. **212/514-7182.** Subway: 2, 3, 4, 5 to Fulton St.

Toys, Gifts & Gadgets

At press time, the big news was the opening of the splashy new **Disney Store** in Times Square (1540 Broadway; **212/626-2910;** www.disneystore.com). With interactive exhibits—including a 20-foot- tall princess castle and magic mirrors—and a 20,000-square-foot sprawl, the store is Disney to its core.

Alphabets The East Village sensibility of this wacky gift-a-torium translates well to more mainstream neighborhoods; central to the concept is lots of campy kids' stuff—Etch A Sketch and Mr. Potato Head, yes, but also some truly goofball stuff like a chess set with the Simpson family (Homer and Bart, that is)—which is probably bought by as many adults as children. Loads of one-of-a-kind T-shirts abound. www.alphabetsnyc.com. (1) 115 Ave. A (at 7th St.). **212/475-7250.** Subway: 6 to Astor Place. (2) 47 Greenwich Ave. (btw. Sixth and Seventh aves.). **212/229-2966.** Subway: 1, 2, 3 to 14th St.

Balloon Saloon ★ All your balloon needs can be met in this store—which does a brisk business supplying balloons and party decor to Manhattan's movers and shakers—but it's also crammed with winning toys, from retro Bozo Bopper punching bags to games, puzzles, and gag gifts like fake moustaches. 133 W. Broadway (near Duane St.). **800/540-0749.** www.balloonsaloon.com. Subway: A, C, E, 1, 2, 3 to Chambers St.

Boomerang Toys This TriBeCa toy store (newly located a few blocks south) is crammed with the latest and greatest stuff for kids from baby to tweens. It's the official flagship store for Bruder Trucks and has a good selection of toy trains, including Thomas and Brio. It has quality dollhouses, castles, tricycles, stuffed toys—the works. A second location is inside the World Financial Center in Battery Park City.

10

SHOPPING WITH YOUR KIDS | Shopping A to Z

www.boomerangtoys.com. (1) 119 W. Broadway (at Duane St.). ✆ **212/226-7650.** Subway: 1, 9 to Franklin St. (2) 2 World Financial Center, 225 Liberty St. ✆ **212/786-3011.** Subway: A, C, E, 1, 2, 3 to Chambers St.

Build-A-Bear Workshop The two-story flagship location of this mall-based chain is quite impressive—in fact, it's the biggest Build-A-Bear Workshop in the whole world. It has a number of only-in-New-York items as well as a full line of international bear outfits and accessories. Both boys and girls have a blast choosing a limp bear form and seeing it stuffed right before their eyes (not to mention getting to put a red satin heart inside, or even a voice box with their own recorded message on it). 565 Fifth Ave. (at 46th St.). ✆ **212/871-7080.** www.buildabearworkshop.com. Subway: S, 4, 5, 6, 7 to 42nd St./Grand Central.

Children's General Store This charming toy boutique is a welcome addition to the shopping at Grand Central Terminal, offering some unusual handmade and imported toys you won't see in most other stores. The emphasis is on well-made toys with a certain imagination-sparking value. (1) Grand Central Station, Lexington Passage. ✆ **212/682-0004.** Subway: S, 4, 5, 6, 7 to 42nd St./Grand Central. (2) 168 E. 91st St. (btw. Lexington and Third aves.). ✆ **212/426-4479.** Subway: 4, 5, 6 to 86th St.

Daily 2.3.5 ★ This is where you find the kind of "where'd you get *that?*" toys and goofy gifts that convince the folks back home that you have traveled somewhere truly cool and wondrous. The collection at this delightful Nolita shop is eclectic, to say the least, with lots of post-retro windup toys, adult gag gifts, light-up tops, and teeny-tiny Horner harmonicas—even freeze-dried astronaut ice-cream sandwiches. Wow! 235 Elizabeth St. (btw. Prince and Houston sts.). ✆ **212/334-9728.** Subway: N, R to Prince St.; B, D to Broadway/Lafayette.

Dinosaur Hill ★ Selling imported toys, mobiles, dollhouses, wooden blocks, art supplies, and puppets—notably an extensive line of handmade marionettes—this newly renovated East Village shop also has a battery of under-$2 stuff so no child will have to leave empty-handed. 306 E. 9th St. (near Second Ave.). ✆ **212/473-5850.** www.dinosaur hill.com. Subway: 6 to Astor Place.

Doodle Doo's ★ This downtown store is both a kids' haircutting salon and a toy store. The toy collection is rich, with lots of the current usual suspects: Melissa & Doug toys and puzzles, Kettler tricycles, and books galore. 11 Christopher St. (near Greenwich Ave.). ✆ **212/627-3667.** www.doodledoos.com. Subway: 1 to Christopher St.

E.A.T. Gifts ★ Next door to the absurdly overpriced E.A.T. cafe, this gift store is crammed with things we find we can't live without—and won't find anywhere else. Little gift books, bath toys, tiny shaped soaps and crayons, chocolate novelties—it's like quicksand for the shopper who has everything. 1062 Madison Ave. (btw. 80th and 81st sts.). ✆ **212/861-2544.** Subway: 6 to 77th St.

FAO Schwarz ★ Risen like a phoenix from the ashes of corporate bankruptcy, this Manhattan toy mecca has reemerged as a sleek, streamlined multistory temple of conspicuous consumption. The focus is on larger-than-life stuffed animals, collectible Barbies and other dolls, antique toys, elegant dress-up clothes, top-of-the-line art kits, high-end electronic cars and robots (what kid doesn't want his or her own mini-Mercedes?), and a panoply of other toys you won't find at any mall. Downstairs is a spacious baby and toddler section, with some yummy clothes and children's books.

Costumed characters, doormen dressed as toy soldiers, story hours, and a soda shoppe add to the fairy-dust ambience. Even if you don't intend to buy, stroll around and gawk to your heart's content; it's one of those only-in-Manhattan experiences your kids will remember. 767 Fifth Ave. (at 58th St.). ✆ **212/644-9400.** www.faoschwarz.com. Subway: N, R, W to Fifth Ave.

Giggle ★   This bright and colorful baby and toddler lifestyle store hits all the hot buttons of the modern urban parent. The designer furniture is clean-lined and thoroughly 21st century; the clothes are smart and fashioned of natural materials (not a stitch of spandex); toys are eco-friendly and educational; and bedding, feeding, bathing, and changing supplies represent the latest in functional chic. All of which, of course, comes at a price. But you can find some nifty toys here, including cool minimalist dollhouses, Manhattan Toy infant playthings, organic cotton plushies, Kettler trikes, and environmentally friendly wooden toys. www.giggle.com. (1) 120 Wooster St. (btw. Prince and Spring sts.). ✆ **212/334-5817.** Subway: R to Prince St. (2) 1033 Lexington Ave. (at 74th St.). ✆ **212/24904249.** Subway: 6 to 77th St. (3) 352 Amsterdam Ave. (btw. 76th and 77th sts.). ✆ **212/362-8680.** Subway: 1 to Broadway/79th St.

Hammacher Schlemmer ★   You want gadgets? They've got gadgets—high-quality gadgets to do everything under the sun, including some things you've never thought of doing before. Older kids and adults get a kick out of the unique and ingenious products, and don't worry if most items are way out of your price range—the ratio of browsers to buyers is usually pretty high. Closed Sunday. 147 E. 57th St. (btw. Lexington and Third aves.). ✆ **212/421-9000.** www.hammacher.com. Subway: 4, 5, 6 to 59th St.

Homboms 👜   Crowded into this storefront is a deep selection of stuff to play with, best for its arts-and-crafts materials, puzzles, board games, PLAYMOBILs, and other small-motor activities. It's definitely a place that rewards a long, slow browse. 1500 First Ave. (btw. 78th and 79th sts.). ✆ **212/717-5300.** Subway: 6 to 77th St.

Ibiza Kidz   Now in its new location on lower Broadway, this Village kids boutique has a small but good selection of toys, as well as books and stuffed animals. You can find Manhattan Toy products for the under-1 set, as well as charming items from Folkmanis puppets, Melissa & Doug, and Radio Flyer. 830 Broadway (btw. 12th and 13th sts.). ✆ **212/228-7990** or 212/375-9984. www.ibizakidz.com. Subway: N, R, W to 8th St.

Kidding Around ★   This shop carries top imports and creative toys in a stuffed-to-the-gills space. If you can't find that special something anywhere else, odds are you'll find it here, in spades. 60 W. 15th St. (btw. Fifth and Sixth aves.). ✆ **212/645-6337.** www.kiddingaroundnyc.com. Subway: N, Q, R, W, 4, 5, 6 to 14th St.; L to Union Square.

Kid O ★   Back in business after a devastating fire, this superb shop sells a wonderful selection of creative preschool toys, blocks, puzzles, and books chosen with great care and ecological sensitivity; it's become a downtown fixture in no time. 123 W. 10th St. (btw. Sixth and Greenwich aves.). ✆ **212/366-KIDO** (366-5436). www.kidonyc.com. Subway: 1, 2, 3, 9 to 14th St.

The LEGO Store ★   Opened in summer 2010 in Rockefeller Center, this is the city's first LEGO-only store and a big, bright play space with interactive play areas, games, and videos. 620 Fifth Ave. (Rockefeller Center). ✆ **212/245-5973.** www.lego.com. Subway: B, D, F, V to 47th–50th sts./Rockefeller Center.

Little Airplane The studio of Little Airplane Productions, home of *The Wonder Pets* and other hot kiddie shows, has a tiny shop on-site that sells toys, Wonder Pets paraphernalia, and collectibles in a historic South Street Seaport structure. Be sure to ask about the studio tours, held twice daily on Tuesdays and Thursdays ($10 per person). 207 Front St. (btw. Beekman and Fulton sts.), 2nd Floor. ℭ **212/965-8999.** Subway: 2, 3, 4, 5 to Fulton St.

Mary Arnold Toys ★ One of the last surviving mom-and-pop businesses in the neighborhood, Mary Arnold's is crammed with good stuff but smartly laid out with nooks where children can fiddle and browse without clogging the aisles. Quality toys—LEGOS, BRIOS, PLAYMOBILs—many shelves of board games, lots of dress-up costumes, and a very impressive doll department make this a never-fail destination to satisfy kids of any age or interest. Closed Sunday. 1010 Lexington Ave. (btw. 72nd and 73rd sts.). ℭ **212/744-8510.** Subway: 6 to 77th St.

Playing Mantis ★★ This TriBeCa toy store is pure, unadulterated joy, selling "toys for life," in this instance, toys crafted from natural materials: charming wood-carved fairy woodland houses, wooden mosaic puzzles, teddy bears recycled from old mink coats, hand-crafted musical instruments, medieval costumes sewn out of jute, and other remarkable finds from around the world. 32 N. Moore St. (btw. Hudson and Varick sts.). ℭ **646/4844-6845.** www.playing-mantis.com. Subway: 1 to Franklin St.

The Scholastic Store ★ Lots of quality educational toys as well as book tie-ins can be found in this airy, bright store downstairs from the publisher's SoHo offices. There's even room to play, and lots of in-store events keep things hopping. Intelligently stocked and refreshingly free of blatant self-promotion. 557 Broadway (btw. Prince and Spring sts.). ℭ **212/343-6166.** www.scholasticstore.com. Subway: R, W to Prince St.

Shoofly ★ If you're looking for party favors, stocking stuffers, or just inexpensive gewgaws to keep the little one amused, this store has a good selection of small toys. How about teeny-tiny Slinkys? Or miniature windup toys? Or light-up rubber hammers? 42 Hudson St. (btw. Duane and Thomas sts.). ℭ **212/406-3270.** www.shooflynyc.com. Subway: A, C, E, 1, 2, 3 to Chambers St.

Soho Baby This dull-looking store has an interesting assortment of toys and gifts, including handmade felt books, top-quality kid-size pianos, and stuffed animals. 251 Elizabeth St. (btw. Prince and Houston sts.). ℭ **212/625-8538.** Subway: R, W to Prince St.; B, D, F, V to Broadway/Lafayette St.

A Time for Children ★ This Upper West Side store has lots of good reasons to stop in, among them the top selection of toys, including giant *Good Night Moon* puzzles and Paddington Bear dolls, as well as Hanna Anderson baby and toddler clothes. But the best reason to shop here is because 100% of the profits go to the Children's Aid Society, a charitable organization that has helped out underprivileged city kids for more than 150 years. 506 Amsterdam Ave. (btw. 84th and 85th sts.). ℭ **212/580-8202.** www.atimeforchildren.org. Subway: 1, 9 to 86th St.

Toys "R" Us The space is huge, bright, sparkling clean, and full of fun, from the amazing scale models of New York landmarks in the LEGO section to the pink Barbie clubhouse to the adorable Candyland-themed sweet shop upstairs. Though the stock is fairly mass market, it has everything on hand, and the prices are (surprise!) not jacked up to pay Manhattan rents. ***One warning:*** There's a menacing animatronic dinosaur out of *Jurassic Park* in the back corner of the second floor, in case you've got a skittish younger child. Oh, and another warning: It can be excruciatingly crowded in high season. 1514 Broadway at 44th St. © **800/869-7787.** www.toysrus.com. Subway: N, Q, R, S, W, 1, 2, 3, 7, 9 to 42nd St./Times Square.

West Side Kids ★   This generic-looking West Side store has lots of LEGOs, T.C. Timber, PLAYMOBILs, some truly elegant dolls and stuffed animals, every crafts kit known to youth, an impressive board game selection, and a whole wall of superb imported infant and toddler items. The staff is knowledgeable, the selection intelligent and responsible. It's great for one-stop shopping. 498 Amsterdam Ave. (at 84th St.). © **212/496-7282.** Subway: 1 to 86th St.

The World of Disney   The Disney Corporation's three-story Fifth Avenue flagship store borrows liberally from Disney theme parks to present a big, glossy stage set of an emporium. You'll find not only tons of Disney-themed merchandise, but also lots of interactive areas: Shoppers can visit the Princess Castle Court for glittery costume jewelry and crafts, Goofy's Candy Company sweets boutique (similar to Candy Land at the Times Square Toys "R" Us), a make-your-own Mr. Potato Head room, a Friendship Room where Disney characters provide several daily photo ops, and a MultiMedia Zone with listening stations and gaming stations for trying out the latest Disney products. 711 Fifth Ave. (at 55th St.). © **212/702-0702.** www. disneystore.com. Subway: F, V to Fifth Ave.

Zittles ★ 🎁   The Zitomer drugstore's toy department just kept expanding and crowded out the second floor; now it's got its own name and a floor all to itself. Finally, this overflowing selection of toys has room to be properly displayed, even with a little flair. For a solid mix of quality items and unsnobby mainstream toys, it's a hidden gem. 969 Madison Ave. (btw. 75th and 76th sts.). © **212/737-2040.** www.zitomer.com. Subway: 6 to 68th St.

11 ENTERTAINMENT FOR THE WHOLE FAMILY

Being the theater capital of the United States doesn't necessarily make New York City the children's theater capital—most of those struggling actors and playwrights and directors are too intent on breaking into the Big Time to pay much mind to kid stuff. On the other hand, the major classical-music venues—Lincoln Center and Carnegie Hall—have in the past few years seen the wisdom of introducing children to music early, perhaps because impresarios realize (with panic) that their core audience is rapidly aging and needs to be replaced. In any case, there's a lot of talent hanging around this city, and when enterprising organizers decide to put on a show for young audiences, the production values are generally high.

New York parents tend to be culture hounds, so plays and concerts for children are usually well attended—which means that, as for adult productions, you've got to reserve in advance. Compared to the $100 you can pay for orchestra seats in the big Broadway theaters, ticket prices for kids' events aren't usually outrageous, though a few major annual events—like the Big Apple Circus and *The Nutcracker*—get away with higher prices.

FINDING OUT WHAT'S ON Both the weekly *Time Out New York* (www.timeoutny.com) and its offspring **Time Out Kids** (www.timeout.com/newyork/kids) have up-to-date, detailed listings of cultural events kids would enjoy, as does the website **www.urbanbaby.com**. We also like **Macaroni Kid** (www.national.macaronikid.com), an exhaustive listing of the goings-on in New York, reported by parent/publishers; you can sign up for the weekly on-line newsletter from the correspondents from the Upper East Side, the Upper West Side, or Downtown—all report on goings-on all over town.

The **Theatre Development Fund** lists current theater offerings online at www.tdf.org. You can get event listings for **Lincoln Center** by calling © **212/546-2656** or visiting www.lincolncenter.org. For events in **city parks,** which are plentiful in summer (and often free!), call © **311** or go to **www.nycgovparks.org** (outside NYC call **212/New York**).

Every Friday the *New York Times* (www.nytimes.com) lists family-friendly weekend events in the "Spare Times" section of the "Weekend" arts section. You may also find useful listings in *New York* magazine (www.nymag. com) and the *Village Voice* (www.villagevoice.com).

For a complete listing of current Broadway and Off-Broadway shows, visit **www. playbill.com**. Not only do they give you all the basic information, but you also can sign up to receive a regular update via e-mail, informing you which shows offer discounted tickets of anywhere from 10% to 50%.

GETTING TICKETS The Radio City Christmas show and seasonal runs like *The Nutcracker*, the Big Apple Circus, and the Ringling Bros. and Barnum & Bailey Circus should be reserved weeks or even months in advance, as should Broadway plays and popular long-running shows. For pro-sports events, ticket availability is a matter of how well the team's been doing lately, though even rotten season records haven't freed up Knicks or Jets tickets, whose venues are long sold out to season ticket holders. You can usually find scalpers hovering around Madison Square Garden, but you'll pay through the nose and might be sold bogus tickets; using a ticket agent would be a safer bet if your youngster desperately wants to see a game.

Madison Square Garden events and major theater productions offer their tickets through Ticketmaster (© **800/755-4000,** 212/307-4100, or 212/307-7171; www. ticketmaster.com) or through **Tele-Charge** (© **800/432-7250** or 212/239-6200; www.telecharge.com). **Madison Square Garden** events also have their own box office (© **212/465-MSG1** [465-6741]; www.thegarden.com). For smaller children's theater companies and puppet shows, contact the box office numbers in separate listings below (some are simply answering machines where you leave your number so the organizer can call you back).

Same-day tickets for many Broadway, Off-Broadway, and Lincoln Center events can be bought in person at the **TKTS booths** (© **212/912-9770;** www.tdf.org) in Midtown on the pedestrian island called Duffy Square at 47th Street and Broadway (evening performances: Mon and Wed–Sat 3–8pm, Tues 2–8pm, and Sun 3pm to half-hour before curtain time; matinees: Wed and Sat 10am–2pm, Sun 11am–3pm). Remember, no evening tickets are sold from 10am to 2pm at Times Square. The **South Street Seaport TKTS** booth, 199 Water St., is located at the corner of Front and John streets, near the Resnick/Prudential building (daily Mon–Sat 11am–6pm, Sun 11am–4pm). At TKTS Seaport, matinee tickets are sold only on the day before the performance. A TKTS booth has opened in **Downtown Brooklyn** (1 MetroTech Center, Jay St. and Myrtle Ave.; Tues–Sat 11am–6pm).

The earlier you line up, the more options you will have. Most tickets are sold at half-price, though some are discounted only 25%, but you'll have to have cash or traveler's checks—no plastic. A $4 TKTS service charge is added. TKTS often has long lines, which move fairly fast but not fast enough for restless small kids. (*Tip:* Window 6, the "PLAY ONLY" window, often has a shorter wait.) The surrounding assemblage of wild lit-up signs can provide some distraction while you're waiting, and sometimes mimes and jugglers and street musicians work the crowd. But if you can swing it, one parent should take the youngsters for a walk while the other hangs out in line.

Another option: BroadwayBox.com, where tickets can be found online for 50% less (and without waiting and standing at the TKTS booth).

THE BIG VENUES

Brooklyn Academy of Music (BAM)   Theater, dance, music, puppetry—an impressively international selection of productions rolls through BAM in the course of a year, with a tendency toward the avant-garde. A handful of reasonably priced performances are suited to youngsters, especially the 2-day BAM Kids Film Festival at BAM Rose Cinemas in the spring. Age levels are specified for each performance. 30 Lafayette Ave., Brooklyn. © **718/636-4100.** www.bam.org. Subway: B, Q, 2, 3, 4, 5 to Atlantic Ave.; C to Lafayette Ave.; G to Fulton St.; D, M, N, R to Pacific St. BAM is within walking distance from the B, C, D, G, M, N, Q, R, 2, 3, 4, and 5 trains.

Lincoln Center   With resident companies including the Metropolitan Opera, New York City Ballet, New York City Opera, New York Philharmonic, Film Society, Jazz at Lincoln Center, and the Lincoln Center Theater (all covered in various sections below), something exciting is always brewing at this world-class arts center—with an increasing amount geared for families. 65th and Broadway. © **212/875-5456.** www.lincoln center.org. Subway: 1 to 66th St./Lincoln Center.

Madison Square Garden   B-ball, hockey, WWE wrestling, the circus, ice shows, and rock concerts occupy this large arena in a grubby part of Midtown. It can be an intimidating space for a small child, but older kids will recognize it for what it is: a big-league venue with lots of urban electricity. This is the home of the NBA's New York Knicks, the WNBA's New York Liberty, and the NHL's New York Rangers. Tickets for most events here are also handled through Ticketmaster. The **Theater at Madison Square Garden** (www.theateratmsg.com), part of the Garden complex, hosts concerts and live touring stage shows. Among the recent family fare: Cirque du Soleil's *Wintuk* and *Yo Gabba Gabba! Live.* 4 Pennsylvania Plaza (Seventh Ave. btw. 31st and 33rd sts.). © **212/465-6741.** www.thegarden.com. 1, 2, 3 to Seventh Ave.; A, C, E to 34th St./Penn Station.

New Victory Theater   This lovely, renovated century-old theater on 42nd Street has an impressive lineup of entertainment totally for kids. In 2008, Americans for the Arts awarded the New Vic with their prestigious National Award for helping change public education through the arts. You'll find high-profile talent such as London's Young Vic Theatre Company, Theater for a New Audience, Circus Oz, Mabou Mines, and the Peking Acrobats, as well as idiosyncratic acts like the Flying Karamazov Brothers, the Flaming Idiots, and Thwack. Target age groups vary, but there are significant offerings for that tricky age group of 8- to 12-year-olds—too old for puppet shows but still too young for many Broadway shows. There are many special workshops and meet-the-cast events as well, especially through the VicTeens program. New York parents have learned to book tickets far in advance, even if they've never heard of the artists; the runs are generally only 3 weeks long and often sell out. The season is September through June, with extra showtimes during holidays and spring vacation. 209 W. 42nd St. (btw. Seventh and Eighth aves.). © **646/223-3020** or 212/239-6200 (Telecharge). www.newvictory.org. Tickets $9–$38. Subway: N, Q, R, S, W, 1, 2, 3, 7 to 42nd St./Times Square; A, C, E to 42nd St./Port Authority.

Radio City Music Hall   The Art Deco interior of this Rockefeller Center showcase is a marvel in itself, but kids probably won't notice—they'll be too busy gaping at the vast proscenium of the stage. Besides mounting its own live stage shows twice a year, including the hugely popular Radio City Music Hall Christmas Spectacular (see "Seasonal Events," below), Radio City hosts concerts, including the occasional family show. For most events children who are 2 years old and older require a ticket. Depending on the event, however, a child who has not reached his or her second birthday usually does not require a ticket but must sit on a parent's or guardian's lap. Please check the specific event before purchasing tickets. For more information, contact Guest Relations at ☎ **212/465-6225.** 1260 Sixth Ave. (at 50th St.). ☎ **212/307-7171** (Ticketmaster). www.radiocity.com. Subway: B, D, F to 47th–50th sts./ Rockefeller Center.

Symphony Space Besides the Just Kidding series, this renovated Upper West Side theater hosts an eclectic variety of events, including international dance troupes, and, in spring, "Selected Shorts," a really great series of short-story readings by famous actors and writers. 2537 Broadway (at 95th St.). ☎ **212/864-5400.** www.symphonyspace. org. Subway: 1, 2, 3 to 96th St.

SEASONAL EVENTS

Big Apple Circus **All ages.** This beloved one-ring circus performs in a tent (heated, of course) at Lincoln Center from October to January. In 2¼ hours, the Big Apple Circus manages to pack in clowns, elephants, trapeze artists, bareback riders, and something for everyone. Skilled circus artists and a sophisticated sense of humor make this a good show for adults who'd rather be charmed than stunned. A splendid time is guaranteed for all. In Damrosch Park behind Lincoln Center, Broadway and 64th St. ☎ **212/307-4100.** (Mailing address: 505 Eighth Ave., 19th Floor, New York, NY 10018.) www.bigapple circus.org. Tickets $38–$125, free for children 1 and under. Subway: 1 to 66th St./Lincoln Center.

Cirque du Soleil **Ages 10 & up.** Not your ordinary big-top show by any means, Cirque du Soleil productions change from year to year, but they're always sophisticated

STREET performers

When former Mayor Giuliani cleared away the vagrants and the squeegee men from New York City streets, the crime rate plummeted, but the number of street performers also dwindled. They're still around, however. Top spots for catching jugglers, acrobats, break dancers, and magicians are at South Street Seaport, by the Statue of Liberty ferry line in Battery Park, by the TKTS line in Duffy Square, on the Central Park pathways just north of the children's zoo around 65th Street, at Bethesda Terrace just north of 72nd Street in Central Park, on the steps leading up to the Metropolitan Museum of Art, and by the fountain in Washington Square Park.

The subways see their fair share of entertainers, and the MTA actually sponsors a successful **"Music under New York"** program, featuring 350 officially vetted musicians (many of them terrific) performing in some 25 station locations throughout the transit system. Otherwise, don't be surprised to hear doo-wop quartets and other "unofficial" musicians break into song as they roam from one subway car to another.

You're under no obligation to give these people money, but if you think they're good, by all means do so.

visual spectacles, a creative blend of acrobatics, dance, music, and traditional clowning with an edgy twist. Shows tend to run 2½ hours long. The Theater at MSG is home to the holiday-season production of *Wintuk*. The Theater at Madison Square Garden. 4 Pennsylvania Plaza (Seventh Ave. btw. 31st and 33rd sts.). ☏ **800/678-5440** or 514/790-1245. www.cirquedusoleil.com. Tickets $30–$220. 1, 2, 3 to Seventh Ave.; A, C, E to 34th St./ Penn Station.

The Nutcracker ★★★   Ages 10 & up. The city's best Nutcracker is staged every December by the New York City Ballet in Lincoln Center, with several stunning effects (like a Christmas tree that grows up out of the stage to ginormous proportions). Although the theater is undergoing renovations, it will not affect the New York City Ballet schedule. At the David H. Koch Theater (formerly the New York State Theater) in Lincoln Center, Broadway and 63rd St. ☏ **212/870-5570.** www.nycballet.com. Tickets $20–$135. Subway: 1 to 66th St./Lincoln Center.

Nutcracker 👪   Ages 3 & up. The New York Theatre Ballet's abbreviated version of Tchaikovsky's holiday classic ballet lasts about 1 hour, cutting out a lot of the first act to focus on the magical elements of the story. Alongside the classical ballet elements, bits of juggling have been thrown in, and Herr Drosselmeyer has some speaking parts to set up the story. Children are allowed—even expected—to make noises and jump out of their seats. A nice introduction to the ballet for younger audiences. Florence Gould Hall, 55 E. 59th St. (btw. Park and Madison aves.). ☏ **212/355-6160** or 212/307-4100 (Ticketmaster). www.nytb.org. Tickets $31 adults, $26 children 12 and under. Subway: 4, 5, 6 to 59th St.

Radio City Music Hall Christmas Spectacular   Ages 3 & up. The Rockettes gotta perform somewhere, and this is it. Radio City's elegant Art Deco interior, with its immense stage, cries out for a stage extravaganza like this—lots of music, lavish effects, corny holiday motifs, and that classic precision kick line. The Christmas Show runs early November to the first week in January, usually one show a day until the holidays loom close, when up to five shows a day are performed. It's an annual tradition, and the magic still works, dazzling the Nickelodeon (and now Noggin) generation. 1260 Sixth Ave. (at 50th St.). ☏ **212/307-1000** (Ticketmaster). www.radiocity.com. Tickets $45–$250. Subway: B, D, F to 47th–50th sts./Rockefeller Center.

Ringling Bros. and Barnum & Bailey Circus   Ages 6 & up. This glitzy, humongous circus takes up residence at the Garden for 6 weeks every spring, beginning in late March, starring death-defying aerialists, wild animal acts, lumbering elephants, snarling bears, hordes of clowns, the whole shebang. Smaller kids may be overwhelmed by the sheer size of the Garden, not to mention the flashing lights and eardrum-blasting music. Adults may be overwhelmed by the barrage of vendors selling junk food and junky souvenirs at wildly inflated prices. Still, it's the Greatest Show on Earth and pretty darn impressive. At Madison Square Garden, Seventh Ave. btw. 31st and 33rd sts. ☏ **800/755-4000,** 212/465-MSG1 (465-6741), or 212/307-7171 (Ticketmaster). www.ringling.com. Tickets $16–$80. Subway: A, C, E, 1, 2, 3 to 34th St.

Shakespeare in the Park   Ages 10 & up. From June to August of each summer, The New York Public Theater produces two free shows at the outdoor Delacorte Theater in Central Park, at least one of them by Shakespeare. Recent years have included the much-loved *A Midsummer Night's Dream,* a musical of *Two Gentlemen of Verona,* and *Macbeth.* The line to get tickets forms early each day (9 or 10am), snaking around the Great Lawn; but once the box office opens it moves quickly, and all tickets are soon distributed. The wait can be tedious, but it's a small price for free theater in a beautiful setting. *Note:* A limited number of tickets are available online the day of the performance. Register at www.publictheater. org. Log on between midnight and 1pm the day of the performance and again from 1 to 6pm to see if you have been selected for a pair of tickets. At the Delacorte Theater, Central Park. ☎ **212/260/2400.** www.publictheater.org. Tickets free (limit 2 per person in line). Subway: B, C to 81st St.

THEATER
Long-Running Shows

It's always hard to predict which Broadway and Off-Broadway shows will still be running by the time you read this (much less by the time you get to New York), but these shows are a pretty safe bet—many have been running for a long time with no sign of letting up. Most of them (except *The Lion King*) are usually available for half-price at the TKTS booth at 47th Street and Broadway. Note that most theaters do not admit children under 4 years of age.

Blue Man Group   **Ages 8 & up.** Faces painted blue, this trio has been committing weird mayhem onstage since 1992, with lots of flashing strobes and percussion effects. The hip performance-art elements are directed to adults, but preteens dig the show, too. It runs slightly under 2 hours. At the Astor Place Theatre, 434 Lafayette St. (btw. E. 4th St. and Astor Place). ☎ **212/254-4370** or 212/307-4100 (Ticketmaster). www.blueman.com. Tickets $74–$04. Subway: 6 to Astor Place.

The Lion King ★★★   **All ages.** Still a hot ticket, this adaptation of a Disney animated movie is worth planning your trip around. Tony-award-winning director Julie Taymor discarded glitzy special effects and made stage magic instead with puppets, dancers, masks, billowing cloths, and imagination, drawing strongly on African folk traditions. This show is genuinely moving, even—dare I say it?—better than the movie. Call for tickets many months in advance, line up outside for same-day returns, or splurge on a ticket agent, but somehow get your children to see this play. At the Minskoff Theatre, 1515 Broadway at 45th St. ☎ **212/307-4747** or 307-4100 (Ticketmaster). www.disney onbroadway.com. Tickets $73–$129. Subway: N, Q, R, S, 1, 2, 3 to 42nd St./Times Square.

Mary Poppins ★   **Ages 5 & up.** Disney's latest brings the cheer of chim-chim-cheree to Broadway. At the New Amsterdam Theatre, 214 W. 42nd St. (btw. Seventh and Eighth aves.). ☎ **866/870-2717** or 212/307-4100 (Ticketmaster). www.disney.go.com/theatre/marypoppins. Tickets $32–$122. Subway: N, Q, R, S, 1, 2, 3 to 42nd St./Times Square.

Stomp   **Ages 8 & up.** What kid hasn't made music by tapping a broom handle on the floor or crashing pot lids together? This troupe of eight athletic-looking dancers does the same sort of rhythmic stuff with everyday objects for an hour and a half, and it's undeniably captivating. Early-evening performances Saturday and Sunday make it possible to see this without being out too late. At the Orpheum Theater, 126 Second Ave. (btw. 7th and 8th sts.). ☎ **800/982-2787** or 212/307-4100 (Ticketmaster). www.stomponline.com. Tickets $40–$73. Subway: 6 to Astor Place.

Wicked ★★   **Ages 8 & up.** This musical has been packing 'em in on Broadway since 2003. It's the tale of the young Wicked Witch of the West and her good

Theater

ENTERTAINMENT FOR THE WHOLE FAMILY

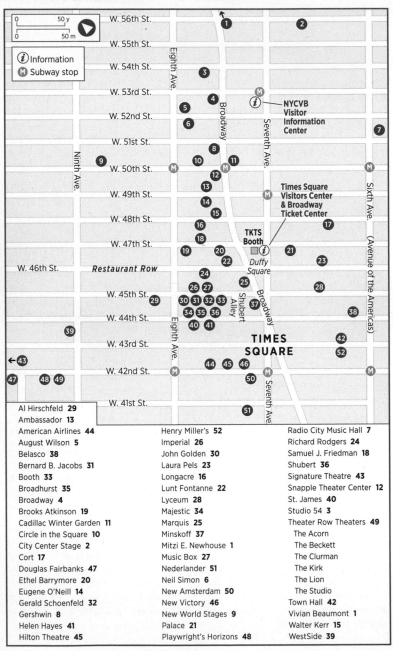

Al Hirschfeld **29**
Ambassador **13**
American Airlines **44**
August Wilson **5**
Belasco **38**
Bernard B. Jacobs **31**
Booth **33**
Broadhurst **35**
Broadway **4**
Brooks Atkinson **19**
Cadillac Winter Garden **11**
Circle in the Square **10**
City Center Stage **2**
Cort **17**
Douglas Fairbanks **47**
Ethel Barrymore **20**
Eugene O'Neill **14**
Gerald Schoenfeld **32**
Gershwin **8**
Helen Hayes **41**
Hilton Theatre **45**

Henry Miller's **52**
Imperial **26**
John Golden **30**
Laura Pels **23**
Longacre **16**
Lunt Fontanne **22**
Lyceum **28**
Majestic **34**
Marquis **25**
Minskoff **37**
Mitzi E. Newhouse **1**
Music Box **27**
Nederlander **51**
Neil Simon **6**
New Amsterdam **50**
New Victory **46**
New World Stages **9**
Palace **21**
Playwright's Horizons **48**

Radio City Music Hall **7**
Richard Rodgers **24**
Samuel J. Friedman **18**
Shubert **36**
Signature Theatre **43**
Snapple Theater Center **12**
St. James **40**
Studio 54 **3**
Theater Row Theaters **49**
  The Acorn
  The Beckett
  The Clurman
  The Kirk
  The Lion
  The Studio
Town Hall **42**
Vivian Beaumont **1**
Walter Kerr **15**
WestSide **39**

sister witch Glenda, and the story and score continue to enthrall older children. At the Gershwin Theatre, 222 W. 51st St. (btw. Broadway and Eighth Ave.). ℂ **212/586-6510** or 212/307-4100 (Ticketmaster). www.gershwintheatre.com. Tickets $56–$251. Subway: N, Q, R to 49th St.; to 50th St.

Children's Theater Companies

Big Red Chair Family Series at the Skirball Center Ages 3 & up. This performing arts center in the heart of the NYU Washington Square "campus" offers theater pieces based on popular children's books. The 2010 season saw the production of *The Adventures of Harold and the Purple Crayon* and *Nobody's Perfect*. The Joffrey Ballet's low-tech version of *The Nutcracker* is also performed here. At the Skirball Center for the Performing Arts, New York University. 566 LaGuardia Place (at Washington Square South). ℂ **212/352-3101**. www.skirballcenter.nyu.edu. Tickets $20–$25. Subway: N, R to 8th St.; A, C, D, E, F, V to W. 4th St.

Galli's Fairytale Theater Ages 3 & up. Modern interpretations of classic fairy tales, with plenty of audience interaction. At the Galli Theater NY, 38 W. 38th St., 3rd Floor (btw. Fifth and Sixth aves.). ℂ **212/352-3101**. www.gallitheaterny.com. Tickets $15–$20. Subway: N, Q, R, S, W, 1, 2, 3 to 42nd St./Times Square.

IMPROV 4 Kids Ages 4 & up. Ever dreamed of raising a little stand-up comic? Here's your chance to see if he or she's got the goods. The official outreach program of the former Laugh Factory comedy group now known as *Eight Is Never Enough* teaches children comedy arts and shows kids a deliciously good time in the process. Shows are Saturdays at 3pm, and you can buy half-price tickets online. Times Square Arts Center, 300 W. 43rd St. (at Eighth Ave.). ℂ **212/352-3101** or 212/568-6560. www.improv4kids.com. Tickets $20. Subway A, C, E to Port Authority Terminal.

Literally Alive Ages 3 to 10. This company performs two to three shows a year showcasing classic children's stories with original music. Past shows include *The Velveteen Rabbit* and Oscar Wilde's *The Selfish Giant*. It also provides preshow arts-and-crafts workshops on Saturday and Sunday beginning at noon before a 1pm show. Check the website for weekday performances during school vacations as well. Currently in residence at the Players Theatre, 115 MacDougal St. (btw. Bleecker and W. 3rd sts.). ℂ **212/866-5170**. www.literallyalive.com. Tickets $25 (www.theatermania.com). Subway: A, C, E, D, F, V to W. 4th St.

Manhattan Theater Source Ages 5 & up. This bustling Greenwich Village theater organization works a few hour-long productions for kids—both musicals and straight plays—into their yearly schedule. 177 MacDougal St. (btw. 8th St. and Waverly Place). ℂ **212/260-4698**. www.theatresource.org. Tickets $15 $18. Subway: A, B, C, D, E, F, V to W. 4th St.

Paper Bag Players Ages 4 to 9. January to March, this veteran troupe presents original 1-hour plays with a pleasant edge of nuttiness, on Saturday at 2pm and Sunday at 1 and 3pm. The company's trademark is using everyday materials like paper bags and corrugated cardboard for all the costumes, sets, and props, giving the productions a homegrown look that somehow makes them very appealing to kids. Each year they perform in various locations throughout the city. ℂ **212/353-2332**. www.paperbagplayers.org. Tickets $10–$25.

Queens Theatre in the Park   Ages 3 to 12. Just a few hundred yards from the Unisphere, the giant steel globe that is the centerpiece of the Flushing Meadows-Corona Park, this Philip Johnson–designed theater features a Kids Corner series of quality children's musicals. Recent productions have included funny and spirited renditions of *Rumplestiltskin* and *Goldilocks and the Three Bears*. ℂ **718/760-0064.** www.queenstheatre.org. Tickets $10–$12.

Shadow Box Theatre   Ages 4 & up. The children's theater-in-residence at the Theatres at 45 Bleecker Street specializes in original musicals with multicultural themes, featuring singing, dancing, and puppetry, both hand puppets and shadow puppets. They perform weekday puppet performances from October to May and holiday-themed shows on weekends October through April. They also do various performances in Brooklyn. At the Theatres at 45 Bleecker Street, 45 Bleecker St., ℂ **212/724-0677.** www.shadowboxtheatre.org. (Mailing address 325 West End Ave., New York, NY 10023.) Tickets $15–$20.

Theater for a New Audience   Ages 8 & up. This top-notch Off-Broadway company devotes itself to the classics, mostly Shakespeare. By no means for children only, its vigorous productions do attract lots of school groups because they're a great way to introduce youngsters to the Bard. From January to April there are two or three productions, playing Tuesday to Saturday nights, with a Saturday matinee. Performing at the Duke, 229 W. 42nd St. (btw. Seventh and Eighth aves.). ℂ **466/223-3010.** www.tfana.org.

TheatreworksUSA   Ages 4 & up. One of the city's top choices for kids, this long-running troupe presents witty, vivid musical versions of classic books like *The Lion, the Witch, and the Wardrobe; Charlotte's Web;* or *The Plant That Ate Dirty Socks,* as well as some original story scripts. They put on a dozen or so plays each year, with several performances of each, so you can count on something every weekend at 2pm from September to March. Children under age 4 are not admitted. The family series musicals are held at the Lucille Lortel Theatre, 1212 Christopher St. (ℂ 212/647-1100 or 800/497-5007). 151 W. 26th St. ℂ **800/497-5007** or 212/647-1100. www.theatreworksusa. org. Subway: 1 to 50th St.; N, R to 49th St.; B, D, E to Seventh Ave.

Thirteenth Street Repertory Theater   Ages 4 & up. Alongside its grown-up productions, this Greenwich Village company puts on two original children's shows on Saturday and Sunday at 1 and 3pm year-round. With recorded music and special effects, shows like *Wiseacre Farm* and *Rumple Who?* are perfectly calibrated for a young audience, with healthy doses of humor. Reservations are recommended a couple of days in advance of the performance. 50 W. 13th St. ℂ **212/675-6677.** www.13thstreetrep.org. Tickets to children's shows $10. Subway: F, V, 1, 2, 3 to 14th St.; A, C, E to W. 4th St.; N, R, 4, 5, 6 to Union Square; L to Sixth Ave.

Tribeca Performing Arts   Ages 3 & up. Offering a mixed bag of events—some starring kids, others with adult performers, others with puppets or dancers or actors performing in sign language—this downtown arts center brings to town a full season of children's entertainment with its Family, Folk, and Fairy Tale series (Oct–June Sat or Sun at 1:30pm). Past productions have included musical versions of classics like *The Lion, the Witch, and the Wardrobe* and *The Reluctant Dragon,* as well as retellings of children's books such as *The House at Pooh Corner.* 199 Chambers St. (btw. Greenwich St. and the West Side Hwy.). ℂ **212/220-1460.** www.tribecapac.org. All tickets $25.

Kids Onstage

City Lights Youth Theatre **Ages 4 & up.** Several times a year, students 7 to 18 who've taken classes at the City Lights school perform—an original play in the winter and a musical (like *Pippin*) in the spring. A junior musical for younger children is performed in May as well as part of the spring performance festival. Other events include stage readings for family audiences. Check the website for directions to current venues. Most performances are held at 630 Ninth Ave. (btw. 44th and 45th sts.). ☎ **212/262-0200.** www.clyouththeatre.org.

New Media Children's Theatre Company **Ages 4 to 18.** The nonprofit New Media Children's Theatre Company performances are by and for kids, with lots of participation from the youthful audience. A new original play is presented every February and March on Saturday at 3pm. The young performers are students at the program's acting workshops. Reservations are essential. 512 E. 80th St. (btw. York and East End aves.). ☎ **212/734-5195.** www.newmediarep.org. Tickets $10. Subway: 6 to 77th St.

TADA! **Ages 3 & up.** The most energetic and successful of NYC's theater schools for kids, the award-winning TADA! has even performed at the White House. A diverse group of professional kid performers, ages 8 to 17, stars in TADA!'s sprightly original musicals. They play weekends in January, March, and December (including one Fri-night show, unusual for children's companies; two Sat matinees; and two Sun matinees). In July—when most other children's entertainment dries up—TADA! comes to the rescue with weekday shows. Even adults without children have been known to see TADA!'s shows, which tells you something about how lively they are. 15 W. 28th St. (btw. Broadway and Fifth aves.). ☎ **212/252-1619.** www.tadatheater.com. Tickets $25 adults, $10 children. Subway: N, R, 1 to 28th St.; A, B, C, D, E, F, 2, 3 to 34th St.

CONCERTS

Brooklyn Center for the Performing Arts **Ages 3 & up.** The Target FamilyFun Series presents five productions a year in the gorgeously renovated Walt Whitman Theatre, plus an annual December *Nutcracker* ballet from the Dance Theatre in Westchester troupe. The weekend matinees are a multicultural grab bag of cultural events appealing to kids—live theater, music concerts, drum ensembles, and ballet. Performances scheduled for the 2010–11 season included productions of *Seussical* and *Beauty and the Beast.* Walt Whitman Theatre at Brooklyn College, 2900 Campus Rd., Brooklyn. ☎ **718/951-4500.** www.brooklyncenter.com. Target Family-Fun tickets $6–$7. Subway: 2 to Flatbush Ave.

Carnegie Hall Family Concerts ♦ **Ages 5 to 12.** Six or seven Saturdays a year, October through May, Carnegie Hall presents hour-long concerts at 1pm and 2pm, preceded by preconcert activities like demonstrations, craft workshops, and storytelling. Performers might include anyone from the Chicago Youth Symphony Orchestra to classical-music stars such as cellist Yo-Yo Ma and clarinetist Richard Stoltzman. Advance reservations recommended. At Carnegie Hall, 881 Seventh Ave. (at 57th St.). ☎ 212/247-7800. www.carnegiehall.org. Tickets $9. Subway: N, R to 57th St./Seventh Ave.

CarnegieKids ♦ **Ages 3 to 6.** These free 45-minute interactive concerts are designed for preschoolers and kindergartners, using storytellers and musicians who interact with the children in the audience, letting them sing and move around to the music. Concerts are held in venues throughout the city Thursday through Sunday from mid-October through October 30 and again from February to early June (times vary). Held in venues throughout the city. ℭ **212/247-7800.** www.carnegiehall.org. Subway: N, Q, R, W to 57th St./Seventh Ave.

Jazz for Young People   Ages 5 & up. Under the aegis of superstar trumpeter Wynton Marsalis, this exciting series consists of two shows (1 and 3pm) on Saturdays at Lincoln Center's Rose Theater in the Time-Warner Center on Columbus Circle. 33 W. 60th St. (at Broadway). ℭ **212/721-6500** for tickets; 212/258-9800 for information. www.jazz atlincolncenter.org. Tickets $12–$32 ($35 for 3-performance series). Subway: A, B, C, D, 1 to 59th St./ Columbus Circle.

Jazz Standard's Jazz for Kids   Ages 4 & up. The Jazz Standard Youth Orchestra, an ensemble of about 20 musically gifted schoolchildren, entertains during a delightful jazz brunch for children, Sunday from 1 to 3pm (shows start at 2pm) from September to June. The food, from the barbecue restaurant **Blue Smoke** downstairs (see chapter 6), is as winning as the music. Reservations recommended. 116 E. 27th St. (btw. Park and Lexington aves.). ℭ **212/576-2232.** www.jazzstandard.com. $5 donation. Subway: 6 to 28th St.

Little Orchestra Society   Ages 3 to 12. Two series—**Happy Concerts for Young People** (ages 6–12) and **Lolli-Pop Concerts** (ages 3–5)—are designed to introduce kids to classical music, using first-class professional artists (moonlighting Philharmonic members, New York City Ballet stars, and the like). This organization has been around since the 1950s, and the quality is top-notch. The Lolli-Pop series, held at the **Kaye Playhouse** at Hunter College (68th St. btw. Park and Lexington aves.), uses cutesy costumed figures to help teach wee ones about music. You can buy a three-concert or a six-concert series with several performance times for each on Saturday and Sunday, and it's popular so you should book early (three-concert series $36 or $90; six-concert series $72 or $150). It's easier to score tickets for Happy Concerts; there are two Saturday performances (11am and 1pm) for each of the three concerts per year, but they are held in a much larger space, Lincoln Center's **Avery Fisher Hall** (Broadway at 65th St.). Happy Concert subscription prices range from $30 to $120; call about prices for individual tickets. The Happy Concert series includes the annual performances of *Peter and the Wolf* and Menotti's *Amahl and the Night Visitors,* a fully staged opera with live animals. Mailing address: 330 W. 42nd, 12th Floor, New York, NY 10036-6902. ℭ **212/971-9500.** www.littleorchestra.org.

Meet the Music!   Ages 6 to 12. The Chamber Music Society of Lincoln Center puts in its bid for young audiences with this upbeat Sunday-afternoon series. Even modern pieces by Aaron Copland or Andrew Lloyd Webber might be performed, as long as they're played by a small group of musicians, one player to a part. With narrators, props, and audience participation, the concerts engage fidgety youngsters admirably. The three-concert series features two concerts at Merkin Concert Hall and one program in Alice Tully Hall. You can purchase series or individual tickets. Lincoln Center, 129 W. 67th St. (btw. Broadway and Amsterdam Ave.). ℭ **212/875-5788.** www.chambermusicsociety.org. Series tickets $41–$66; individual tickets $15–$25. Subway: 1 to 66th St./Lincoln Center.

Young People's Concerts **Ages 6 to 12.** Want to turn your kid into a hard-core classical-music fan? Four Saturdays a year the New York Philharmonic trots out musicians like violin prodigy Sarah Chang and conductors Kurt Mazur and Leonard Slatkin to introduce kids to major selections from the classical repertory—not just the chestnuts like *Eine kleine Nachtmusik,* but also pieces by moderns like George Gershwin and Charles Ives. Topping it off, free 12:45pm interactive Kidzone Live! music fairs precede the 2pm concerts. Want to start 'em a little younger? Head to the **Very Young People's Concerts** (ages 3–5), interactive concerts on Sundays and Mondays at Merkin Concert Hall (series subscription $57–$72). Older kids (12–17) can graduate to **Phil Teens,** which gives them free pre-performance workshops and discounted seats ($12) to the orchestra's Friday-evening concerts. Avery Fisher Hall, Lincoln Center, Broadway and 64th St. ℂ **212/721-6500** or 212/875-5656. www.nyphil.org. Young People's Concerts series tickets $40–$128; individual tickets $5–$25. Subway: 1 to 66th St./Lincoln Center.

FILMS

If it's standard feature-film fare you want, Manhattan is packed with cinema screens, including the busy 13-screen **AMC Loews Lincoln Square complex** at 68th and Broadway, where each theater entrance evokes a different classic New York movie palace; and the multiplex **Regal E-Walk Stadium 13** and **AMC Empire 25** cinemas, both located on West 42nd Street between Broadway and Eighth Avenue. For more unusual films geared to a young audience, here are your choices:

AMC Loews IMAX Theater **Ages 3 & up.** Not just IMAX but 3-D IMAX—awesome. The screen is eight stories high, and a cool headset puts you in the extraspatial dimension. Needless to say, there isn't a lot of film material for this format and some of the offerings aren't 3-D. But AMC Loews has managed to get movies that go beyond documentaries into actual storytelling features—like *Across the Sea of Time,* which tells of a young Russian immigrant boy searching for relatives in Manhattan (think of it as a live-action *An American Tale*). Most shows run about 45 minutes to an hour. Target ages for the scheduled films vary, so check ahead—and as always with IMAX, consider whether your youngster is suited to the medium's heightened sensory impact. Other IMAX theaters are found in **AMC Loews Kips Bay 15** (570 Second Ave.; ℂ 212/447-0638); **AMC Loews 34th Street 14** (312 W. 34th St; ℂ 212/244-4456); and **AMC Empire 25** (234 W. 42nd St.; ℂ **212/398-2597**). At AMC Loews Lincoln Square, Broadway and 68th St. ℂ **212/336-5000.** Tickets $18–$20 adults, $15–$17 children 12 and under. Subway: 1 to 66th St./Lincoln Center.

American Museum of Natural History IMAX Theater **Ages 4 & up.** The screen at the Natural History Museum isn't quite as huge as the one at the AMC Loews Lincoln Square IMAX (see above), but unless you get out your measuring tape, you'd never know. The main thing is that your whole field of vision is occupied, which somehow doubles the sensory impact of a movie—something to consider before you take young, skittish children inside. You have a choice of dazzling 3-D

IMAX movies every day, some more intense than others, though all have an educational bent. Whether you're in outer space, underwater with prehistoric sea monsters, or deep in the rainforest, the sights and sounds tend to include a speeding camera taking you on a visual thrill ride that swoops over rising and falling terrain, the hallmark of the IMAX experience.

An IMAX ticket includes admission to the museum and the Rose Center; you can buy the combination ticket when you enter, or stop by the ticket counter near the museum's 77th Street entrance. There's a movie every 45 minutes or so, though school groups get first dibs on seats weekday mornings (the public is then admitted on a first-come, first-served basis). The museum is open daily year-round, except on Thanksgiving and Christmas. At the American Museum of Natural History, Central Park West at 79th St. ℂ **212/769-5200.** www.amnh.org. Tickets (includes museum admission) $24 adults, $18 seniors and students over 12, $14 children 2–12. Subway: B, C to 81st St./Museum of Natural History; 1 to 79th St.

BAMKids Film Festival   Ages 2 to 13. For 2 days each spring (generally a weekend in late Feb), BAMKids treats its young audience to an array of international feature-length films and shorts. Selections have ranged from animated favorites like *Babar: King of Elephants* to quality classics like *The Red Balloon.* Guest appearances by featured animators and directors make the experience for youngsters even more meaningful. At the Brooklyn Academy of Music (BAM) Rose Cinemas, 30 Lafayette Ave., Brooklyn. ℂ **718/636-4100.** www.bam.org. Tickets $12 adults, $8 kids 13 and under. Subway: B, Q, 2, 3, 4, 5 to Atlantic Ave.; C to Lafayette Ave.; G to Fulton St.; or D, M, N, R to Pacific St.

New York International Children's Film Festival   Ages 3 & up. This excellent festival brings a wide range of films and videos, from commercial features to animation to shorts and documentaries from around the world, screened at venues around town. The NYICFF Awards Ceremony is held in March, and young viewers get to vote to award festival prizes for certain portions of the program. Way cool. In addition, the festival hosts special screenings of kids' films (new and old) all year long. 295 Greenwich St. (at Chambers). ℂ **212/349-0330.** www.gkids.com. Ticket prices for individual films vary.

DANCE

American Ballet Theatre   Ages 8 & up. On this enormous stage, the spring season (May–June) features both modern works and some classic story ballets like *Swan Lake, Giselle,* and *Sleeping Beauty*—just the thing for budding ballerinas. Check the website for hands-on workshops for youngsters, occasionally held in conjunction with performances. Metropolitan Opera House, Lincoln Center, Broadway and 64th St. ℂ **212/362-6000.** www.abt.org. Tickets $28–$145. Subway: 1 to 66th St./Lincoln Center.

Dance Theater Workshop   Ages 4 & up. One of the city's leading promoters of modern dance, the workshop presents, among other things, a **Family Matters Series,** Sunday matinee showcased appropriate for parents and kids of all ages (not necessarily purely dance). The season usually runs September to June. 219 W. 19th St. (btw. Seventh and Eighth aves.). ℂ **212/924-0077.** www.dancetheaterworkshop.org. Tickets $15–$25; free for children 12 and under. Subway: C, E to 23rd St.; 1 to 18th St.

Ice Theatre of New York ✦ **Ages 5 & up.** Unlike typical ice-show companies, Ice Theatre leads figure skating strongly in the direction of dance, even commissioning noted nonskating choreographers to create new pieces for their lyrical, intriguing performances. The theater's home is the **Sky Rink** at Chelsea Piers (23rd St. at the Hudson River). With guest artists like Nancy Kerrigan and David Liu, the skaters take to the ice in free lunchtime shows at rinks all over town, including **Rockefeller Center;** the **World Ice Arena,** in Flushing, Queens; and the **Riverbank State Park** (145th St. and Riverside Dr.). ℂ **212/929-5811** or 212/307-7171 (Ticketmaster). www. icetheatre.org.

Joyce Theater **Ages 6 & up.** This Chelsea theater devoted to modern dance does an admirable job of bringing in young audiences. Touring dance companies booked into the Joyce are asked to design special Saturday family matinees, with dancers showing up in the lower lobby afterward, still in costume, to meet audience members and give autographs. Two performances are held in Chelsea; a third, the "Special Family Matinee Event," is held at the Joyce SoHo Theater, a converted firehouse (155 Mercer St.; ℂ **212/431-9233**). 175 Eighth Ave. (at 19th St.). ℂ **212/242-0800** or 212/691-9740. www.joyce.org. Tickets $10–$75. Subway: C, E to 23rd St.; 1 to 18th St.

New York City Ballet **Ages 10 & up.** For technique, many critics feel this troupe surpasses its Lincoln Center cousin, the ABT (see above), but young balletomanes may not get the point of NYCB's more abstract pieces, following the tastes of founder George Balanchine. Still, the dreamy costumes and sets may be enchantment enough. Plus, this is where the city's best *Nutcracker* is staged every December (see "Seasonal Events," earlier in this chapter). Check out the children's online activities under "Kids & Families" on the NYCB website. The ballet offers two seasons—April through June and Thanksgiving through February—with nightly performances (except Mon) and weekend matinees. New York State Theater, Lincoln Center, Broadway and 64th St. ℂ **212/870-5570.** www.nycballet.com. Tickets $20–$135. Subway: 1 to 66th St./Lincoln Center.

New York Theater Ballet **Ages 5 & up.** Besides its splendid condensed *Nutcracker* (see "Seasonal Events," earlier in this chapter), this classical dance troupe presents three other fairy tale–based ballets each season, in the "Once Upon A Ballet" series. The quality of the dancing is excellent, and costumes are lovely, though sets are minimal on this relatively small stage. Geared for young audiences, these productions stress the storytelling elements of dance and are only 1 hour in length—which makes them a great introduction to traditional ballet. At Florence Gould Hall, 55 E. 59th St. (btw. Park and Madison aves.). ℂ **212/355-6160** (theater box office), or 212/307-4100 (Ticketmaster). www.nytb.org. Tickets $15–$46. Subway: 4, 5, 6 to 59th St.; N, R, W to Lexington Ave./59th St.

MAGIC SHOWS

Monday Night Magic **Ages 10 & up.** A fabulous showcase for serious magicians, *Monday Night Magic* varies from week to week; some performances are less appropriate for children than others (they won't admit anyone age 7 and under), so go on the website to see what this week's program offers. Acts range from hilarious to eerie to borderline raunchy, with card tricks, knife throwing, balloon tricks, and all the sleight of hand you could want. Performances run year-round, every Monday night at 8pm. The Bleecker Street Theater, 45 Bleecker St. (east of Lafayette St.). ℭ **212/615-6432** or www.telecharge.com for tickets. www.mondaynightmagic.com. Tickets $34–$39. Subway: B, D, F, V to Broadway/Lafayette; R, W to Prince St.; 6 to Bleecker St.

PUPPET SHOWS

Los Kabayitos Puppet & Children's Theater **Ages 4 & up.** Well-known tales are presented in Spanish and English simultaneously and performed with giant life-size puppets. 107 Suffolk St., 2nd Floor. ℭ **212/260-4080,** ext. 14. Subway: F, J, M, Z to Delancey St.

Puppetworks 🎭 **Ages 3 to 7.** Using both hand puppets and marionettes, these puppeteers retell such classic children's stories as *Beauty & and the Beast* and *Alice in Wonderland.* The season runs year-round, with performances on weekends at 12:30 and 2:30pm. Reservations are required. 338 6th Ave., Brooklyn. ℭ **718/965-3391.** www.puppetworks.org. Tickets $8 adults, $7 children. Subway: F to 7th Ave.

Swedish Cottage Marionette Theatre 🎭 **Ages 3 to 10.** This alpine-looking cottage holds a small stage where near-life-size marionettes prance and caper in hour-long productions of classic fairy tales—recorded soundtrack, spotlighting, full scenery, the works. A puppeteer prefaces performances with a helpful miniseminar on puppetry. The pace is leisurely, and the sense of humor is gentle. Call 3 or 4 weeks in advance for a reservation—there are usually one or two shows a day, but they fill up fast with school groups and birthday parties. In Central Park (West Dr. at 81st St.). ℭ **212/988-9093.** www.cityparksfoundation.org or www.centralpark.com. Tickets $8 adults, $5 children; reservations required. Closed mid-Aug through Sept. Subway: B, C to 79th St.

SPECTATOR SPORTS

Public transportation to the major sports arena in the New York metropolitan area just keeps on getting easier and easier. For the latest on "taking the train to the game," go to the sports page on the **Metropolitan Transportation Authority (MTA) website** (www.mta.info/mta/sports) for the latest info.

Brooklyn Cyclones 🎭 **Ages 6 & up.** The hardest-to-get sports ticket in town just may be for this Mets-affiliated Class A minor-league franchise out in Brooklyn, which debuted in Coney Island in 2001. Folks line up before dawn the day season tickets go on sale, and individual tickets often sell out within an hour after online ticketing opens. However, in keeping with the Cyclones' populist profile, there are always a limited number of general admission tickets offered at the box office at 10am on home game days. KeySpan Park strives for the way-back-when feel of the Brooklyn Dodgers' old Ebbets Field, with only 7,500 seats, alcohol-free sections, billboards advertising local small companies, and a view of Coney Island's boardwalk. A great place to spot good young players on their way up, and to recapture the charm that made baseball America's Game. KeySpan Park, 1904 Surf Ave. (btw. W. 17th and 19th sts.), Coney Island. ℭ **718/449-8497.** www.brooklyncyclones.com. Tickets $8–$16. Subway: D, F, N, Q to Coney Island/Stillwell Ave.

New Jersey Devils **Ages 8 & up.** Winners of the 1995 and 2000 Stanley Cups, the Devils have stolen the thunder from the New York area's older hockey teams, the Rangers and the Islanders. The season runs from October to mid-April, and though much of the arena gets sold out with season tickets, individual tickets for cheaper seats may be available. It's always worth checking the day of a game to see if some seats have been released. Prudential Center, Newark. ℰ **201/507-8900,** 212/307-7171 (for single-game tickets). http://devils.nhl.com. Tickets $20–$90. Parking $8. For game-time bus service from Manhattan's Port Authority Bus Terminal, call New Jersey Transit at ℰ 800/772-2222.

New Jersey Nets **Ages 8 & up.** The 2001–02 season was a magical one for the Nets, who won the Eastern Conference championship and battled the L.A. Lakers for the national title. It's been sorta downhill from there. Now with new ownership (the second-richest guy in Russia is the principal owner), a new GM (Billy King, former Duke Blue Devil), and the promise of a new home—the construction of a new Nets arena in Brooklyn, Barclays Center, was underway at press time—the Nets are in serious rebuilding mode. The regular season runs from November to mid-April. Prudential Center, Newark, NJ. ℰ **800/7NJ-NETS** (765-6387), 201/935-3900 (for single-game tickets), or 201/507-8900 (Ticketmaster). www.nba.com/nets. Tickets $18–$500. Parking $8.

New York Giants **Ages 8 & up.** With their spectacular win over the undefeated New England Patriots in Super Bowl 2008, Eli and company made a lot of New Yorkers Giants fans overnight. We'll see how the team fares in its new stadium in the Meadowlands, which will hold more than 80,000 seats—it's still roofless, however, which means it can get cold late in the season. Because football teams play only once a week, there are few home games in the course of their September-to-December season, and just about the whole stadium goes with season ticket holders—to get tickets you have to know somebody, *be* somebody, or spring for a scalper. Now you can **"take the train to the game"** from Manhattan with a new Meadowlands rail line that travels between the Hoboken terminal and the Frank R. Lautenberg Station in Secaucus Junction (just take the PATH train to Hoboken and then hop on a NJ Transit rail to the Meadowlands Sports Complex Station); round-trip tickets are $7.75 from the PATH train at Penn Station/33rd Street to Secaucus. On game days, a New Jersey Transit bus travels from Port Authority Terminal, Eighth Avenue between 40th and 42nd streets—call ℰ **212/564-1114** for information. At New Meadowlands Stadium in the Meadowlands, East Rutherford, NJ. ℰ **201/935-8222** or 201/935-3900 for single-game tickets. www.giants.com. Tickets $40 and $50. Parking $10.

New York Islanders **Ages 8 & up.** A lively force in recent NHL seasons, the Islanders skate on their home ice out on Long Island (hence the name) from October to mid-April. Take the Long Island Rail Road from Penn Station, Seventh Avenue between 31st and 33rd streets, to Hempstead (bus service nearby) or Westbury (take a taxi to the Nassau Coliseum). To reach the coliseum by car, take the M4 exit off the Meadowbrook Parkway. At Nassau Veterans Memorial Coliseum, Hempstead Tpk., Uniondale, NY. ℰ **800/882-ISLES** (882-47537), or 631/888-9000 (Ticketmaster). http://islanders.nhl.com. Tickets $35–$220.

MILESTONES IN NEW YORK sports history

In all the major pro sports, the lucrative New York area market sustains at least two teams, and at some periods (baseball in the 1950s, hockey today), three teams. New Yorkers, spoiled by years of sports success, aren't big on rooting for underdogs (with the exception of the 1969 Mets). Then again, we aren't used to having underdogs, maybe because New York money enables team owners to buy the best talent available, from Babe Ruth to Wayne Gretzky to Alex Rodriguez. New York fans, hooked on those championship titles, still can't get enough. Here's the sort of thing we're talking about:

- **1921–23:** Two New York baseball teams—the Giants and the Yankees—meet in the World Series for 3 consecutive years. The Giants win the first 2 years; the Yankees finally take the title in 1923, establishing a taste for victory they'll never shake.

- **1927–28:** Two consecutive World Series victories for the Yankees, both of them four-game sweeps. Babe Ruth sets his home run record at Yankee Stadium in 1927.

- **1928:** New York Rangers win hockey's Stanley Cup for the first (but not the last) time.

- **1936–37:** Two more Yankees-Giants World Series matchups— the Yankees win both times.

- **1938–39:** The Yankees continue their streak, sweeping the Cubs and then the Reds to make four World Series titles in a row.

- **1941:** The Yankees beat the Brooklyn Dodgers in the World Series.

- **1947:** Another Dodgers vs. Yankees Series; the Yankees win.

- **1949–56:** New York dominates baseball, with one of its teams winning the World Series every year—the Yankees for 5 years straight, and then the Giants in 1954 and the Dodgers in 1955

New York Jets   **Ages 8 & up.** Playing in the same brand-new stadium as the Giants, the Jets have had some loser seasons in the recent past; but Jets fans are die-hards, and both individual and season tickets are totally sold out—you'll need connections, ticket agents, or a scalper to attend a game, and rest assured that they will take their profits off the top. Now you can **"take the train to the game"** from Manhattan with a new Meadowlands rail line that travels between the Hoboken terminal and the Frank R. Lautenberg Station in Secaucus Junction (just take the PATH train to Hoboken and then hop on a NJ Transit rail to the Meadowlands Sports Complex Station); round-trip tickets are $7.75 from the PATH train at Penn Station/33rd Street to Secaucus. On game days there's a New Jersey Transit bus from Port Authority Terminal, Eighth Avenue between 40th and 42nd streets—call ✆ **212/564-1114** for information. The regular season runs September through December. At New Meadowlands Stadium in the Meadowlands, East Rutherford, NJ. ✆ **516/560-8200.** www.newyorkjets.com. Tickets $55 and $70. Parking $10.

New York Knicks   **Ages 8 & up.** The Knicks play 41 regular-season home games a year from November to mid-April. Though the team has suffered from injuries and whirlwind managerial changes the past few volatile seasons, getting (finally beating the Yankees!), only to have the Yankees vanquish the Dodgers again in 1956. Six World Series in this 8-year period are "Subway Series"—the Yankees face the Dodgers five times and the Giants once.

- **1961:** Yankee Roger Maris breaks Babe Ruth's home run record.
- **1969:** The New York Jets win the Super Bowl; the "Miracle" Mets win the World Series.
- **1970:** The New York Knicks take the NBA championship (and again in 1973).
- **1980–83:** The New York Islanders dominate hockey, winning the Stanley Cup 4 years in a row.
- **1986:** The Mets win another World Series.
- **1987:** The Giants win the Super Bowl (and again in 1991).
- **1994:** The Rangers win another Stanley Cup.
- **1995:** This year, it's the New Jersey Devils' turn to win the Stanley Cup.

- **1998–2000:** The Yankees make regular World Series visits, winning three in a row, including the first-ever Subway Series against the Mets in 2000.
- **2000:** The New Jersey Devils win another Stanley Cup.
- **2001:** In a highly emotional post–September 11 end of season, the Yankees win their fourth consecutive World Series berth— only to lose in the seventh game to the Arizona Diamondbacks.
- **2003:** The New Jersey Devils win the Stanley Cup once more.
- **2008:** The New York Giants, with Eli Manning at the helm, win the Super Bowl.
- **2009:** In their first season in the new Yankee Stadium, the New York Yankees win their 27th World Series title; less than a year later, cantankerous Yankees owner George Steinbrenner dies at the age of 80.

tickets is still tough, unless you're Spike Lee. There's still hope: On the day of the game, the box office sometimes releases a small number of tickets (call ℭ **212/465-6040**), and there are always scalpers who'll be happy to let you pay top dollar for tickets. At Madison Square Garden, Seventh Ave. btw. 31st and 33rd sts. ℭ **212/465-MSG1** (465-6741), 212/465-JUMP (465-5867), 800/4NBA-TIX (462-2849), or 212/307-7171 (Ticketmaster). www.nyknicks.com. Tickets $40–$285. Subway: A, C, E to 34th St./Penn Station; 1, 2, 3 to 34th St.

New York Liberty Ages 5 & up. The success of professional women's basketball surprised all the pundits, who never expected the public to respond so immediately to its brand of clean, fast, non-trash-talking basketball. Kids, especially girls, have been an important part of the Liberty's audience all along (it helps that its June–Aug season coincides with school vacation); plenty of on-court activities during the breaks, along with a lively dog mascot who patrols the stands looking for kids to shake paws with, boosts the entertainment quotient for younger ones. At Madison Square Garden, Seventh Ave. btw. 31st and 33rd sts. ℭ **212/465-MSG1** (465-6741) or 877/WNBA-TIX (962-2849; Ticketmaster), 212/564-WNBA (564-9622) for info. www.nyliberty.com. Tickets $10–$260. Subway: A, C, E to 34th St./Penn Station; 1, 2, 3 to 34th St.

New York Mets　**All ages.** The Mets have become National League contenders in a big way. The regular season runs mid-April through early October; throughout this stretch, 81 home games will be played at the home of the Mets, **Citi Field.** Tickets are best purchased in advance, but you may still be able to get tickets at the stadium on game day if you don't care about sitting close. The food is served in multiple sit-down, climate-controlled restaurants, a majority with field views and a wide range of menu choices. The family-friendly environment includes the **2KSports FanFest** family entertainment area on the field level in Center Field, open 2½ hours prior to game time and through the 7th inning—it has a Mets Kiddie Field (a miniature replica of Citi Field), two batting cages, and a speed pitch/dunk tank. At Citi Field, located at the north end of Flushing Meadows Corona Park in Queens on Flushing Bay. ✆ **718/507-METS** (507-6387) or 718/507-TIXX (507-8499). www.mets.com. Tickets $5–$117. Free for children under 32 in. Subway: 7 to Mets/Willets Point Station.

New York Rangers　**Ages 8 & up.** The Rangers play 41 hockey games, mostly at night, at Madison Square Garden during their season, from October to mid-April. Celebrities and CEOs pay big bucks for prized behind-the-bench seats, but in "Blue Heaven"—the cheap seats high above the ice—true hockey fans make Rangers games an audience-participation sport. Rangers tickets usually sell out a couple of months before the season starts, so buy in advance. At Madison Square Garden, Seventh Ave. btw. 31st and 33rd sts. ✆ **212/465-MSG1** (465-6741) or 212/307-7171 (Ticketmaster), 212/465-4459 for info. www.newyorkrangers.com. Tickets $37–$288. Subway: A, C, E to 34th St./Penn Station; 1, 2, 3 to 34th St.

New York Red Bulls　**Ages 6 & up.** Playing in its new 25,000-seat arena, the Red Bulls have built an audience among all those kids and parents who've been bitten by the soccer bug through youth leagues. Games are played from March to October, generally Wednesday nights or weekend days or evenings. The most convenient way to get to the arena from Manhattan, Newark, and Hoboken is to take the PATH train, which stops in Harrison; the Red Bull Arena is 4 blocks from the PATH station. For game-time bus service from Manhattan's Port Authority Bus Terminal, call **New Jersey Transit** (✆ **800/772-2222**). At Red Bull Arena in the New Meadowlands Stadium in the Meadowlands, Harrison, NJ. ✆ **201/935-3900;** for tickets 888/4-METROTIX (463-8768), or 212/307-7171 and 201/507-8900 (Ticketmaster). www.redbulls.com. Tickets $22–$50. Parking $10.

New York Yankees　**All ages.** Yankees fans have never minded watching their team roll effortlessly over all the competition—and in 2009 the Yanks captured the World Series crown for the 27th time. Only Derek Jeter is left from the halcyon days of the team that won consistently from 1996—and now even bombastic owner George Steinbrenner has gone on to greener pastures (he died in 2010 at the age of 80). New York's American League team plays 81 home games at the 21st-century version of Yankee Stadium, designed by HOK Sport and completed in 2008. The diamond has a replica of the beautiful copper frieze that once lined the old stadium's inner wall, and at a new Monument Park beyond the center field wall, kids can gaze at the retired jersey numbers and plaques of the Yankee heroes of yesteryear. The new ballpark has indoor and outdoor food courts. From mid-April to early October; order tickets in advance or buy them at the stadium ticket office on game day (when they're playing well, ticket availability gets tight toward fall). Show up a couple of hours early and you may be able to watch batting practice. To make it a really special outing, take the **NY Waterway's *Yankee Clipper* ferry,** which leaves from four different departure sites to the stadium ($25 adults, $18 children 11 and under; free for kids 2 and under); call 🕐 **800/533-3779** or order from www.nywaterway.com. Ferries depart from Weehawken, New Jersey; South Street Seaport; 34th Street at the East River; and 90th Street at the East River. At E. 161 St. and River Ave. 🕐 **718/293-6000** or 212/307-1212 (Ticketmaster). www.yankees. com. Tickets $15–$65. Subway: D, 4 to Yankees–East 153rd St. Station.

Staten Island Yankees 🏊 **Ages 6 & up.** The Yankees' Class A minor-league team hasn't quite achieved the retro glamour of their local rivals, the Brooklyn Cyclones; but the quality of play is high, and their ballpark is a pleasantly low-key place to watch the major-league stars of tomorrow show off their goods. Best of all, it's easy to get to, being within walking distance from the Staten Island Ferry terminal (all this and a cool boat ride too!). Richmond County Bank Ballpark at St. George, 75 Richmond Terrace, Staten Island. 🕐 **718/720-9200.** www.siyanks.com. Tickets $5–$16. Parking $5.

STORY HOURS

Barnes & Noble   Ages 2 to 7. Many of these bookstores hold lively, well-attended weekend story hours. Call ahead, or check www.bn.com to make sure of dates and times, but in general the East 86th Street branch holds Saturday and Sunday story hours at 11am, Union Square Sunday at 2:30pm, and TriBeCa Wednesday and Thursday at 11am and 4pm. (1) 240 E. 86th St. (btw. Second and Third aves.). 🕐 **212/794-1962.** Subway: 4, 5, 6 to 86th St. (2) 2289 Broadway (at 82nd St.). 🕐 **212/362-8835.** Subway: 1 to 79th St. (3) 675 Sixth Ave. (at 21st St.). 🕐 **212/727-1227.** Subway: F, V to 23rd St. (4) Union Square, 33 E. 17th St. (btw. Broadway and Park Ave.). 🕐 **212/253-0810.** Subway: N, R, 4, 5, 6 to 14th St.; L to Union Square. (5) 396 Sixth Ave. (at 8th St.). Subway: B, C, D, E, F, V to W. 4th St.

Books of Wonder   Ages 3 to 7. This great Flatiron shop runs friendly story hours on Sunday at noon. 18 W. 18th St. (btw. Fifth and Sixth aves.). 🕐 **212/989-3270.** www.booksof wonder.net. Subway: 1 to 18th St.

Borders Books   ** At these large, welcoming chain stores, well-stocked children's departments usually hold weekly story hours for preschoolers: Columbus Circle holds two on Wednesdays at 10am and 2pm, and the Second Avenue store has them at 3:30pm on Thursdays. Check www.borders.com for updates. (1) 10 Columbus Circle (at Eighth Ave.). 🕐 **212/823-9775. Subway A, B, C, D, 1 to 59th St./Columbus Circle. (2) 550 Second Ave. (at 32nd St.) in Kips Bay Plaza. 🕐 **212/685-3938.** Subway: 6 to 33rd St. (3) 2 Penn Plaza (7th Ave. and 31st St.). 🕐 **212/244-1814.** Subway: 1, 2, 3 to 34th St. (4) 100 Broadway (at Pine St.). 🕐 **212/964-1988.** Subway: 2, 3, 4, 5 to Wall St.

Hans Christian Anderson Statue, Central Park   Ages 5 & up. June through September, there are story hours here every Saturday from 11am to noon, rain or shine. At the Hans Christian Andersen Statue, on the west side of Conservatory Water (at 74th St.). www.centralparknyc.org. Subway: 6 to 77th St.

New York Public Library 🏊 **Ages 2 to 8.** Nearly every weekday, some Manhattan branch library holds a story hour or shows short films about children's books or holds some kind of cool workshop—and it's all free. You can contact the NYPL at 8

W. 40th St., New York, NY 10018 (© **212/221-7676**), for a monthly brochure of events for children, or visit its website at www.nypl.org/events. Better yet, stop by the **Humanities and Social Science Library** at Fifth Avenue and 42nd Street, 20 W. 53rd St. (© **212/930-0830**), to see the original Winnie-the-Pooh animals on display. Various branches around Manhattan.

Story Time at the Scholastic Store   Weekly story hours are held Tuesdays, Wednesdays, and Thursdays at 11am at the big, bright SoHo flagship of the Scholastic publishing house. Saturdays often feature author readings or interactive events planned around Scholastic titles—which happily include such winners as the Harry Potter books, Clifford the Big Red Dog, the adventures of Captain Underpants, and the 39 Steps interactive series. Check events by clicking on "Scholastic Store SoHo" at www.scholasticstore.com. 557 Broadway (btw. Prince and Spring sts.). © **212/343-6166.** Subway: N, R to Prince St.

SIDE TRIPS FROM NEW YORK CITY

Though New York City has enough attractions to keep even the most active child busy and interested, sometimes it's a relief to get away from the jangle of honking horns and crowded streets for a little while. When the weather's nice, a day trip from Manhattan can be just the ticket.

The following places are all within an hour of the city. A car would be the most convenient way to travel, but all are also reachable by train (or even, in the case of Philipsburg Manor, boat).

If you're interested in exploring farther afield, you might want to check out *Frommer's Wonderful Weekends from New York City* or *Frommer's Great Escapes from NYC Without Wheels.*

THOMAS EDISON NATIONAL HISTORICAL PARK

45 min. W. of Manhattan

"I always invented to obtain money to go on inventing," Thomas Edison once said. Yes, he was a gifted chemist and visionary, but he was also a shrewd businessman who amassed a fortune. The **Edison Laboratories** in West Orange, New Jersey, reopened in 2009 after extensive renovations. Just a mile from the labs is **Glenmont,** Edison's imposing mansion, which gives you a personal glimpse into the life of this man whose very name became synonymous with "genius."

Essentials

If you're driving, take either the Lincoln or Holland tunnels and take either the Garden State Parkway or the New Jersey Turnpike to I-280 westbound (exit 145 from the Garden State, exit 15-W from the NJ Turnpike). Follow I-280 west to exit 10; turn right at the end of the exit ramp, go to the end of the street, and make a left onto Main Street. At the second light, Park Way, you can turn left to reach the Edison home, Glenmont (pass through a gatehouse, follow Park Way to Glen Ave., turn right, then left onto Honeysuckle Ave.). If you continue on Main Street 2 more blocks, you will reach Lakeside Avenue and the Edison Laboratories.

New Jersey Transit (© **800/772-2222;** www.njtransit.com) bus no. 21 takes you to the Mississippi Loop in West Orange; it's a pleasant quarter-mile stroll through a private gated community from there to Glenmont; or you can take a cab to Glenmont from the bus station.

What to See & Do

Glenmont Already a successful inventor and businessman, Edison bought this grand 29-room red Queen Anne–style mansion in Llewellyn Park for his second wife, Mina. All the original furnishings are here. Downstairs rooms reflect the formal Victorian style of the era, with lots of ornate carved wood, damask wall coverings, and stained-glass windows; things get comfier upstairs in the family living room, where Edison's children sometimes helped him look up scientific references in shelves full of books. In the master bedroom, you can see the imposing bed where all three Edison children were born, and where Edison himself died. An heiress in her own right, Mina presided over the elegant mansion, raising their children and throwing lavish dinner parties, which workaholic Thomas did his best to avoid. As a businessman, Edison saw the benefits of putting on a high-class social front, but he didn't enjoy socializing. One thing's for sure: This was probably the first house in the neighborhood with a phonograph, let alone the Home Projecting Kinetoscope—the Edison children must have been very popular for play dates. Tickets to the house tours, offered between noon and 4pm, are limited and distributed on a first-come, first-served basis.

Honeysuckle Ave., Llewellyn Park, West Orange, NJ. © **973/324-9973.** www.nps.gov/edis. Admission (includes Glenmont and Laboratory Complex) $7 adults, free for those 16 and under. June 9–Sept 5 Wed–Sun 9am–5pm; grounds daily 11:30am–5pm. Closed Dec 25 and Jan 1.

The Edison Laboratories Though Edison's first lab was in Menlo Park, New Jersey, this larger West Orange complex was in operation for over 40 years and accounted for over half of his patents. Notice how closely the ivy-covered red-brick buildings are set together—Edison designed it this way so he wouldn't waste too much time scurrying from chemistry lab to machine shop to drafting room. Kids may be surprised to learn that, of the 1,093 patents credited to Edison—the most any American has ever obtained—many were actually invented by other scientists who worked for him. Walking around the restored lab complex, you can visualize his team of some 200 researchers, hired to refine and improve existing inventions. There were light bulbs before Edison's, but his was more reliable, long-lasting, and easy to manufacture; the telegraph, the phonograph, the stock ticker, and the movie camera and projector were all devices that other scientists pursued at the same time, but Edison's versions *worked better.* Another 10,000 workers in the attached factory (not part of the historic site) then mass-produced these inventions for commercial sale—he controlled the entire cycle. Accessories, too—there's a music recording studio you can peek into, where Edison engineers made sure phonograph customers would have something to play on their new machines.

211 Main St., West Orange, NJ. © **973/736-0550.** www.nps.gov/edis. Admission (includes Glenmont and Laboratory Complex) $7 adults, free for those 16 and under. Wed–Sun 9am–5pm.

GARDEN CITY, LONG ISLAND

50 min. E of Manhattan

Across the road from the Nassau Coliseum, one of the New York area's best-kept secrets is quietly growing into a museum powerhouse. Eventually, this Mitchel Field complex—referred to as "Museum Row"—will include a science-and-technology museum and even a vintage carousel. If your kids are enamored with fireman and fire trucks, the **Nassau County Firefighters Museum** (© 516/572-4177; www. ncfiremuseum.org; Tues–Sun 10am–5pm; $4 adults, $3.50 kids 2–12) has interactive exhibits in a 10,000-square-foot facility. But the complex's two major museums—**The Long Island Children's Museum (LICM)** and the **Cradle of Aviation Museum**—definitely make this worth the hour's drive from Manhattan. You could spend a day here—the morning at the children's museum, the afternoon at the aviation museum—and it still wouldn't be enough time to see and do everything.

Essentials

If you're driving, take the Long Island Expressway to exit 38 for the Northern Parkway. You'll quickly see signs for the Meadowbrook Parkway South (exit 31A). From the Meadowbrook, take exit M4 West, which will take you onto Charles Lindbergh Boulevard. The museums are on the right side after the traffic light.

Long Island Rail Road (© 718/217-5477; www.mta.nyc.ny.us/lirr) trains from Penn Station will take you to the Garden City station or the Mineola station. One-way adult fares are $6.75 to $9.25 (onboard fares higher), depending on time of travel. A cab ride from either station to the museum costs about $6.

What to See & Do

The Long Island Children's Museum (LICM)   The two-story LICM echoes with children's excitement. The ground floor is geared for the younger set, with a special **TotSpot** play area for under-5s, the ever-popular **bubble room,** and a maze-like climbing structure called **ClimbIt@LICM** (which cleverly has a ramp, so it's wheelchair accessible). The **ToolBox** area attracts young tinkerers to its carpentry worktables, where kids can discover the principles of simple machines, and **Sandy Island** is much more of a science lab than you might think—various stations demonstrate wave motions, sediment patterns, and erosion, with plenty of sand samples to peer at under microscopes.

Older kids will gravitate upstairs. In the **Communication Station,** kids explore various modes of communication, from speaking tubes to Morse Code telegraphs to telephones. The **mock TV station** is a big hit—your kids may want to see themselves projected on a giant TV screen as big-time news broadcasters—and the adjacent radio station lets them practice being DJs and putter around with sound effects. We had a ball in the **mUSic Gallery,** testing different drums and xylophones; in the **Bubbles** gallery you can not only step inside a giant bubble but also make a huge bubble honeycomb. **It's Alive!** focuses on animal habitats (including human ones), and **Bricks & Sticks** is full of young block-builders. Children 6 and up enjoy an exhibit called **Changes & Challenges,** which aims to sensitize kids to disabilities: There are wheelchairs and crutches to experiment with, Braille to touch, lenses showing what the world looks like to people with diminished sight, a phone that plays only muted conversation, and writing as it might appear to a dyslexic child. The **Pattern Studio** sounds simple—computer monitors and wooden blocks where you can fiddle around with recurrent visual images—but it's a favorite among kids and parents alike.

Like all children's museums, this one can get noisy and chaotic at times, depending on the ages of the school groups milling around. The ticket policy is set up to prevent overcrowding, though, so call in advance to get a time slot.

11 Davis Ave., Garden City, NY (museum entrance on Charles Lindbergh Blvd.). ✆ **516/224-5800.** www.licm.org. Admission $10, free for children under 1 and members. Tickets are sold for specific time slots when crowded; in inclement weather, call ahead for schedule. Sept–June Tues–Sun 10am–5pm; July–Aug daily 10am–5pm.

Cradle of Aviation Museum ★ 👔 Right next door to the Long Island Children's Museum, this is like a miniversion of Washington's Air and Space Museum, fascinating but not overwhelmingly big. It's focused on Long Island's aviation history—this site is, after all, where Lindbergh took off on his historic flight to Paris. Famed aviatrix Harriet Quimby trained here, and major companies like Curtiss and Grumman were located a stone's throw away. The local-history hook really means something.

Walk into the glass atrium and there's a supersonic F-11 Tiger suspended overhead; from the gallery's catwalk entrance, you can gaze straight ahead at an authentic 1909 Bleriot monoplane, a *Spirit of St. Louis* sister plane, and Grumman Wildcats, Hellcats, and Tomcats; around the corner, in the space exploration section, there's an original 1972 lunar landing module displayed in a rugged mock moonscape. Inside a hangar you can see even more of the collection's really big aircraft, including an F-14 and the nose of a speed-record-setting El Al 707. There are plenty of hands-on activities—a hot-air balloon you can inflate, cockpits you can climb into, and a mesmerizing monitor displaying current air traffic across the U.S. For an additional $2 you can spend 20 minutes executing a simulated mission to Mars, an activity that includes 4 minutes on a better-than-average motion simulator. There's also an IMAX show every hour. Loads of volunteers, many of them retired engineers and pilots, mill about, eager to share their knowledge; a number of them personally helped to restore the planes on display.

1 Davis Ave., Garden City, NY (museum entrance on Charles Lindbergh Blvd.). ✆ **516/572-4111.** www.cradleofaviation.org. Admission $9 adults, $8 kids 2–12; IMAX tickets $8.50–$14 adults, $6.50–$12 kids 2–12. Tues–Sun 9:30am–5pm (daily in summer); IMAX open daily. Closed Dec 25 and Jan 1.

Where to Eat

The Long Island Children's Museum has a cafeteria space, but you'll have to bring your own food or buy snacks at the vending machines. The Cradle of Aviation is better equipped foodwise, with the **Red Planet Cafe** selling sandwiches, packaged salads, and drinks. Otherwise, you can drive to the end of Charles Lindbergh Boulevard, keeping right at the fork, and turn left onto Stewart Avenue for the usual mix of chain restaurants in strip malls.

PLAYLAND

50 min. N of Manhattan

Remember the movie *Big*, when Tom Hanks's younger self made his fateful wish to be big after missing the height requirement for a roller coaster? That was shot at Playland. A pleasant antidote to the big, overhyped mega theme parks that proliferate all over the country, this old-timey collection of rides and games in a conveniently close seaside suburb is like a window into a kinder, gentler past.

Essentials

By **car,** take I-95 north to exit 19 in Rye (Playland Pkwy.) and then follow the signs to Playland. Parking costs $5 Tuesday to Friday, $7 Saturday and Sunday, and $10 holidays. Senior citizens with a valid ID pay only $1 except on holidays.

Metro-North Railroad trains take about 45 minutes from Grand Central Terminal to the Rye station. Adult one-way fares are $10 peak and $7.50 off-peak; children travel $5 peak and $4.75 off-peak. From the Rye station, take bus no. 75 to Playland. Metro-North also organizes seasonal Playland packages, which include train and bus fare and a book of Playland tickets. These packages are likely to be cheaper than buying train tickets and Playland tickets separately; call Metro-North (© **800/METRO-INFO** [638-7646] or 212/532-4900; www.mta.nyc.ny.us/mnr) for details.

Enjoying the Park

No mere rinky-dink midway, Playland is actually listed on the National Register of Historic Places. In 1923, the Westchester County Park Commission decided to create an "unequaled seaside public park to provide clean, wholesome recreation for the people of Westchester County"; Playland opened in 1928, right on Long Island Sound, and has lived up to its promise ever since. It's been kept up beautifully, with neat landscaping, landmark Art Deco buildings, and old-fashioned charm: striped awnings, painted wooden fences enclosing the rides, and festive-looking ticket booths.

Playland features so many rides, food stalls, games, and other amusements, I can't list them all. Kids 5 and under should be steered straight to **Kiddyland,** which has rides tailored to their size like the Kiddy Whip, Kiddyland Bumper Cars, and the Demolition Derby. For older kids, the most thrilling rides are probably the vintage wooden **Dragon Coaster** (tame by Busch Gardens standards, but enough to make me lose my lunch), the **Super Flight,** the **Log Flume,** and **Double Shot.** Great fun are retro rides like the **Ferris wheel,** the **Kiddy Whip,** and the **Carousel.** Plan on several hours here; your kids will insist on it.

In addition to the rides, Playland has a beach, a pool, an ice rink, minigolf, a boardwalk, and a lake for boating, which are open seasonally.

Playland Pkwy., Rye, NY. © **914/813-7010.** www.ryeplayland.org. $30 unlimited rides, $20 Kiddyland unlimited rides, $5 spectator admission (no rides). May–Sept; hours vary daily (check website for details).

Where to Eat

Playland offers many types of food in **concession stands**—such as Burger King, Nathan's Hot Dogs, Popeyes, Cocina Fresca, Carvel, Pizza Village, and Wrap City. There are also attractive picnic areas.

12 PHILIPSBURG MANOR

45–50 min. N of Manhattan

Leafy, suburban Tarrytown is one of those Hudson Valley towns that has been around since colonial days and still maintains pockets of quiet charm. It's a great place to visit the past, since there are four historic homes in relative proximity: Philipsburg Manor, Sunnyside (Washington Irving's home), Van Cortlandt Manor in Croton-on-Hudson, and the Rockefeller estate, Kykuit. Of the four, Philipsburg offers the most for children, but you could easily visit two homes in 1 day if your crew has the stamina.

Essentials

By **car,** take I-95 or the Henry Hudson Parkway/Saw Mill River Parkway north to the New York State Thruway (I-87), and go west toward the Tappan Zee Bridge. Get off I-87 at exit 9, Tarrytown, the last exit before the Tappan Zee Bridge. Go left on NY 119 and then take a quick right onto U.S. 9 north. Philipsburg Manor is 2 miles north on the left.

    Metro-North (© **800/METRO-INFO** [638-7646] or 212/532-4900; www.mta. nyc.ny.us/mnr) offers local train service from Grand Central Terminal directly to Philipsburg Manor (a 50-min. ride) or express train service to Tarrytown (a 40-min. ride). One-way adult fares are $8.25 to $11, depending on when you travel; children's fares are $4 to $5.50 (ages 5–11 with an adult). If you get off at the Philipse Manor station, you can walk to your destination (⅓ mile). From the Tarrytown station, you'll need to take a cab, which costs about $6. Call for details.

    For information on children's workshops and special events at any of the four historic homes in the area, check out **Historic Hudson Valley's** website at **www. hudsonvalley.org**.

Visiting the Manor

An 18th-century colonial farm with a working gristmill, a yard full of animals, a farmhouse, and a tenant house, Philipsburg Manor fascinates school-age children. A long wooden bridge crosses the millpond near the entrance, leading on to the main house; long and close to the water, the bridge is fun to run across, sweeping you straight into the 18th century once you reach the other side.

    Guides decked out in 18th-century dress demonstrate various farm activities of that era (milling, sheep shearing, plowing, and dairying) and give regular **tours of the farmhouse,** where the wealthy Philipse family once lived. The **stone manor house,** built between 1682 and 1720, includes interesting details of colonial life, including a night box to guard candles from rat attacks and a big white mound in the kitchen you later learn is sugar (the guide allows kids several guesses on that one). However, it was African slaves who actually worked the property for the

Philipse family, laboriously threshing their wheat and grinding it into flour (there was indeed slavery outside of the South, folks), and their lives centered more on the **barnyard.** Children 7 and under, who may have started to weary during the house tour, will perk up when they see the sheep, chickens, cows, and cats wandering about the barnyard, though they won't be allowed to pet the animals. Just be aware that with the pond and the stream so close, parental supervision is necessary at all times.

U.S. 9, Sleepy Hollow, NY. © **914/631-3992** or 631-8200. www.hudsonvalley.org. Admission $12 adults, $10 seniors, $6 children 5-17, free for children 4 and under. Apr 1-Oct 31 Wed-Mon 10am-5pm; Nov 1-Dec 26 Sat-Sun 10am-4pm. Closed Thanksgiving, Dec 25, and Jan-Mar.

Where to Eat

The **Tastefully Yours Cafe** offers panini, made-to-order sandwiches, salads, and desserts with views of historic Philipsburg Manor.

MARITIME AQUARIUM AT NORWALK

1 hr. NE of Manhattan

Focusing on the marine ecology of Long Island Sound, the **Maritime Aquarium** is just as pleasant a place to view marine life as the New York Aquarium in Coney Island (p. 178), and if you've got a car, it's perhaps easier to get here; it's certainly easier to get here from Manhattan than it is to visit the superb Mystic Aquarium at the other end of Connecticut.

Essentials

By car, take I-95 heading east/north to the South Norwalk exit (exit 14) off I-95 and follow the signs to the Maritime Center; it's about a 6-minute drive from the highway. Or take the Hutchinson River Parkway north, which becomes the Merritt Parkway in Connecticut; take exit 39A, and follow the signs on U.S. 7 to the Maritime Center. Parking at the center costs up to $5.

Metro-North trains (© **800/METRO-INFO** [638-7646] or 212/532-4900; www.mta.nyc.ny.us/mnr) to South Norwalk cost $9.75 to $13 for adults, $5 to $6.50 for children 5 to 11, and free for children 4 and under. Travel time is about 60 minutes. From the South Norwalk station, take a short taxi ride or walk—it's only about 3 blocks. When you get off the train, turn left, and go down the stairs at the end of the platform; turn right at the bottom of the stairs, walk under the bridge, and go 1½ blocks to the first traffic light, at the intersection of Main and Monroe streets. Turn left onto Main Street, and go to the next traffic light; then turn right onto Washington Street. Go under another bridge, and continue past shops and restaurants to the next traffic light, at the corner of Washington and Water streets. You'll see the large red-brick Maritime Aquarium on your left.

Exploring the Aquarium

Go up free-standing stairs in the lobby and across a midair bridge to the second-floor entrance, where carpeted walkways lead through a softly lit series of **20 marine**

habitats, progressing from salt marsh to the ocean depths. You'll see a thousand or so marine creatures of more than 125 species, all native to Long Island Sound, including sleek speckled harbor seals that flop around an indoor/outdoor pool in the lobby (check the feeding times) and bright-eyed otters in the woodland shoreline habitat. Sand tiger sharks circle and glare at you through the glass in enormous ocean tanks; immense, primeval-looking loggerhead turtles paddle like wise old grandpas in another tank; and jellyfish shimmer seductively in the Jellyfish Encounter. Kids who want to get really close to sea creatures—sea stars, horseshoe crabs, whelks—can linger at the **Touch Tank** or, if they're bold enough, pet a live ray at the **Ray Touch Pool.** On Saturday and Sunday between 11am and 3pm, kids can take a toy-boat-making workshop ($5 per child).

Two-story **Maritime Hall** has loads of interactive educational displays on fish, as well as displays on navigation and a wooden-boat workshop. The second-floor **Ocean Playscape** is a colorful marine-themed play area for children 4 and under. Aside from regular exhibits, the aquarium always has on tap some intriguing traveling exhibit or other, as well as an **IMAX theater** with a rotation of megascreen natural-history films. An excellent gift shop lies in wait at the end of your day.

N. Water St., Norwalk, CT. © **203/852-0700.** www.maritimeaquarium.org. Admission $13 adults, $12 seniors, $9.95 children 2–12; IMAX tickets $9–$12 adults, $8–$11 seniors, $6.50–$9.50 children 2–12. Daily 10am–5pm (to 6pm July–Aug). Closed Thanksgiving and Dec 25.

Where to Eat

The **Cascade Café** on the second floor offers clam chowder, burgers, chicken fingers, pizza, sandwiches, and salads at reasonable prices. It's open daily from 10am to 4pm.

KINGDA KA ROLLER COASTER AT SIX FLAGS GREAT ADVENTURE

90 min S. of Manhattan.

If riding the subway is only a whisper of a thrill for your brood, head to Six Flags Great Adventures, where the Kingda Ka roller coaster will leave them either screaming or speechless.

Essentials

By car, take the Holland Tunnel to New Jersey and head for I-95 South. Stay on I-95 South for approximately 44 miles to exit 7A. Proceed on I-195 East until exit 16A, then go one mile west on Rte. 537 to Six Flags.

New Jersey Transit (© **800/772-2287** or 973/275-5555; www.njtransit.com) offers bus service to the park via the 308 and 318 bus lines.

Experiencing Kingda Ka

As soon as one roller coaster sets a record, another new coaster is built to break it. Recently, the crown passed from Cedar Point to **Six Flags Great Adventure** in New Jersey, where the Kingda Ka debuted in 2005. It's almost as if a designer went down a list of stats from the previous record holder, the Top Thrill Dragster, and nudged each one just a tick higher. At the time we went to press, this one held all the records.

Using hydraulic technology, the Kingda Ka launches from 0 to *128 mph* in a breathtaking 3.5 seconds, then climbs 458 feet at a 90-degree angle—nearly 40 feet higher than Top Thrill. Making a neat quarter turn at the top of its green steel track, the ride hesitates—just long enough for you to realize where you're going and wonder why you ever thought this was a good idea—then whooshes back down the whole 458 feet, torquing into a 270-degree spiral. This is followed by a fast-paced camel hump and a banked left turn, before you glide back to the start, shaken if not stirred. The whole episode lasts less than a minute—50.6 seconds, to be exact—and you probably stood in line an hour to do it. And you'll probably do it again.

For those who prefer wooden coaster action—where the heights may be less but the sensation more intense—Six Flags Great Adventure has **El Toro.** This out-and-back wood coaster drops at a record-breaking 76 degrees on its first 188-foot hill, followed by three more hills in rapid succession (112 ft., 100 ft., and 82 ft.), all at a speed of 70 mph.

As you'd expect from this homogenized theme-park franchise, the New Jersey Six Flags has an overwhelming number of top-class rides—wood coasters, steel coasters, dark rides, soak rides, free-falls and flumes, and a Ferris wheel, many of them with licensed-character tie-ins (Batman: The Ride and Superman Ultimate Flight are two of the most popular). There are a cable car, a large section of rides scaled for younger kids, and plenty of pocket-emptying food and souvenir stands. Lines are a fact of life, and it doesn't come cheap—but for East Coast roller coaster addicts, this is an essential visit.

1 Six Flags Blvd. (off I-195), Jackson, NJ 08527. ✆ **732/928-1821;** www.sixflags.com. $59.99 adults, $34.99 under 54 inches tall, free 2 and under, from $36.99 online. Daily June–Aug; Sat–Sun Apr–May and Sept–Oct.

FAST FACTS: NEW YORK CITY

Area Codes The area codes for New York City are 212, 646, 718, 917 (cellphones), and 347. Make sure to dial 1 plus the area code before your call, even if you are in the same area.

ATM Networks See "Money & Costs," p. 35.

Babysitting Many New York hotels provide babysitting services or keep a list of reliable sitters. If your hotel doesn't, call the **Baby Sitters Guild** (*C* **212/682-0227;** www.babysittersguild.com; cash or travelers' checks only). This 60-year-old service provides in-room child-care and on-request trips to the playground, the Central Park Zoo, and so on, for children of all ages, with licensed, bonded, insured sitters (baby nurses are trained in CPR) who speak a range of languages.

Business Hours The city that never sleeps truly doesn't. Most stores stay open to 7pm or so, with drugstores and groceries usually going strong until 9pm or later, and delis and corner produce markets lasting on into the wee hours. Most stores (except for Midtown and Upper East Side boutiques) are open on Sunday, though they may not open until 11am or noon. **Restaurants** stay open late, at least until 11pm, and most are open 7 days a week. Many **museums** are closed on Monday, but several have late hours—until 9 or 10pm—on Thursday, Friday, or Saturday. **Banks** are generally open Monday to Friday 9am to 5 or 6pm and Saturday mornings.

Car Rentals See "Getting Around," p. 49.

Currency The most common bills are the $1 (a "buck"), $5, $10, and $20 denominations. There are also $2 bills (seldom encountered), $50 bills, and $100 bills (the last two are usually not welcome as payment for small purchases).

Coins come in seven denominations: 1¢ (1 cent, or a penny); 5¢ (5 cents, or a nickel); 10¢ (10 cents, or a dime); 25¢ (25 cents, or a quarter); 50¢ (50 cents, or a half dollar); the gold-colored Sacagawea and nearly identical Presidential coin, worth $1; and the rare silver dollar.

For additional information see "Money & Costs," p. 35.

Doctors The **NYU Downtown Hospital** offers physician referrals at *C* **888/698-3362.**

Drinking Laws The legal age in New York for purchase and consumption of alcoholic beverages is 21; proof of age is required and often requested at bars, nightclubs, and restaurants. Beer is sold in grocery stores and delis 24 hours a day except Sunday before noon. Liquor and wine are sold in licensed liquor stores that are open 6 days a week, with some opting to open Sundays. You can also be fined for drinking publicly from an open container—which means if you do want to enjoy a bottle of beer or wine during a picnic in Central Park, be certain it's covered in a brown paper bag.

Driving Rules See "Getting Around," p. 49.

Drugstores Numerous **CVS** and **Duane Reade** stores are open 24 hours a day; www.cvs.com and www.duanereade.com lists them all. **Walgreens** is a growing presence in the city; go to www.walgreens.com for 24-hour locations. For **Rite-Aid** 24-hour locations, consult www.riteaid.com.

Electricity Like Canada, the United States uses 110 to 120 volts AC (60 cycles), compared to 220 to 240 volts AC (50 cycles) in most of Europe, Australia, and New Zealand. Downward converters that change 220–240 volts to 110–120 volts are difficult to find in the United States, so bring one with you.

Embassies & Consulates All embassies are located in the nation's capital, Washington, D.C. Some consulates are located in major U.S. cities, and most nations have a mission to the United Nations in New York City. If your country isn't listed below, call for directory information in Washington, D.C. (𝄐 **202/555-1212**) or check www.embassy.org/embassies.

The embassy of **Australia** is at 1601 Massachusetts Ave. NW, Washington, DC 20036 (𝄐 **202/797-3000;** usa.embassy.gov/au).

The embassy of **Canada** is at 501 Pennsylvania Ave. NW, Washington, DC 20001 (𝄐 **202/682-1740;** www.canadianembassy.org). Other Canadian consulates are in Buffalo (New York), Detroit, Los Angeles, New York, and Seattle.

The embassy of **Ireland** is at 2234 Massachusetts Ave. NW, Washington, DC 20008 (𝄐 **202/462-3939;** www.irelandemb.org). Irish consulates are in Boston, Chicago, New York, San Francisco, and other cities. See website for complete listing.

The embassy of **New Zealand** is at 37 Observatory Circle NW, Washington, DC 20008 (𝄐 **202/328-4800;** www.nzembassy.com). New Zealand consulates are in Los Angeles, Salt Lake City, San Francisco, and Seattle.

The embassy of the **United Kingdom** is at 3100 Massachusetts Ave. NW, Washington, DC 20008 (𝄐 **202/588-7800;** www.britainusa.com). Other British consulates are in Atlanta, Boston, Chicago, Cleveland, Houston, Los Angeles, New York, San Francisco, and Seattle.

Emergencies Call 𝄐 911 for police, fire, and ambulance service. Fires can also be reported in Manhattan by dialing 𝄐 212/628-2900 or 212/999-2222. The 24-hour **Poison Control Center** can be reached at 𝄐 800/222-1222 toll-free or 212/764-7667. If you encounter serious problems, contact **Traveler's Aid International** (𝄐 202/546-1127; www.travelersaid.org) to help direct you to a local branch. This nationwide, nonprofit, social-service organization geared to helping travelers in difficult straits offers services that might include reuniting families separated while traveling, providing food and/or shelter to people stranded without cash, or even emotional counseling.

Gasoline (Petrol) At press time, in the U.S., the cost of gasoline (also known as gas, but never petrol) was around $2.80 per gallon. Taxes are already included in the printed price. One U.S. gallon equals 3.8 liters or .85 imperial gallons. Fill-up locations are known as gas or service stations.

Holidays Banks, government offices, post offices, and many stores, restaurants, and museums are closed on the following legal national holidays: January 1 (New Year's Day), the third Monday in January (Martin Luther King Day), the third Monday in February (Presidents' Day), the last Monday in May (Memorial Day), July 4 (Independence Day), the first Monday in September (Labor Day), the second Monday in October (Columbus Day), November 11 (Veterans Day/Armistice Day), the fourth Thursday in November (Thanksgiving Day), and December 25 (Christmas). The Tuesday after the first Monday in November is Election Day, a federal government holiday in presidential-election years (held every 4 years, and next in 2012).

For more information on holidays, see "Kids' Favorite New York City Events" in chapter 3.

Hospitals The following hospitals have full-service emergency rooms:

Downtown: New York Downtown Hospital, 170 William St., between Beekman and Spruce streets (☏ **212/312-5106** or 312-5000); and **Beth Israel Medical Center,** First Avenue and 16th Street (☏ **212/420-2000**).

Midtown: Bellevue Hospital Center, 462 First Ave., at 27th Street (☏ **212/562-4141**); **New York University Medical Center,** 550 First Ave., at 33rd St. (☏ **212/263-7300**); and **St. Luke's/Roosevelt Hospital,** 425 W. 59th St., between Ninth and Tenth avenues (☏ **212/523-4000**).

Upper West Side: St. Luke's Hospital Center, 1111 Amsterdam Ave. at 114th Street (☏ **212/523-4000**); and Columbia Presbyterian Medical Center, 622 W. 168th St., between Broadway and Fort Washington Avenue (☏ **212/305-2500**).

Upper East Side: New York Presbyterian Hospital, 525 E. 68th St., at York Avenue (☏ **212/472-5454**); **Lenox Hill Hospital,** 100 E. 77th St., between Park and Lexington avenues (☏ **212/434-2000**); and **Mount Sinai Medical Center,** 1190 Fifth Ave. at 100th Street (☏ **212/241-6500**).

Hot Lines For information on theater, music, and dance performances, check out **NYC On Stage** online at www.tdf.org. Review current offerings at **Lincoln Center** (☏ 212/LINCOLN [546-2656]; www.lincolncenter.org). For all **New York City Parks & Recreation information,** simply dial (☏ 311) or go to www.nycgovparks.org; the parks department also provides up-to-the-minute updates on Twitter and Facebook). To find out about outdoor concerts and performances and special arts events in city parks, call the **City Parks Foundation Arts Hotline** (☏ 212/360-8290). Listings of commercial films are available through **Moviefone** (☏ 212/777-FILM [777-3456]) and **Fandango** (☏ 800/326-3264), which allows you to prepurchase movie tickets via credit card. **Sports Scores** (☏ 212/976-1717) gives updates on the most recent pro sports events.

Internet Access The **Times Square Visitor Information Center,** 1560 Broadway, between 46th and 47th streets (☏ **212/768-1560**; open daily 7am–7pm), has computer terminals that you can use to send e-mails courtesy of Yahoo!. In Times Square, **easyInternetCafé,** 234 W. 42nd St., between Seventh and Eighth avenues (☏ **212/398-0775**; www.easyeverything.com), is open 24/7. Most hotels have Internet access in their public spaces.

Legal Aid If you are "pulled over" for a minor infraction (such as speeding), never attempt to pay the fine directly to a police officer; this could be construed as attempted bribery, a much more serious crime. Pay fines by mail, or directly into the hands of the clerk of the court. If accused of a more serious offense, say and do nothing before consulting a lawyer. In the U.S. the burden is on the state to prove a person's guilt beyond a reasonable doubt, and everyone has the right to remain silent, whether he or she is suspected of a crime or actually arrested. Once arrested, a person can make one telephone call to a party of his or her choice. International visitors should call their embassy or consulate.

Libraries At any branch of the **New York Public Library,** you can pick up a monthly brochure listing all the kids' activities planned—films, story hours, puppet shows, and the like—at the system's many branches. These are usually wonderful programs, and they're absolutely free. The magnificent **Stephen A. Schwarzman Building** at Fifth Avenue and 42nd Street (✆ 212/930-0830), is a good place to start. Branches with good children's rooms (and story hours) include **Jefferson Market,** 425 Sixth Ave., at West 10th Street (✆ 212/243-4334); **Yorkville,** 222 E. 79th St. (✆ 212/744-5824); **Epiphany,** 228 E. 23rd St. (✆ 212/679-2645); and **St. Agnes,** 444 Amsterdam Ave., at 82nd Street (✆ 212/877-4380).

Lost & Found Be sure to tell all of your credit card companies the minute you discover that your wallet has been lost or stolen and file a report at the nearest police precinct. Your credit card company or insurer may require a police-report number or record of the loss. Most credit card companies have an emergency toll-free number to call if your card is lost or stolen; they may be able to wire you a cash advance immediately or deliver an emergency credit card in a day or two. Visa's U.S. emergency number is ✆ **800/847-2911** or 410/581-9994. American Express cardholders and traveler's check holders should call ✆ **800/221-7282.** MasterCard holders should call ✆ **800/307-7309** or 636/722-7111. For other credit cards, call the toll-free number directory at ✆ **800/555-1212.**

If you need emergency cash over the weekend when all banks and American Express offices are closed, you can have money wired to you via **Western Union** (✆ **800/325-6000;** www.westernunion.com).

Mail At press time, domestic postage rates were 28¢ for a postcard and 44¢ for a letter. For international mail, a first-class letter of up to 1 ounce costs 98¢ (75¢ to Canada and 79¢ to Mexico). For more information go to www.usps.com and click on "Calculate Postage."

If you aren't sure what your address will be in the United States, mail can be sent to you, in your name, c/o General Delivery at the main post office of the city or region where you expect to be. (Call ✆ **800/275-8777** for information on the nearest post office.) The addressee must pick up mail in person and must produce proof of identity (driver's license, passport, and so on). Most post offices will hold your mail for up to 1 month, and are open Monday to Friday from 8am to 6pm, and Saturday from 9am to 3pm.

Always include zip codes when mailing items in the U.S. If you don't know your zip code, visit www.usps.com/zip4.

Newspapers & Magazines New York City has three vigorous daily newspapers: the well-known *New York Times* and the tabloids the *New York Daily News* and the *New York Post.* The *Wall Street Journal* is also published here (with daily and weekend editions), though its scope is national rather than local. Weekly newspapers include the downtown-oriented *Village Voice* and the uptown-oriented *New*

York Observer, the latter printed on distinctive peach-colored paper. Weekly magazines with excellent comprehensive cultural listings include the weeklies *New York Magazine, Time Out New York,* and the *New Yorker,* and the monthly *Time Out New York Kids.*

Passports   See www.frommers.com/planning for information on how to obtain a passport. See "Embassies & Consulates," above, for whom to contact if you lose yours while traveling in the U.S. For other information, please contact the following agencies:

For Residents of Australia   Contact the **Australian Passport Information Service** at © **131-232,** or visit the government website at www.passports.gov.au.

For Residents of Canada   Contact the central **Passport Office,** Department of Foreign Affairs and International Trade, Ottawa, ON K1A 0G3 (© **800/567-6868;** www.ppt.gc.ca).

For Residents of Ireland   Contact the **Passport Office,** Setanta Centre, Molesworth Street, Dublin 2 (© **01/671-1633;** www.irlgov.ie/iveagh).

For Residents of New Zealand   Contact the **Passports Office** at © **0800/225-050** in New Zealand or 04/474-8100, or log on to www.passports.govt.nz.

For Residents of the United Kingdom   Visit your nearest passport office, major post office, or travel agency or contact the **United Kingdom Passport Service** at © **0870/521-0410** or search its website at www.ukpa.gov.uk.

For Residents of the United States   To find your regional passport office, either check the U.S. State Department website or call the **National Passport Information Center** toll-free number (© **877/487-2778**) for automated information.

Police   Dial **911.**

Post Offices   The **main post office** at Eighth Avenue between 31st and 33rd streets (© **212/330-3668**) is open daily 24 hours. There are many other branches around town. Call the **Postal Answer Line** at © **800/ASK-USPS** (275-8777) for information.

Restrooms   See "Finding a Restroom," in chapter 4.

Safety   New York has become one of the safest cities in the world, with major crimes at a historic low at press time. But that doesn't mean you should take a stroll through Central Park in the wee hours of the morning, leave unsecured valuables in your car, or flash wads of cash in Times Square. No, no, and no. Avoid being the victim of petty crime by using common sense: Store your wallet in a safe place; wear your purse so it's not snatchable; lock up any valuables in the hotel safe; and avoid low-trafficked areas, especially at night. The NYPD has a comprehensive **Crime Prevention Tips list** on the NYC.gov website www.nyc.gov/html/nypd.

Smoking   New York's laws against smoking in public places are among the country's strictest. There is no smoking allowed on all public transportation and inside restaurants, bars, taxis, theaters, museums, stores, and the lobbies of hotels and public buildings.

Taxes   The United States has no value-added tax (VAT) or other indirect tax at the national level. New York City's **sales tax** is 8.875%; this tax will not appear on price tags. You do not have to pay sales tax on groceries, takeout food, or any clothing and shoe purchases of $110 or less. **Hotels** add a 14.25% hotel tax (plus a $3.50-per-night occupancy tax) to room rates.

Telephones   For directory assistance, dial ⓒ **411** or [area code] + 555-1212. There are public phones on every other street corner in Manhattan, though not all are in what you'd call working order; large hotels generally have a bank of public phones off the lobby, too. A local call costs 50¢. Pay phones do not accept pennies, and few will take anything larger than a quarter.

Generally, hotel surcharges on long-distance and local calls are astronomical, so you're better off using your **cellphone** or a **public pay telephone** (if you can find one). Many convenience groceries and packaging services sell **prepaid calling cards** in denominations up to $50; for international visitors these can be the least expensive way to call home. Many public phones at airports now accept American Express, MasterCard, and Visa credit cards.

Most long-distance and international calls can be dialed directly from any phone. **For calls within the United States and to Canada,** dial 1 followed by the area code and the seven-digit number. **For other international calls,** dial 011 followed by the country code, the city code, and the number you are calling.

Calls to area codes 800, 888, 877, and 866 are toll-free. However, calls to area codes 700 and 900 (chat lines, bulletin boards, "dating" services, and so on) can be very expensive—usually a charge of 95¢ to $3 or more per minute, and they sometimes have minimum charges that can run as high as $15 or more.

For **reversed-charge or collect calls,** and for person-to-person calls, dial the number 0 and then the area code and number; an operator will come on the line, and you should specify whether you are calling collect, person-to-person, or both. If your operator-assisted call is international, ask for the overseas operator.

Telegraph and telex services are provided primarily by Western Union. You can telegraph money, or have it telegraphed to you, very quickly over the Western Union system, but this service can cost as much as 15% to 20% of the amount sent.

Most hotels have **fax machines** available for guest use (be sure to ask about the charge to use it). Many hotel rooms are even wired for guests' fax machines. A less expensive way to send and receive faxes may be at stores such as **The UPS Store** (formerly Mail Boxes Etc.).

Time   New York City is in the **Eastern Time Zone.** (The continental United States has four time zones, each 1 hr. apart: Eastern, Central, Mountain, and Pacific, with Alaska and Hawaii having their own zones.) From November to early March, it is on Eastern Standard Time **(EST),** which is 5 hours behind Greenwich Mean Time; **daylight saving time (EDT)** takes effect at 2am the second Sunday in March and holds sway until 2am the first Sunday in November, moving the clock 1 hour ahead of standard time.

Tipping   Tips are a very important part of certain workers' income, and gratuities are the standard way of compensating them for services provided. In hotels, tip **bellhops** at least $1 per bag ($2–$3 if you have a lot of luggage) and tip the **chamber staff** $1 to $2 per day (more if you've left a disaster area for him or her to clean up). Tip the **doorman** or **concierge** only if he or she has provided you with some specific service (for example, calling a cab for you or obtaining difficult-to-get theater tickets). Tip the **valet-parking attendant** $1 every time you get your car.

In restaurants, bars, and nightclubs, tip **service staff** 15% to 20% of the check (25% in cheaper restaurants—especially if your waiter has provided extra attention to keep your children happy—or for food deliveries). Tip **checkroom attendants** $1 per garment, package, or stroller.

Tip **cab drivers** 10% to 20% of the fare; tip **skycaps** at airports at least $1 per bag ($2–$3 if you have a lot of luggage); and tip **hairdressers** and **barbers** 15% to 20%.

Toilets   See "Finding a Restroom," in chapter 4.

Useful Phone Numbers   U.S. Dept. of State Travel Advisory: ✆ **202/647-5225** (manned 24 hr.).

U.S. Passport Agency: ✆ **202/647-0518.**

U.S. Centers for Disease Control International Traveler's Hotline: ✆ **404/332-4559.**

For local **time** and **weather,** call ✆ **212/976-2828** or 976-4111 (you'll also get current winning lottery numbers).

Visas   For information about U.S. visas go to http://travel.state.gov and click on "Visas." Or go to one of the following websites:

Australian citizens can obtain up-to-date visa information from the **U.S. Embassy Canberra,** Moonah Place, Yarralumla, ACT 2600 (✆ 02/6214-5600), or by checking the U.S. Diplomatic Mission's website at http://canberra.usembassy.gov.

British subjects can obtain up-to-date visa information by calling the **U.S. Embassy Visa Information Line** (✆ 0891/200-290) or by visiting the "Visas to the U.S." section of the American Embassy London's website at www.usembassy.org.uk.

Irish citizens can obtain up-to-date visa information through the **Embassy of the USA Dublin,** 42 Elgin Rd., Dublin 4, Ireland (✆ 353/1-668-8777; or by checking the "Visas to the U.S." section of the website at http://dublin.usembassy.gov.

Citizens of **New Zealand** can obtain up-to-date visa information by contacting the **U.S. Embassy New Zealand,** 29 Fitzherbert Terrace, Thorndon, Wellington (✆ 644/472-2068), or get the information directly from the website at http://wellington.usembassy.gov.

AIRLINE WEBSITES

Air Canada
www.aircanada.ca

Air France
www.airfrance.com

Air India
http://home.airindia.in

Air New Zealand
www.airnewzealand.com

AirTran Airlines
www.airtran.com

Alaska Airlines
www.alaskaair.com

Alitalia
www.alitalia.com

American Airlines
www.aa.com

British Airways
www.britishairways.com

Caribbean Airlines
www.caribbean-airlines.com

Continental Airlines
www.continental.com

Delta Air Lines
www.delta.com

Emirates
www.emirates.com

Frontier Airlines
www.frontierairlines.com

JetBlue Airlines
www.jetblue.com

KLM
www.klm.com

Lufthansa
www.lufthansa.com

Mexicana
www.mexicana.com

Olympic Air
www.olympicair.com

South African Airways
www.flysaa.com

Southwest Airlines
www.southwest.com

Spirit Airlines
www.spiritair.com

TACA
www.taca.com

TAM Airlines
www.tamairlines.com

United Airlines
www.united.com

US Airways
www.usairways.com

Virgin Atlantic Airways
www.virgin-atlantic.com

WestJet
www.westjet.com

13

FAST FACTS: NEW YORK CITY | Airline Websites

Index

GENERAL INDEX

Staten Island Children's Museum, 174–175
Staten Island Ferry, 53, 176
Staten Island Yankees, 281
Staten Island Zoo, 179
State Shuttle, 32
STA Travel, 40
Statue of Liberty, 159
  quiz, 158
Steinhardt Conservatory (Brooklyn), 180
Stephen A. Schwarzman Building, 170
Stettheimer Dollhouse, 168
Stomp, 267
Story hours, 281–282
Story Time at the Scholastic Store, 282
The Strand, 236
Strawberry Fields, 201–202
Street fairs, 234
Street people, 3
Street performers, 265
Strollers, 27
Student travel, 40
The Studio Museum in Harlem, 171
  workshops, 229
Studio tours, 187
Stuyvesant Street, 193
Subway, 50–51
  safety tips, 37
Subways, from the airport, 32–33
Subway stations, art in, 51
SummerStage, 23
Sunrise Mart, 113
SuperShuttle, 30–31, 39
Sutton Place Park, 214
Swedish Cottage Marionette Theatre, 161, 276
Swimming, 225–226
Swimming pools, hotels with, 56, 64

T

TADA!, 271
Tannen's Magic, 252
Tavern on the Green, 201
Taxes, 296
Taxis, 52–53
  from the airport, 29–30
  for disabled travelers, 39
Teachers College, 195
Teardrop Park, 216
Tecumseh Playground, 213
Telegraph and telex services, 297
Telephones, 41, 297
Temperatures, average, 20
Tenement Museum, Lower East Side, 166–167
Tennis, 226
Thanksgiving Day Parade, Macy's, 25

Theater, 267–271
Theater at Madison Square Garden, 264
Theater District, 48
Theater for a New Audience, 270
TheatreworksUSA, 270
Thirteenth Street Repertory Theater, 270
30 Rockefeller Plaza (30 Rock), 190
Thomas Edison National Historical Park (New Jersey), 283–284
Thompson Street Playground (Vesuvio Playground), 216
Three Bears (statue), 212
Tiffany & Co., 256
A Time for Children, 260
Time Out New York, 40
Time Square Planet Hollywood, 140
Times Square, 48
  walking tour, 190–191
Times Square Alliance, 43
Times Square Visitors Center, 42, 43, 191
Time zones, 297
Tiny Doll House, 249
Tipping, 297–298
Tip Top Kids, 255–256
Tisch Children's Zoo, 153
TKTS booths, 191, 263
Toho Shoji, 247
Tompkins Square Park, 193, 216
  minipools at, 225
Tom's Diner, 196
Top of the Rock, 162, 190
Torly Kids NYC, 243
Totally Kid Carousel, 165
Toys, 257–261
Toys "R" Us, 191, 260–261
Toys "R" Us Ferris Wheel, 176–177
Toy Tokyo Showroom NYC, 247
Trading cards, 246–248
Trainland, 248
Train travel, 34
Transportation, 49–54
Trapeze School New York, 226–227
Travel CUTS, 40
TriBeCa, 47
  clothing, 243
  playgrounds, 216–217
  restaurants, 136–138
  shopping, 232
Tribeca Performing Arts, 270
Tribeca Treats, 109
Triborough Bridge, 49
Trico Field, 242–243
Trinity Church, 14, 191–192
Tudor City playground, 214
Tunnels, 49
Turtle Island, 204

Turtle Pond, 204
Tutti Bambini, 245
TV shows, 17
2KSports FanFest, 280
Two Little Red Hens, 109

U

Umberto's Clam House, 194
Union Square
  food zone, 123
  shopping, 232
Union Square Greenmarket, 215, 234
Union Square playground (Evelyn's Playground), 215
Union Theological Seminary, 195
Uniqlo, 240
United, 28
United Nations, 159–160, 190
Upper East Side, 48
  accommodations, 66–68
  clothing, 243–246
  playgrounds, 214
  restaurants, 106–110
  shopping, 232
Upper West Side, 48
  accommodations, 58–66
  clothing, 246
  playgrounds, 213
  restaurants, 101–105
  shopping, 232
Uptown neighborhood stroll, 195–197
US Airways, 28
USIT, 40–41
U.S. Open Tennis Championships (Queens), 24
USS Intrepid Sea, Air & Space Museum, 161, 166
U.S.T.A. Billie Jean King National Tennis Center (Queens), 226

V

Van Cortlandt Park (the Bronx), 199, 223
Very Young People's Concerts, 273
Vesuvio Park, minipools at, 225–226
Vesuvio Playground (Thompson Street Playground), 216
Victorian Gardens at the Wollman Rink, 177
Village Chess Shop, 251
Village Kids Foot Wear, 256
Visas, 25–26, 298
Visa Waiver Program (VWP), 25–26
Visitor information, 43
Voice over Internet Protocol (VoIP), 41

W

Accommodations

Restaurants